# REAL-WORLD
# NETWORKING
## with NT 4

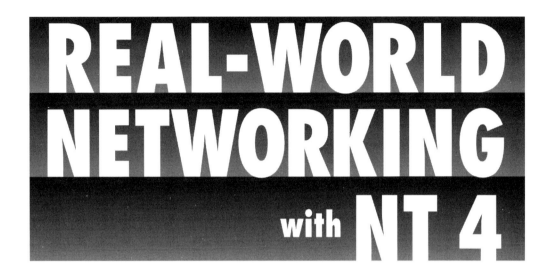

# William Holderby

CORIOLIS GROUP BOOKS

| | |
|---|---|
| **Publisher** | Keith Weiskamp |
| **Project Editor** | Toni Zuccarini |
| **Copy Editor** | Jenni Aloi |
| **Proofreader** | Mary Millhollon |
| **Indexer** | Caroline Parks |
| **Cover Artist** | Gary Smith |
| **Cover Design** | Anthony Stock |
| **Interior Design** | Bradley Grannis |
| **Layout Production** | ProImage |

The Coriolis Group, Inc.
7339 E. Acoma Drive, Suite 7
Scottsdale, AZ 85260
Phone: (602) 483-0192
Fax: (602) 483-0193
Web address: http://www.coriolis.com

ISBN 1-57610-055-3: $39.99

Printed in the United States of America

10 9 8 7 6 5 4 3 2 1

# Contents

# Chapter 2    Internal Networking    37

# Chapter 3    Installing and Configuring Windows NT 4 Networking    77

# Chapter 4    Network Security    131

# Part 2

# Chapter 5    Remote Networking    173

# Chapter 6    Network Planning    223

# Part 3

# Chapter 7   Built-In Maintenance   275

# Chapter 8   Testing and Troubleshooting the NT Network    313

# Part 4

## Chapter 9   Configuring NT for the Internet   343

# Chapter 10    NT 4 in the Multivendor Environment    407

# Part 5

# Chapter 11    Network Performance    481

# Acknowledgments

A book containing as wide a technical content as this one is not the product of a single person. It definitely requires a team effort. I was lucky to have an excellent team of writers, agents, editors, and proofreaders working to help produce this book. First, I would like to thank my lovely wife of thirty-two years, Lois, for providing me with the necessary inspiration. She also contributed her ability to decipher my thoughts on paper and turn them into clear, intelligible sentences. Next, I would like to thank my agent, Valda Hilley. She provided me with assistance and encouragement all the way through to the completion of this book. I would also like to thank Toni Zuccarini, my project editor, for the help she has provided to me throughout this project. I would like to thank Jenny Aloi, my copyeditor, for all the effort she put forth in reviewing and editing the many manuscript pages. I would also like to acknowledge and thank Entergy Corporation and Compaq for their support.

A special thanks goes to my associate writers Bob Crisp, Arshia Tayyab, and John West. Bob wrote Chapter 10, which exhibits his extensive knowledge in adapting NT 4 to multi-vendor systems. Arshia wrote Chapter 9, contributing her special Internet knowledge to a timely presentation of today's fast moving technology. John wrote Chapter 2, bringing with him an abundant knowledge of a difficult and detailed subject.

Robert Crisp is a network designer by profession. His areas of expertise include cable plant design and internetworking technology. He has a B.S. with honors in Computer Science from the University of Glamorgan and is a BiCSi certified Registered Communications Distribution Designer (RCDD) LAN Specialist. British by birth, he now resides in Panama City Beach, FL, with his wife Jane.

Arshia Tayyab has a BS in Computer Science from the University of Maryland, European Division, and an MBA from Pepperdine University. She is the owner and President of Computer Consultants International, Inc.(CCI); a small computer consulting firm located in Des Moines. Arshia does consulting extensively all over the country and internationally. You can reach her at **74561.2062@compuserve.com** or through CCI's website at **http://ourworld.compuserve.com/homepages/cci**, which will be changing to **http://www.cciinet.com**.

Since 1989, John West has been providing solutions for clients using the best in networking and application operating systems. As a Microsoft Certified Systems Engineer, Mr. West has installed client/server and mid-range integration solutions for companies such as Entergy, Lockheed Martin, and Siemens Corporation. Mr. West has experience using OS/400, Novell Netware, Windows NT, and the Internet. He currently works as a Technical Analyst for Paranet, a premiere provider of installation, support, and management of distributed computer environments. You can reach John West by sending email to **jwest@wild.net**.

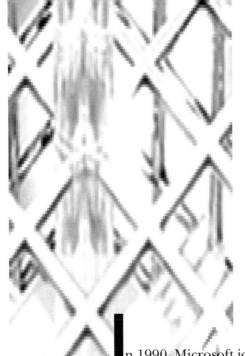

# Introduction

In 1990, Microsoft joined the systems network parade by releasing Windows NT 3.1. Their theory of trying to maintain compatibility with many of the existing network operating system leaders was a good one. While their initial release received mixed reviews for its open-system design, it generated an ample amount of interest from people who had used other Microsoft software products.

This same open-system design that was first criticized as being too generic has now evolved into an effective new release called Windows NT 4. Because of that much-criticized compatibility, along with a user-friendly design, NT 4 has been able to replace many well-entrenched network operating systems. This same strategy has also enabled NT to gain a foothold in many large pre-existing LAN installations, because the LAN administrators didn't have to make expensive replacement decisions. NT 4 also includes network compatibility with not only Microsoft's LAN Manager network, but also Novell's NetWare, Banyan's Vines, OS/2, and Unix. NT also shows a distinct command of many areas, such as security, peer-to-peer networking, and a firm integration with the predominant desktop client, Windows.

# Who This Book Is For

This book is intended for the reader who is not familiar with NT 4 and may or may not be familiar with networking. As each new concept is being explained, I will try to make no assumptions of prior knowledge, because, like any exceptional product, NT 4 will be of value to you only if you really understand how to use it.

The goal of this book is to present NT 4's networking capabilities in an easy-to-read format. That is why I have broken it down into five parts.

# Part 1: Understanding NT Networking

This first section contains four chapters that explain the concepts behind NT 4's networking capabilities. I think it is important at this first stage to understand just how NT 4 has integrated networking into its operating system.

The information in this first section:

- Presents an overview of NT 4's architecture.

- Expands on the protocols and technologies that will be important in later chapters.

- Describes the network installation of several selected protocols, services, and server functions. (Each installation is accompanied by all of the information you will need to make the necessary installation decisions.)

- Introduces NT 4's network security framework, and explains the concepts and mechanisms needed to create a secure operating system.

# Part 2: Planning and Designing Your NT Network

The next two chapters, contained in the second part of this book, describe how, as a client, you can remotely access an NT 4 workstation or server. This section also includes the tools offered by the operating system that will allow a remote client to manage both server and workstation functions.

I also present a detailed method of designing a network that makes the best use of NT 4's functionality and includes overall project plans. Then I show you the types of problems that are likely to be encountered during the planning and installation of that network.

# Part 3: Maintaining Your Network

This section contains two chapters designed to help keep you on top of networking problems and allow you to solve them. I am, of course, talking about tools. I discuss the various types of tools available with NT 4, and then I cover the options, configurations, and use of these tools.

The information contained in this section:

- Presents the built-in NT 4 tools that either come standard with NT or are included in the NT Resource Kit.

- Shows a series of common network problems and how to use the built-in tools to troubleshoot, diagnose, and repair these problems.

# Part 4: Extending Your NT Network

Part 4 provides two chapters that will help you configure NT 4 to interface the Internet, intranet, and/or be integrated into a mixed network with Unix, Novell, and Banyan.

The information presented in this section covers:

- NT 4's interface with the global Internet. Plus, the latest Microsoft Internet software is described and previewed in this chapter.

- The installation of NT 4 on either new or existing networks that contain more than one NOS. Additional information describes NT 4's relationships with several popular NOSs in a multivendor environment.

# Part 5: Reviewing Your Network's Performance

The two chapters in Part 5 deal with tools and techniques you can use to predict performance from your NT 4 servers and networks. In addition to performance predicting, we'll also cover benchmarking and the use of performance benchmarking tools to create, test, and predict network operation under different loading conditions.

I describe real LAN designs, operations, maintenance, and administrative issues on NT 4 workstations and servers. I also show you many different types of problems that you might encounter. By reading this book, you will become acquainted with the tools and procedures necessary to correct common LAN problems.

# What's in It for You

This book is neither full of code samples nor does it delve deeply into the NT 4 operating system's inner workings. Each chapter stays focused on real-world issues that confront both the client and the user. Because there is a good possibility that you will be in either one of these positions at one time or another, this book gives you an excellent troubleshooting advantage to learn what to look for on either side.

I hope the information contained in this book will be useful to you. I have tried to stay close to the real problems, procedures, and solutions that you are likely to face in the networking world. Basically, I wrote the book that I would want to have close by. Read it carefully, keep it near, and good luck.

PART

1

# Windows NT Networking
# Introduction

**W**indows NT 4 is, as the name explains, the fourth release of Microsoft's NT product. The initial release, NT 3.1, occurred in 1990 and signaled Microsoft's opening salvo in the Network Operating System (NOS) race with Novell, Banyan, and IBM's OS/2. NT 3.1 opened to mixed reviews and found critics accusing Microsoft's open-systems NT design as a jack of all trades and master of none.

However, this open-systems design enabled subsequent Microsoft NT releases to replace well-entrenched NOSes and to work effectively in the same local area networks (LANs) with the industry leaders. This strategy enabled NT to gain a foothold in many large LAN installations without requiring the LAN administrators to make expensive replacement decisions. NT includes network compatibility with not only Microsoft's LAN Manager network, but also with Novell's NetWare, Banyan's Vines, OS/2, and Unix.

Now in its fourth release, NT shows a definite mastery of many areas. Specifically, these are security, peer-to-peer networking, and a firm integration with the predominant desktop client, Windows.

While NT is the direct descendent of both the MS-DOS and Windows operating systems, the operating system has maintained backward compatibility while overcoming many MS-DOS-inherent problems (for example, 640 K byte addressing). In each additional NT release, other user problem areas have been addressed. For example, in the 3.51 NT release, 16-bit Windows applications gained the ability to operate in their own address space. The newest release, NT 4, has some new features that affect not only the user, but how NT interfaces networks.

In order to understand NT networking, you must first understand the NT operating system from a high level. Many of the terms and subsystems used in the following chapters often relate to non-networking portions of the operating system. At first glance, NT networking appears confusing because it doesn't fit extremely well into the NOS standards. In NT, Microsoft has sought to fully comply with standards and good network design practices. This chapter presents a high-level view of the overall NT architecture and its subsequent networking components.

# The Top-Level NT Architecture

To understand NT networking, we need to first review the basic operating system high-level structure. Figure 1.1 provides a functional hierarchy of NT OS subsystems and components. This hierarchy has undergone some fundamental changes since the last NT (3.51) release. At the highest level, NT operates in two modes: User mode and Kernel mode.

## User Mode

The NT 4 User mode supports a variety of applications by creating an environment that matches the type of application being executed. User mode creates environmental subsystems that emulate different operating system environments. For example, the Virtual DOS Machine (NTVDM) appears to MS-DOS applications as a fully functional DOS environment.

The User mode also provides generic services that all environment subsystems can use to perform basic OS functions. Each subsystem produces an environment that meets the specific needs of its client applications. Let's take a moment to briefly discuss each of these subsystems.

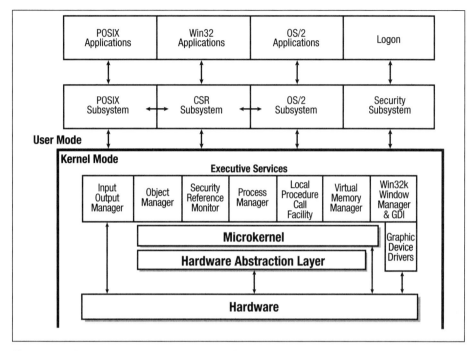

**Figure 1.1**    NT 4 uses two primary modes of operation, the User mode and the Kernel mode. Application software runs in User mode and the operating system executes in Kernel mode.

## POSIX APPLICATIONS

Portable Operating System Interface (POSIX) is a set of 12 standards for applications that are portable across Unix environments. The Windows NT POSIX subsystem is designed to run POSIX applications and meets the requirements of POSIX 1. POSIX 1 is a specification that defines a standard source-code level C-language application programming interface (API) for operating systems such as NT.

## POSIX SUBSYSTEM

The POSIX subsystem provides a compatible operational environment for POSIX 1-compliant applications. The subsystem interfaces the User mode applications to the Executive Services Kernel.

## WIN32 APPLICATIONS

NT 4 supports Win32 applications written for Windows 95, Windows 3.x, MS-DOS, and Windows NT.

## CSR SUBSYSTEM

In previous versions of NT, Win32 applications and console operations were conducted through the Win32 subsystem. This subsystem contained the Console, Windows Manager, Graphics Device Interface, Graphics Device Drivers, and Win32 API functions. The subsystem was contained within the CSRSS.EXE file.

In NT 4, this Win32 subsystem has been replaced with the Client/Server subsystem and is now only responsible for console interface and hard error handling. For purposes of efficiency and speed, the other tasks have been moved into the Kernel mode.

## OS/2 APPLICATIONS

The NT support for OS/2 applications is limited to OS/2 1.x character-based applications and runs only on Intel x86-based computers. However, NT 4 does not support the OS/2 High Performance File System (HPFS) that was supported in previous versions.

## OS/2 SUBSYSTEM

The OS/2 subsystem is started when the first OS/2 application is loaded. The subsystem shares address space with each OS/2 application and handles the communication and peripheral interactions between the OS/2 application and the NT Executive Services Kernel.

## LOGON

Before a user can use NT Workstation or Server, he must supply a user ID and password to the Logon screen. The logon process is the first milestone in NT's security. This information is processed by the Security subsystem.

## SECURITY SUBSYSTEM

The security subsystem accepts a user's ID and password, creates a token, and compares that token against a system security database. The details of the security subsystem, tokens, and the Security Accounts Manager (SAM) database are described in Chapter 4. Passing NT's security checks enables a user to logon to the workstation or server.

## KERNEL MODE

When NT switches to Kernel mode, all memory becomes accessible and all restricted (Level 0) instructions can be executed. Kernel mode executes with elevated thread priorities and, with the higher privileges, can clean up misbehaving applications and execute timed or critical tasks without lower priority software interference.

## EXECUTIVE SERVICES

The Executive is a collection of high-priority, Level 0 modules that conduct basic OS services supporting the User mode subsystems and network access. These modules include the following seven components, each managing a particular set of system services:

- *Input Output (I/O) Manager*—The I/O Manager manages fundamental operating system data movement to and from attached hardware devices. Its role is to manage driver communication and oversee the operation of all hardware and network drivers. This module oversees NT's networking.

- *Object Manager*—The object manager defines what an object is and what operations can be performed upon it. The Object Manager sets rules for object retention, naming, and security. It also creates object handles that act as programmable object pointers.

- *Security Reference Monitor*—This module oversees internal and external network and program access to the operating system. It checks user rights before allowing access to files and other security objects. Before granting you access, the Object Manager asks the Security Reference Monitor to compare your access token against the Access Control List (ACL). When you see the Access Denied message box, the Security Reference Monitor has determined that you do not have sufficient rights.

- *Process Manager*—The Process Manager manages the creation and deletion of processes and their associated threads. It standardizes process and thread creations for each subsystem environment.

The Process Manager also works in conjunction with the Security Reference Monitor and the Virtual Memory Manager to provide inter-process protection. This is accomplished by assigning each process a *security access token* to be used in order to gain access to objects.

- *Local Procedure Call (LPC) Facility*—In order to communicate and coordinate actions, the User and Kernel mode subsystems must pass messages and data. The inter-subsystem message-passing is managed by the LPC facility. Applications communicating with environment subsystems also pass messages via the LPC facility.

- *Virtual Memory Manager (VMM)*—The VMM manages NT's real and virtual memory. The VMM provides a flat 4 GB memory space for the NT 4 operating system and the applications running on either the workstation or server. When memory is required, the VMM maps memory pages between the virtual and physical memory. Once mapped, the VMM can page (transition) the mapped applications to a paging file on the hard drive, providing memory space for other applications.

- *Win32K Window Manager & GDI*—Manipulating large screen buffers coupled with the time required to build and rebuild SVGA and XVGA graphics screens is time consuming. In earlier versions of NT, the subsystem that performed these functions was known as the Win32 subsystem and executed in User mode. In NT 4, this function was moved to the Kernel mode and renamed as the Win32K Executive Service. These changes have resulted in the Win32 subsystem being replaced by the CSR Subsystem, which has reduced responsibilities. As a direct result of these changes, applications with highly intensive graphics can see a significantly improved display performance.

    This module includes:

    - The Window Manager, which controls displayable windows

    - The Graphics Device Interface, which is the graphics engine that creates and manages displayed and printed graphics

    - The Graphics Device Drivers, which directly interface the graphics hardware; these drivers are created as a result of the cooperation between Microsoft and the graphics hardware manufacturers

## MICROKERNEL

The Microkernel is NT 4's version of its predecessor's Kernel. The Kernel is located at the bottom of NT's layered architecture and maintains the highest OS priority to execute Kernel mode operations, such as thread dispatching, multiprocessor synchronization, and hardware exception handling.

## HARDWARE ABSTRACTION LAYER (HAL)

The Hardware Abstraction Layer (HAL) is a layer of software designed to shield applications from differences in hardware and device drivers. Abstracting devices reduces the need to tailor the operating system to the wide variation in hardware components. Using the abstraction concept allows NT to run on multiple platforms (for example, MIPS, Alpha, and PowerPC).

# NT 4's New Features

These are the new features that you can expect to find in the latest version of Windows NT. After four revisions, Microsoft is still carefully enhancing NT's network capabilities by adding features aimed at global networks and network management.

## DNS NAME SERVER (SERVER ONLY)

NT 4 contains a new Domain Name System (DNS) server that is compliant with RFCs 1034 and 1035. A DNS is a database of network names that resolves a host's IP address to its given network name. The NT 4 DNS database can be accessed by both client computers and other DNS servers. This means that you can easily add your local DNS to a distributed set of domain DNS databases. Microsoft has designed the DNS service to work in conjunction with Windows Internet Name Service (WINS) to resolve host names.

## MICROSOFT'S INTERNET INFORMATION SERVER (SERVER ONLY)

Microsoft includes an integrated version of the new Internet Information Server (IIS) linked into the NT 4 Server. The IIS provides Internet access as a configurable option to the NT 4 setup.

## MULTI-PROTOCOL ROUTING (SERVER ONLY)

Using two network interface cards, NT 4 can be used as a router to inter-connect two LANs. The new Multi-Protocol Routing service can connect a LAN to a wide area network (WAN) using either IP or IPX.

## DHCP RELAY AGENT (SERVER ONLY)

Using the DHCP Relay Agent, NT 4 can relay DHCP messages from one LAN to another. This eliminates the need for multiple DHCP agents to be present on each LAN. The DHCP Relay Agent is compatible with RFC 1542.

## DNS AND WINS COMPATIBILITY (SERVER ONLY)

The DNS and WINS servers provided with NT 4 have resolved their naming differences to allow DNS domain naming to be used in WINS. This feature enables the NT workstations to access NT Servers across WANs and the Internet.

## WINDOWS UNIFORM NAMING CONVENTION

The Windows Uniform Naming Convention (UNC) has been updated to support DNS names. In the UNC naming convention, "\\server\share" users can use a DNS domain name for the server portion. A typical UNC version of a DNS name would be \\Able.baker.delta\system, which specifies that the system folder in the baker.delta domain is located on the Able server.

## WINDOWS 95 COMPATIBLE USER INTERFACE

NT 4 Server and Workstation support the Windows 95 compatible user interface. NT 4 makes use of the same control set allowing users to start programs, open documents, and administer files using Win95's optimized user interface control set.

## INTERNET EXPLORER

Microsoft has packaged their Internet Explorer as a configurable option with NT 4. The Internet Explorer is a well-designed, efficient tool for accessing and searching Internet Web sites.

## WINDOWS EXPLORER

Windows Explorer is the Windows 95 and NT 4 answer to the Windows 3.1 File Manager. The Explorer allows a user to open files, run applications, and quickly navigate the local and network drive's file hierarchy.

## WINDOWS MESSAGING SUBSYSTEM (NT-WMS)

NT 4 includes a newly revised messaging subsystem (NT-WMS) that includes the exchange client, Messaging API (MAPI) support, and email. The new messaging subsystem services both local and remote (dial-up) clients. During NT 4 setup, you can specify which mail system will be installed. The selections include Internet Mail, Microsoft Mail, or both.

## HARDWARE PROFILES

NT 4 has incorporated the Hardware Profiles capability that was first introduced in Windows 95. If your workstation changes frequently (you have a dockable laptop, or you often change, attach, and re-attach peripherals), you can create bootable profiles that NT will use to test your hardware configuration during system bootup.

## MICROSOFT EXCHANGE

Microsoft Exchange is an updated and greatly expanded version of the previous Microsoft email utility. With Exchange, you have a full-featured, networked mail system, including addressing and folders, that is easier to use and more efficient. NT 4 includes the Exchange Universal Inbox, which supports incoming mail and fax messages.

## CLIENT/GATEWAY SERVICES FOR NETWARE 4.x

NT 4 has revised its client and gateway services to interface with Novell's current NetWare 4.x servers. This modification includes shared object capability supported by the new NetWare Directory Services (NDS). The new NDS client enables the NT 4 workstation to use NetWare logon scripts and file/print capabilities, however, it does not extend to include the NetWare VLM support.

## DISTRIBUTED COMPONENT OBJECT MODEL

NT 4 has extended the Component Object Model (COM) capabilities from local applications to also include networked and Internet applications.

DCOM was originally known as NetOLE. In previous versions of NT, OLE was restricted to using only local objects. With NT 4's DCOM, network objects are now accessible.

## Direct X API

NT 4 now supports the new Direct X APIs for both Microsoft and third-party software applications. Direct X applications control sound, video, and other desktop services.

## Enhanced Meta File Spooling

Enhanced Meta File (EMF) Spooling is a technology that was developed for Windows 95. EMF decomposes a graphic image into components that can be efficiently processed by the graphics subsystem and spooled to a printer.

## Peer Web Services

Microsoft Peer Web services is an Internet Server API (ISAPI)-compliant personal Web server that runs on NT 4 workstations. We'll discuss ISAPI and the Peer Web services in more detail in Chapter 9.

## Point-to-Point Tunneling Protocol Client

Point-to-Point Tunneling Protocol (PPTP) is a newly installed protocol that enables a Remote Access Service (RAS) client to access resources on a WAN through an Internet connection to a Windows NT RAS. PPTP can establish connections either through an Internet Service Provider or directly to the Internet.

## Dial-Up Logon

A user logging into a RAS-connected Windows NT 4 workstation can connect and conduct encrypted logon authentication transactions with a domain controller. We'll cover dial-up logon in Chapter 4.

## A Revised Internal Architecture

As we have previously discussed, NT 4 has revised the Win32 subsystem by adding its repetitive, time-consuming functions to the higher-priority Kernel mode Executive Services.

## Two Flavors of NT

Your first impression of NT may be one of confusion because NT has two flavors—the NT Workstation (client) and the NT Advanced Server (server). Other factors can also lead to confusion because, although the names are different, many of their functions appear to be the same (for example, the server supports all workstation functions and the workstation supports some server functions). Each flavor can share files across networks using peer-to-peer network connections. Table 1.1 describes the similarities and differences between the two flavors of NT.

| Table 1.1 Comparison between the NT Workstation and the NT Advanced Server | | |
| --- | --- | --- |
| **Features** | **NT Workstation** | **NT Server** |
| Minimum Memory Requirements | 12 MB | 16 MB |
| System Services | — | Optimized Thread Allocation |
| 16-Bit Applications | Optimized | Peer-to-Peer Concurrent Client Connections |
| 10 Inbound | Unlimited Outbound | Unlimited Inbound and Outbound |
| Data Caching | — | Optimized |
| Symmetric Multiprocessing | 2 Processors | 4 Processors |
| Remote Access Service | 1 Session | 256 Sessions |
| Directory Replication | Import Only | Import and Export |
| Domain Logon Validation | No | Yes |
| Primary or Backup Domain Controller | No | Yes |
| File and Printer Sharing | — | Optimized |
| Services for Macintosh | No | Yes |
| Disk Fault Tolerance | No | Yes |

*(continued)*

**Table 1.1    Comparison between the NT Workstation and the NT Advanced Server (continued)**

| Features | NT Workstation | NT Server |
|---|---|---|
| DHCP Services | Client | Client/Server |
| WINS Services | Client | Client/Server |
| DNS Services | Client | Client/Server |

## NT WORKSTATION

The Windows NT Workstation has been designed to operate as a desktop client. NT's workstation operation is optimized to support three primary functions:

- *Human Interaction*—The workstation recognizes that it must support two masters, the user and the network. Thus, the user interface is a primary design driver for the workstation.

- *Foreground Execution*—The workstation is tuned to provide faster, more efficient support of foreground tasks. The background and network support is run at lower default priority levels.

- *Support for Both 16- and 32-Bit Applications*—While both the NT Workstation and Server will run MS-DOS and 16-bit Windows applications, the workstation's internals are optimized for the NT Virtual DOS Machine (NTVDM). In plain language, this means that these applications will run more efficiently on the workstation than on the server.

The workstation design enables NT to run in a minimum memory model of 12 MB, versus the 16 MB required for the Server. As shown in Table 1.1, the workstation can service only 10 attached clients, versus the Server's unlimited capacity.

## WINDOWS NT SERVER

The server is designed to support optimized network responsiveness, which is accomplished by increasing the execution priorities of those tasks that support the network. For example, the server is optimized to more efficiently utilize cached memory for handling large data blocks.

Basically, the four distinct types of NT Server operations are:

- *Domain Controllers*—NT 4 now manages network logons and user databases, and oversees LAN security.

- *File and Print Service*—The server is dedicated to handling incoming and outgoing data traffic, sharing data files, and managing print queues for attached printers.

- *Application Server*—NT 4 is configured to execute dedicated server applications, such as Database Server, Mainframe Front End applications, and CAD. NT Server is optimized for 32-bit server type applications, such as MS-SQL Server.

- *Remote Access Server*—NT 4 is configured as a remote server managing low-speed serial lines, remote network traffic, and providing a LAN gateway to WAN users.

Depending on speed, the number of attached users, and data traffic, a server can support all of these tasks within the same hardware platform.

# NT in Today's Local Area Networks

Microsoft created NT to both fit into existing installation and become the backbone of new installations. Many existing LANs use the dedicated service approach where servers with dedicated functions already exist. Many smaller LANs see limited use for dedicated servers and make maximum use of the Peer-to-Peer networking features to reduce cost and maximize cooperative file sharing.

## Dedicated Service Model

Dedicated File servers have been used extensively in Novell LANs to centralize management of resources and to control resources that affect many users. These dedicated servers can be classified into three groups: file servers, print servers, and applications servers.

### FILE SERVERS

Historically, the personal computer LAN model grew out of the mini-computer and mainframe worlds—both of which effectively use a Dedicated Service model. In this model, networked PC LAN topology consists of attaching multiple workstations to file, print, and applications servers through the network. File servers are often mainframe computers or large scale mini-computers with vast amounts of mass storage and resources. Individual workstations can share network data only with those file servers. Specifically, if you wish to share a file with someone, you must first log onto the file server, then store the data file in a common directory. The workstation wanting to share this data must also log onto that server before it can retrieve the stored file from the shared directory. This results in the file server being involved in virtually every network data transaction.

## PRINT SERVERS

In the Dedicated Service model, network printing is constrained to dedicated print servers. One or more printers are attached to a network print server. The print server manages one or more print queues. To print, you send your print file to one of the print queues and the print server then sends the queued print files to the attached printers. The dedicated server approach works very well in large LANs, as it makes efficient use of expensive printing equipment by sharing it among the LAN workstations. Even today, special color printers and high-density mass storage is prohibitively expensive. Another consideration is that these costly resources are under the scrutiny and management of a LAN administrator. The administrator oversees usage, can clear printing problems, and remind you to purge your directories of unwanted files. This model is still very effective on middle to larger networks (hundreds of users).

## APPLICATIONS SERVERS

In the Dedicated Service model, applications are also run on network application servers. To use a word processor, spreadsheet, or database application, you must log onto the application server and access the software residing on that server. You effectively share the application with other users. Application cost and vendor control are major factors in this design. Vendors can more carefully restrict access to the applications through the use of license fees and limitations to the number of concurrent users for each application. This model is still effective today for high-end, expensive, or difficult-to-administer applications.

## Peer-to-Peer Networking Model

Dedicated servers work very well in a centralized controlled environment, but they are expensive. The Peer-to-Peer model reduces costs by eliminating the need for many of the servers through sharing. This makes the Peer-to-Peer networking model well suited to small or distributed networks.

### FILE SHARING

The Peer-to-Peer Networking Model resulted, in part, from the reduction of costs for printers and mass storage. In the peer-to-peer model, each workstation on the network has essentially the same set of resource rights and capacities. The peer-to-peer model creates a local workstation environment that views network resources, files, printing, and applications as if they were local. To share a file, you simply attach your workstation to another workstation with shared directories and move files in either direction. I will explain these mechanisms in more detail later in this chapter.

### PRINT SHARING

Peer-to-peer printing involves attaching printers to the local user workstations and using the facilities of the local workstations' operating system to share these printers with other network users. A remote user can connect to your local workstation and attach to its local printer. The remote user's workstation then executes and spools the print job, but the print stream still utilizes resources on the local workstation.

### APPLICATION SHARING

Peer-to-peer applications have evolved in much the same way as peer-to-peer printing. To use a network-compatible application on another workstation, the application has to be in a network-shared directory. The using workstation attaches to the shared directory and begins executing the program located in that directory. The application actually executes on the local workstation and appears to be a local application, but is really located on another networked computer. Note that not all applications are network capable. Some applications still restrict unlimited access and some require extensive network utilization.

The limitations of peer-to-peer networking are decreased network security, diminished workstation capacity, and more intensive LAN management.

The sheer number of interconnections between workstations in larger networks can make the network impossible to manage. The less restrictive, non-dedicated access to shared resources found in peer-to-peer networks make security difficult, if not impossible, to manage.

## NT's Role in Both Models

In a Dedicated Service network, NT has sufficient power and resources to operate effectively as file, print, and application servers. This has enabled NT to gain a foothold in existing large networks. The NT Server supports security, effectively restricts file access, and has the disk capacity (terabytes) to be a file server. NT Server printing has been streamlined in its later releases and, through the use of EMF and PostScript drivers, can be effectively used as a print server. Application server capability has lagged behind the other two service types, but with the release and acceptance of MS-SQL server by many large corporations, NT is quickly catching the pack. Third-party software vendors have either written new applications or modified existing Unix or mainframe applications to run on NT.

When configured in the Peer-to-Peer Networking Model, NT is very cost effective for small to mid-sized networks (fewer than 500 users). NT workstations can effectively share mass storage among networked workstations for file sharing, and NT's ability to attach local printers and share the printers with other networked workstations works well on smaller networks. Both NT Workstation and NT Server are built to participate in peer-to-peer networking. As both workstation and server, each has incorporated a Redirector (RDR) function and Server (SVR) function into its default architecture (see Figure 1.2). The NT 4 Workstation can support 10 simultaneous incoming user connections, but the NT 4 Server can service an unlimited number of incoming connections. Both the NT Workstation and Server can theoretically connect to an unlimited number of outgoing connections.

# The Seven Layer OSI Model

In 1984, the International Organization for Standardization (ISO) created the Open Systems Interconnection (OSI) reference model as a better way to describe the complex network layering. It has become widely used

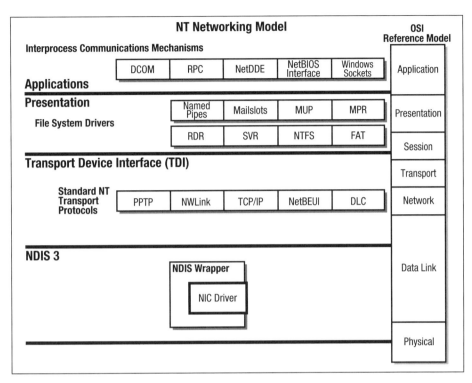

**Figure 1.2** NT's networking architecture is contained within four layers, which are described in the context of the seven layer OSI Reference Model.

to describe the flow of data between the various network layers and the user application. NT has made a few changes to the basic model, but it is useful to compare the OSI model with NT's version.

NT 4 uses a design that can't be precisely mapped on the OSI seven layer model. Figure 1.2 describes a relative mapping of each OSI function to the internal NT networking architecture. Each function described by the OSI model exists in NT's networking architecture, but representing NT's software models to each layer can be confusing. Take a good look at the figure and then we'll go through a quick overview of each layer's responsibilities, to clear up any confusion.

## *Physical Layer*

The Physical Layer is where the proverbial rubber (Network Interface Card [NIC]) meets the road (the network cable). The NIC transfers data frames to and receives data from other computers on the network. Determining which NIC to use is based on the physical network media, which may be fiber, copper, infrared, or even an antenna transmitting and receiving Radio Frequency (RF) data. Two major design criteria for the media choice are how far and how fast you need to send data. Masking the physical media, the Physical Layer connects the Data Link Layer to the network.

## Data Link Layer

In a transmitting computer, the Data Link Layer sends data frames that are received from the Network Layer to the Physical Layer. The Data Link Layer is responsible for the error-free transfer of data from one computer to another through the network.

In a receiving computer, the Data Link Layer organizes data bits received from the Physical Layer into Network Layer-compatible data frames. Depending on the protocol used, the Data Link Layer passes a data frame to the Physical Layer and waits for a receipt acknowledgment. If a data frame is not sent and a receipt acknowledgment is not returned, the Data Link Layer retransmits the data frame. Of course, the number and timing of these waits and retries are governed by the protocol and communications settings.

To make this a bit more clear, let's consider a real-world analogy: faxing a letter. Faxing requires you to place the letter in the fax machine and then enter the telephone number (address). The next step is to let the fax machine (Data Link Layer) send the letter through the phone lines in its standard format (data frame). If the fax is not received correctly, the fax machine must resend it.

The Institute of Electrical and Electronics Engineers (IEEE) extended this layer by dividing it into two sub-layers—the Media Access Control (MAC) and the Logical Link Control (LLC)—created by the IEEE 802 Project. These two sub-layers split the Data Link Layer's responsibilities.

The LLC manages communications services through the use of Service Access Points (SAP). An SAP is a vector to the upper-layer protocol initiating the data transfer. Using SAPs, the LLC can identify where to send the data in the upper-model layers. The LLC is also responsible for error handling. Given a notification of network error by the MAC, the LLC is programmed to perform error recovery and retransmission.

In the 802 modified model, the MAC is responsible for the error-free transmission and reception of data frames to and from the Physical Layer. The MAC is a lower-level sub-layer and contains the NIC and its software driver. Network errors are detected at the MAC layer, which notifies the LLC. The MAC specification requires a unique physical address for each NIC.

## Network Layer

The Network Layer is a traffic cop that manages traffic problems on the network, including switching, routing, and controlling data congestion. The Network Layer supervises the network message traffic and translates node names into physical (network) addresses. The Network Layer also assembles small data frames together for transmission across the network and restructures large frames into smaller packets. On the receiving end, the Network Layer reassembles the data packets into their original frame structure.

## Transport Layer

The duty of the Transport Layer is the error-free transfer of data between the higher levels of the model and the network. In any communications, there must be a sender and a receiver. The duties of the Transport Layer depend on whether the computer is transmitting or receiving.

When transmitting, the Transport Layer is responsible for reconciling the data packets and recovery if errors are detected. The layer monitors messages and, in those protocols which are deterministic, verifies data delivery. In the event that a packet is not delivered, the Transport Layer notifies the application of the event.

At the receiving end, the Transport Layer unpacks the messages, removes the messages, checkpoints, reassembles the original messages, and sends a receipt acknowledgment.

## Session Layer

The Session Layer manages computer-to-computer interchange by establishing a communications link called a *session*. In order to establish sessions, the layer executes functions to perform name and user rights recognition. To increase data security, this layer creates data checkpoints and controls which computer has clear access for sending network data.

In Figure 1.2, the File System Drivers, RDR, and SVR bridge both the Session and Presentation Layers, as some of these layer's functionality is contained in these drivers. Remember, the OSI model is only a reference. The value of the model is in determining what tasks have to be performed. NT and other operating systems determine the final implementation, including where the modeled tasks are to be performed.

## Presentation Layer

The Presentation Layer translates data obtained from the Applications layer into its own intermediate format. When intermediate data is received from the lower layers, the Presentation Layer performs reverse translation and passes the result to the waiting applications. The Presentation Layer's intermediate format is designed to reduce overhead by packing data (compression) to reduce the number of bytes transmitted, resulting in increased throughput. In addition to compression, the Presentation Layer is equipped to convert protocols, switch the character set of ASCII data, and expand the graphics data. This layer also performs data security management, including data encryption, an important feature for password and domain management.

## Application Layer

The Application Layer contains the application processes that use network services. The Application Layer also contains the Application Programming Interfaces (API) that are used by those processes to communicate with NT's network hierarchy. The API is a library of standard functional utilities that can be used by the following application types:

- Standard NT Packaged Software (Notepad, Wordpad, Explorer)—These software applications come as a part of the NT operating system, but, in reality, are not part of NT's internal operating system.

- End-User Created Software Applications (Visual Basic, Powersoft, C++)—These software applications are created by the final NT end-user.

- Third-Party Software Applications (Word, WordPerfect, CorelDraw)— These are packages created by a third party (not Microsoft and not the end-user).

One major requirement that all three of these categories share is their expectation that the software they create will run reliably under the NT standard operating system. This means that they use the standard API functions whenever possible and they expect the functions to be standardized to effectively mask changes to the hardware platform or NT's software internals.

# The NT Networking Model

NT's internal design contains specific components which we'll be covering in the following sections. I'll introduce you to each of these components and explain their relative layer location and role in NT's networking architecture. The component discussions contain a number of acronyms and build on themselves, so you need to start at the beginning and work your way through or you might find yourself quite confused. We'll develop these topics more in later chapters.

## *Application Layer*

Software has typically lagged behind hardware development. Today's modern networked workstation has been capable of executing 32-bit applications since the introduction of the 80386 technology. But, only recently has there been an operating system and an application suite to make use of this power.

Network software has also lagged. As users demand more features and capabilities from their desktop PCs, applications have grown ever larger. Consider the growth in size from the MS-DOS Word version 5 to today's Word 7 running under NT. The desktop applications have outgrown the desktop workstation. While hardware costs have dropped, the user's needs have grown ever faster. To meet today's expectations, the workstation must be networked and its applications suite fully integrated with networking capability.

Desktop applications have grown to the point where additional capabilities and features must be an outgrowth of networking. Newer applications will be released within the next few years that will run on the desktop workstation, but will acquire enhanced features, sharing data and remote resources through the local area network. Network applications must be capable of sharing text, graphics, and even sound and video between remote devices. Cooperative applications make use of the Peer-to-Peer Network Model we discussed earlier. Consider the word processor user that must obtain information from spreadsheet data located on another workstation or add graphics from a presentation stored in a library.

The Windows software that you recognize—Write, Word, and Excel—resides at the Application Layer. To communicate with the network and other networked computers, these software applications use Interprocess Communication (IPC) mechanisms provided through Application Programming Interfaces (APIs). An IPC is a set of API functions that runs on networked workstations to cooperatively exchange data.

## DISTRIBUTED COMPONENT OBJECT MODEL

In earlier versions of NT, Microsoft created Object Linking and Embedding (OLE) to make it easier to handle objects within documents by enabling the user to link an object to the application that created it. OLE also allowed an object to be embedded into a document that can be updated or modified using the controls of the creating application. OLE worked very well, but it had one stumbling block: The objects, containers (documents), and creating applications had to be physically located on one platform (all located on your workstation).

NT 4, however, makes use of Distributed Component Object Model (DCOM), which is an applications-level protocol for object-oriented IPC. With DCOM, or what was termed in early NT literature Networked Dynamic Data Exchange (NetDDE), the local restriction has been lifted. DCOM enables a user to manipulate objects across a network and even across the Internet.

In Windows 95 and NT 3.X, NetDDE is the primary technology to the user-oriented method of exchanging data between networked applications. Many in the industry believe that DCOM will eventually replace NetDDE as the IPC Windows standard of choice for users.

## REMOTE PROCEDURE CALLS

Remote Procedure Calls (RPC) is defined as part of the Open Software Foundation's (OSF) Distributed Computing Environment (DCE) specification. RPC is an IPC that resides at the Applications Layer. RPC enables individual application procedures to execute on systems anywhere on the network. This means that you can write a program that will run on your NT Workstation while executing portions of its procedures on other workstations. RPC is a true client-server mechanism, as either the application's client or server portion must reside on a computer to execute.

The benefit of RPC is that it allows potentially time-consuming functions to execute on remote computers, sharing the computational burden. As you will see when we discuss clustering, burden sharing can significantly speed up some applications, such as database operations.

RPC applications are created in a special language called the Interface Definition Language (IDL). Using IDL, programmers can readily develop network applications without the burden of writing special interface drivers. RPC already incorporates these drivers as part of the NT operating system. Programs written in IDL can readily use the existing RPC linkage between networked workstations.

RPC is able to use other IPC mechanisms to establish communications between the computers on which portions of the application exist. If the client and server are both on the same computer, the Local Procedure Call (LPC) mechanism can be used to transfer application data. RPC is an extension of the LPC and effectively integrates with the LPC. This makes RPC one of the most flexible and portable of NT's IPC mechanisms.

Many developers who create networked applications prefer RPC because there is more control and flexibility than with named pipes (we'll get to named pipes in just a moment).

## NETDDE

Dynamic Data Exchange (DDE), in which client and server are on one workstation, enables the user to link data in one file to data in another file. Applications can then dynamically exchange that data as changes occur. For example, consider a client spreadsheet that is linked to other server spreadsheets. As data in the server spreadsheets change, the client's spreadsheet can be either automatically or manually updated to reflect the changes.

Network Dynamic Data Exchange (NetDDE) is a network extension of that same mechanism. NetDDE is a client/server IPC that enables applications to share data between files located on networked computers.

## NETBIOS INTERFACE

NetBIOS at the Application Layer is an API that allows interconnections with remote computers. NetBIOS works in conjunction with TCP/IP and NWLink to send and receive networked data. NetBIOS is a legacy IPC from MS-DOS and earlier versions of Windows.

## WINDOWS SOCKETS

Windows Sockets is an IPC that resides at the Applications Layer. Sockets provide functional calls to enable computers to connect a socket or pipe between networked computers. Once connected, the computers share the socket to exchange data. The Windows Sockets (referred to simply as Sockets) API also resides at the Applications Layer. Sockets is an NT standard programming interface that works with NT's TCP/IP and IPX transport protocols. Windows NT Sockets is a public specification, based on the Berkeley Unix Sockets specification.

## *Presentation Layer*

As in the OSI model, the Presentation Layer translates, manages security, and compresses data. The following mechanisms are used, in varying degrees, to perform these tasks.

## NAMED PIPES

Named pipes provide connection-oriented messaging services that allow applications to share memory over the network. Windows NT provides a special API that increases security when using named pipes.

Unlike the Application Layer IPC mechanisms, named pipes (and mailslots, which we'll get to next) were created as file systems. The named pipes are treated internally as Named Pipes File System (NPFS). Local processes can use named pipes to communicate without involving the lower network layers. Remote access to named pipes is provided through the redirector (RDR).

As with the Application Layer IPCs, named pipes requires both a client and a server to form a connection. A pipe is nothing more than a communication duct with two ends. Each end must have a Windows handle (an internal reference used by processes) and direction. A pipe may be designated as either read-only, write-only, or two-way.

Although a pipe can be created to support several clients located on different machine, every named pipe can only service one communication. So, a party line among three or more machines, all using the same pipe, cannot cross-communicate. When two clients connect to the server pipe of a third machine, each client has independent conversations with the server.

## MAILSLOTS

Mailslots are used to provide connectionless messaging services on a local area network. However, delivery of connectionless messages is not guaranteed. Mailslots APIs in Windows NT are a subset of those in Microsoft OS/2 LAN Manager. As with named pipes, mailslots are implemented as a file system—Mail Slots File System (MFSF). Windows NT implements second-class mailslots which are used most commonly for:

- Registration of computer, workgroup, or domain

- Identification of user names on the network

- The Computer Browser service, which browses the network for names

- Sending broadcast messages to computers or users

## MULTIPLE UNIVERSAL NAME CONVENTION PROVIDER

The Multiple Universal Name Convention Provider (MUP) is responsible for decoding UNC names. When a process makes I/O calls using UNC names, these requests are passed to MUP. MUP then selects the appropriate UNC network RDR to handle the I/O request. If the MUP has not seen the UNC name in the recent time period, the MUP will send the name to each of the UNC providers registered with it. The MUP negotiates with each redirector to find out which one can process the UNC name. MUP identifies the redirector with the highest priority response claiming it can establish a connection to the UNC. This connection remains as long as there is activity.

## MULTI-PROVIDER ROUTER

The Multi-Provider Router (MPR) supports applications that do not use UNC names in their I/O requests. These applications may use WNet APIs or third-party APIs.

MPR is similar in function to the MUP. This layer receives non-UNC commands, determines the appropriate redirector, and passes the command to that redirector. Often, different network vendors use special interfaces for communicating with their redirector. This requires that a series of special vendor-provided DLLs be included between the MPR and the redirectors. The special DLLs expose a special interface so that MPR can communicate with the redirectors, and, in turn, the redirectors use the DLLs to understand how to act on the request from the MPR. The vendor DLL libraries must be supplied by the third-party vendor and installed with the redirector.

## THE NETWORK WORKSTATION

The redirector (RDR) is the Presentation Layer component that finds data. In NT's Executive Services there is an object named the Local Procedure Call (LPC) facility. The purpose of this facility is to execute procedure calls within the local NT operating system. The RDR is a remote version of this facility. If a user wishes to move a file from one location to another, the applications program—File Manager or Explorer—sends the request to the LPC. If the LPC does not find the file locally, it forwards the request to the RDR to seek a network location. The RDR redirects the request across the network to another remote networked computer containing the file. The RDR request is processed by the remote computer's server (SVR).

The Windows NT RDR allows connection to MS-Net servers, such as NT Workstations, NT Servers, Windows for Workgroups, LAN Managers, and LAN Servers. As shown in Figure 1.2, the RDR is contained in a layer above the Transport Driver Interface (TDI) and sends its request through the transport protocols.

The redirector is an NT file system driver that is accessed by applications through API calls. Since the RDR is a file system, NT uses the same kernel software to manage both local and remote (redirected) files.

## THE NETWORK SERVER

Windows NT uses a server (SVR) component to interact with network data requests. The SVR, residing at the Presentation Layer, directly interfaces the file systems (FAT, NTFS) to gain access to the system's mass storage. Like the redirector, SVR is responsible for satisfying network input/output (I/O) requests for file access.

Like the workstation RDR, the server service exists in two forms in the NT system:

- *Server*—An NT process that runs as part of the NT services.

- *SRV.SYS*—The server's file system driver that interfaces both the TDI Transport Layer protocols and the various file system devices which read and write files.

## NT's FILE SYSTEM (NTFS)

NTFS is NT's file system of choice for volumes requiring security and fault tolerance, which makes it an excellent choice for servers. NTFS supports 8.3 file names for compatibility with MS-DOS and other networked clients, including AppleShare, OS/2, and Unix. NTFS supports security to ensure that only users with sufficient permissions may gain access to your files. RAID 5, disk striping with parity, is a fault tolerant disk technology that uses NTFS to reduce or eliminate the effects of a disk crash on your data.

## MS-DOS' FILE SYSTEM

The NT 4 File Allocation Table (FAT) file system is a revved up version of the original MS-DOS FAT file system. Its design has been enhanced to support larger disk capacity and operating system changes, but it stays compatible with legacy MS-DOS applications and MS-DOS specifications. The FAT file system does support network drives and, beginning with NT 3.51, FAT extended it's original 8.3 file name restriction to NT's 255 character limits.

## *Transport Layer*

The Transport Driver Interface (TDI) is not a single program but a specification to which the transport protocol device drivers are written. At this layer, networking software provides a virtual connection between RDR and the remote destination's RDR. Similar connections are made between the server and the sources of the requests it receives.

The RDR and the SVR are designed to be compliant with the TDI. This compatibility arrangement shields the file systems from the details of the underlying network transports. TDI is a Kernel-mode programming interface.

## THE POINT-TO-POINT TUNNELING PROTOCOL

The Point-to-Point Tunneling Protocol (PPTP) is a new addition to NT 4. The PPTP supports virtual private networks (VPN). VPNs are private networks set up to interact with the Internet. Using PPTP, a user may log onto a private network over the Internet while maintaining company security. PPTP communicates by tunneling encrypted data in one of the standard NT transport protocols (IP, IPX, and NetBEUI).

Using PPTP, a remote user could make a local dial-up call to a local Front End Processor. The Front End Processor would then communicate across the Internet or a corporate WAN to the appropriate NT Server.

## THE NWLINK PROTOCOL

NWLink is an IPX/SPX-compatible protocol for Windows NT. It can be used to establish connections between Windows NT computers and MS-DOS, Windows, or other NT computers. Access to files or printer queues on a NetWare server requires an additional redirector, such as Microsoft's Client Service for NetWare (CSNW). NWLink is needed to interface NT with NetWare client-server applications. The client portion can be run on a Windows NT computer by accessing the server portion on a NetWare server.

## THE TCP/IP PROTOCOL SUITE

TCP/IP stands for Transmission Control Protocol/Internet Protocol, and is an industry-standard suite of protocols designed for wide-area networking.

The TCP/IP protocol suite includes the Transmission Control Protocol (TCP), Internet Protocol (IP), User Datagram Protocol (UDP), Address Resolution Protocol (ARP), and Internet Control Message Protocol

(ICMP). The PPP and Serial-Line IP (SLIP) protocols used for dial-up access to TCP/IP networks are also included. TCP/IP supports application interfaces, including Windows Sockets 1.1, RPC, NetBIOS, and NetDDE.

Basic TCP/IP utilities (Finger, FTP, LPR, RCP, REXEC, RSH, Telnet, and TFTP) are included to allow Windows NT to interact with non-Microsoft hosts, such as Unix workstations. TCP/IP diagnostic tools (arp, hostname, ipconfig, lpq, nbtstat, netstat, ping, route, and tracert) are included to detect and resolve TCP/IP networking problems.

Additional services and related administrative tools, including FTP Server service, Windows Internet Name Service (WINS), Dynamic Host Configuration Protocol (DHCP) service, and TCP/IP printing for accessing Unix printers are included within NT's TCP network suite.

## THE NETBEUI PROTOCOL

The NetBEUI protocol, first introduced by IBM in 1985, was written to the NetBIOS interface. It was designed as a small, efficient protocol for use on department-sized LANs of 20 to 200 workstations. The NetBEUI protocol provides powerful flow control and tuning parameters, plus better-than-average error detection.

## THE DATA LINK CONTROL PROTOCOL

Unlike the other NT protocols, the Data Link Control (DLC) protocol is not used as a primary protocol for use between personal computers because it does not support a NetBIOS interface. DLC is used to support network printers that are configured with their own NIC. The network requires only direct access to the Data Link Layer, not the NT RDR. For example, DLC can be configured on a print server interfacing a network card-equipped Hewlett-Packard printer. The server transmits print data to the printer and the printer responds with the proper acknowledgment and status or fault information.

## *The Data Link Layer*

Network Driver Interface Specification (NDIS) version 3 is a standard that describes the requirements to enable NT to use multiple NICs and multiple transport protocols. Because NT supports the NDIS, it can support one or more NDIS-compliant cards running one or more transport protocols within the same platform.

In theory, NDIS 3 permits an unlimited number of network adapter cards to a computer running an unlimited number of protocols. Unlimited is, of course, an unbounded term. In the real world, the number of protocols and NICs is limited. Because each card occupies one bus slot and multiple protocols impose a communications overhead, the real limitation is the hardware platform's ability to support a realistic communications data throughput and the number of physical platform connections.

NDIS permits the transport protocol to remain independent of the NIC through use of a standard interface. All transport protocols use the NDIS interface to access data to and from the network adapter cards.

The NDIS 3 boundary layer is the interface that NDIS exposes to the transport protocols. This interface, or wrapper, shields the detailed workings of the network adapter card drivers from the upper-layer protocols. In later chapters, we'll define how NT binds the protocols with the network interface cards to result in a protocol stack that is both versatile and robust.

## Conclusion: Using the Network

In the preceding sections, I presented a topical overview of NT networking, which was designed to introduce you to the names and concepts that we'll encounter in the remainder of this book.

The modules, services, and layers associated with NT networking are all designed to produce a result. Often, as you pour through pages of text describing software processes, you lose the broader perspective. For this reason, I have decided to conclude this chapter with a real-world example of how NT processes data. Most of you have, at one time or another, connected to a networked workstation or server to copy a file. The file access scenario uses all layers of the NT network architecture and shows how each layer cooperates with the layers above and below to move the data file from one computer to another. I'll continue to use this example in succeeding chapters, including more detail as we cover each topic. At this point, the example is simply designed to show how the architectural layers interact throughout the process.

## File Access Example

Our example involves two workstations, the client and the server, as shown in Figure 1.3. The server contains a file that the client needs to access. Both client and workstation exist on a local area network and each supports the TCP/IP transport protocol. As you step through the example, you'll probably have questions concerning security and network functionality that I have not yet covered. In order to expedite the example, I've included the answers to the questions which we'll cover in subsequent chapters.

The following represents the questions that need to be asked when copying a file from the server to the client:

- The client and the server are both on the same network, but does the client have access rights to the server?

- Is the file to be copied contained within an NTFS or a FAT file structure?

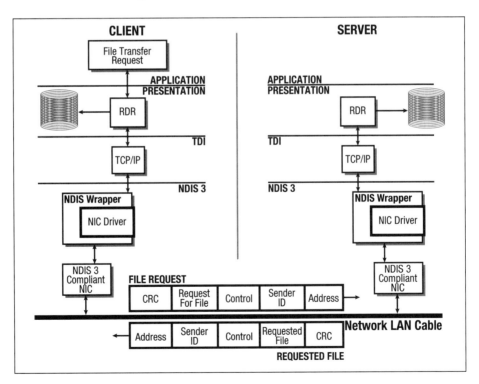

**Figure 1.3** The transfer of file information between a client and a server requires the interaction of all layers of the NT network architecture.

- Assuming an NTFS file structure, if the client does have rights to the server, is the server exposing the directory where the file exists to the network?

- If the directory is exposed to the network, does the client have sufficient rights to the share and the file within the shared directory?

If the client does have rights to the file, then the client must attach the server's shared directory as a network drive. This process enables the client's system to see the drive and search the contents of the shared directory. Using NT's Explorer or File Manager, the user must specify the UNC address of the server along with its shared directory name. Using the browser feature of the File Manager, the user identifies and links the server's shared directory as a network drive. The steps that follow are:

1. The user makes a file copy request using drag and drop to copy the file into a local directory.

2. The file transfer request is transferred, along with the UNC name of the server, the shared directory, and the file name to the Win32 API by the File Manager as a function call.

3. The function calls are passed to the I/O Manager to request that the file be opened.

4. The I/O Manager recognizes that the request is for a file on a remote computer, so it passes the request to the RDR.

5. The Presentation Layer RDR receives the request and verifies the file's address is not contained within the local client's workstation. The MUP is used to identify the UNC name.

6. The RDR then interfaces the TDI Layer's transport protocol to start a network transmission.

7. The TCP/IP transport protocol creates a network frame and adds the destination address, the sender's workstation identity, control information to checkpoint the transmission, and the request for file code.

8. TCP/IP passes the completed data frame to the NDIS wrapper at the NDIS 3 Layer for transmission.

9. The NDIS 3 wrapper creates and appends the data frame's Cyclical Redundancy Check (CRC), then passes the data frame to the NIC's driver. The driver queues the data frame and waits for the opportunity to transmit the data frame to the destination address.

10. The data frame is transmitted over the LAN cable and arrives at the appropriate server.

11. The server's NIC reads the address and accepts the data frame.

12. The NIC transfers the data frame to the NDIS wrapper.

13. The server's NDIS wrapper verifies that the data frame was received with the correct CRC and passes the data frame to the TCP/IP transport protocol.

14. TCP/IP breaks the data frame into its individual parts and passes the request to the SVR. TCP/IP recognizes that the request will require a response and maintains the sender's ID.

15. The SVR receives the file request and verifies the requester network security access contained in the data frame's control. If the requester has sufficient security privilege, then the SVR processes the command by requesting the file from the NTFS file system.

16. The NTFS file system reads the file from the disk and transfers the file's contents to the SVR.

17. The SVR sends the file to the transport layer, where it is broken into many data frames for retransmission back to the client workstation. These data frames are sequentially sent to the NDIS wrapper where their CRC codes are appended and then subsequently sent to the NIC for network transmission.

18. The client's NIC receives the data frames and passes them to the NDIS wrapper, which checks for and acknowledges a valid transmission. In the event that an error is detected, a retransmission request is returned to the server where a subsequent retransmission of the flawed data frame is made.

19. The NDIS wrapper passes the data frames to the Transport Layer protocol as they are successfully received.

20. The Transport Layer strips the additional data frame information from the file data and passes the data to the RDR.

21. The RDR interfaces with the NTFS file system, which stores the data as it is received.

22. Upon completion, the RDR notifies the Application Layer that a successful retrieval has taken place.

After all this effort, finally the file is moved from server to workstation. As I mentioned earlier, I noted the security aspects because nothing happens on NT without security. It has definitely become a major part of the architecture. Basically, you must have permission to access named objects in NT. A named object can be a file, an application, or a directory. We'll cover security in Chapter 4.

As you can see, NT does a lot of work to complete a relatively simple task. While the NT operating system was designed with inherent networking capability, it must support modern networking requirements and continue to grow. One of the principal strengths of the NT network operating system is its ability to adapt to changing requirements and to include third-party protocols and file system components.

This chapter has provided you with a brief overview of the NT version 4 and, at a high level, its networking architecture. In the following chapters, NT networking is presented in more detail, with an emphasis on the important aspects required to tie NT 4 into existing and new LANs.

CHAPTER

# 2

# Internal Networking

**W**indows NT uses a modular network design that allows the operating system to support a large assortment of network protocols and redirectors. The purpose of this chapter is to introduce you to the components of the Windows NT operating system and how they work. We are going to first take a look at the components that make up the core of Windows NT networking: the system, the redirector, the server, and the providers. We will then review the protocols that allow the network system to speak in a language the network can understand. From there, we will cover the NDIS 3.0 interface. This interface takes the network protocols and gets them transmitted on the network. After giving you the information you need to understand how NT communicates with the network, we are going to take a look at third-party products that expand on NT's capability of running more than one network redirector. Then, I will introduce you to a network communications standard which is beginning to gain popularity: the Distributed Computing Environment (DCE). We will wrap up this chapter with an introduction to the NT Registry and familiarize you with the files NT uses for the network components we have covered. Let's get started.

# NT's Network Redirector, Server, and Providers

NT's flexibility and openness to multiple network standards can be attributed to its modular network design. Each aspect that we will be examining in NT's networking process is broken down into individual user and kernel mode components. The individual components work together to complete the networking process, as shown in Figure 2.1. We are going to look at the components that make up the network process and examine their roles and functions. We will keep the order of the examination as close as possible to the order an application would take when making a call to the network.

First, we will examine the Input/Output Application Programmers Interface (I/O API) and the WNet Application Programmers Interface (WNet API) to see how the application determines which one of these two interfaces to use for network requests. The next step in the network request involves the use of either the Multiple UNC Provider or the Multiple Provider

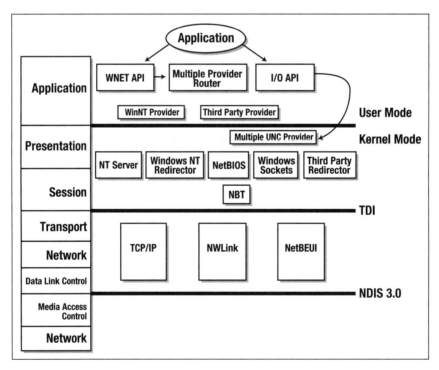

**Figure 2.1**   Network components.

Router; we will examine their uses and the differences between the two. The next section describes the provider layer, which is the interpreter NT uses to communicate with network redirectors. All network requests end up in a redirector, and we will see how the redirector handles the network request and the tools it uses to complete it. Toward the end of the section, we will cover how the redirector uses the Transport Device Interface (TDI) to communicate with the network, and finally, we will see how network requests from client machines are processed by the server.

## I/O API

When a program tries to access a file located on a machine on the network, and the data request is made using the Universal Naming Convention (UNC), the request from the program is passed to the I/O API. The I/O API, a user -mode application, then determines whether the request made by the application is indeed for a file located on the network. Once the I/O API determines that the request is for a networked file, the request is sent to the Multiple UNC Provider.

## WNet API

If a request is made by an application using the WNet API, a slightly different process occurs. The WNet API is a user-mode process that takes the network request from the application when the application uses a WNet API call to request network data. Unlike a data request that uses a UNC, the request is not sent to the Multiple UNC Router; instead, the WNet API passes its request to the Multiple Provider Router. For more information on the WNet API, see the section of the same name later in the chapter.

## The Multiple UNC Provider

The Multiple UNC Provider (MUP) is a kernel mode process that takes network requests from the I/O API. The MUP determines first whether it has a redirector that has already been recorded as being able to service the network request. If there is no record of a redirector handling this request, the MUP asks each of the installed redirectors if they can process the network request. Once a redirector acknowledges being able to handle the request, the MUP passes the request to the redirector and makes a record of which redirector services those types of network requests for future reference.

## Multiple Provider Router

The Multiple Provider Router (MPR) is a user-mode process that services WNet commands. WNet is part of the Win32 API and is specifically designed to allow Windows NT applications to connect, browse, and transfer data to and from multiple networks. The MPR takes the network request from the application and determines which provider the request should be passed to. Once the proper provider is determined, the MPR forwards the network request to it.

## The Provider

The provider is the user-mode component that takes requests from the Multiple Provider Router. Whenever a redirector is installed, a provider dynamic link library (DLL) is installed with it. The provider takes requests from the MPR, formats the request for the redirector, and passes the request to the redirector. The provider layer, shown in Figure 2.2, is the interpreter NT uses to communicate with other network redirectors. By default, Windows NT installs a provider that allows connections to Windows NT, LAN Manager, LAN Server, and MS-Net networks. Windows NT also ships with the Client Service for NetWare and the Gateway Service for NetWare, which can be installed with the default NT redirector to provide connectivity to NetWare resources. The Windows NT design allows multiple providers to be installed and used at the same time.

## The Redirector

The network redirector in NT, shown in Figure 2.3, is a 32-bit service designed to act just as any other file system in NT. This means that Windows

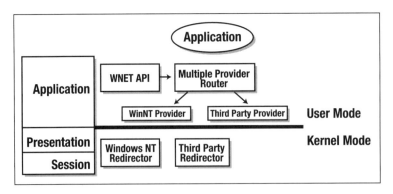

**Figure 2.2**   The provider layer.

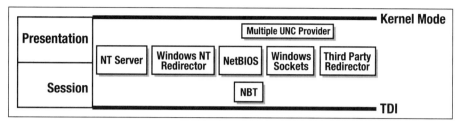

**Figure 2.3** The redirector model.

NT handles a call to the network just like it would handle loading a file on the local system. This approach gives the redirector certain advantages, including the ability to load and unload dynamically, work easily with other redirectors, and gain access to NT optimization items, such as the cache manager, which can help improve performance. The redirector is in charge of managing the network request across the network and re-establishing connectivity to network resources in the event of a failure. When the redirector receives the request from either the MUP or a provider, it takes the request and converts it into a system message block (SMB). System message blocks are a command set that contains the commands necessary for communicating with other SMB-compliant systems on the network. SMBs can be broken down into four message groups:

- *Session Control Messages*—These messages contain the commands that establish and end a redirector's communication session with a system on the network.

- *File Messages*—The file messages are used by the redirector to manipulate files on a system on the network.

- *Printer Messages*—The printer messages contain the commands to send information to a network print queue or to receive information from that queue.

- *Message Messages*—The message messages allow network clients to send messages to one another.

When the redirector creates the necessary system message request to carry out the network commands, it creates a pointer for the protocols to reference for access to the SMB. This pointer is known as the network control block (NCB). Once the SMB is prepared and the NCB is created, the redirector uses the Transport Driver Interface to hand control of communication over the network to the protocol layer.

## The Transport Driver Interface

The TDI was developed to provide an application breakpoint at the session layer of the OSI model. The TDI is not a program, but a specification that handles how to communicate with the network protocol that is compatible with the TDI installed on the NT server. This means that all the services above the TDI that want to communicate with the network only need to make sure that they are compliant with the TDI specification. The redirector and server components of NT are written to the TDI spec, and the major protocols of NT, TCP/IP, NetBEUI, and NWLink can all be used by components designed to be compliant with the TDI specification, regardless of the protocol installed or used. The TDI specification prevents the services from having to worry about customizing calls for certain protocols so that they can complete their requests. The redirector and server components use the TDI specification to access the network protocols to finish processing their network requests. To learn more about the TDI, you can check out the Windows NT device driver kit, which is part of the developers' network.

## Server

While the redirector handles requests for retrieving information across the network, it is up to the Server service to handle incoming requests from redirectors. The Server service sits right above the TDI layer and waits for network requests to be passed to it from the TDI, as shown in Figure 2.4. This service takes an incoming request and passes it on to the I/O manager. The I/O manager then determines the medium the file is stored on and passes it to the appropriate file system. The file system retrieves the data requested and returns it to the I/O manager. The I/O manager takes the retrieved data and returns it to the server component. The server component completes the circle by returning the retrieved information to the TDI so that it can be passed back to the workstation that requested the information via the network.

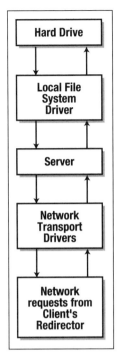

**Figure 2.4**   The server process flow.

# The NetBIOS and Windows Sockets Specifications

In addition to the redirectors that TCP/IP can receive network requests from, it is possible for protocols to receive NetBIOS or Windows Sockets calls. These API specifications sit in the kernel mode, right next to the redirector. Applications designed to use the redirector do not have to go though the NetBIOS interface, because the redirector provides a translator that converts NetBIOS names into TDI equivalents. Application calls that are written to use either the NetBIOS or Windows Sockets specification bypass the redirector and pass straight to protocols specified by the application.

NetBIOS is an older programming specification used by many applications, including the networking services of most Windows network operating systems. The use of the NetBIOS specification with TCP is referred to as NetBIOS over TCP/IP (NBT or NetBT). NetBIOS is used by Windows

NT to find systems available on the network. The NetBIOS specification is used by all Windows networking products to publish their system names and available services on the network. The Windows Internet Naming Service (WINS) makes use of the NetBIOS specification. In order for other systems to be able to see each other in a Windows network, it is necessary for them to publish NetBIOS names. TCP/IP as a protocol has no built-in mechanism to publish NetBIOS names to the network. This is why it is necessary to use WINS or broadcasts in a network—to determine the NetBIOS name of a network provider using the TCP/IP protocol. When an application wishes to use NT networking system functions to communicate across the network to another machine, it establishes a single NetBIOS session between the machines based on the system's name. The application then makes all network requests using the NetBIOS name that has been assigned to the network resource. All additional network calls occur within the context of this session.

Windows Sockets is another API used by most new applications and is the preferred method for developing Internet applications. Unlike applications written to the NetBIOS specification, applications written to the Windows Sockets specification are not dependent on published network names. This approach allows the application greater freedom and accessibility to systems that are not running a NetBIOS name provider. Applications written to the Windows Sockets specification use predetermined socket numbers to communicate data to network resources. These applications located on the network resource machine are designed to listen to the agreed upon socket. When a message is received by the socket, the data is processed and any return information is sent out to a specified socket on the system requesting the information.

We have now seen NT take network requests from an application, through the network components of NT, to their return. You have seen how NT's modular design provides network processing to provide performance and flexibility. In the next section, we will see how NT's modular design pays off by giving the system an open design that easily accommodates network redirectors from third parties.

# Protocols

Protocols are the set of rules that computers on networks use to communicate with one another. Just like people communicate in different languages, like English, French, or German, networks communicate with different protocols, like TCP/IP, IPX/SPX, and NetBEUI. In order for computers to communicate with each other, they must be speaking with the same protocol.

Network protocols have been created and refined over the years. Most of the major protocols in use today were created by a specific vendor to allow communications to occur between networked systems running the vendor's software. For example, IPX/SPX was created by Novell to allow communications between the clients and servers of Novell NetWare operating systems. NetBEUI was created by IBM in conjunction with Microsoft so that their operating systems could function in a network. DLC was created by IBM to allow communications with IBM mainframes in SNA networks. And AppleTalk was created by Apple Computer Corporation to network Apple's line of computers. The only non-vendor-specific protocol in wide use today that we will cover is TCP/IP. TCP/IP was created by a task force whose goal was to create a protocol that could link many different types of systems over a series of wide area network links. As shown in Figure 2.5, Windows NT is capable of running and supporting all of the previously mentioned protocols. This means that Windows NT is protocol independent. All Windows NT services will work with virtually any of the protocols that we may want to use. We will be going over the architectural details of TCP/IP and the other network protocols I mentioned in the following sections.

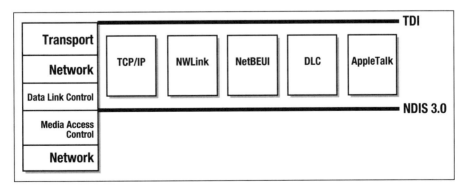

**Figure 2.5**  The protocol layer.

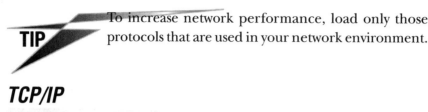

**TIP** To increase network performance, load only those protocols that are used in your network environment.

## TCP/IP

TCP/IP has developed into one of the most widely used protocols available today. As a result of its vendor independence, robust design, and multiplatform support, this protocol is used on over 20 million workstations worldwide. Because of its popularity and the sudden surge of growth in its use, I am going to cover a lot of detail on TCP/IP. When you get done with this section, you should have a good idea of the components of TCP/IP, how Windows NT NetBIOS computer names are resolved to addresses, and what the services are that NT provides to make managing TCP/IP easier. With this in mind, let's get started.

TCP/IP is not really a single protocol but a suite of protocols grouped together under one name, as shown in Figure 2.6. Transmission Control Protocol (TCP) and Internet Protocol (IP) are only two of the members of the TCP/IP suite. IP provides the packet delivery of all TCP/IP protocols and uses a connectionless best-effort delivery system. This means that IP has no way of knowing if the target system is listening or if it even receives the data that IP is transmitting correctly. The TCP works in conjunction with IP. TCP includes the ability to guarantee packets are delivered to the intended recipient and that the packets are delivered and reassembled in the proper sequence. If a packet has a problem, it is up to TCP to make sure that the data that had the transmission problem is re-sent. While TCP

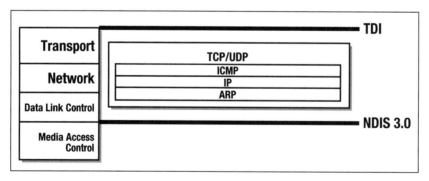

**Figure 2.6**   The TCP/IP model.

ensures data is properly received, it does generate additional network traffic and reduces the overall speed of the network. If you are working in a fairly reliable network environment, you may want to consider using the User Datagram Protocol (UDP).

**TIP** To get better performance from IP in a reliable network environment, try using applications that make use of UDP/IP instead of TCP/IP. This protocol does not use tools to verify data delivery and reduces network traffic.

## User Datagram Protocol (UDP)

The User Datagram Protocol is similar to TCP in that it uses IP as its delivery mechanism. However, UDP has the ability to not use checksums or require acknowledgments for packet delivery. If you are working in a highly reliable network environment, UDP may be used to help increase the speed with which you deliver your network data.

## Address Resolution Protocol (ARP)

Address Resolution Protocol (ARP) is another component of the TCP/IP suite of protocols. ARP is used to provide a method to determine the hardware address of the machine that data needs to be delivered to. This information is necessary for TCP/IP or UDP/IP to be able to deliver data. IP uses an ARP request packet, which contains the IP address of the system it is trying to communicate with. All the systems in the local subnet have the ability to respond to this request, and the system that has the target IP address will respond with its hardware address. The requesting system then receives this data and stores it in an ARP cache for future use.

## Internet Control Message Protocol (ICMP)

The Internet Control Message Protocol(ICMP) is used by IP for error message and status information notification between two networked workstations. The information provided by ICMP is necessary for higher-level protocols like TCP to be able to recover from errors during the transmission of data. Because of this special ability, ICMP is required for any implementation of TCP/IP.

Together, these five protocols make up the TCP/IP suite.

## Managing TCP/IP

One of the more restrictive issues associated with using TCP/IP is the work traditionally necessary to manage it. In the past, a computer running TCP/IP required a unique ID and other information to be individually entered on each machine in the network. If any of the machines moved around in the network, or the network TCP/IP configuration changed, an administrator would have to go to every machine that was affected and update its configuration. This type of management could be very time consuming for administrators of large network environments. Microsoft helps address this problem by providing services such as Windows Internet Naming Service (WINS) and Dynamic Host Configuration Protocol (DHCP).

## Windows Internet Naming Server (WINS)

WINS is a database that client computers are set up to use. When a client computer comes online, it registers with the WINS server. The WINS server stores the client system's NetBIOS name (for example PC1) and the client's IP address. When another client on the network configured for WINS tries to connect to PC1, the system first goes to the WINS server and asks if WINS knows the IP address of PC1. Because PC1 is registered in the WINS database, the WINS server is able to successfully look up the name in its database and find out the IP address for PC1. The WINS server then passes this information to the network client that made the original request. The network client then uses the IP address to connect to PC1. There are other methods of determining a client's IP address without having a WINS server. We'll talk about those methods in the next section.

In order for friendly names that identify computer systems on the network to appear in the browser list when using the TCP/IP protocol, it is necessary to encapsulate the NetBIOS command calls into the TCP/IP protocol. This type of encapsulation is referred to as NetBIOS over TCP/IP (NBT). Depending on how your network is configured, NBT can use any one of four possible modes.

- *b-node*—Uses broadcast to resolve names.

- *p-node*—Uses point-to-point communications with a name server to resolve names.

- *m-node*—Uses b-node first and then the p-node if the b-node fails to resolve the name.

- *h-node*—Uses p-node first for name queries and b-node second if the name service is unavailable or if the name is not registered in the WINS database.

Let's look at these modes in a bit more detail.

The b-node method of address determination uses broadcasts to get or resolve a client's address. Basically, if PC2 was using b-node to connect to PC1, PC2 would start transmitting broadcasts that all computers on the subnet would hear. It would then be up to PC1 to respond to the broadcast and give PC2 the IP address it is looking for. PC2 would then use the IP address to connect to PC1.

**TIP** b-node broadcasts do not transmit over routers. In order to be able to browse network resources across a wide area network using TCP/IP, it is necessary to have WINS servers set up on the network to resolve addresses.

In a p-node environment, all the machines are configured to register with a WINS server, which handles resolving all network names into IP addresses. For machines to be visible on the network, it is necessary to configure each system for WINS.

m-node uses a combination of b-node and p-node. In an m-node environment, a system first tries to use b-node. If b-node fails, it will then switch to p-node. Using m-node will definitely raise your traffic levels. While this method will allow you to communicate across a router in a wide area network, its choice of creating unnecessary network traffic does not make it the preferred method.

**TIP** To get the best network performance and reliability use p-node. p-node uses WINS servers first and then uses broadcasts if the WINS server fails.

h-node is a standard that still uses both b-node and p-node to resolve names, but it uses p-node first. This reduces overall network traffic and makes a lot more sense. In addition to using p-mode as its default IP resolution method, if p-node fails, h-node will not only use b-node as a backup, it will continue to poll the WINS server until it comes back online. h-node will then switch back to p-node for resolution. This makes for a much cleaner network solution.

Listing 2.1 shows a portion of a network sniff that shows a WINS client registering itself with a WINS server. A network sniffer is an application that allows you to see network traffic that has occurred on the wire. A network sniffer is included in Windows NT 4 and allows you to see network traffic sent by and received by the system it is running on. A more robust network sniffer, Network Monitor, is available in Microsoft's System Management Server Application.

## Listing 2.1 A WINS client registering with a WINS server.

```
Source IP           Dest IP          Prot    Description
205.219.176.124     205.219.177.254  NBT     NS: Registration req.
                                             for PC1<00>
+ FRAME: Base frame properties
+ ETHERNET: ETYPE = 0x0800 : Protocol = IP: DOD Internet Protocol
+ IP: ID = 0x300; Proto = UDP; Len: 96
+ UDP: Src Port: NETBIOS Name Service, (137); Dst Port: NETBIOS Name
Service (137); Length = 76 (0x4C)
NBT: NS: Registration req. for PC1<00>
NBT: Transaction ID = 32770 (0x8002)
NBT: Flags Summary = 0x2900 - Req.; Registration; Success
NBT: 0............... = Request
NBT: .0101.......... = Registration
NBT: .....0......... = Non-authoritative Answer
NBT: ......0........ = Datagram not truncated
NBT: .......1....... = Recursion desired
NBT: ........0...... = Recursion not available
NBT: .........0..... = Reserved
NBT: ..........0.... = Reserved
NBT: ...........0... = Not a broadcast packet
NBT: ...........0000 = Success
NBT: Question Count = 1 (0x1)
NBT: Answer Count = 0 (0x0)
NBT: Name Service Count = 0 (0x0)
NBT: Additional Record Count = 1 (0x1)
NBT: Question Name = PC1<00>
```

```
NBT: Question Type = General Name Service
NBT: Question Class = Internet Class
NBT: Resource Record Name = PC1<00>
NBT: Resource Record Type = NetBIOS General Name Service
NBT: Resource Record Class = Internet Class
NBT: Time To Live = 300000 (0x493E0)
NBT: RDATA Length = 6 (0x6)
NBT: Resource Record Flags = 57344 (0xE000)
NBT: 1............... = Group NetBIOS Name
NBT: .11............. = Reserved
NBT: ...0000000000000 = Reserved
NBT: Owner IP Address = 205.219.176.13
```

## *Dynamic Host Configuration Protocol (DHCP)*

Dynamic Host Configuration Protocol (DHCP) allows administrators to use a central database to store all IP information. In addition, network clients can be configured to receive their configuration information from the DHCP server. DHCP allows administrators to easily maintain a TCP/IP environment. For example, if a user's machine moved to a new subnet in a non-DHCP environment, it would be necessary for the network administrator to reconfigure the settings of the machine manually. In a DHCP environment, the system will obtain new IP information from the DHCP server. Let's take a look at how the DHCP is able to accomplish the reduction of work an administrator faces with the TCP/IP protocol.

When a client configured to use DHCP is booted for the first time, it goes through a series of steps to obtain its TCP/IP configuration information to gain a *lease*, as shown in Figure 2.7. A lease is a completed TCP/IP configuration that has been received from a DHCP server. It is called a lease because the configuration information received from the DHCP server is usually renewed after a time specified by the server. The following steps outline the process of obtaining a lease from a DHCP server.

- Initialization

- Selection

- Requesting

- Binding

Let's review these steps in more detail.

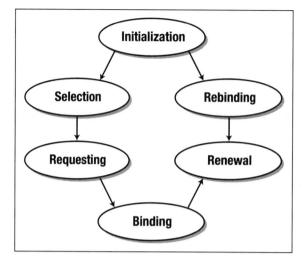

**Figure 2.7** DHCP client steps.

## INITIALIZATION

When a DHCP client boots, it starts out with its IP address set to nothing. The DHCP client then sends out a DHCPDISCOVER message to its local subnet. The DHCPDISCOVER message contains the clients Media Access Control (MAC) address and the client's system name. A MAC address is a unique address that all network cards have burned into them. By using the MAC address in its message, the client ensures that it is uniquely identified on the network. Listing 2.2 shows a network trace of a DHCPDISCOVER message.

## Listing 2.2  A network trace of a DHCPDISCOVER message.

```
Time     Source IP    Dest IP             Prot    Description
0.000    0.0.0.0      255.255.255.255     DHCP    Discover(xid=68256CA8)

+ FRAME: Base frame properties
 ETHERNET: ETYPE = 0x0800 : Protocol = IP: DOD Internet Protocol
   + ETHERNET: Destination address : FFFFFFFFFFFF
   + ETHERNET: Source address : 0040051376D9
 ETHERNET: Frame Length : 342 (0x0156)
 ETHERNET: Ethernet Type : 0x0800 (IP: DOD Internet Protocol)
 ETHERNET: Ethernet Data: Number of data bytes remaining = 328
    (0x0148)
 IP: ID = 0x0; Proto = UDP; Len: 328
 IP: Version = 4 (0x4)
```

```
IP: Header Length = 20 (0x14)
 + IP: Service Type = 0 (0x0)
IP: Total Length = 328 (0x148)
IP: Identification = 0 (0x0)
 + IP: Flags Summary = 0 (0x0)
IP: Fragment Offset = 0 (0x0) bytes
IP: Time to Live = 32 (0x20)
IP: Protocol = UDP - User Datagram
IP: CheckSum = 0x99A6
IP: Source Address = 0.0.0.0
IP: Destination Address = 255.255.255.255
IP: Data: Number of data bytes remaining = 308 (0x0134)
UDP: IP Multicast: Src Port: BOOTP Client, (68); Dst Port: BOOTP
  Server (67); Length = 308 (0x134)
UDP: Source Port = BOOTP Client
UDP: Destination Port = BOOTP Server
UDP: Total length = 308 (0x134) bytes
UDP: CheckSum = 0x4A0E
UDP: Data: Number of data bytes remaining = 300 (0x012C)
DHCP: Discover  (xid=68256CA8)
DHCP: Op Code  (op) = 1 (0x1)
DHCP: Hardware Type (htype) = 1 (0x1) 10Mb Ethernet
DHCP: Hardware Address Length (hlen) = 6 (0x6)
DHCP: Hops (hops)  = 0 (0x0)
DHCP: Transaction ID  (xid)  = 1747283112 (0x68256CA8)
DHCP: Seconds  (secs)  = 0 (0x0)
DHCP: Flags (flags) = 0 (0x0)
DHCP: 0.............. = No Broadcast
DHCP: Client IP Address (ciaddr) = 0.0.0.0
DHCP: Your  IP Address (yiaddr) = 0.0.0.0
DHCP: Server IP Address (siaddr) = 0.0.0.0
DHCP: Relay IP Address (giaddr) = 0.0.0.0
DHCP: Client Ethernet Address (chaddr) = 0040051376D9
DHCP: Server Host Name (sname) = <Blank>
DHCP: Boot File Name (file)  = <Blank>
DHCP: Magic Cookie = [OK]
DHCP: Option Field (options)
DHCP: DHCP Message Type = DHCP Discover
DHCP: Client-identifier = (Type: 1) 00 dd 01 07 57 15
DHCP: Host Name = DAVEMAC4
DHCP: End of this option field
```

## SELECTION

When a server running DHCP receives the DHCPDISCOVER message from the client, it will respond with a DHCPOFFER message. This message is sent directly to the client; it is not a broadcast message. The DHCPOFFER message contains the client's MAC address, an offered TCP/IP address, a subnet mask, and the IP address of the DHCP server. The DHCP server then puts a temporary hold on the address it has sent to the client via the DHCPOFFER and waits for confirmation from the client that it is going to take the address.

If a DHCP client does not receive a DHCPOFFER messages from a DHCP server during bootup, it will try to communicate with a DHCP server five times every five minutes. The four retries are sent at 2, 4, 8, and 16 second intervals, and one random interval between 0 and 100 milliseconds. The sniff in Listing 2.3 shows how this looks on the network.

## Listing 2.3    A network trace of a DHCPOFFER message.

```
Time     Source IP        Dest IP          Prot    Description
0.165    205.219.177.254  205.219.176.13   DHCP    Offer (xid=68256CA8)

+ FRAME: Base frame properties
 ETHERNET: ETYPE = 0x0800 : Protocol = IP: DOD Internet Protocol
   + ETHERNET: Destination address : 0040051376D9
   + ETHERNET: Source address : 00000C1AEBC5
 ETHERNET: Frame Length : 590 (0x024E)
 ETHERNET: Ethernet Type : 0x0800 (IP: DOD Internet Protocol)
 ETHERNET: Ethernet Data: Number of data bytes remaining = 576
    (0x0240)
 IP: ID = 0x906; Proto = UDP; Len: 576
 IP: Version = 4 (0x4)
 IP: Header Length = 20 (0x14)
   + IP: Service Type = 0 (0x0)
 IP: Total Length = 576 (0x240)
 IP: Identification = 2310 (0x906)
   + IP: Flags Summary = 0 (0x0)
 IP: Fragment Offset = 0 (0x0) bytes
 IP: Time to Live = 31 (0x1F)
 IP: Protocol = UDP - User Datagram
 IP: CheckSum = 0xAF0D
 IP: Source Address = 205.219.177.254
 IP: Destination Address = 205.219.176.13
 IP: Data: Number of data bytes remaining = 556 (0x022C)
 UDP: Src Port: BOOTP Server, (67); Dst Port: BOOTP Client (68); Length
    = 556 (0x22C)
 DHCP: Offer (xid=68256CA8)
```

```
DHCP: Op Code  (op) = 2 (0x2)
DHCP: Hardware Type (htype) = 1 (0x1) 10Mb Ethernet
DHCP: Hardware Address Length (hlen) = 6 (0x6)
DHCP: Hops (hops)  = 0 (0x0)
DHCP: Transaction ID  (xid)  = 1747283112 (0x68256CA8)
DHCP: Seconds  (secs)  = 0 (0x0)
DHCP: Flags (flags) = 0 (0x0)
DHCP: 0.............. = No Broadcast
DHCP: Client IP Address (ciaddr) = 0.0.0.0
DHCP: Your  IP Address (yiaddr) = 205.219.176.13
DHCP: Server IP Address (siaddr) = 0.0.0.0
DHCP: Relay IP Address (giaddr) = 205.219.176.1
DHCP: Client Ethernet Address (chaddr) = 0040051376D9
DHCP: Server Host Name (sname) = <Blank>
DHCP: Boot File Name  (file)  = <Blank>
DHCP: Magic Cookie = [OK]
DHCP: Option Field (options)
DHCP: DHCP Message Type = DHCP Offer
DHCP: Subnet Mask  = 255.255.255.0
DHCP: Renewal Time Value (T1) = 1 Days, 12:00:00
DHCP: Rebinding Time Value (T2) = 2 Days, 15:00:00
DHCP: IP Address Lease Time = 3 Days, 0:00:00
DHCP: Server Identifier = 205.219.177.254
DHCP: End of this option field
```

**TIP**    In order for a DHCP broadcast to be heard by DHCP servers and clients located on a wide area network, you need to make sure your router can act as an RFC 1542 (BootP) relay agent. With this type of router, it is possible for a single DHCP server to service multiple subnets.

## REQUESTING

When the DHCP client receives DHCPOFFER messages, it makes a decision regarding which message it is going to use. This is usually the first message it receives. It is possible for a client to receive more than one DHCPOFFER message if you have more than one DHCP server in your network. The client then prepares a DHCPREQUEST message to send to the DHCP server. This message lets the server know that the DHCP client accepts the offered TCP/IP address and whether the client needs any additional configuration information, like a default gateway address.

Because the client has not yet confirmed with the DHCP server that it has accepted the TCP/IP address, it is still using a broadcast message based on the MAC address of the server to deliver the DHCPREQUEST to the DHCP server. A broadcast message is used so that if you have other DHCP servers in your network and they have supplied DHCPOFFER messages to the client, they will now release the address they reserved back into the pool of available addresses. Listing 2.4 shows how this looks under Network Monitor.

## Listing 2.4    A Network trace of a DHCPREQUEST.

```
Time       Source IP    Dest IP            Prot    Description
0.172      0.0.0.0      255.255.255.255    DHCP    Request (xid=08186BD1)

+ FRAME: Base frame properties
+ ETHERNET: ETYPE = 0x0800 : Protocol = IP: DOD Internet Protocol
+ IP: ID = 0x100; Proto = UDP; Len: 328
+ UDP: IP Multicast: Src Port: BOOTP Client, (68); Dst Port: BOOTP
 Server (67); Length = 308 (0x134)
 DHCP: Request  (xid=08186BD1)
 DHCP: Op Code  (op) = 1 (0x1)
 DHCP: Hardware Type (htype) = 1 (0x1) 10Mb Ethernet
 DHCP: Hardware Address Length (hlen) = 6 (0x6)
 DHCP: Hops (hops)  = 0 (0x0)
 DHCP: Transaction ID  (xid)  = 135818193 (0x8186BD1)
 DHCP: Seconds  (secs)  = 0 (0x0)
 DHCP: Flags (flags) = 0 (0x0)
 DHCP: 0.............. = No Broadcast
 DHCP: Client IP Address (ciaddr) = 0.0.0.0
 DHCP: Your  IP Address (yiaddr) = 0.0.0.0
 DHCP: Server IP Address (siaddr) = 0.0.0.0
 DHCP: Relay IP Address (giaddr) = 0.0.0.0
 DHCP: Client Ethernet Address (chaddr) = 0040051376D9
 DHCP: Server Host Name (sname) = <Blank>
 DHCP: Boot File Name  (file)  = <Blank>
 DHCP: Magic Cookie = [OK]
 DHCP: Option Field (options)
 DHCP: DHCP Message Type = DHCP Request
 DHCP: Client-identifier = (Type: 1) 00 dd 01 07 57 15
 DHCP: Requested Address = 205.219.176.13
 DHCP: Server Identifier = 205.219.177.254
 DHCP: Host Name = PC2
 DHCP: Parameter Request List = (Length: 7) 01 0f 03 2c 2e 2f 06
 DHCP: End of this option field
```

## Binding

When the DHCP server that is servicing the DHCP client receives the DHCPREQUEST from the client, it will reply to the DHCPREQUEST with a DHCPACK message. This message lets the client know that it now has a valid lease. The server uses a directed message to send DHCP information to the client. Once the client receives the DHCPACK, it completes its configuration and becomes a fully leased DHCP client. Listing 2.5 shows the network sniff of a DHCPACK conversation.

## Listing 2.5    A Network trace of a DHCPACK.

```
Time      Source IP         Dest IP          Prot    Description
0.061     205.219.177.254   205.219.176.13   DHCP    ACK  (xid=08186BD1)


+ FRAME: Base frame properties
+ ETHERNET: ETYPE = 0x0800 : Protocol = IP: DOD Internet Protocol
+ IP: ID = 0xA06; Proto = UDP; Len: 576
+ UDP: Src Port: BOOTP Server, (67); Dst Port: BOOTP Client (68);
 Length = 556 (0x22C)
 DHCP: ACK  (xid=08186BD1)
 DHCP: Op Code   (op) = 2 (0x2)
 DHCP: Hardware Type (htype) = 1 (0x1) 10Mb Ethernet
 DHCP: Hardware Address Length (hlen) = 6 (0x6)
 DHCP: Hops (hops)  = 0 (0x0)
 DHCP: Transaction ID  (xid)  = 135818193 (0x8186BD1)
 DHCP: Seconds  (secs)  = 0 (0x0)
 DHCP: Flags (flags) = 0 (0x0)
 DHCP: 0............... = No Broadcast
 DHCP: Client IP Address (ciaddr) = 0.0.0.0
 DHCP: Your  IP Address (yiaddr) = 205.219.176.13
 DHCP: Server IP Address (siaddr) = 0.0.0.0
 DHCP: Relay IP Address (giaddr) = 205.219.176.1
 DHCP: Client Ethernet Address (chaddr) = 0040051376D9
 DHCP: Server Host Name (sname) = <Blank>
 DHCP: Boot File Name  (file)  = <Blank>
 DHCP: Magic Cookie = [OK]
 DHCP: Option Field (options)
 DHCP: DHCP Message Type = DHCP ACK
 DHCP: Renewal Time Value (T1) = 1 Days, 12:00:00
 DHCP: Rebinding Time Value (T2) = 2 Days, 15:00:00
 DHCP: IP Address Lease Time = 3 Days, 0:00:00
 DHCP: Server Identifier = 205.219.177.254
 DHCP: Subnet Mask  = 255.255.255.0
```

```
DHCP: Domain Name  = (Length: 22) 63 73 77 61 74 63 70 2e 6d
   69 63 72 6f 73 6f 66 ...
DHCP: Router = 199.199.40.1
DHCP: NetBIOS Name Service  = 205.219.177.254
DHCP: NetBIOS Node Type = (Length: 1) 08
DHCP: End of this option field
```

# DHCP Lease Renewal

Once a DHCP client has its lease, it is necessary to renew the lease after a certain amount of time. The time period that determines when the lease expires is set by the DHCP server when the client system first receives its lease. Depending on the time necessary for the system to receive a renewal confirmation from the DHCP server, the client will go through either one or two steps to get its lease renewed. The steps used for renewal are Renewal and Rebinding. Let's take a moment to discuss these steps in more detail.

It may be necessary to release a DHCP lease before the lease has expired. To do this, you first run the ipconfig/release command to have the lease released. Next, you run the ipconfig/renew to establish a new DHCP lease for the client.

## RENEWAL

A DHCP client begins the process of renewal when 50 percent of the lease time has been used. At this point, the client sends out a DHCPREQUEST message. Notice that the request is a message, not a broadcast. This is because the DHCP client currently has a TCP/IP configuration and can use the protocol for communications to the server. Unless a restriction has been placed on the DHCP client, the server will automatically renew the client lease and will confirm this with the client by sending a DHCPACK message.

## REBINDING

The DHCP client only goes into the rebinding state if the DHCP client has not renewed its lease by the time 87.5 percent of the lease has been used. At this point, the DHCP client will attempt to contact any DHCP server by broadcasting DHCPREQUEST messages to the network. It is then possible for the DHCP server to respond with either a DHCPACK, which will automatically renew the lease, or with a DHCPNACK, which will force the DHCP client to begin the acquisition process again.

## Domain Name Service (DNS)

DNS is used by Internet systems to resolve friendly names into usable TCP/IP addresses. For example, if you type www.bitnet.net, your computer goes out to a server running the Domain Name Service. The DNS server then looks in its database to resolve the name into an IP address, for example 205.219.176.1. This address is then passed back to your computer, which uses the address to establish the connection with www.bitnet.net. This is the method that systems attached to the Internet use to resolve addresses. The drawback to this system is that all data stored in most DNS databases are static. This means that some administrator (usually you) is responsible for making sure that every time a new host is added to your network, their DNS name (www.bitnet.net) and IP address (205.219.176.1) are added to the DNS database. Windows NT 4 solves this issue by integrating DNS with WINS. Whenever the Windows NT DNS server is unable to resolve an address request, it passes the request to WINS. If WINS has the information, it resolves the address and passes the information back to the DNS server. The DNS server passes the information back to the client which carries out its connect request. Couple DNS and WINS with DHCP, and the tasks that are usually faced by administrators of TCP/IP networks are greatly reduced.

## NWLink (IPX/SPX)

NWLink is the NetBIOS compatible extension of the IPX/SPX protocol. IPX/SPX is the protocol used by Novell NetWare. I must point out that NWLink by itself does not support connecting to other NetWare servers, nor does it allow the NT server to act as a file and print server for NetWare clients. What NWLink does allow is NetBIOS or Sockets-based applications to access to the NWLink transport for use in communications. NWLink on NT offers standard support for network frame types like 802.2 and 802.3. The 802.2 is the default protocol used by Novell servers 3.12 and higher (Novell Servers 3.11 and below use 802.3 as their default). NT offers a feature that allows the frame type to be selected automatically. NT accomplishes this by listening to the network and determining what frame type is in use.

The NWLink protocol can be enhanced by adding the Client Services for NetWare. This service installs a redirector and a provider that allows network requests to be packaged in control blocks readable by NetWare servers (NCPs). The Client Service for NetWare does not install a server component that allows NetWare clients to access the NT server's file and print services. This function is provided by a Microsoft product called File and Print Services for NetWare.

When an application makes calls to network resources, the MUP or MPR forwards the request to the NetWare redirector. The NetWare redirector serves the same function as the default redirector that comes with Windows NT, except that it packages its messages using NCPs. When the NetWare server receives the requests from the NT client, it treats the NT client like any other NetWare client requesting access to resources.

## NetBEUI

NetBEUI is a small and fast network protocol useful for small non-routed networks that have 20 to 100 users. The protocol is easy to configure. All that is necessary for the protocol is a unique system name. The problem with this protocol is that it does not allow itself to be routed, which means that it is not useful for large network implementations. In Windows NT, NetBEUI is referred to as NBF (NetBEUI Frame).

NetBEUI can support both connection-based and connectionless traffic. Connection-based traffic is created by commands like **net use**, which establish and maintain a connection to a network resource. Connectionless traffic is created by commands like **net view**, which query the network for information and wait for a result set to be returned.

NetBEUI works in conjunction with NetBIOS to establish connections to other network resources. Keep in mind that NetBIOS is used by NT as a method of assigning names to network resources. When a client specifies a **net use** command, the system must first send out a request using unnumbered information (UI) frames, which then cause a response from the intended client. Once the name has been retrieved, the system is able to establish a link between the two systems for the SMBs to be sent over.

## AppleTalk

AppleTalk is provided to allow communications between Windows NT Server and Macintosh clients. This protocol is installed by NT when you install the Services for Macintosh software component. This protocol, which works very well on NT, allows Windows NT to appear as an Apple file server in an AppleTalk network.

## Data Link Control (DLC)

DLC is a protocol used to give an application direct access to the data link layer. This protocol bypasses the redirector, so Windows NT does not use it for file or print sharing. Generally, the DLC protocol is used to provide access to IBM mainframe and midrange networks and is also used by HP Jet Direct cards to perform network printing functions.

## NDIS 3.0

Network Device Interface Specification, shown in Figure 2.8, is a standard that allows multiple protocols and adapters to communicate with each other. NDIS is broken into two parts: the NDIS wrapper and the NDIS NIC driver. The NDIS wrapper is implemented on NT in a system driver called NDIS.SYS. The NDIS NIC driver is provided by the network card hardware provider to allow access to the network card. The wrapper takes all calls from the network protocols and passes them to the NDIS NIC driver. This gives the protocols a consistent interface to work with no matter which network interface card is used. By using NDIS, network cards can

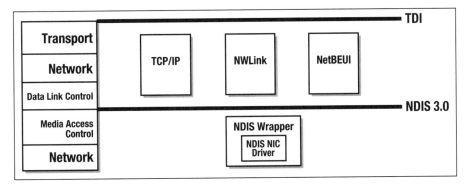

**Figure 2.8**   The Network Device Interface Specification.

be changed without NT having to worry about the cards' compatibility, providing the manufacturer writes to the NDIS 3.0 standard.

# Network Services

NT groups the functions that it offers, such as the multiple redirectors and server processes, into services. Services can be started and stopped independently of each other on NT, so if one component fails (for example, the Workstation service), the other components (for example, the Server service) will continue to operate. In this section, we'll discuss the major services used by Windows NT.

## Server Service

The Server service is responsible for taking in all network requests and returning the result set the client requests. The Server service makes use of the server kernel mode process to fulfill the incoming network requests. Services can be started and shut down via the Control Panel's Services box, as shown in Figure 2.9.

## Workstation Service

The Workstation service includes the redirectors and providers, which I mentioned previously, that are used to make requests to network resources. Shutting down the Workstation service will prevent the machine from accessing resources across the network.

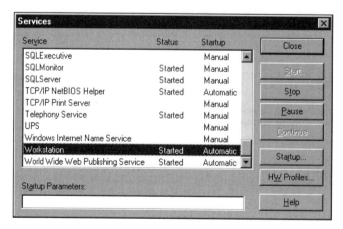

**Figure 2.9** The Services tab.

**TIP** If the Workstation service on a server fails, check to see if the Server service is still working by connecting to the network server from another network client. You can use the client and Server Manager to properly shut down other application services like SQL Server. This technique will help prevent data corruption from occurring due to an improper shutdown.

## Remote Access Service

The Remote Access service (RAS) is used by Windows NT to provide access for clients over phone lines to the network. RAS is broken down into two components: the remote access server and the remote access client.

### REMOTE ACCESS SERVER

The remote access server component is used by Windows NT to receive calls from remote access clients and attach them to the network. The remote access server can be configured to use one or all network protocols available on the network. When a system calls into a RAS server, the following sequence occurs:

- The RAS server uses the Point-to-Point Protocol (PPP) specification to establish the connection to the incoming client.

- The RAS server uses a WAN wrapper to take incoming physical layer information.

- The WAN wrapper passes the information to the TCP/IP and IPX/SPX router or the NetBEUI gateway, depending on the protocol that it uses.

- The data is then passed up through the rest of NT's internal networking components and is treated as if the network request was coming from a machine located on the local area network.

### THE REMOTE ACCESS CLIENT

The remote access client is available on most of Microsoft's popular networking clients. The client is responsible for establishing and maintaining the connection with the RAS server. Figure 2.10 gives you an idea of the

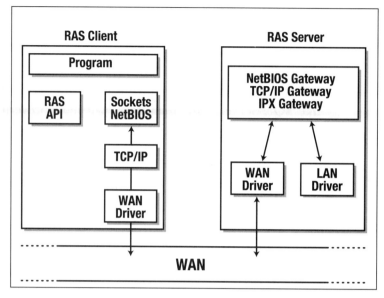

**Figure 2.10**  The remote access model.

process flow of Remote Access on the client. The process used to establish and route communications via remote access is as follows:

- The client software uses the RAS API to initiate, negotiate, and maintain the RAS connection to the remote access server.

- Once the connection is made, protocols wishing to establish network calls can use the WAN wrapper to send their data to the remote access server.

- The data is then receive by the server where it is forwarded across the network as if the client was located on the local area network.

## *Browser Service*

The Browser service is used by all Windows networking clients to efficiently locate all available resources on the network.

# Third-Party Redirectors

NT's inherent flexibility from its modular design allows third-party programmers to easily add their own network functionality to Windows NT.

The products listed in this section are just a few of the programs available that provide additional network capabilities for Windows NT.

## DEC Pathworks

DEC Pathworks is a middleware product designed to take the file and print resources of multiple operating systems and make them usable by all. This gives administrators the ability to support and manage all desktops and servers with a common set of tools. This also gives users a common set of resources to access no matter which platform they are sitting in front of. DEC provides Pathworks in both server and clients versions, which means that you can both share resources to and access resources from the Pathworks network. You can check out DEC's Web site at **www.dec.com** or call them a 1-800-DIGITAL for more information on Pathworks or other DEC products.

## Novell Netware 4.1 Client

While NT does ship with the Client Services for NetWare and the Gateway Services for NetWare, giving NT clients access to Netware file and print services, these services do not provide NT the services available to a fully functional Novell client. Novell NetWare is currently offering a public beta of a NetWare client for NT. This client allows NT to use enhanced features of the Novell operating system that the client software from NT does not support. The services include:

- Support for NDS

- The ability to use the NetWare graphical utilities to map network drives and printers

You can obtain additional information about this client from Novell's Web site at **www.novell.com**.

## Novell Directory Services

In a July 15, 1996 press release, Novell announced that it would be providing the Novell Directory Services (NDS) for Windows NT. NDS is currently used by Novell's Netware 4.1 operating environments to synchronize user and file management into a single directory tree for multiple servers. This will allow NT and Novell servers to be grouped under one tree and will greatly

reduce the amount of management usually required in a multiserver and multiplatform environment. Keep your eye on this product. For more information about NDS, check out the Novell home page at **www.novell.com**.

## NFS

NFS redirector and server components allow Windows NT to act as both a Unix client and server. There are quite a few vendors who are currently making or have made NFS products for Windows NT. Table 2.1 lists some of the manufacturers and their contact numbers.

# Routing Information Protocol

Routing Information Protocol (RIP) is used by routers in self-contained (autonomous) networks to dynamically maintain routing information. Basically this means that if you have a network with more than one router, these routers can share information using RIP to let each other know which networks they are servicing. Windows NT 4 can route between multiple network cards installed in the system and update available routes using RIP. This allows Windows NT to act as a router. RIP updates can occur on either TCP/IP or NWLink.

By using RIP routing, changes that happen in the network will be updated automatically. RIP updates occur every 30 seconds. RIP is good for small or medium-sized networks that use high-speed LAN links. Because RIP

**Table 2.1   NFS Vendors**

| Vendor | Contact Numbers |
| --- | --- |
| Beame and Whiteside | (919) 831-8989 |
| Distinct Corporation | (408) 741-0781 |
| Esker, Inc. | (415) 341-9065 |
| Frontier Technologies Corp. | (414) 241-4555 |
| FTP Software | (508) 685-4000 |
| Intergraph | (205) 730-5499 |
| Lanera Corporation | (408) 956-8344 |
| NetManage, Inc. | (408) 973-7171 |
| SunSelect | (508) 442-2300 |

uses broadcasts for updates, you may encounter problems if you use it on low-bandwidth connections. Windows NT 4 uses RIP version 1, which does not include subnet information in its packets. While this does not mean that you can not use subnets, you will have to subnet the same address. For example, you can subnet 205.219.176.0 between the routers in your autonomous system; however, you cannot subnet the addresses 205.219.176.0 and 206.150.78.0 at the same time between your internal routers.

# WNet API

Being able to support multiple network redirectors is a terrific feature for users, but has the potential to be a programmer's nightmare. To make sure programmers can easily code products to work with any redirector installed, Microsoft included the WNet API. The WNet API is offered by Windows NT so programmers do not need to know which provider they are working with when writing applications. The API contains functions to establish and cancel network connections and to gather information about the network. Table 2.2 outlines the WNet commands and their functions. For more information, refer to the Microsoft Developers Network, a quarterly subscription offered by Microsoft which uses a set of CDs to deliver details on programming APIs and developer kits.

**Table 2.2　WNet Functions**

| Function | Description |
| --- | --- |
| **Connection Functions** | |
| WNetAddConnection | Enables the calling application to connect a local device to a network resource. A successful connection is persistent, meaning that Windows automatically restores the connection during subsequent logon operations. This function is provided for compatibility with earlier versions of Microsoft Windows. For new applications, use the WNetAddConnection2 function. |

*(continued)*

**Table 2.2 WNet Functions** *(continued)*

| Function | Description |
|---|---|
| **Connection Functions (continued)** | |
| WNetAddConnection2 | Makes a connection to a network resource. The function can redirect a local device to the network resource. The WNetAddConnection2 function supersedes the WNetAddConnection function. If you pass a handle to a window that the provider of network resources can use as an owner window for dialog boxes, use the WNetAddConnection3 function. |
| WNetAddConnection3 | Makes a connection to a network resource. The function can redirect a local device to the network resource. The WNetAddConnection3 function is similar to the WNetAdd Connection2 function. The main difference is that WNetAddConnection3 has an additional parameter, a handle to a window that the provider of network resources can use as an owner window for dialog boxes. |
| WNetCancelConnection | Breaks an existing network connection. The function is provided for compatibility with earlier versions of Microsoft Windows. For new applications, use the WNetCancelConnection2 function. |
| WNetCancelConnection2 | Breaks an existing network connection. It can also be used to remove remembered network connections that are not currently connected. This function supersedes WNetCancelConnection. |
| WNetConnectionDialog | Starts a general browsing dialog box for connecting to network resources. |
| WNetDisconnectDialog | Starts a general browsing dialog box for disconnecting from network resources. |
| WNetGetConnection | Retrieves the name of the network resource associated with a local device. |
| **Enumeration Functions** | |
| WNetCloseEnum | Ends a network resource enumeration started by the WNetOpenEnum function. |

*(continued)*

**Table 2.2   WNet Functions** *(continued)*

| Function | Description |
|---|---|
| **Enumeration Functions (continued)** | |
| WNetEnumResource | Enumerates a network resource. |
| WNetOpenEnum | Starts an enumeration of network resources or existing connections. |
| WNetGetLastError | Retrieves the most recent extended error code set by a Windows network function. |
| **Resource Functions** | |
| WNetGetResource-Information | Retrieves enumeration information for a network resource. You typically use this function when the user types in the remote name of the specified object. Call this function in conjunction with WNetGetResourceParent to determine the placement and nature of the resource in the browse hierarchy. Unlike WNetGetResourceParent, WNetGetResource-Information always tries to determine the network provider that owns the resource and the type of the resource, although it might not currently be accessible (or even exist, if the type of the resource was specified by the caller). |
| WNetGetResourceParent | Lets you navigate up from a resource. This function enables browsing to commence based on the name of a network resource. This function also allows navigating up from a browsed resource to find connectable resources. Unlike WNetGetResourceInformation, if the resource syntactically has a parent, the parent is returned by WNetGetResourceParent, whether or not the parent actually exists. |
| WNetGetUniversalName | Takes a drive-based path for a network resource, and obtains a data structure that contains a more universal form of the name. |
| **User Functions** | |
| WNetGetUser | Retrieves the current default user name or the user name used to establish a network connection. |

# Distributed Computing Environment

The Distributed Computing Environment (DCE) was developed by the Open Software Foundation (OSF) to provide a common set of application services that could work across a wide range of operating systems. The theory behind DCE is that you can mix, manage, and operate multiple operating systems as if they were one unified network. The basis of communications in DCE is the Remote Procedure Call (RPC). The RPC used in Windows NT is similar and is, in fact, based on the RPC standard used by DCE. There are some differences, however, which are covered in detail later in this section.

In order to meet DCE compliance, you need a few more services in addition to RPC. These services come in both client and server-side flavors. The minimum services necessary to be DCE compliant are the RPC service, Distributed Directory service, Distributed Security service, Threads service, and Time service. These services, which we'll cover in detail in a moment, are often referred to as the secure core services.

## Remote Procedure Call

When Microsoft was in the process of developing the RPC standards in NT, the OSF DCE standards did not meet Microsoft's needs. Microsoft then set out using the OSF DCE standard as a model, meeting the DCE specifications and adding their own enhancements. The results were an RPC service that is compatible with most aspects of the OSF DCE RPC except in the area of security. The bottom line is that to get complete DCE compliance, it is necessary to purchase a third-party product that either translates or replaces the NT RPC service. Third-party products are available for Windows NT from companies such as DEC and Gradient technologies.

In the DCE model, RPCs are used for communicating across the different operating systems for information on security updates, time synchronization, and application services. The RPC service accomplishes this by allowing applications and services to execute components of the application on systems across the network. The application or service makes a call to *stub code*, which replaces the local procedure. The stub code takes application calls and packages them for use by the RPC service. The stub code then uses the RPC service to communicate with the remote systems, and handles getting the data processed and returning the result set to the requesting application. You can see how an application uses RPCs by taking a look at the diagram shown in Figure 2.11.

## *Distributed Directory Service*

The Distributed Directory service is responsible for managing the publication of available network resources. Resources are published using friendly names that users can remember easily. These names are not machine specific, they are network specific, which means that you can move a share file system from a less powerful or crashed server to a more robust or reliable server and the users would not know the difference (they might notice the improved performance, however). The Distributed Directory services also make use of *replication*, which allows you to keep copies of mission-critical data across less reliable links. In the event of a failure, the user can continue to work as if nothing has happened. Transport independence, which is another feature of the Distributed Directory service, allows you to easily span mixed environments. For security, the Distributed Directory services are integrated with the Distributed Security service, discussed next, providing on-the-fly authentication to any system within the network.

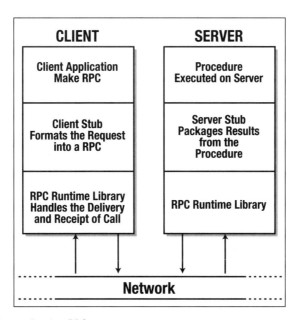

**Figure 2.11**   An application RPC.

## Distributed Security Service

Access to resources across a network of multiple operating systems requires an authentication system functional in each environment. The Distributed Security service (DSS) provides this and is responsible for three critical security services: authentication, authorization, and user account management.

The DSS uses authentication standards based on the Kerberos system. Kerberos is a trusted service that confirms a user's identity, preventing users from faking an identity. Authorization is treated on a user-by-user basis to network resources. A user is first authenticated and then passed to the authorization process. The authorization process determines if the user has access to the resources they are requesting and grants or rejects access accordingly.

To maintain users in environments that are diverse in nature, a central area for user IDs is necessary. The user registry provides this area. The user registry acts as a central repository for user accounts for the entire network. This way, accounts can be managed centrally without worry of account duplication. Additional properties, such as group, login, and system properties for users, are also stored here.

Together, these features provide a powerful and flexible security service.

## Threads Service

With the power of an entire network to tap into, programmers want the ability to process concurrent threads at the same time. The Threads service fills this need. Threads allow multiple instructions to be run concurrently in applications and services. Threads are what allow concurrent user requests to be processed while RPCs are being made. This feature is important to allow the power of distributed computing to be fully utilized.

## Time Service

In order for distributed applications to work, they all have to synchronize their watches. The distributed Time service is responsible for making sure that all systems in the network match each other's clocks as closely as possible. This service works in conjunction with the RPC, DSS, and DDS. For even higher precision, the Time service supports obtaining time from outside sources, such as atomic clocks.

In summary, DCE is a robust standard for developing and writing applications in for distributed networks. This standard is starting to pick up momentum in the network community and has a lot of potential. I encourage you to go to the OSF home page at **www.osf.org** to learn more about DCE.

# The Registry

The NT Registry is the area where all settings for hardware and software are stored. Basically, every aspect concerning the Windows NT operating system is stored in the Registry. You can change most of the settings in the Registry using graphical tools, such as the Control Panel. However, certain settings can only be accessed via the Registry.

You use UNC-type names when describing a path to a particular setting in the Registry. For example, to describe the location for the entry item order, which is located in the Hkey_Local_Machine, system folder, CurrentControlSet folder, Control folder, NetworkProvider folder, you would use HKEY_Local_Machine\system\currentcontrolset\control\networkprovider\order. Refer to Appendix B for a detailed listing of network items located in the Registry.

# Network Files

The Windows NT Server and Workstation network components are composed of a number of drivers (SYS files) and dynamic link libraries (DLL files). The driver files are used by the NT operating system to provide an interface to the system's hardware. Dynamic link libraries store programming procedures, such as APIs, which contain the details of application calls. We'll discuss the details of each network function and its associated SYS and DLL files in the following sections.

## *Redirector*

Redirectors are what allow NT to access resources stored on computers across the network. To provide maximum compatibility with other operating systems, Windows NT has the ability to run multiple redirectors. The redirector that comes with Windows NT uses the driver RDR.SYS and provides access to machines running Windows NT, MS-Net, LAN Manager, and LAN Server. A more in-depth discussion about the redirector was presented earlier in this chapter.

## RAS

NT's Remote Access service allows computers to dial in to the server via a modem or ISDN line and appear to be on the network. Device driver files used by RAS include RASARP.SYS and RASHUB.SYS. Dynamic link libraries used by RAS include RASADMIN.DLL, RASAPI16.DLL, RASAPI32.DLL, RASAUTH.DLL, RASBCP.DLL, RASCCP.DLL, RASCFG.DLL, RASCHAP.DLL, RASFIL32.DLL, RASGPRXY.DLL, RASIPCP.DLL, RASIPHLP.DLL, RASIPXCP.DLL, RASMAN.DLL, RASMSG.DLL, RASNBFCP.DLL, RASNBIPC.DLL, RASPAP.DLL, RASPPP.DLL, RASPPPEN.DLL, RASRES.DLL, RASSAUTH.DLL, RASSER.DLL, RASSPAP.DLL, RASTAPI.DLL, and RASTRS.DLL.

## NWLink

The NWLink protocol provides NetBIOS services for IPX/SPX clients. The driver files used by NWLink include NWLNK.SYS, NWLNKB.SYS, NWLNKRIP.SYS, and NWNBLINK.SYS. Dynamic link libraries used by NWLink include IPXCFG.DLL, NWAPI16.DLL, NWAPI32.DLL, NWCFG.DLL, NWEVENT.DLL, NWLNKCFG.DLL, NWLNKMSG.DLL, NWNBLINK.DLL, NWPROV- AU.DLL, NWSAP.DLL, and NWWKS.DLL.

## TCP/IP

Windows NT uses a 32-bit TCP/IP implementation. TCP/IP uses the driver files TCPIP.SYS and STREAMS.SYS and the dynamic link libraries INETMIB1.DLL, TCPIPCFG.LL, and TCPIPSCV.DLL.

## NetBIOS

NetBIOS is an API used to assist applications in locating resources through the use of friendly names. NetBIOS is protocol independent and is available using TCP/IP, NWLink, or NetBEUI. NetBIOS uses the device drivers NBT.SYS and NWNBLINK.SYS, and the dynamic link libraries used by NetBIOS are LMHSVC.DLL, NBTSVC.DLL, NDDENB32.DLL, NWNBLINK.DLL, and WSHNETBS.DLL.

## NetBEUI

NetBEUI is a fast network protocol useful for small local area networks. NetBEUI is limited in that it can't be routed. This precludes its use from large multisegmented networks. NetBEUI uses the driver file NBF.SYS.

# Conclusion

Well, we've gotten a pretty good look at the Windows NT operating system. You should now have a good understanding of how NT connects, retrieves, and sends network information. You saw how protocols take the information from the TDI and publish it to the network. You also found out where to go if you have to work on tweaking the system in the Registry. And you now know which files in NT are used by networking services. In the following chapters, you are going to get a chance to put the theory you have learned here to practice.

# 3

# Installing and Configuring Windows NT 4 Networking

**B**efore you can use NT Networking, you must first install the network services, adapters, and protocols. To do this successfully, you'll need to have a firm grasp of the NT network installation tools. I can hear you now, "But isn't every installation basically the same?" Actually, no. Every NT release uses a different installation procedure, look, and feel. Version 4 is no different. The tools make use of the new Graphics User Interface (GUI) controls introduced in Windows 95. In addition to the new controls, NT uses a new menu structure that is quite different and somewhat more efficient than the network menus found in the NT 3.51 release.

Sounds like a lot to tackle, but I've provided you with all the necessary background information to get you started. Once you have installed NT Networking, I will step you through all the possible configuration options. How you will configure your application will depend on your needs.

## NT 4 Installation of Network Resources

NT 4 uses the Installation Wizard, pioneered by Microsoft in Windows 95, to install its components. During the NT 4

77

installation, the Installation Wizard requests information and decisions from the installer as it prepares to load specific services and code from the CD. Installation Wizard offers you the option of installing all of the networking components during the installation process, or waiting until after NT is fully installed. After the installation, you may then install the various components using the Networks icon from the Control Panel. However, you may choose specific services and protocols to be included in the installation to save time later during configuration.

Prior to installing NT, you will need to make some decisions regarding which services are needed and what protocols will be necessary to meet your LAN requirements. However, as in most real-world scenarios, specific requirements can quickly change, causing the need for additional services or different protocols. For this reason, I'll describe the configuration of most of the NT Networking components later on in this chapter.

As I hinted at earlier, to install any NT services during the initial installation, you must use the Installation Wizard. Simply follow the directions provided for the necessary information to complete the installation. Typically, I install TCP/IP, as it requires the most time and the most entries. Use the Installation Wizard if you are not familiar with IP addressing.

## GUI Controls: Some Basic Ground Rules

While you may be familiar with the NT 4 GUI, we need to first review the basic control set. Microsoft has embraced the "Tab control" and uses it extensively throughout NT installation. The Tab control can contain many tabs, each with a distinctive heading. Each heading describes the functions and commands on that particular tab (the View tab includes commands that pertain to your view of the screen, the Save tab includes commands about Windows NT's various save features, etc.). The placement signifies its relative order or priority. Tabs contain a variety of controls also gleaned from the new GUI. You will often come across controls that are *grayed out* or *ghosted.* A grayed-out control indicates that a control is not available for some reason. Unfortunately, NT doesn't always indicate why it's not available. Some of the controls you will see are:

- *Control Buttons*—Control buttons are a simple point-and-click control emblazoned with a self-descriptive name. Control buttons that are usually included are: Add, Delete, Edit, OK, and Cancel. Control buttons' names generally include one underlined letter which indicates the hot key for accessing the button. For example, pressing Ctrl+A will activate the Add button.

- *Radio Buttons*—Radio buttons allow a user to select one, and only one, item from a list of multiple choices. When you select a radio button, the fill color changes.

- *Check Boxes*—Check boxes are square controls that allow you to select one or all of the possible choices. When you select a check box option, an "X" appears in the box.

- *List Boxes*—NT installation and configuration makes extensive use of list boxes, which appear as rectangular controls with a down arrow next to them and a default choice contained within the control. You can click on the down arrow to see what other choices are available. Once you see the desired item, highlight it with the cursor. The list box will now contain your selection.

## What Happens If You Make a Mistake?

It's very possible to make a mistake during the installation process. However, networking mistakes can be easily corrected after the installation has been completed. Following the network installation, you may go back and change virtually all of the initial settings. While the selections made during installation or subsequent configuration are vital to NT operation, and making the wrong choices will undoubtedly affect networking performance, mistakes can be quickly remedied after they are detected. Because the NT networking architecture is complex and services are interrelated, we recommend that you limit your configuration changes and test the new configuration after each change. This will verify that your changes did not adversely affect any other service or protocol.

Because a workstation usually supports only one person, reconfiguration on the workstation requires little more than a quick reboot of the operating system to register the changes. Servers, however, may be a bigger problem, because a server supports many clients and a simple reboot can result in an undesired outage. This is always a consideration when working with operational servers.

Because you install the workstation and server from their own unique CDs, confusion about the particular type of NT has been effectively eliminated. While many of the installable workstation and server network components are the same, the server can install additional services not available to the workstation. I will point out these services as we come across them in our discussion.

NT is designed to be installed in either a standalone or network installation. In a standalone configuration, you are present to make changes and answer questions. During a network installation, the workstation or server is installed with the expectation that the specific network settings will be changed later. For this reason, Microsoft has made it easy to change or remove extra or unwanted protocols and services following installation. In this chapter, I assume a standalone configuration.

# NT 4 Network Configuration

NT 4's network configuration tool is available as an *applet* located in the Control Panel. An applet is a small application that performs a specific function. In this case, the Networks applet starts the Network tabbed menu. The Network tabbed menu has five tabs: Identification, Services, Proto-

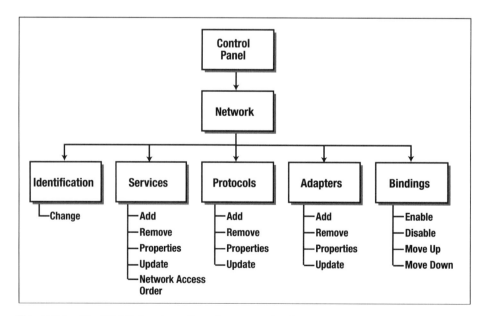

**Figure 3.1**   The NT 4 Network configuration menu structure.

cols, Adapters, and Bindings. Figure 3.1 presents an overview of NT 4's menu structure. Each tab contains controls to be used to manage its particular subject. The menu structure was designed to allow you to easily move through your network configuration. In the following sections, we'll cover each tab in detail.

## The Identification Tab

The Identification tab provides the tools necessary to identify your computer, server, or workstation to the network, as shown in Figure 3.2. The Identification tab displays the name of your computer and the workgroup to which it is attached. This tab provides one button control, Change, which allows you to modify the displayed information. Select the Change button to display the Identification Changes menu shown in Figure 3.3.

This menu provides you with the tools to change one or all of the following: the Computer Name, the Workgroup, and the Domain. If you have sufficient domain privileges, you may also use this screen to create an account on the domain. To create a domain account, check the Create a Computer Account in the Domain option and then supply a valid user name (with the proper domain privileges) and a password. Click on OK to save your changes and exit the menu, or click on Cancel to exit without saving the changes.

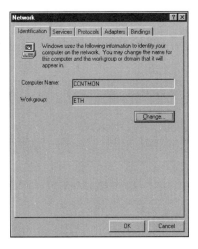

**Figure 3.2** The Identification tab shows your computer's network ID.

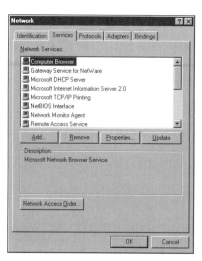

**Figure 3.3** The Identification Changes menu includes all the controls required to change your computer's ID and domain or workgroup membership.

## The Services Tab

The Services tab allows you to indicate which services you want installed or configured, as shown in Figure 3.4. The tab lists all of the network services that are currently configured on the computer and includes the Add, Remove, Properties, and Update buttons to manage and configure the

**Figure 3.4** The Services tab displays a list of your computer's currently configured network services.

services shown in the list box. In addition, the Services tab contains the Network Access Order button that enables you to specify the relative priorities NT will use in accessing your various network connections.

The Add button displays the Select Network Service menu, shown in Figure 3.5, which contains a list of standard NT 4 network services from which you can choose. In addition to these standard services, NT also provides you with the Have Disk button, which allows you to specify third-party network services from a floppy disk or CD.

The standard network services provided with NT 4 (Beta 2) are shown in Table 3.1.

**Table 3.1    NT 4 Standard Network Services**

| Service | Description |
| --- | --- |
| DHCP Relay Agent | Allows a computer to relay IP protocol DHCP messages across a LAN. |
| Gateway (and Client) Services for NetWare | IPX/SPX-compatible service and NetWare-compatible redirector that enables NT computers to access file and print resources on NetWare servers. |

*(continued)*

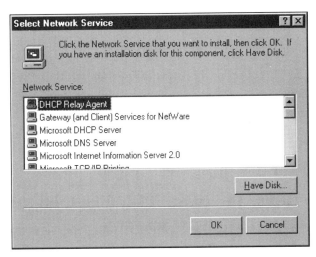

**Figure 3.5**    The Select Network Service menu contains a list of the standard NT services that can be configured on your computer.

**Table 3.1    NT 4 Standard Network Services** *(continued)*

| Service | Description |
| --- | --- |
| Microsoft DHCP Server | Provides leased IP addresses to network clients. |
| Microsoft DNS Server | Allows users to access domain names for remote domains and hosts. |
| Microsoft Internet Information Server 2.0 | A World Wide Web server tightly integrated into the Windows NT 4 Server operating system. |
| Microsoft TCP/IP Printing | Supports direct network printing. |
| NetBIOS Interface | Provides a NetBIOS mapping layer between NetBIOS applications and the transport protocols. |
| Network Monitor Agent | Interfaces with the Microsoft Network Monitor and captures network statistics. |
| Network Monitor Tools and Agent | Allows monitoring of the network and the individual NT nodes. |
| Remote Access Service | Enables a user to remotely access a computer and share files, printers, and applications using a range of devices, from a low-speed modem connection up to an ISDN connection. |
| Remoteboot Service | Enables an administrator with sufficient privilege to perform a system re-boot from a remote location. |
| RIP for Internet Protocol | Supports dynamic interchange of IP routing information between routers. |
| RIP for NWLink IPX/SPX Compatible Transport | Supports dynamic interchange of IPX/SPX routing information between routers. |
| RPC Configuration | Supports DNS, WINS, and Remote Procedure Calls. |
| RPC Support for Banyan | Supports Remote Procedure Calls for the Banyan Vines Network. |
| SAP Agent | Used for NetWare-compatible file servers or SQL servers. |
| Server | Provides server and file access functions for network clients. |

*(continued)*

**Table 3.1    NT 4 Standard Network Services** *(continued)*

| Service | Description |
| --- | --- |
| Services for Macintosh | Provides file sharing and network services for the Macintosh client. |
| Simple TCP/IP Services | A suite of TCP/IP protocols including Chargen, Echo, Quote, Discard, and Daytime. |
| SNMP Service | Monitors network operations and detects workstation and server failures. |
| Windows Internet Name Service | Includes a distributed database for supporting the conversion of network names to IP addresses. |
| Workstation | NT Client and Redirector service. |

The Remove button removes the currently selected service (the service that is highlighted in the list box). When you remove a service, the Services tab requests confirmation of the deletion. If NT restricts the service, it will notify you that the selected service cannot be deleted until the Adapter card has been removed. This is true of three of the services: server, workstation, and browser. To remove these services, you must first delete the Adapter card to which they are linked.

Clicking on the Properties button displays the properties associated with the currently highlighted service. We'll cover the service property screens in detail in later sections.

The Update button enables you to configure an up-to-date version of the service from another source, such as floppy disk or CD.

Choosing the Network Access Order control button displays the Network Access Order menu, shown in Figure 3.6. This menu displays the currently attached networks and the relative order that NT uses for access. The Move Up and Move Down controls allow you to change the relative position of a highlighted network.

## The Protocols Tab

The Protocols tab, shown in Figure 3.7, is used to install both NT standard and third-party protocols. The Protocols tab lists the currently configured

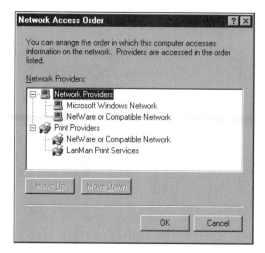

**Figure 3.6**  The Network Access Order menu allows you to change NT's network access order.

network protocols and includes the Add, Remove, Properties, and Update buttons to manage and configure these and other protocols. Let's take a detailed look at the tasks each of these buttons performs.

Clicking on the Add button displays the Select Network Protocol menu, shown in Figure 3.8, which lists the default NT protocols from which you can select. NT 4 provides six standard protocols (Beta 2), as shown in Table 3.2.

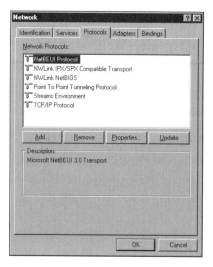

**Figure 3.7**  The Protocols tab contains a list of configured protocols and the tools to add, remove, or configure them.

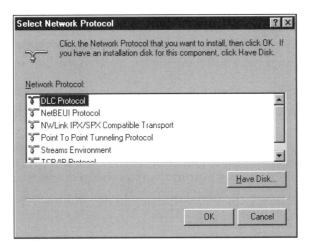

**Figure 3.8** The Select Network Protocol menu contains a list of the standard NT protocols.

**Table 3.2 NT 4 Standard Protocols**

| Protocol | Meaning | Description |
|---|---|---|
| DLC | Dynamic Link Control Protocol | Primarily used for interfacing network printers. |
| NetBEUI | NetBIOS Extended User Interface Protocol | Compatible with legacy software; fast, non routable protocol suitable for small local area networks. |
| NWLink IPX/SPX Compatible Transport | Internet Packet Exchange/Sequenced Packet Exchange Protocol | Supports NT's NetWare compatibility. |
| PPTP | Point-to-Point Tunneling Protocol | Used to provide a secure Wide Area Networking protocol to allow users to remotely access Virtual Private Networks (VPN). |
| Streams Environment | | A Unix-based protocol that supports Streams-based network drivers. |
| TCP/IP | Transport Control Protocol/Internet Protocol | A routable, high-performance protocol. |

To select a new protocol, simply choose one from the list and then click on OK. You can also use this menu to select a third-party protocol by clicking on the Have Disk button and entering the path to the new protocol.

Clicking on the Remove button removes the currently selected protocol—the protocol that is highlighted in the list box. When you remove a protocol, the Protocol tab requests confirmation of the deletion. Click on OK to delete the protocol or on Cancel to exit without deleting the protocol.

Clicking on the Properties button displays the properties associated with the highlighted protocol. We'll cover the protocol property screens in detail later in this chapter.

The Update button enables you to configure an up-to-date version of the protocol from another source, such as a floppy disk or CD.

## The Adapters Tab

The Adapters tab, shown in Figure 3.9, is used to install or configure one or more network adapters. The Adapters tab lists the currently configured network adapters and includes the Add, Remove, Properties, and Update buttons to manage and configure these adapters. Let's take a closer look at the buttons provided on the Adapters tab.

Clicking on the Add button displays the Select Network Adapter menu of default NT adapters, as shown in Figure 3.10. To select a new adapter, simply choose one from the list and then click on OK. The Select Network

**Figure 3.9**   The Adapters tab contains a list of the network adapters currently attached to your computer.

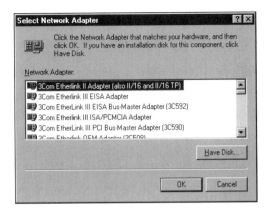

**Figure 3.10**   The Select Network Adapter menu contains a list of the standard NT network adapters.

Adapter menu also allows you to select additional adapters not contained in the NT 4 installation (Beta 2) database by clicking on the Have Disk button and entering the path to the new adapter's information file (.INF) and drivers.

The Remove button allows you to remove the currently selected adapter—the adapter that is currently highlighted in the list box. When you remove an adapter, the Adapters tab requests confirmation of the deletion. Click on OK to delete the adapter, or click on Cancel to exit without deleting the adapter.

**TIP**   When switching between different physical media or adapter types (Token Ring to Ethernet, for example), you should totally remove and reload the adapters and services. Reinitiating the network setup results in a cleaner protocol stack and reduces sporadic network problems.

Clicking on the Properties button displays the properties associated with the currently highlighted adapter. The properties screen that displays depends on which adapter you are using; many NT properties are device-specific to allow you to configure third-party products. Certain NICs allow you to specify an IRQ, base address, and other configuration items. Other NICS are automatically configured and the settings shouldn't be changed unless there is a conflict with another peripheral device.

The Update button enables you to configure an up-to-date version of the adapter's information file and drivers from a floppy disk or CD.

## The Bindings Tab

The Bindings tab, shown in Figure 3.11, is used to define which services are bound to which protocols, and which protocols are bound to which adapters. This tab includes controls for managing how NT will link or "bind" the services, protocols, and adapters together.

A service must be bound to a network adapter by one or more protocols. The Bindings tab shows the bindings that NT has created for the given set of services, protocols, and adapters. The tab also includes controls for changing the default bindings.

Notice that the Bindings tab uses a hierarchy menu to display bindings. A plus sign on the left-most column designates that the item contains additional, hidden information that you can view. Select the plus sign to expand the item revealing the hidden information. In Figure 3.11, several bindings are shown with their lower-level elements displayed. Notice also that the Gateway Service for NetWare shows only a link to the NWLink

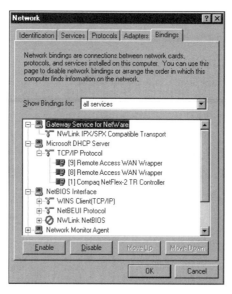

**Figure 3.11**   The Bindings tab contains a hierarchy of the various services, protocols, and adapters.

IPX/SPX Compatible Transport, whereas the NetBIOS Interface shows a link to WINS Client (TCP/IP) and, at the next level, the network adapter.

Some services do not link directly to the network adapter. The Show Bindings for list box has three viewing options: All Services, All Protocols, and All Adapters. Each selection allows you to view the protocol stack from a different perspective.

- *All Services*—Shows the protocols and adapters linked to each service.

- *All Protocols*—Shows the services and adapters linked to each protocol.

- *All Adapters*—Shows the protocols and services linked to each adapter.

You can enable or disable specific bindings or certain parts of bindings. In the example shown in Figure 3.11, the NWLink NetBIOS connection has been disabled, as indicated by the circle with a diagonal line. To enable a binding, you must first highlight a disabled service or protocol, and then click on the Enable button. Enabling a disabled service or protocol causes NT to rebind and restore the item to the protocol stack. Restoring a service or protocol naturally requires an NT reboot.

To disable a service or protocol, select one of these items and click on the Disable button. Check the complete hierarchy prior to disabling to be sure you are will not be adversely affecting network operation. NT will not allow you to disable certain services, including the workstation, server, and browser. Again, you must reboot NT before the action will take effect.

You can use the Move Up and Move Down buttons to change the position of a service within the protocol stack. Notice that in Figure 3.11, these buttons are grayed out. This is because the Show Bindings for list box indicates that "all services" is selected, so moving individual services is not possible. You must first choose a specific service before you can change its position.

 I strongly recommend that you change only one item in the Bindings tab at a time, allowing NT to bind, reboot, and test the selection before you change additional bindings. While this process may be time consuming, it will prevent unwanted interactions and will force NT to completely rebind.

# Adding and Configuring Network Components

In the following sections, we'll cover the configuration of the strategic protocols and services for NT. Specifically, we will configure:

- The Server Service

- The NetBIOS Interface Service

- TCP/IP Transport Protocol, including its subprotocols

- DHCP Server

- NetBEUI Transport Protocol

- IPX/SPX Transport Protocol

Installing these services and protocols will enable you to understand NT's methodology for configuring any standard protocol or service.

## *The Server*

NT was designed to minimize the amount of tuning required to set up and manage the operating system over a wide range of applications. However, no single set of parameters will meet every need. Therefore, NT has a few adjustable parameters besides the Systems Registry. The Server Service is one of these. In previous versions of NT, the System icon in the Control Panel would lead you to the NT Tasking menu, which would allow you to tune the way NT conducts its foreground and background services. In version 4, NT has changed the Systems menu. It now uses a slide bar control that allows you to change the foreground's priority. And the ability to adjust network performance has been moved to the Server menu.

Foreground priority is the priority that NT uses to run your desktop applications and those applications that directly interface with the user. Network applications and services run in the background. NT 4 has reached a compromise—NT Workstation is designed to give priority service to the foreground applications, while NT Server is designed to provide better support to background and network applications.

In NT 4, the Server menu, which is shown in Figure 3.12, is used to adjust the way the server handles network support. The NT server can act as a file server, providing files to network clients, or an applications server, running MSSQL Server. Each use of the server function requires different server priorities. You may use the Server menu to set the priority that provides you with the best performance, given your applications and hardware platform limitations. As indicated in Figure 3.12, the following choices are available to you:

- *Minimize Memory Used*—Uses allocated memory for a limited number (10 to 12) of user connections. This choice is usually made to prevent network transactions from using up RAM needed by other server applications. The memory being allocated is non-paged memory, which absorbs more physical memory than paged memory, which can be swapped out.

- *Balance*—Allocates memory for many more connections (default is 50 to 70) by balancing the use of existing physical memory.

- *Maximize Throughput for File Sharing*—Allows as many connections as needed by allocating larger chunks of non-paged memory from the physical memory pool. Of course, the number of connections is ultimately limited by the amount of physical memory available.

- *Maximize Throughput for Network Applications*—Allocates more memory to the network applications rather than network connections. Network users log into network applications and require fewer server memory resources.

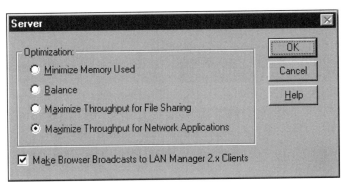

**Figure 3.12**   The Server menu controls how NT will prioritize its network operations.

## CONFIGURING THE SERVER SERVICE

Before you jump right in and start tweaking with the server configuration options, monitor your server's network operations and obtain a sample set of readings for a sufficient period of time to characterize its performance. Once you have collected a good deal of data, follow these steps to configure the server:

1. Double click on the Network icon in the Control Panel.

2. Select the Services tab from the Network tabbed menu.

3. Highlight the Server service.

4. Click on the Properties button to display the Server menu, shown in Figure 3.12.

5. Select the Optimization choice that best represents your needs. Note that these are radio buttons and you may only choose one.

6. Select the Make Browser Broadcasts to LAN Manager 2.x Clients check box if your system supports LAN Manager 2 clients.

7. Click on OK.

8. Rebind and reboot your computer.

Once you've completed these steps, monitor your server's network operations and compare the results with your initial tests to see if the value you selected has improved or worsened the server's performance.

## *The NetBIOS Service*

NetBIOS is widely used as a legacy service to maintain NT's compatibility with MS-DOS and LAN Manager network applications. NetBIOS uses LAN Adapter (LANA) numbers to segregate adapters and their stacked protocols.

You can assign a LANA number to each network route and each adapter card. A network route is a combination of a protocol driver and an adapter card. Therefore, your NT system can have multiple LANA assignments. NT can stack several protocols on several adapters. As a result, you have many LANA numbers.

Unfortunately, some MS-DOS and LAN Manager programs are hard coded to specific LANA numbers (single protocol, single adapter) and do not have the ability to be reconfigured (for example, many MS-DOS-based applications send their requests to LANA 0). Adding adapters and protocols may connect LANA 0 to a protocol adapter combination that is not necessarily compatible with the MS-DOS application. Because there is no automatic way to arrange the LANA numbers, NT uses the NetBIOS configuration to manually move protocols to specific LANA numbers to eliminate problems with older applications.

While this is not a dark secret, the LANA compatibility fix is not always obvious. When researching an incompatibility problem, you may come across the statement that the protocol must be linked to LANA 0 or 1. By using the NetBIOS Configuration menu shown in Figure 3.13, you can move the appropriate protocol and adapter combination to the required LANA number.

## Configuring NetBIOS

Assuming your application requires a LANA 0 value to run, you must change the existing NetBIOS configuration in order meet this requirement. Here are the steps to follow:

1. Double click on the Network icon in the Control Panel.

2. Select the Services tab from the Network Tabbed menu.

**Figure 3.13**  The NetBIOS Configuration menu controls which LANA number a given protocol and adapter will use.

3. Highlight the NetBIOS Interface service.

4. Click on the Properties button to display the NetBIOS Configuration menu, shown in Figure 3.13. The NetBIOS Configuration menu shows the protocol and adapter order for each of the installed protocols.

5. Highlight the current LANA 0 and click the Edit button. The number will become editable.

6. Change the number to a higher, unique number.

7. Select the LANA number that will be linked to your application. Click on the Edit button and change the number to the 0.

8. Rebind, reboot, and test the changed LANA order.

## Configuring the TCP/IP Transport Protocol

Transport Control Protocol/Internet Protocol (TCP/IP) is a major NT protocol. TCP/IP is not one, but many protocols and utilities unified under one name. In Windows NT 4, TCP/IP contains the following:

- The IP Protocol

- File Transfer Protocol (FTP)

- Simple Network Management Protocol (SNMP)

- TCP/IP Network Printing

- Dynamic Host Configuration Protocol (DHCP)

- Domain Naming Service (DNS)

- TCP/IP utilities

Before you install Microsoft TCP/IP on a Windows NT computer, you will need to know the following information:

- If there is not a DHCP server attached to your network, you must have a network card IP address and subnet mask for each installed network adapter card in your computer.

- The IP address of the local IP router.

- Will this computer be a DHCP server? Only NT servers can be configured as DHCP servers.

- Will this computer be a WINS proxy agent?

- Will your computer use a Domain Name System (DNS)? If it will, you must know the IP addresses of the DNS servers available on your network. You may select one or more DNS servers.

- If a WINS server is available on the network, you must know its IP address. As with DNS, you can configure multiple WINS servers.

The Protocols tab lists the currently configured transport protocols. To configure TCP/IP, highlight the protocol in the list box and then click on the Properties button to display the Microsoft TCP/IP Properties menu, shown in Figure 3.14. This menu contains five tabs: IP Address, DNS, WINS Address, DHCP Relay, and Routing. Each tab contains controls to install and configure a portion of the TCP/IP suite.

## TCP/IP REQUIREMENTS

To configure TCP/IP on your NT computer, you must first determine if you want the system to lease its IP address from a DHCP server or have a permanent IP address that you enter manually in the Microsoft TCP/IP

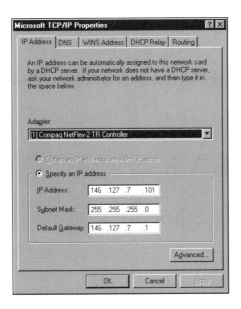

**Figure 3.14** The Microsoft TCP/IP Properties menu lets you set your computer's IP address.

Properties menu. To receive and deliver packets successfully between hosts, TCP/IP relies on the configured IP address, subnet mask, and default gateway.

Although an IP address is a single value, it contains two pieces of information: the network ID and the host ID for your computer. The network ID identifies whether or not a new computer system is connected to your network. The host ID uniquely identifies your computer as a host within that network. Your network uses the network ID and host ID to determine which packets should be received or ignored. Because the sender's IP address is included in every outgoing IP packet, the receiving computer can determine the originating network ID and host ID from the IP address field. This is done by using subnet masks.

Subnet masks are 32-bit binary values that allow your computer to decipher IP addresses of other networked computers. The IP address is combined with the subnet mask to separate the network ID portion of the IP address from the host ID. Like an IP address, the value of a subnet mask is represented in IP address notation—four groups of three digits, each group followed by a period. Each of the four groups can contain a decimal number between 0 and 255. The subnet mask allows your computer to determine if an IP address is located on the local subnet or on a remote network.

When compared, a 1 in the subnet mask indicates that a corresponding 1 in the IP address is part of the network ID. The subnet mask changes if your network is one of the following:

- Class A subnets have a subnet mask of 255.0.0.0 and can decode 126 network IDs and 16.7 million host IDs.

- Class B subnets have a subnet mask of 255.255.0.0 and can decode 16,384 network IDs and 65,534 host IDs.

- Class C subnets have a subnet mask of 255.255.255.0 and can decode 2 million network IDs and 254 host IDs.

For example: when the IP address is 148.190.35.10 and the subnet mask is 255.255.0.0, you have a Class B address. The address decodes to the network ID of 148.190 and the host ID of 35.10. If your local network addresses all start with 148.190 then this is a local address. If you are still unclear as to what subnet mask to enter, ask your LAN administrator what class of IP address is licensed to your site, then use the class information listed previously to enter your correct subnet mask.

TCP/IP networks are connected by gateways that regulate the flow of addresses over the network and subnets. A subnet is really a local area network separated from another LAN by a router. In this book, a router refers an IP gateway that transfers your data packets from your local network to a larger local or wide area network.

A default gateway contains a list of the IP addresses contained in the networks to which it is connected. Each IP host (server or workstation) maintains a static destinations routing table. A default gateway is used to find remote destinations. This is why the address of the default gateway is required.

When an IP host prepares to send a packet, it inserts its source IP address and the destination address in the packet's header. The Transport layer verifies that the network ID of the destination matches the network ID of the source. If they match, the packet is sent to the destination computer on the local network. If the destination address does not match local network IDs, the host's static routing table is consulted for static routing information. If no matches are found, the packet is forwarded to the default gateway for delivery.

The default gateway can be a computer or a complex dedicated router that is connected to your subnet on one side and other networks beyond your gateway. Because the default gateway knows the network IDs of other networks, it can route your data packets to other gateways. The packet is eventually delivered to a gateway connected to the specified destination. If delivery is impossible, the packet eventually dies.

If for some reason the default gateway becomes unavailable, your computer will be limited to addresses within its own subnet. To prevent this from happening, you can assign multiple default gateways so that packets can be routed outside the subnet, even in the event of a default gateway failure.

## INSTALLING AND CONFIGURING TCP/IP

Now that you are aware of the requirements, we can go ahead and configure TCP/IP on your computer. Here are the steps to follow:

1. From the Control Panel, double click on the Network icon.

2. Select the Protocol tab from the Network tabbed menu to display the Microsoft TCP/IP Properties menu, shown in Figure 3.14.

3. Verify that the Adapter list box indicates the network adapter card that you wish to bind with TCP/IP. If it does not, click on the downward-pointing arrow and scroll down to find the appropriate network adapter. This step is important because it is possible to assign the wrong IP address to an adapter when your system supports several adapters.

4. Using the information we covered in the previous section, determine if you wish to use the Dynamic Host Configuration Protocol (DHCP) to provide an IP address and subnet mask. If the answer is yes, then select the "Obtain an IP address from a DHCP server" radio button; DHCP will automatically lease an IP address for this computer. If the answer is no, and you plan to manually enter your IP address, then select the "Specify an IP address" radio button.

5. If you chose to manually enter your IP address, enter your 12-digit IP address in the IP Address text box. Make certain to correctly enter the digits. This is especially true of addresses with blanks or zeros. If in doubt, verify your IP address with your LAN administrator. If you are the LAN administrator, just be careful. The same two IP addresses on the network can cause problems with both computers.

6. Enter your subnet mask in the Subnet Mask text box. Again, be careful to enter the proper digits in the correct sequence.

7. Enter the IP address of your local router or bridge into the Default Gateway text box. Again, be careful to enter the proper digits in the correct sequence. If your network has several gateway routers, then choose the Add button to display the TCP/IP Gateway Address menu. Enter the appropriate IP addresses for each gateway.

8. Click on the Advanced button to display the Advanced IP Addressing menu, shown in Figure 3.15.

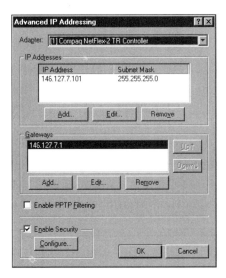

**Figure 3.15**    The Advanced IP Addressing menu sets the additional IP addresses and IP security.

Before we move on, verify your IP address and subnet mask contained in the IP Addresses text box. You can use the Edit and Remove buttons to modify these values, if necessary. You can also enter additional IP addresses and subnet masks for the displayed adapter card or for any other Network Interface Cards (NIC) in your computer.

Next, verify your default gateway's address in the Gateways text box. You can use the Edit and Remove buttons to modify these values. For multiple gateways, you can specify the priority of each gateway by moving its IP address higher or lower in the list corresponding to increased or decreased priority. NT uses the first (top) gateway address and sequences through the addresses until it finds a gateway that will service a destination address.

PPTP is a tunneling protocol that enables WAN users to access multiprotocol Virtual Private Networks (VPN) by wrapping a secure protocol within standard network data packets. VPNs are secure corporate networks that can extend services across unsecured wide area networks (for instance, the Internet). Choose this option to select the PPTP protocol. Once selected, the PPTP protocol will only accept PPTP packets. The PPTP Filtering is covered further in Chapter 9.

9.  Check the Enable Security check box to display the TCP/IP Security menu, shown in Figure 3.16.

    The TCP/IP Security menu allows you to restrict the network traffic that will be handled by your computer. Specifically, you can restrict traffic from specific TCP ports, User Datagram Protocol (UDP) ports, and traffic using specific Internet Protocols. Although the TCP/IP Security menu is used principally for restricting access and trouble-shooting problems associated with any one of the three ports, another application is to speed up host network operation in networks with high volumes of unwanted traffic.

10. For initial configuration, click on the Permit All radio button for TCP Ports, the Permit All radio button for UDP Ports, and the Permit All radio button for IP protocols.

11. Click on OK to return to the Advanced TCP/IP Properties menu.

12. Click on OK to return to the IP Address tab in the TCP/IP Properties menu.

Congratulations, you have completed the installation of TCP/IP on your workstation.

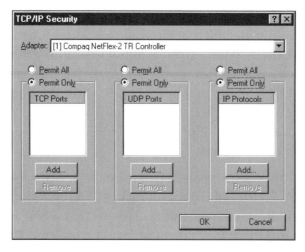

**Figure 3.16**   The TCP/IP Security menu allows you to restrict certain types of network traffic from your computer.

# DNS

Domain Name System (DNS) is designed for the user that prefers to use network names rather than IP addresses. DNS is a naming service that provides standard naming conventions for IP computers. DNS supports Windows Sockets, FTP, and TCP/IP utility applications when connecting to hosts that are unknown on your network.

If you choose to use DNS, you must configure how your computer will use DNS and the HOSTS file. The HOSTS file is located in your WINNT\ SYSTEM32\DRIVERS\ETC\ directory. Microsoft includes a copy of a sample HOSTS file, named HOSTS.SAM. A HOSTS file contains an IP address followed by a computer's network name. Also, you must install TCP/IP (shown in the previous section) before you set up the DNS connectivity. DNS configuration covers all network adapters installed on the same computer.

## Configuring DNS

The following steps provide instructions for configuring DNS:

1. Select the Protocols tab.

2. Select TCP/IP Protocol and then click on the Properties button to display the Microsoft TCP/IP Properties menu.

3. Select the DNS tab to display the DNS menu, shown in Figure 3.17.

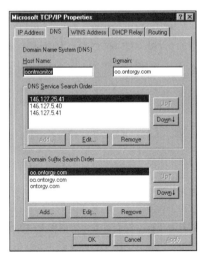

**Figure 3.17**   The DNS tab allows you to set your DNS server locations and the order used to search for DNS names.

4.  Enter your computer's network name in the Host Name text box.

5.  Enter the name of your Domain name in the Domain text box. This DNS domain name is used with the host name to create a fully qualified domain name (FQDN) for the computer. The FQDN is the host name followed by a period (.) followed by the domain name.

6.  Under DNS Service Search Order, click on Add. The TCP/IP DNS Server dialog box appears. Type the IP address of the DNS server that will provide name resolution.

7.  If you have additional DNS servers, click on Add to move the address to the DNS Service Search Order box. You can only configure three DNS server IP addresses. The servers running DNS will be searched in the order listed, from top to bottom. To change this order, select an address to move, and then select Up or Down. To remove an IP address, highlight it, and then click on Remove. To make a change to one of the addresses, first highlight it, and then click on Edit.

8.  Under Domain Suffix Search Order, click on Add. A TCP/IP Domain Suffix dialog box appears. Enter the DNS domain suffix to be appended to the host names during name resolution, and click on Add to list the suffix in the Domain Suffix Search Order box.

9.  You can add a maximum of six domain suffixes. The suffixes will be used in the order listed. To change this order, highlight a suffix to move, and then choose Up or Down. To remove a domain suffix, highlight it, and then choose Remove. To make a change to one of the suffixes, first highlight it, and then choose Edit.

10. When you are done setting DNS options, click on OK two times, then click on Close. The settings will take effect after you restart your computer.

## WINS Service

Windows Internet Naming Service (WINS) is an efficient way to find named servers and workstations connected to a Microsoft TCP/IP network. WINS servers can only be installed on NT Servers. A WINS server consists of an NT Server configured with a TCP/IP protocol stack and running the WINS server application.

The WINS server contains a distributed database of IP addresses and network computer names. The word *distributed* is important to understanding WINS. It means that more than one WINS server can exist and that each WINS server can jointly use their combined database resources to resolve names and IP addresses.

If a network client is configured to use WINS, unknown network names are automatically resolved into IP network addresses. This enables the client to append the IP address into the destination field of its transmitted data frames.

WINS has several beneficial features:

- WINS interfaces with the NetBIOS Interface faster and is more flexible then DNS.

- Configuring a client to use WINS virtually eliminates the need to support an LMHOSTS file on every workstation. This makes LAN management easier and eliminates the need for constant workstation updates. If a client workstation needs an address, it can obtain one from the centrally managed WINS server.

- Using WINS reduces the need to use broadcast packets to obtain network names, which results in improved network performance.

- WINS enables domain browsing across routers.

- The WINS service can grow with your network. The distributed database feature means that additional WINS servers can be added as network requirements dictate.

- When DHCP issues a new IP address for computers moving between subnets, the addresses are automatically updated in the WINS database.

Before you can configure the WINS service, you must know:

- That your server has been configured with TCP/IP.

- The primary (and secondary, if required) WINS server's IP addresses.

- If you wish to use an LMHOSTS file for local configuration control.

## CONFIGURE **WINS** ADDRESSING

The following steps provide instructions for configuring WINS addressing:

1. From the Control Panel, double click on the Network icon.

2. Select the Protocols tab. Select TCP/IP Protocol and then click on the Properties button to display the Microsoft TCP/IP Properties menu.

3. Choose the WINS Address tab from the TCP/IP Properties menu. The WINS Address tab is shown in Figure 3.18.

4. Enter the primary WINS server's IP address.

5. Enter the secondary WINS server's IP address, if required.

6. If you have configured DNS, choose the Enable DNS for Windows Resolution check box.

7. If you want to maintain local control over a limited number of network addresses, choose the Enable LMHOSTS Lookup check box. The LMHOSTS file is contained in the WINNT\SYSTEM32\ DRIVERS\ETC\ directory. Microsoft includes a sample LMHOSTS. SAM file which can be used. This file contains network IP addresses

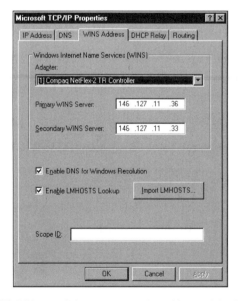

**Figure 3.18** The WINS Address tab lets you enter the address of the WINS servers.

followed by host names, followed by a #PRE. The definition of #PRE is cryptic. In most applications, the # signifies a comment. In the LMHOSTS file, it tells NT to preload the computer names and addresses from this file.

**TIP** Create a new LMHOSTS file from scratch, using the sample as a guide.

8. If your network has a centralized LMHOSTS file, click on the Import LMHOSTS button. NT will request the network path to the file. Enter the appropriate path, or find the path using a supplied browser window. The imported file will be copied to your computer and stored in the appropriate directory.

9. The Scope ID is required if your system is only using NetBIOS over TCP/IP in the bindings to communicate. If this is the only protocol between your computer and others on the network, then you must enter the Scope ID that matches the other computers' Scope ID. In order for computers running that protocol to find each other, their Scope ID's must match.

10. Reboot your computer to complete the WINS configuration changes.

## Configuring the DHCP Relay

If you have chosen to use the Dynamic Host Configuration Protocol server to provide you with an IP address, then you may update the information contained in the DHCP Relay tab. This menu is used to configure your NT computer as a DHCP relay agent. A relay agent is a software agent that forwards DHCP and BOOTP packets between subnets—that is, across a router. Usually, this configuration is only applicable if you have enabled IP routing on this computer. To configure the DHCP relay agent, set the following options:

1. From the Microsoft TCP/IP Properties menu, choose the DHCP Relay tab, shown in Figure 3.19, which contains two variable settings and an address box. The Seconds threshold value sets the time to wait between discovery broadcasts on the local subnet. The Maximum Hops limits the number of hops that the broadcast can make to relay broadcast messages. The default value for these variables is both 4. This

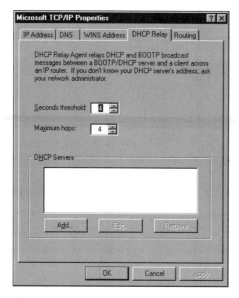

**Figure 3.19**   The DHCP Relay tab contains the information NT needs to find its local DHCP servers.

information is compliant with the Request For Comments (RFC) 1542 document, which is available from **www.internic.com**. Before you change these values, check with your network administrator.

2. Click on Add and enter your DHCP Server's address in the DHCP Servers Address text box.

3. Click on OK to close the menu. This completes the DHCP Relay setup configuration.

## Configuring IP Routing

Click the Routing tab on the Microsoft TCP/IP Properties menu. The Routing tab is the final TCP/IP Properties menu. This tab only contains a single check box control that allows you to enable IP forwarding. IP Forwarding allows packet routing between networks. The IP forwarding check box is only available if you have two or more NIC cards installed in your computer. Choose this option only if your NIC cards are attached to different networks and if you wish to use NT to perform IP routing between the two networks.

## *SNMP*

Simple Network Management Protocol (SNMP) is a network tool for monitoring network operation. SNMP is a structured, extensible protocol that specifies standard information blocks from each network device. The protocol is extensible because new network devices and monitoring points can be easily added and monitored. The SNMP service enables NT 4 to accept network inquiries from other hosts to report its operation and condition. Before installing SNMP, you should know:

- The network community names to which the computer will be connected.

- A trap destination IP address for each community name.

- The IP address of any SNMP management host attached to your network.

### INSTALLING THE **SNMP** SERVICE

To install the SNMP service, follow these steps:

1. Log on to your workstation or server as a member of the Administrators group.

2. From the Control Panel, double click on the Network icon, and then select the Services tab.

3. Click on the Add button to display the Select Network Service menu.

4. In the Network Service dialog box, select SNMP Service and then click on OK.

5. NT Setup now displays a message requesting the full path to the distribution files.

6. Enter the correct path. Be sure to enter both the drive and full path details (for example, E:\i386).

7. Click on the Continue button.

8. NT Setup copies the appropriate files to your computer from the selected path and then displays the SNMP Properties dialog box, as shown in Figure 3.20.

Now, we're ready to configure the SNMP service.

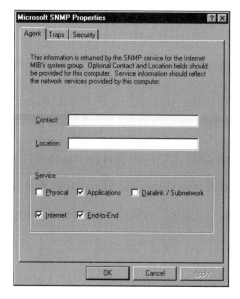

**Figure 3.20**    The SNMP Properties dialog box is used to configure the computer's SNMP agent.

## SETTING THE AGENTS TAB OPTIONS

Our first task is to set the options on the Agents tab. Follow these steps:

1. Select the Agents tab.

2. Enter the computer user's name in the Contact box and the computer's physical location in the Location box. These are comments that will be used as text and cannot include embedded control characters.

3. Select the services to report in the Service box. Check all boxes that indicate network capabilities provided by your Windows NT computer. SNMP must have this information to manage the enabled services.

   - Select the Physical option if this NT computer manages any physical TCP/IP device, such as a repeater.

   - Select the Applications option if this NT computer contains any applications that make extensive use of TCP/IP. If you are in doubt, select this option.

   - Select the Datalink/Subnetwork option if your computer manages a TCP/IP network device such as a bridge or RIP router.

- Select the Internet option if this Windows NT computer acts as an IP gateway.

- Select the End-to-End option if this computer is an IP host. Select this option for all installations.

4. When you have made all the necessary service choices, click on OK.

5. When the Network dialog box appears, choose the Close control button. If you are installing SNMP for the first time, the settings will only take effect after you reboot the computer. If you are configuring SNMP, the Agent Options changes take effect immediately—one of the few times NT doesn't require you to reboot the computer.

## SETTING THE TRAPS OPTIONS

Our next step is to set the Traps options. The SNMP Traps tab provides the tools required to change the SNMP communities and trap destinations, as shown in Figure 3.21. The screen controls allow you to add or remove *community* names. A community is nothing more than a group of SNMP hosts that communicate using a common heading. You can set your computer to belong to one or more of these communities. The pur-

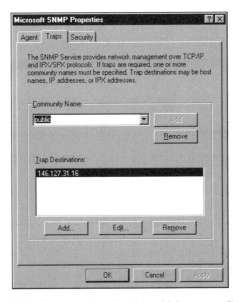

**Figure 3.21**  The Traps tab allows you to determine which community will receive traps from this computer.

pose of belonging to a community is that the community name is included in your SNMP trap packet and can be recognized by other members of the community.

The Traps tab also allows you to add, edit, or remove *trap destinations.* Trap destinations identify the SNMP hosts to be sent SNMP traps from your computer. Of course, the destinations you specify must belong to the same community, or they will generate their own "Authentication Failure" traps. The default community "public" is usually specified. Other community names can be specified if you intend to cause network events to occur, such as sending information to SNMP management servers. The SNMP community names are case sensitive, so *Public* does not equal *public.*

Follow these steps to set your Trap options:

1. Select the Traps tab.

2. Identify each community to which you want this computer to send traps by entering the name in the Community Name box and clicking on Add after each entry to add the name to the list. If you make a mistake and need to delete an entry, highlight the text, and click on Remove.

3. If you want to specify one or more hosts for each community, be sure that the community name is still highlighted, then, under Trap Destinations, click on Add. Enter the host IP address, and then click on Add.

4. If you need to make changes to an entry in the list, first highlight it, and then click on Edit.

5. When you have completed all entries, click on OK. When the Network dialog box reappears, click on Close.

If you are installing SNMP for the first time, the settings will only take effect after you reboot the computer. If you are configuring SNMP, the changes take effect immediately; you will not need to reboot the computer.

## SETTING THE SNMP SECURITY OPTIONS

Our next step is to set up SNMP security. The Security tab, shown in Figure 3.22, allows you to specify the communities and network hosts from which

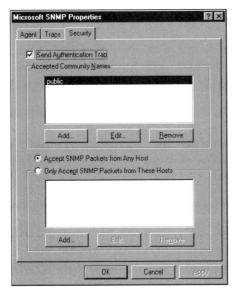

**Figure 3.22**   The Security tab contains several controls to set SNMP security options.

your computer will accept requests. The Security tab also provides tools to authorize authentication traps. Setting the Send Authentication Trap option tells your computer to send a trap whenever it receives a request for information from an unauthorized community or host computer. Authentication traps identify to you or your LAN administrator that unauthorized requests for access are taking place. They may also indicate that LAN security is being breached.

Follow these steps to set up security for SNMP:

1. Select the Security tab.

2. Select the Send Authentication Trap check box to verify or add information.

3. Under the Accepted Community Names list box, click on Add to display the Security Configuration dialog box.

4. In the Accepted Community Names list box, enter a community name from which your computer will accept requests. Click on Add to move the name to the Accepted Community Names list. Repeat this process for additional community names. Remember, a host must belong to a

community that appears in this list for the SNMP service to accept requests from that host.

5. If you need to make changes to an entry in the Accepted Community Names list, highlight the community name, and then click on Edit.

6. To delete an entry in the Accepted Community Names list, highlight the community name, and then click on Remove.

7. Select whether your computer will accept SNMP packets from any host or only from specified hosts.

   • Checking the Accept SNMP Packets From Any Host option allows all packets access.

   • Checking the Only Accept SNMP Packets From These Hosts option restricts packet acceptance to the listed hosts. If you choose this option, you must then click on the Add button and add the names or addresses of the hosts from which your computer will accept requests in the IP Host text box. If you need to make changes to an entry, highlight the name, and then click on Edit.

8. To delete an entry in the list, highlight the name, and then click on Remove.

If you are installing SNMP for the first time, the settings will only take effect after you reboot the computer. If you are configuring SNMP, the changes take effect immediately without the need to reboot the computer.

# TCP/IP Printing Services

Using TCP/IP Printing services, Microsoft Network users can print to printers that are directly connected to the network or connected through a Unix print server. Directly connected printers are configured with their own adapter card and internal software. A directly connected printer must be able to:

• Recognize its unique network address

• Accept or reject print jobs

• Queue print jobs until the printer can create the hard-copy page

- Reject any print job that it cannot queue or is improperly sent

- Print using the information sent by NT

- Provide a status back to NT of the current and queued print jobs

TCP/IP printing services also allow Unix users to print to a Windows NT computer with shared printing. The TCP/IP printing services is RFC 1179 compliant. In addition to interfacing network printers, NT can host a printer and provide the print capability to the network as a print server.

## Overview of TCP/IP Printing

Mixed networks can include Windows for Workgroups, Unix print servers, NT Workstations, NT Servers, or LAN manager servers. NT provides a printing service that enables other network computers running non-TCP protocols to access NT print services. The other computers can send print jobs to the NT print server using any protocol they share with the NT server. Only NT requires TCP/IP.

## Before You Install TCP/IP Printing

You need to know the following information in order to install TCP/IP printing on NT:

- The IP identifier of the host where the printer is connected. This can be the DNS name or the IP address.

- An IP address for each printer (for directly connected network printers).

- If your network printer is configured with an HP JetDirect card, it must support LPD (Line Printer Daemon from Unix), or TCP/IP printing will not work properly.

- The printer name of the host (if your printer is attached to a Unix host).

- TCP/IP installed on the NT computer you are configuring.

## Configuring TCP/IP Printing

Now, we're ready to get down to business and configure the TCP/IP printing services. Here are the steps to follow:

1. From the Control Panel, double click on the Network icon, and select the Services tab.

2.  Click on Add to display Select Network Service menu.

3.  From the Select Network Service menu, select Microsoft TCP/IP Printing, and then click on OK.

4.  NT Setup will request the full path to your distribution files. Enter the path, and click on Continue.

5.  When NT finishes copying the appropriate files to System32 directory, click on Close.

You will see the Bindings status box appear, binding the new service to the TCP/IP protocol. If NT discovers any problems with the configuration, it will notify you with a diagnostic message stating the cause of the problem. If there is a problem with the configuration, reopen the Select Network Service menu, and remove the TCP/IP printing by selecting the service and then clicking on Remove.

If the bindings complete successfully, you must reboot the computer for the changes to take effect. NT is now ready to create a TCP/IP printer.

# DHCP Server

The Dynamic Host Configuration Protocol (DHCP) is a mechanism to automatically assign and manage network IP address information. Your LAN administrator must submit and be granted a range of IP addresses. These addresses are distributed to each workstation, server, router, and other network computers. You may enter these fixed addresses into NT. From that point on, this becomes your network address. Unfortunately, the number of addresses granted may be insufficient to allow everyone on the network to have their own address.

DHCP relies on the fact that not everyone needs a static address all the time. The DHCP server leases the addresses to your computer, the client, for a "Lease Period" of time. If your computer moves to another network, you will pick up a leased address from that network's DHCP server. When your lease runs out, you will be granted a new lease. If you don't need the address any longer, it is moved to the DHCP server's pool of available addresses.

While DHCP is not a cure for the lack of available addresses, it is very effective in some networks. The address leasing process conserves the time and efforts of both the workstation user and the LAN administrator involved in adding and removing IP addresses. DHCP can also maintain a higher level of utilization for the available supply of IP addresses. Depending on lease periods, if a computer user is on vacation or inactive, the leased address can be issued to an active user.

## DHCP Operation

DHCP operates using these four main processes:

- *The Discovery Process*—If your computer is configured as a DHCP client, it sends a broadcast discover message to the local network during startup. All of your network's DHCP servers receive the broadcast message. They each respond with an offer message containing an IP address and valid configuration information to your computer.

- *The Selection Process*—Your computer's NT DHCP agent receives these offers and chooses one of them. Your computer sends a request message that specifies which of the DHCP servers' offer has been chosen. The rejected DHCP servers that made outstanding offers return the offered addresses to their available address pools.

- *The Acknowledgment Process*—The selected DHCP server acknowledges the acceptance and includes in that acknowledgment the address that it has previously sent during the Discovery Process. In addition to the address, it includes a valid lease for the address and client configuration parameters.

- *The Binding Process*—Once your computer receives the acknowledgment, it is bound to the DHCP server and the leased address. Your computer is configured to participate on the TCP/IP network. Depending on your DHCP lease rate and the network requirements, your computer will reuse the address for subsequent startups. Once the lease period has expired, your computer must once more go through the Discovery Process.

## Installing a DHCP Server

Before installing the DHCP server, you must first install TCP/IP. The installation procedure will eventually notify you that you can't install DHCP without TCP/IP, so don't waste your time. DHCP service will only install on an NT server. Here are the steps to follow:

1. Log into the computer with Administrator's privileges.

2. From the Control Panel, double click on the Network icon, and select the Services tab.

3. Click on Add to display the Select Network Service menu.

4. In the Select Network Service menu, select Microsoft DHCP Server, and click on OK.

5. NT Setup will now request the full path to the NT distribution files. Enter the path, and click Continue.

   All necessary files will be copied to your system's hard disk. If your computer was not configured for static TCP/IP, then you must complete all the required procedures for manually configuring TCP/IP. See the *Configuring and Installing TCP/IP* section earlier in the chapter for detailed instructions on configuring TCP/IP. Do not try to use DHCP to configure a new DHCP server because a new DHCP server is only described by its static IP address, which has yet to be identified.

6. When you are done, click on OK.

7. In the Microsoft TCP/IP Properties menu, click on OK.

8. In the Select Network Service menu, click on Close.

All the appropriate DHCP software is ready for use after you restart the computer.

## Configuring the DHCP Server

Before you can configure your DHCP server, you must know the range of network addresses that you plan to manage under DHCP. This does not mean that you must have a contiguous string of addresses. You may exclude a set of IP addresses within the range of managed addresses. You must also decide if you wish to award each computer an "Unlimited Lease" or if you wish to restrict the leases to a fixed time period. This information must be entered to complete the DHCP server configuration.

The following steps provide the instructions for configuring the DHCP server:

1. Start the DHCP Manager. The DHCP Manager is contained in the Start|Programs|Administrative Tools menu.

2. Double click on the Local Machine icon.

3. Open the Scope pull-down menu, and select Create to display the Create Scope (Local) menu, shown in Figure 3.23.

4. Enter the beginning DHCP address in the Start Address text box, and enter the ending DHCP address in the End Address text box.

5. Enter the Subnet Mask that is appropriate to the range of addresses you are configuring.

6. If your range of managed addresses contains any that should be excluded, click on Add, and enter those start and end addresses in the Exclusion Range text box. You may specify more than one range of excluded addresses.

7. If you wish to permanently lease the IP addresses to the network computers, select the Lease Duration: Unlimited radio button. If you wish

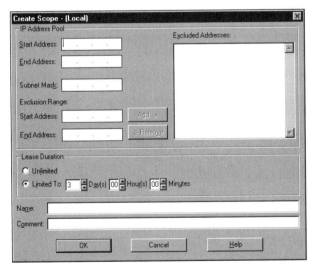

**Figure 3.23**   The Create Scope menu is the DHCP server's configuration menu for your server.

to restrict how long the network computers can maintain their IP addresses, select Lease Duration: Limited To. Set the leasing time period using the scroll boxes for Days, Hours, and Minutes. When you first set this value, observe how the network is used. For networks that are frequently adding or removing workstations, a lower value is more practical. For networks that are stable and are seldom changed, higher values can be used.

8. In the Name text box, enter your name or the name of the LAN administrator.

9. In the Comment text box, enter any comments, such as a telephone or extension.

10. Exit the DHCP Manager, and reboot NT to enter the configuration.

This completes the configuration of the DHCP server.

# Installing NetBEUI

This section provides a step-by-step guide for installing the NetBEUI components on NT 4. This section also includes the necessary background material so that you can perform a knowledgeable installation of the NetBEUI protocol. The material relates the installation parameters to the protocol variable shown in Chapter 1.

1. From the Control Panel, double click on the Network icon, and select the Protocols tab.

2. Click on Add to display the Select Network Protocol screen, which identifies NT's standard suite of protocols.

3. Highlight the NetBEUI protocol, and click on OK.

4. NT Setup will request the full path to your distribution files. Enter the path, and click on Continue.

5. After NT copies the appropriate NetBEUI protocol files to the System32 directory, click on Close.

You have successfully completed the installation of the NetBEUI protocol.

# Installing NWLink IPX/SPX Compatible Transport

Novell NetWare and Microsoft Network are not entirely compatible. They require additional software in the form of an NT protocol or a Novell Redirector. This added requirement allows NetWare and NT Clients to see each other's servers and workstations. Because NT is an extensible operating system, you can purchase a third-party (Novell) Redirector, or you can use the protocol and services provided as standard with NT. In this section, we'll install and configure NT's interfaces to the NetWare environment.

Some of the terminology in this section may be confusing, so I've provided a brief summary of the terms you'll need to know:

- *The NWLink IPX/SPX compatible transport for NetWare*—Supports IPX/SPX NetWare applications and clients. The transport is a standard NT protocol that can be installed on both the NT workstation and server.

- *The Client Service for NetWare*—A service that allows an NT client to communicate with a NetWare server. The Client Service for NetWare can only be installed on an NT workstation.

- *The Gateway Service for NetWare*—Allows Microsoft Network clients attached to the NT server to access file and printer services located across the network on a NetWare server. This service can only be installed on the NT server.

- *NWLink NetBIOS*—A NetBIOS protocol that enables legacy NT applications to use the NetBIOS Application Programming Interfaces (API) to attach to NetWare networks. The NWLink NetBIOS is installed automatically on both the NT workstation and server when you install any other NetWare component.

## NWLink IPX/SPX Compatible Transport

When NetWare clients need access to NT applications, such as SNA or MSSQL Server, NT must emulate the NetWare environment using a compatible protocol. The IPX/SPX Compatible Transport protocol allows NT's applications to emulate a NetWare Loadable Module (NLM). NLM applications are native to NetWare clients. Configuring this protocol enables NT applications to appear, at least to the NetWare client, as if they are running on a Novell NetWare server. Before you configure the NWLink IPX/SPX Compatible Transport protocol, check with your LAN administrator to see if you need to configure an Internal Network Number. If the answer is yes, your LAN administrator must supply the number to configure the protocol.

The following steps will guide you through the configuration of the NWLink IPX/SPX Compatible Transport protocol:

1. From the Control Panel, double click on the Network icon, and select the Protocols tab.

2. Click on Add to display the Select Network Protocol menu.

3. Highlight the IPX/SPX Compatible Transport Protocol, and click on OK.

4. NT Setup will request the full path to your distribution files. Enter the path, and click on Continue.

5. After NT copies the appropriate IPX/SPX Compatible Transport and the NWLink NetBIOS protocol files to the System32 directory, you will be returned to the Protocols tab.

   Note that both the IPX/SPX Compatible Transport and NWLink NetBIOS have been added to the list of configured Network Protocols.

6. Highlight the NWLink IPX/SPX Compatible Transport protocol and click on Properties to display the NWLink IPX/SPX Properties menu, shown in Figure 3.24.

7. If you are required by the LAN administrator to install an eight-digit hexadecimal Internal Network Number, enter the value in the Internal Network Number text box. The Internal Network Number must be set if you are using NT Server as an application server using the SAP protocol (for example, applications such as MSSQL Server).

8. Select the appropriate NIC adapter from the Adapter text box to bind the protocol.

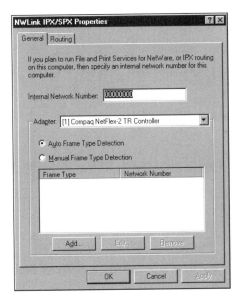

**Figure 3.24**    The IPX/SPX Properties General tab contains the controls for configuring your server's adapter to perform frame detection.

9. Select the type of frame detection you need.

Auto Frame Type Detection allows NT to determine the IPX frame type being used on the network and automatically configure it. This is the default setting. Unless you are experiencing frame error problems, leave this choice selected. Manual Frame Type Detection is used only in the event that you are having frame error problems or if you are configuring several different frame types to be attached to a single adapter card. If this is the case, click on Add and select the appropriate frame type from a list that NT provides.

10. Select the Routing tab from the NWLink IPX/SPX Properties menu.

The Routing tab, shown in Figure 3.25, has only one control. If you have installed the RIP Routing service, the Enable RIP Routing check box will be displayed. If you have not installed the service, the check box will be grayed out. RIP routing enables an NT server to route IPX packets.

11. If you have installed the RIP service, select the Enable RIP Routing check box to enable routing. Once you have finished, click on the

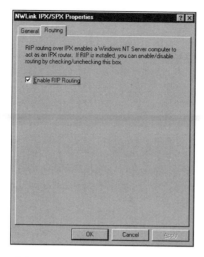

**Figure 3.25**   The Routing tab has only one choice: to enable or disable your NT server to act as an IPX router.

Apply button to immediately apply the choices you have selected in the properties menu. Apply only works for configuring an already installed and bound protocol. If you have just installed the protocol, you should click on OK. The choices will be entered and completed during the binding process. If you don't want to apply your changes, click on Cancel.

12.  At the Select Network Service menu, click on Close.

If you have just installed the protocol, NT will begin its binding process and display any errors discovered. Once the binding process is complete, NT will notify you that it should be rebooted to complete the installation.

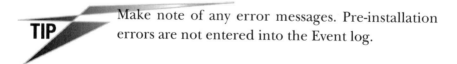

**TIP**   Make note of any error messages. Pre-installation errors are not entered into the Event log.

Following the reboot, notice if any services failed to start. If NT issues a diagnostic screen indicating that an error did occur, check the event log to determine if it was a networking problem associated with the IPX/SPX protocol.

If no errors have occurred, you have successfully completed the installation of the IPX/SPX Compatible Transport protocol.

## *Client Service for NetWare*

The Client Service for NetWare enables an NT workstation to connect to NetWare file and print servers. The Client Service also empowers users, who are logged in with NetWare, supervisory rights to run administrative utilities for purposes of configuring their network environment and updating scripts on NetWare servers. Let's set up the Client Service.

1. From the Control Panel, click on the Network icon, and select the Services tab.

2. Click on Add to display the Select Network Service menu.

3. Select the Client Service for NetWare, and click on OK.

4. NT Setup will request the full path to your distribution files. Enter the path, and click on Continue.

5. After NT copies the appropriate Client Service for NetWare and the NWLink NetBIOS protocol files to the System32 directory, you will be returned to the Services tab.

6. Select Client Service for NetWare, and click on Properties to display the NWLink IPX/SPX Properties menu, shown in Figure 3.26.

7. In the Adapter list box, choose the correct NIC adapter to bind to the Client services.

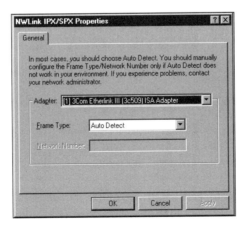

**Figure 3.26**    The General tab contains three controls to specify which adapter you are configuring.

8. Select the type of frame detection you need.

   Auto Frame Type Detection allows NT to determine the IPX frame type being used on the network and automatically configure it. This is the default setting. Unless you are experiencing frame error problems, leave this choice selected. Manual Frame Type Detection is used only if NT is unable to properly choose the type of frames being transmitted over the network. If you choose the Manual Frame Type Detection, you will be allowed to enter an eight-digit hexadecimal number to address your NIC. Leave the Network Number blank unless your LAN administrator specifies the number.

9. Click on OK to return to the Select Network Service menu.

10. Select the Bindings tab, and allow NT to perform a bindings analysis on the new entry. Once the bindings analysis is complete, select the Protocols tab to view the configured network protocols. If the service was properly configured, two additional protocols will be included in the protocol stack. These are the IPX/SPX Compatible Transport and NWLink NetBIOS.

11. Click on Close. NT will notify you that it should be rebooted to complete the installation. Following the reboot, notice if any services failed to start. If NT issues a diagnostic screen indicating that an error did occur, check the event log to determine if it was a networking problem associated with the Client Service for NetWare. If the Client Service is indicated, remove then reinstall the service.

If no errors have occurred, you have successfully completed the installation of the Client Service for NetWare.

## Gateway Service for NetWare

The Gateway Service for NetWare (GSNW) is a gateway between NetWare file and printer servers and Microsoft network workstation clients. Using the NT Gateway, a non-NetWare client can access NetWare server files, print to NetWare print spools, and even read the status of the print jobs. The Gateway account also enables a Microsoft Networks client to access Novell's NetWare Directory Services (NDS).

Before you can configure a GSNW, you must know:

- A Gateway User Name and Password

- A preferred NetWare server name

- A default tree and context, if required

- If a Login Script has been written and attached to the Gateway account

- If the Gateway will be providing printing service access; and, if so, what are the printing options

Once you've gathered this information together, you are ready to install the Gateway account. The Gateway account is a security barrier to control access between Microsoft Network clients and NetWare servers. The Gateway service can be completely managed and can quickly turn on and off the gateway access.

## INSTALLING THE GATEWAY SERVICE FOR NETWARE

Follow these steps to install GSNW:

1. From the Control Panel, click on the Network icon, and select the Services tab.

2. Click on Add to display the Select Network Service menu.

3. Select Gateway Service for NetWare, and click on OK.

4. NT Setup will request the full path to your distribution files. Enter the path and click on Continue.

5. After NT copies the appropriate GSNW, Client Service for NetWare, and the NWLink NetBIOS protocol files to the System32 directory, click on Close.

NT will perform a bindings analysis on the new entry and display any errors discovered. Following the bindings analysis, NT will notify you that it should be rebooted to complete the installation. Reboot your computer and take note of any services that failed to start. If NT issues a diagnostic screen indicating that an error did occur, check the event log to determine if it was a networking problem associated with the Gateway Service for NetWare. If the Gateway Service for NetWare is indicated, remove then reinstall the service.

## CONFIGURING GATEWAY SERVICE FOR NETWARE

Follow these steps to configure the newly installed Gateway Service for NetWare, which now appears with its own icon in the Control Panel:

1.  Select the GSNW icon and NT will display the Gateway Service for NetWare configuration menu, shown in Figure 3.27.

    The Gateway Service for NetWare screen contains a set of controls that allow you to configure a default NetWare file server and print queue. The default NetWare server will contain the logon identification for the users of the NT clients.

2.  Select the Preferred Server radio button.

3.  Enter the name of a preferred network server in the Select Preferred Server text box or use the pull-down control to select one of the servers listed.

4.  If your NetWare server security specifies a specific network path, then select the Default Tree and Context option, and enter the appropriate information in the Tree and Context text boxes.

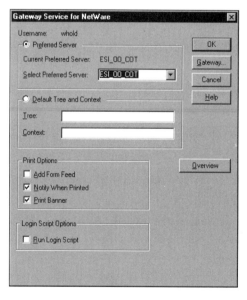

**Figure 3.27**  The Gateway Service for NetWare configuration menu contains the controls necessary to identify which NetWare server will be interfaced.

5.  If your Gateway account is providing print queue access, select the appropriate printing options for the network printing being accessed. There are three check boxes: Add Form Feed, Notify When Printed, and Print Banner. Older printers may require an added form feed to know when to eject a page. Notify When Printed instructs NT to notify the client when a print completion has occurred in the NetWare print queue. The Print Banner tells NT to supply a supplemental print banner signifying the start of a print job.

6.  If the NetWare server starts a Login Script when the Gateway account opens, select the Run Login Script check box.

7.  Click on the Gateway button. NT will display the menu show in Figure 3.28.

8.  Choose the Enable Gateway check box to enable the gateway.

9.  Enter the Gateway Account user's name in the Gateway Account text box.

10. Enter and confirm the account's password. This information is used by NT to secure access to the NetWare server.

11. Click on Add, and enter any shared directories from the NetWare server. Once the share names have been entered, select each, and enter the appropriate group permissions by choosing the Permissions control button.

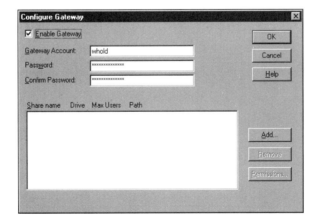

**Figure 3.28**   The Configure Gateway menu contains a quick disconnect to enable or disable the GSNW.

12. Click on OK, and return to the Gateway Service for NetWare menu. Click on OK again, and return to NT.

If you were able to access the NetWare, you have successfully completed the installation and started the Gateway Service for NetWare.

## Chapter Conclusion

In this chapter, we discussed installing and configuring NT networking services and protocols. As you are now aware, there are many and varied services that you can add to NT. Each has a special set of configuration requirements. Because of space limitations, the services I chose to review represent some of the major networking issues. Here's a brief recap.

We installed such services as DHCP server, Gateway Services for NetWare, and TCP/IP printing to show the planning and information that you must obtain prior to installation. Installing and configuring NetBIOS demonstrated that, on many servers, you have to consider legacy applications and adjust certain parameters accordingly. Configuring the Server service showed where NT tuning and performance is a factor. This example also showed how important it is to take computer memory into consideration when adjusting configuration settings.

We will discuss and use all these services and protocols in later chapters.

# Network Security

In the world of computers, security is defined as the level of safety that you place on programs or files to prevent unauthorized use, access, tampering, or destruction. You will find that NT offers a broad level of security designed to ensure safety from both prying eyes and innocent program or operator error. While security can often be unwieldy to use and difficult to manage, once you understand how Microsoft has designed NT's security and what level of security your system needs, you will be able to implement and manage that security.

In this chapter, we'll cover NT security from top to bottom. You'll be able to identify potential security threats and what measures you can take to make your network as secure as possible.

## Threats to Security

You should first realize why the need for security exists. An excellent example that immediately comes to mind is the good old (or new) computer virus. Every year, hundreds of very creative viruses are being constructed and distributed. Unfortunately, you will discover (or, maybe you already have) that the principle target of these viruses is your workstation. Although the method of infection can vary, floppy disks or downloaded programs are the usual carriers. Thanks to the never-ending viral progression, even the seemingly innocent DOC file can now contain a virus. Viruses, however, are not your only potential security problem. Table 4.1 shows the majority of categories of intrusive threats your computer faces. I say majority because even this list is not totally complete. New threats are constantly being hatched by creative minds. The table shows a wide variety of threats that can affect the operation of your standalone or networked computer. As you can see, security is not only a network issue, but more fundamentally, a workstation issue.

This chapter focuses primarily on the security of networked computer systems. In order to understand network security, you must first be familiar with the general subject of NT security. So, let's examine security, first at the workstation level and then at the network level.

**Table 4.1   Computer System Threat Categories**

| Category | Description |
| --- | --- |
| Virus | Random malicious destruction of file data, programs, and operating system objects. |
| Unauthorized Access | Unwanted access to programs, data, and objects, resulting in file copying, compromising secure data, and contents tampering. |
| Operator Error | Improper changes to programs, operating system objects, and data files, resulting in data/file corruption and loss of software functionality. |
| Unauthorized Changes | Unwanted changes to operating system objects, data, or application program operation. |
| Data Movement | Movement of data to and from the workstation or server is subject to unwanted capture or corruption. |
| Object Monopolization | Restriction of access to resources, resulting in the prevention of other normal programmatic execution. |
| Erratic Program Execution | Software application errors resulting in the destruction of disk files, memory images, data, other programs, and operating system components. |

When properly designed and maintained, you'll find that security can eliminate or significantly reduce the effects of the threat categories shown in Table 4.1. By "properly designed," I mean that you must understand the level of security required and design the security to meet both level and user requirements. Too tight security will result in the users working around what they consider to be bothersome restrictions or bottlenecks to get their work accomplished. When you study Table 4.1, remember that the level of safety required by a standalone computer increases significantly when that computer is connected to a network, due to the increased quantity of potential threats.

When it comes to security, most of us think of the U.S. Government and the Department of Defense (DOD). Microsoft is no different. Windows NT was designed to support DOD's C2-level security standard. The C2 standard contains a set of requirements that an operating system must meet to nullify the threats shown in Table 4.1. To meet C2 requirements, NT must provide the following safeguards:

- Restrictive mechanisms must be in place to actively permit or limit user access to objects and resources.

- The software must provide personnel using the operating system with the facilities to uniquely identify themselves before being granted access to system resources or objects.

- The operating system must support an audit trail for tracking access to and use of resources, objects, and actions. All actions being audited must identify the user performing the action, and access to audit trail data must be able to be limited to specific personnel.

- The contents of the system's memory must be cleared after being freed by a process, so that its contents cannot be compromised.

- The operating system must include restrictive mechanisms to protect itself from tampering or being compromised by external systems or personnel.

# NT Security Entities

Figure 4.1 shows a domain model which includes all the functional entities contained within a domain. Every domain must contain a *Primary Domain Controller* (PDC). The domain model shown forms a security bond between workstations, servers, the Primary Domain Controller, and one or more *Backup Domain Controllers* (BDC). Beyond the single domain exists other domains, workgroups, or WAN connections. To offer adequate protection, security must be designed to work and exist at every level. Like the proverbial chain, NT security is only as strong as its weakest link.

Before we go any further, I'd like to define a few key terms for you:

- *Workgroup*—contains two or more computers. Each workgroup computer independently maintains its own user and group security accounts. To share files or printing services, a user must have an account on any of the workgroup computers that will share files. The workgroup is useful if you do not have an NT server.

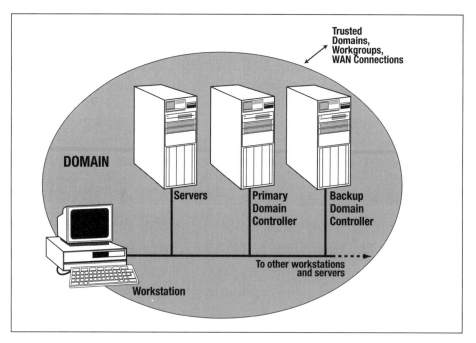

**Figure 4.1**  A typical domain contains workstations, servers, and domain controllers to oversee security management.

- *Domain*—consists of a group of servers and workstations that share common user accounts and policies. Domain security is centralized and reduces efforts to maintain and manage the user account and security policy databases. Each domain contains at least one primary domain controller and, optionally, one or more backup domain controllers. Domains can be interconnected and can form "trust relationships" with other domains for purposes of sharing data and managing user logons.

- *Primary Domain Controller*—an NT server that is responsible for maintaining the user account and security policy databases for the entire domain. Figure 4.2 illustrates the PDC's functions.

- *Backup Domain Controller*—an NT server that contains a replicated copy of the PDC's user account and security policy databases.

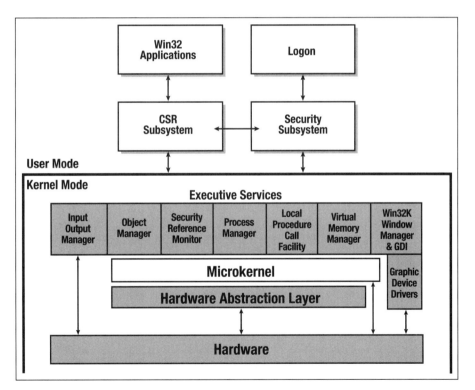

**Figure 4.2** The principle NT modules (in white) are responsible for managing security and interacting with the user during logon.

A BDC can be quickly switched to become a PDC in the event of a PDC failure.

- *Trusted domains*—independent domains that can share users, files, applications, and printing facilities between domain boundaries. Trusted domains have their own PDC and BDC.

- S*tand-alone NT Server*—an NT server that functions independently of any domain or workgroup. The stand-alone server manages its own user account and security policy databases.

- W*orkstation*—a client computer that can be an NT workstation, Windows, Windows for Workgroups, or even an MS-DOS-based client. A workstation can function either as a standalone or connected to a workgroup or domain. An NT workstation maintains a local copy of its user account and security policy databases.

## The Internal NT Security Model

Workstation security is the most familiar to the user. This is the security you come into contact with every day and is your window to the NT security environment. Your workstation faces every one of the threats described in Table 4.1.

Security at the server, however, is more critical. These facilities serve many users and usually contain data that is more highly valued than data at a single user's workstation. Let's take a look at how security works internally:

- *Windows NT logon process* (WINlogon)—accepts the user's ID and password. This process includes the initial interactive logon, which displays the initial logon dialog box to the user, and remote logon processes, which allow access by remote users to a Windows NT server process.

- *Local Security Authority* (LSA)—shown in Figure 4.3, this verifies the user's right to access NT. Once the user has entered the user ID and password, LSA creates an access token, and, using that token, describes the user to the local system, network servers, and the domain controller. LSA audits the user's logon and any messages

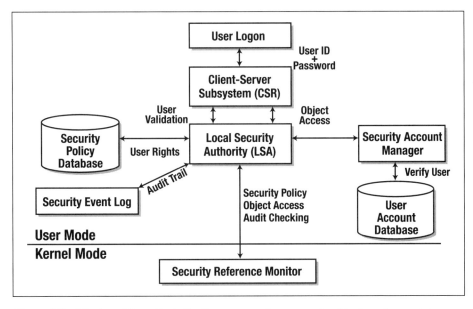

**Figure 4.3**    The Local Security Authority manages the access to objects and resources.

generated, for example, the too often seen "Unable To Logon" or "Denied Access."

- *Security Account Manager* (SAM)—maintains a user accounts database called the SAM database. SAM contains user and group accounts information which are used by the LSA for WINlogon validations.

- *Security Reference Monitor*—verifies that a user has the necessary permission to access objects or processes.

- *Security Policy Database*—contains the operating system security rights and privileges for users and groups.

- *Security Event Log*—captures audit trail events as assigned by the Audit Configuration in the User Manager setup.

- *Client Server Subsystem* (CSR)—contains the console and principle interface between NT and user. NT security uses the CSR to pass and receive transactions with the user. For more information on the CSR, see Chapter 1.

- *User Account Database*—contains all users who have authorized permission to use the system, including their associated group(s).

# Event Audit Policy

One of security's main requirements is the ability to maintain an audit trail which contains user identifications and actions. The NT event log is comprised of three sections: system events, application events, and security events. The system and application event logs are automatically configured and start accepting data as soon as NT is installed. However, the security event log requires a user with the administrator authority to access and clear the log.

Although NT 4 will track macro events (for example, logons or logoffs), it does not automatically begin auditing these events; they must be configured as "audit policies." To set these events, perform the following steps:

1.  Open the User Manager or User Manager for Domains.

2.  Select Policies|Audit to display the Audit Policy dialog box shown in Figure 4.4.

3.  Select the Audit These Events radio button.

4.  Select the actions you want audited by checking the Success or Failure check boxes for each option. The options and their associated events are:

    *   *Logon and Logoff*—A user performed a logon or logoff at the local workstation, domain, or network connection.

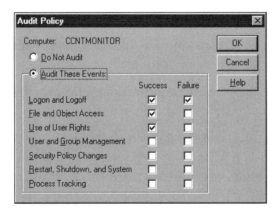

**Figure 4.4** The Audit Policy dialog box allows the administrator to specify which actions will be included in the security event log.

- *File and Object Access*—A user accessed a file, object, or directory that has been designated by the administrator or owner as audited.

- *Use of User Rights*—A user exercised one of the user rights belonging to the group to which he is a member. This does not include exercising logon or logoff rights.

- *User and Group Management*—A user account, group, or password was changed, added, or deleted.

- *Security Policy Changes*—A change was made to the user rights, audit, or trust relationships.

- *Restart, Shutdown, and System*—A system shutdown occurred, caused by either a user command or a system event.

- *Process Tracking*—Auditing a process from initial execution until shutdown.

5. Click on OK to begin auditing.

 Changing the audit policy in the primary domain controller affects the security logs of all backup domain controllers. Changing the audit policy of an NT workstation or NT server affects only that computer.

Audit entries are written in the security event log, accessible through the Event Viewer. If you anticipate large security logs, then set the log size to accommodate the expected number of entries. The log can also be set to recycle space after a set number of days or overwrite itself. You must set these options using the Event Viewer.

# User Groups

Creating security on an NT workstation or server computer requires an administrator. The administrator creates user accounts for each person who will access the computer. As the administrator creates each account, the account is associated with a local group. The rights and privileges of each user are dictated by which group he or she belongs to. These rights dictate what rights and privileges the user has over objects and resources within NT.

Creating security in a domain requires the services of a domain administrator (DA) to both design and manage domain security. The job of the DA is not a small task. However, if the initial security design is done properly, the task of managing the domain becomes much less complex.

The DA must first create user accounts. Users are grouped and entered into the user accounts database. The DA also chooses which group is included into which security policy. The results of these efforts are entered into the security policy database. Once these tasks are completed, the access to each server and workstation by each user must be created. We'll discuss user rights a little later on in this chapter.

To better understand these tasks, let's look at the options involved in the DA's job. First, you need to understand which groups are included as standard within NT. Although new groups can be created and added, NT has a set of default groups.

## Local Groups

A local group can contain user accounts and global groups from different domains. However, the local group's rights and privileges are valid only within its own, or local, domain. If a local group is created on an NT workstation or server, the group is only available on that computer. NT's default local groups are shown in Table 4.2.

**Table 4.2   NT's Default Local Groups**

| Group | Definition |
|---|---|
| Administrators | The Administrators group controls all of the NT resources. Members of this group are granted default rights to create user accounts and/or enter the system into a domain. Administrator rights do not include, as a default, access to all objects. |

*(continued)*

**Table 4.2 NT's Default Local Groups** *(continued)*

| Group | Definition |
| --- | --- |
| Backup Operators | Backup Operator group members have permission to backup and restore files on the computer, even though they may not have the rights to access these files to read, write, or change them. Backup Operator rights are limited only to backup and restore operations using NT's backup utility. |
| Creator Owner | The Creator Owner is a special group that contains the account of the individual user that created or has ownership of an object. |
| Everyone | The Everyone group contains all of the users who have accounts in any of the other groups on this computer. |
| Guests | The Guests group contains temporary users who are granted specific privileges to access local objects. |
| Interactive | The Interactive Group contains users who interactively logon to a local computer. |
| Power Users | The Power Users have all the rights enjoyed by users. Additionally, they have a subset of the Administrator's rights. This group is not available on either primary or backup domain controllers. |
| Network | The Network Group is a special account that includes all network users who are currently logged onto a shared resource on this computer. |
| Replicator | Members of the Replicator group have special rights associated with the creation and management of the replication of NT security databases to other computers (for example, the BDC). |
| Users | Members of the Users group have sufficient rights to logon and use the computer as a workstation. |
| Account Operators | Members of the Account Operators group can modify and change user and group accounts. However, the Account Operators group cannot change the Administrators and Backup Operators groups. This account is only available on NT servers configured as either primary or backup domain controllers. |

*(continued)*

**Table 4.2   NT's Default Local Groups** *(continued)*

| Group | Definition |
|---|---|
| Print Operators | Users assigned to the Print Operators group are allowed to manage local and shared domain printers. This account is only available on NT servers configured as either primary or backup domain controllers. |
| Server Operators | Server Operators are allowed to share printer and file server resources, lock the server, backup/restore files, and shut down the server. This account is only available on NT servers configured as either primary or backup domain controllers. |

## Global Groups

Global groups contain individual user accounts from their native domain. These groups can span domain boundaries and be granted rights in their local domain or any trusted domain. Global groups can only be configured on an NT server acting as a primary domain controller. Table 4.3 describes NT's default global groups.

## Global and Local User Accounts

Using the NT User Manager, the DA can create user accounts as either global or local. Global accounts can be used across any trusted domains, NT domain workstations, and NT servers. Local user accounts can only be used on an NT workstation or server within the creating domain.

**Table 4.3   Default Global Groups**

| Group | Definition |
|---|---|
| Domain Administrators | The Domain Administrators group is added to the administrators local group on every Windows NT workstation and server throughout the domain. They have Administrator privileges on all workstations and servers in the domain. |
| Domain Users | The Domain Users group bundles the user accounts in a domain and grants user privileges on all NT workstations within the domain. |

## User Rights

As a user, you must be accorded a set of rights to work in the NT environment, and you'll belong to one or more groups. Access to NT objects is determined by comparing the user's group memberships with permissions required by the object. Some user activities are task oriented and are not covered by object access (for example, backups). Users must then have certain predefined rights or privileges to perform these tasks based on the same groups memberships that allowed them object access.

Each group has a specified set of rights that entitles its members to perform a limited number of tasks. Table 4.4 contains a list of user rights, along with the groups that NT grants these rights to by default. While these user rights can be changed, you must be logged on as the administrator and should be very careful not to eliminate the Administrators group.

**Table 4.4   Normal and Advanced User Rights**

| User Rights | Defaults | Description |
| --- | --- | --- |
| Access this computer from the network | Administrators, Everyone, Power Users | The right to access this computer from another network server or workstation. When administering a domain, this right applies to the entire domain. If granted at the workstation level, this right only extends to the single workstation. |
| Act as part of the operating system | No Defaults | The right to run a process in secure mode with the same rights and privileges as operating system processes. |
| Add workstations to the domain | Domain Administrators | This right is effective at the domain level. It allows the domain administrator to add additional workstations and their associated accounts to the domain. |

*(continued)*

**Table 4.4   Normal and Advanced User Rights** *(continued)*

| User Rights | Defaults | Description |
| --- | --- | --- |
| Back up files and directories | Administrators, Backup Operators | The right to back up files and directories using the NT backup utility. |
| Bypass traverse checking | Everyone | The right to change directories and access files while being prevented access to higher-level directories. |
| Change the system time | Administrators, Power Users | The right to change the system's time from the Control Panel or from a command prompt. |
| Create a pagefile | Administrators | This right has no current effect. |
| Create permanent shared objects | No Defaults | The right to create permanent shares of operating system objects. |
| Force shutdown from a remote system | Administrators, Power Users | The right to order this computer to perform a shutdown command from a remote workstation or server using remote boot utilities. On NT 4 this is currently listed as not implemented and reserved for future use. |
| Increase quotas | No Defaults | This right has no current effect. |
| Increase scheduling priority | Administrators, Power Users | The right to increase thread execution priorities, making process execution faster. |
| Load and unload device drivers | Administrators | The right to install and remove device drivers from the operating system. |

*(continued)*

**Table 4.4    Normal and Advanced User Rights *(continued)***

| User Rights | Defaults | Description |
|---|---|---|
| Lock pages in memory | No Defaults | The right to specify that additional memory pages be allocated to the non-page memory pool, eliminating NT's ability to pageout the memory to disk. |
| Log on as a batch job | No Defaults | This right has no current effect. |
| Log on as a service | No Defaults | This right allows the user to make a process a service. |
| Manage auditing and security log | Administrators | This right allows the user to access, delete, and configure security event logs. A user with this right can access the Security tab on a properties menu to configure an audit trail for the associated objects. |
| Modify firmware environment variables | Administrators | This right allows a user to install a service pack that upgrades flashrom or firmware modules which affect computer system operation. |
| Profile single process | Administrators, Power Users | This right has no current effect. |
| Profile system performance | Administrators | This right allows a user to use NT Performance Monitor, locally or remotely, to monitor operating system and process performance. |

*(continued)*

**Table 4.4 Normal and Advanced User Rights** *(continued)*

| User Rights | Defaults | Description |
| --- | --- | --- |
| Replace a process level token | No Defaults | This right allows the user to modify a process' security access token to change access rights. |
| Restore files and directories | Administrators, Backup Operators | This right restore files and directories using the NT backup utility. |
| Take ownership of files or other objects | Administrators | This right allows the user to take over ownership rights for NT objects. If required, this allows administrators to oversee and manage all processes and files, even those that they have not been granted rights to. |

# Domains and Domain Trust Relationships

A domain centralizes user accounts and enables users anywhere in the domain to be quickly acknowledged. However, what happens when you need to obtain information from outside your domain? Domain trust relationships are a communications mechanism that allows users to interact, manage user account security, and share information across domain boundaries.

Determining your optimum domain configuration is not an easy task. As always, the initial design criteria is usually a combination of cost versus security. Remember that for each domain you create, you will incur a cost of at least one server, the PDC. If reliability is also a top priority, then you must also include a BDC, which, as I mentioned earlier, contains a replicated version of the PDC's account databases and can assume the PDC role in the event of a failure.

The domain logon requires that each user enters a name and password, and receives a validation from the PDC. Slow logon responses will not be acceptable if a user has to wait for minutes every time he logs on to the system. This means that communications is also a significant factor in the choice of domains. The number of users who can be administered by one domain is 10,000. This limit may also play a part in the domain design decision.

Domain design and tradeoffs are a fundamental part of NT design and installation. In this chapter, I am only providing a brief overview of the domain models as they relate to network security. We will discuss domains further in a later chapter.

## One-Way Trusts

Trust relationships are defined in only one direction—like a one-way street. This means that a trust relationship between two domains does not automatically extend to another trusted domain. For example, if Domain A trusts Domain B, and Domain B trusts Domain C, Domain A's trust relationship does not extend to Domain C. Domain A would have to explicitly establish a trust relationship with Domain C. Therefore, for a complete trust relationship to exist between two domains, two one-way trusts must be created.

## Secure Communications Channel

Before two NT computers can pass sensitive data, they must set up a *secure communication channel* (SCC). To create an SCC, each computer challenges the other computer. The challenges involve identifying the computer at the other end of the channel as an NT system with the ability to secure a data channel. After resolving these challenges, they establish an SCC.

Secure channels are only set up between NT workstations and servers within a domain, and only NT servers located in trusted domains. Workstation and server SCCs are used to logon users using the logon verification located in the PDC and BDC. Using the SCC, NT sends API calls and Netlogin data to the PDC. The most important SCC data includes the user ID and encrypted password to authenticate logons.

## Single Domain Model

The Single Domain model contains only one domain. This model is applicable to NT networks where the majority of information needed by domain users is contained within the domain. Security management is convenient and centralized. If your organization does not plan to share data between domains, the Single Domain model is an excellent choice. Many organizations today are considering multiple single domains with any outside information being shared through an intranet connection, which is carefully screened through a firewall.

## *Master Domain Model*

When domain information needs to be shared across several domains, the Master Domain model may be appropriate. A Master Domain model consists of two or more domains with established trust relationships to a master domain. Although the other domains may or may not trust each other, the master domain is trusted by all other domains and contains the security accounts for all domains. It centralizes logon and user account administration into one manageable PDC. In Figure 4.5, Marketing, Finance, and Sales all have established trust relationships with the master domain.

This model is effective because it combines the advantages of centralized management with organizational autonomy. From a security and user account standpoint, there is really only a single domain—the master

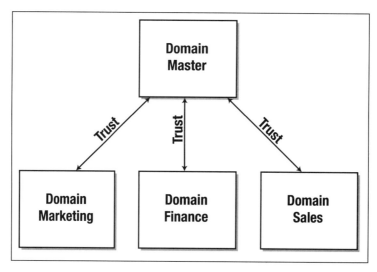

**Figure 4.5** The Master Domain model—each domain establishes a trust relationship with a single master domain.

domain, which stores and manages all the user accounts and global groups. Marketing, Finance, and Sales are resource domains that allow members of each domain to share resources within their respective domains.

Only the PDC and BDC of the master domain contain copies of the user accounts. The other domains contain local user accounts and groups. Master domains are applicable to organizations with no more than 10,000 users and are segregated into multiple domains. Data access can be effectively limited and managed within the confines of each trusting domain. So, this model does not negate the inherent advantages of domain security; it only places the burden of account management at a central point.

The Netlogon service is an NT service that is used by a workstation or server to communicate with a master domain PDC. Netlogon is responsible for the security database replication from the master domain PDC to all BDCs. On each NT domain server, the Netlogon service synchronizes the user account and security policy databases when a master domain PDC is installed or restored to service.

## Complete Trust Domain Model

Within the Complete Trust Domain model, every domain maintains a two-way trust of every other domain. Also, every domain maintains its own user accounts and global groups. These accounts can still be used in every other domain. This enables users to access resources without regard to domain security.

The number of trust relationships that have to be created for the Complete Trust domain model are characterized by the equation $N*(N-1)$. This means that if you have four domains, the number of relationships to be created is $4*(4-1)$ or 12. In the four-domain model shown in Figure 4.6, to add a fifth domain, you must establish eight new relationships. While the labor to construct these relationships is not extensive, this model requires personnel in each domain be assigned the continuing task of maintaining the domain user accounts.

But, there is an expense consideration. For each domain, you must have at least one PDC and a recommended BDC. For this model, you now have eight servers burdened with account responsibilities.

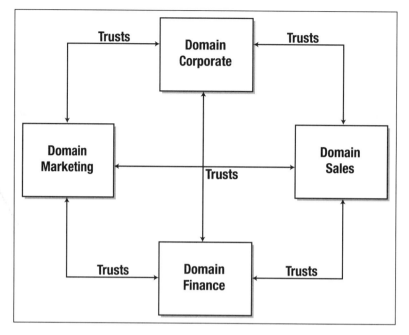

**Figure 4.6**    The Complete Trust Domain model has no centralized master domain.

## Multiple Master Domain Model

Figure 4.7 shows the multiple master domain in practice. Engineering, Manufacturing, and Stock trust one master domain, which maintains the user accounts and global groups for the three trusting domains. The other master domain maintains the account information for Marketing, Finance, and Sales.

The Multiple Master Domain model works well when the domain groups are widely separated geographically and the two master domains are connected by a T1 or other high-speed communications link.

## Establishing Trust Relationships between Two Domains

Now, imagine that you are responsible for creating a one-way trust relationship between the Engineering and Sales Domain. The Engineering Domain will trust the Sales Domain. Here are the steps you would follow to create this relationship:

1. In the User Manager For Domains on each domain's PDC, select Policies|Trust Relationships.

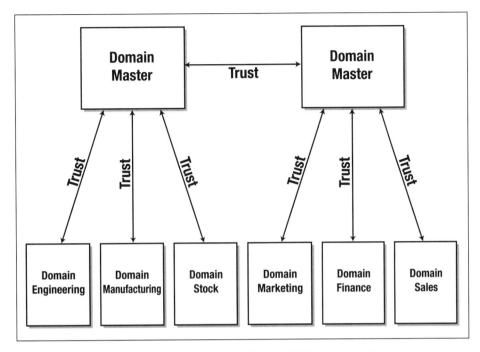

**Figure 4.7** The Multiple Master Domain model has multiple domains with trust relationships to two or more master domains.

2. Add the Sales Domain to the list of domains that the Engineering Domain trusts.

3. Add the Engineering Domain to the list of domains that trust the Sales Domain.

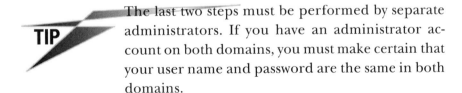

**TIP** The last two steps must be performed by separate administrators. If you have an administrator account on both domains, you must make certain that your user name and password are the same in both domains.

See, that wasn't too complex. But, now you're told that the relationship you've created between Engineering and Sales is too one-sided. (Sales can obtain specifications, but Engineering can't readily obtain forecasts.) You must now change the one-sided trust relationship to a two-way trust.

To complete the two-way trust relationship, you must complete the next three steps:

1.  In the User Manager For Domains on each domain's PDC, select Policies|Trust Relationships.

2.  Add the Sales Domain to the list of domains that trust the Engineering Domain.

3.  Add the Engineering Domain to the list of domains that the Sales Domain trusts.

This completes the creation of the two-way trust relationship between Engineering and Sales.

 **TIP** On the Engineering Domain's PDC, modify the LMHOSTS file found in \WINNT\SYSTEM32\ DRIVERS\ETC\ to include the IP address and the name of the Sales Domain's PDC. Modify the LMHOSTS file on the Sales Domain's PDC to include the Engineering Domain's PDC. This prevents network problems from delaying the completion of the trust relationships.

# The NT File System

If file security is a major requirement for you, then you must format one or more logical or physical drivers using the NT File System (NTFS). The File Allocation Table (FAT) file system does not support file-level security. At the file level, you may wish to allow a user to read a file, but not to change it. Another requirement may be that a user authorized to read only particular files and not have any access to other files. Using NTFS, you can specify file-level security to accomplish these tasks.

Permissions for access rights to files and directories can be specified to include one or more of the following:

•   Domain Users

•   Local Groups

- Global Groups

- Global Groups in Trusted Domains

- Users in Trusted Domains

- Everyone

- System

- Network

- Interactive

- Creator Owner

When the NTFS volume is first created, NT sets default permissions on all directories and files. For directories, the default is for Administrators and Owners Creator to have full control over the directory structures. The Everyone group has "change" control over directories. On servers, the Server Operator group is also granted directory change control rights. Tables 4.5 and 4.6 contain a detailed listing of directory and file rights under the NTFS.

## Setting Directory and File Security

To set permissions on a directory, that directory must first exist on an NTFS formatted drive. If that requirement is met, then perform the following steps:

1. Open the Windows Explorer.

2. Select the directory or file whose permissions you wish to set.

3. Select File|Properties to display the Properties tabbed menu.

**Table 4.5  User Rights Associated with NTFS Directories**

| Directory Rights | Explanation |
| --- | --- |
| No Access | A user cannot access the directory. |
| List | A user can list the files of this directory and branch down to a subdirectory. |

*(continued)*

**Table 4.5   User Rights Associated with NTFS Directories** *(continued)*

| Directory Rights | Explanation |
|---|---|
| Read | The user can read the files located in this directory. |
| Add | The user can add files to this directory, but cannot read or change the files once saved in the directory. |
| Add & Read | The user can add and read files in this directory, but cannot change any of the added files once saved in the directory. |
| Change | The user can read, add, and change files in this directory. |
| Full Control | The user can read, add, change, and delete files in this directory and take ownership of the directory and its files. |

4. Select the Securities tab to display the Securities menu shown in Figure 4.8. This menu offers you three options: Permissions, Auditing, and Ownership.

## SETTING FILE AND DIRECTORY PERMISSIONS

We'll begin by setting permissions:

1. From the Securities menu, click on the Permissions button.

**Table 4.6   User Rights Associated with NTFS Files**

| File Rights | Explanation |
|---|---|
| No Access | The user cannot access the file. |
| Read | The user can read the file, but cannot change the file's contents. If the file is an application, the user can execute it. |
| Change | The user can read, change, or delete the file. |
| Full Control | The user has full change rights to read, change, or delete the file. In addition, the user can set permissions for the file and take file ownership. |

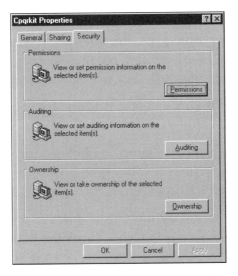

**Figure 4.8** The Security tab provides the controls to set permissions, auditing, and ownership for NTFS files and directories.

Depending on whether you're setting file or directory permissions, the appropriate permissions menu will appear. While Figure 4.9 shows the Directory Permissions menu, the File Permissions menu is basically the same.

The default permission, Everyone, provides all users with full control rights; however, you may set specific user groups to have lesser control

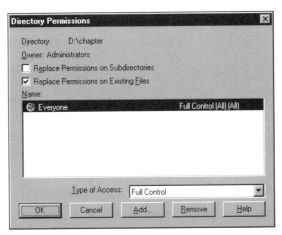

**Figure 4.9** The Directory Permissions menu lets you designate which user or group has permission to access the highlighted directory or file.

over the selected directory or file. Changes take effect immediately. Users who are accessing the directory or file at the time are not affected; however, unless authorized, these users will not be able to re-enter or regain access once they release the file or directory.

2. Adjust the permissions using the Add and Remove buttons. (Remember, Cancel allows you to exit the menu without saving changes.)

3. If you want to place the same level of security on the directories below the one chosen, check the Replace Permissions on Subdirectories check box.

4. If you want to secure all the files within the directory at the same group access and permission level, check the Replace Permissions on Existing Files check box. If you checked the Replace Permissions on Subdirectories check box, you will also place the selected access and permission levels on the files located in all subdirectories.

**TIP**  Be careful not to exclude yourself from access. A good rule is to always include the Administrator, as well as your group, to prevent locking out all access to a file or directory.

## SETTING FILE AND DIRECTORY AUDITING

Our next step involves setting file and directory auditing. The following steps are specific to directory auditing, but the procedure for file auditing is the same:

1. From the Securities menu, click on the Auditing button to display the Directory Auditing menu, shown in Figure 4.10.

2. Click on Add to add users and groups who will be audited. NT displays the Add Users and Groups menu, shown in Figure 4.11. Initially this menu will contain only group entries. Selecting the Show Users control will augment the list by adding users whose accounts are located in the system. Note the List Names From list box. This control contains the names of the local computer, local domain, and any of its trusted domains.

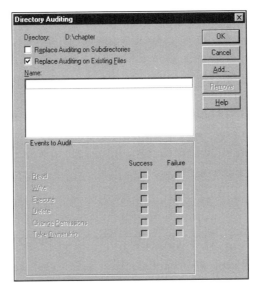

**Figure 4.10** The Directory Auditing menu allows you to specify what level of auditing will be placed on the chosen directory or file.

3. Select one or more users or groups and click on the Add button to add your choices to the Names list.

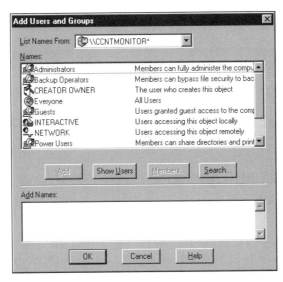

**Figure 4.11** The Add Users and Groups menu lets you select local, local domain, or trusted domain users and groups.

**TIP** If you need to find a specific user's account you can do so by selecting a group, then clicking on the Members button to display a list of the group's members. Then click on the Search button. The Find Account menu allows you to find the group to which a user belongs in the local workstation, local domain, or any trusted domain, and also allows you to specify the domains that it will search to find the appropriate account.

4.  Once all of the users to be audited have been added to the Names list box, click on OK to return to the Directory Auditing menu.

5.  Select the events that you wish to audit by checking the Success or Failure check boxes for each event.

6.  If you wish to audit subdirectories, select the Replace Auditing on Subdirectories check box.

7.  If you wish to audit the files contained in the directory, select the Replace Auditing on Existing Files check box.

8.  Click on OK.

Auditing takes place immediately. The record of audited events can be found in the security event log.

You are now able to specify which directories and files NT 4 will audit. Remember, you must specify that NT can audit these events. In the User Manager or User Manager for Domains, select Policy|Audit and select the Audit These Events and the File and Object Access (Success or Failure) options.

## SETTING DIRECTORY OWNERSHIP

Creating a file or directory makes you its default owner. You can grant permission to another user to take ownership of a file or directory by assigning that user "Full Control" permission. The only other way to take ownership of a file or directory is to be logged on as an Administrator.

**TIP** Use the Ownership button on the Securities menu to check the ownership of critical files regularly. If you see the ownership change without your permission, someone may have violated your file permissions.

1. From the Securities menu, click on the Ownership button to display the Owner menu, shown in Figure 4.12. If you have sufficient permission (Full Control or Administrator), then the Take Ownership button is available. If the button is grayed out, then check with the directory's Owner.

2. If you have selected more than one directory, NT will display an information screen asking if you want to take ownership of all files and subdirectories in the trees of the selected directories. Click on Yes if you do or No if you do not.

3. To change a file's ownership, first choose one or more files, then perform the take ownership tasks. The final ownership will automatically be limited to the selected files.

## Moving or Copying Files and Directories

When a file is copied to a new destination, all file permissions are replaced with the permissions currently in effect in the new or receiving directory. The user who copied the file is now the owner of the copied file. The previous ownership of the source file is unaffected by a copy command.

The same process takes place when a directory is copied. The new copy (destination) receives the default directory and file permissions of the destination directory.

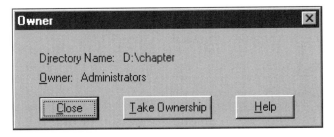

**Figure 4.12**    The Owner menu allows the Administrator to take ownership of the directory.

When you move files and directories within a logical partition, they retain the permissions and owners in effect at the time of the move. This means that if you move a file or directory within drive C, you only change the hierarchical location of the file, not the ownership or permissions. If you move a file or directory to drive D, then the file is reborn with the current permissions in effect on drive D. The ownership belongs to the user who executed the move command. Moving a file is simply copying that file, then deleting the source file.

# Shared Directories

Under Windows NT 4, if you are a member of the Administrator, Power User, or Server Operator group, you may create shared directories. A shared directory simply allows you to share a directory on your computer with other networked computers within your local domain or its trusted domains.

Sharing a directory involves allowing other networked users to have access to your local data and application program files. This adds a new dimension to security because not only do you have to protect your local files from access on your workstation, but now, remote access users can also copy, execute, or change your files.

To create a shared directory under NT 4, use the Windows Explorer to perform the following steps:

1.  Select the directory to be shared.

2.  Select File|Properties. The Properties tabbed menu appears. If you have chosen the root directory, the menu will have three tabs: General, Sharing, and Security. If you chose a non-root directory, only two tabs display: General and Sharing.

3.  Select the Sharing tab, shown in Figure 4.13.

4.  Select the Shared As radio button to expand the menu.

5.  Enter a name for the shared drive in the Share Name text box.

6.  Enter any comments to identify the reason or purpose behind sharing this drive in the Comment text box.

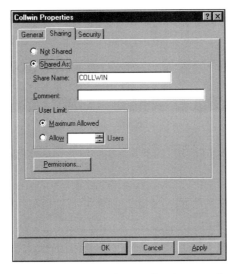

**Figure 4.13**   The Sharing tab allows you to share a directory, require permissions, and set a limit to the number of network users.

7.   If you wish to specify a limit for the number of users who can simultaneously share this directory, enter a number in the Allow Users text box. NT 4 Workstation places a 10-user limitation on this share. NT 4 Server has no mandated limit.

8.   If you do not wish to place a limitation on user access, leave the Maximum Allowed radio button selected.

9.   Click on the Permissions button to display the Access Through Share Permissions menu, shown in Figure 4.14.

     Note that the default value for shared directories is Everyone, enjoying the privilege of Full Control. Clicking on the Add button displays the Add Users and Groups menu. As we discussed earlier, this menu contains the groups and users who are local to your server or workstation, local domain, or trusted domain. You may specify different groups with different Types of Access. In order for the selected users or groups to share this directory, they must have, as a minimum, the List permission (see Table 4.5). If the user or group does not have sufficient permission, they will not be able to access this share.

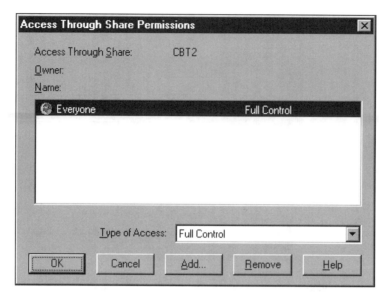

**Figure 4.14**   The Access Through Share Permissions menu lets you set the level of
permissions for anyone accessing this shared drive.

10. Specify the users and groups you wish to access your share and click
    on OK to return to the Sharing tab menu.

11. Click on OK to register your share with NT.

The shared directory is not available to be attached by network users. To
see the share, the network user may use the command line

```
net view \\your workstation name
```

or click on NT 4's Network Neighborhood icon.

## Granting User Rights on Shared Directories

Once you have a shared directory, it's important to review the rights and
privileges that you wish to extend to the network users on the directory.
Many administrators create two directories:

- A Read-Only Directory, where even a user with full privileges is limited
  to reading a file or executing an application.

- A Full Control Directory, where a share user with the appropriate permission level can exercise reading, writing, and changing files.

These two directories allow you to segregate your files to be shared by network users into the two categories. This makes it easier to avoid mixing up which files have which permissions. Remember, don't place anything in the Full Control directory that you can't afford to lose.

On occasion, it makes sense to leave a shared directory available, but to hide that share from prying network eyes. To hide a shared directory, access the Properties and Share tabs. Modify the share's name by placing a "$" after the name—change *myshare* to *myshare$*, for example. Although the share is hidden from any network browser, it still exists and can be accessed by you over the network.

## *Stop Sharing*

To stop sharing a directory, you must repeat the first six steps you used to share that directory, only this time, the last step is for you to choose the default value. If network users are currently attached to the shared drive, stopping the shared drive will affect their operation and could cause them to lose data. So, how do you know if the share is currently supporting users? You can view share users through the Server Manager. Here's how:

1.  Select Start|Programs.

2.  Select Administrative Tools and then select the Server Manager to display the current server.

3.  Double click the local server to display a Properties menu, then click the Shares button.

4.  In the Shared Resources on your workstation or server name menu, select the shared directory that you wish to disconnect.

5.  The menu will display all users connected to the share in the Connected Users list box. If you recognize the user, then you may choose to inform him that the share is being terminated. If you do not know who the users are who are sharing the drive, use the User Manager NT utility program to identify the individual users. The User Manager will display a list of their account names. By double clicking on a single account name, the user's proper name will be displayed.

6.  If you wish to disconnect all users, choose the Disconnect All button. If you wish to disconnect only certain users, highlight those users and click on the Disconnect button.

7.  Close the Server Manager and open the Windows Explorer.

8.  Select the shared directory you want to change.

9.  Select File|Properties to display the Properties tabbed menu.

10. Select the Sharing tab to display the Sharing tab menu.

11. Select the Not Shared radio button.

12. Click on OK to terminate the network sharing of this directory.

# The Logon Process

Windows NT requires a mandatory logon before a user can access local or network resources. NT prompts you to initialize the logon process by simultaneously pressing the Ctrl+Alt+Delete keys. This is the old warm boot sequence that is all too familiar to Windows 3.1 users. In a sense, the NT is initialized or warm booted. This sequence is used to prevent viruses or capture programs from reading the logon sequence data.

NT next displays a Welcome menu and requests the user to enter a user name and password. If the workstation is part of a domain, the user will also need to make a selection in the From list box.

NT processes the logon data by using the Security Accounts Manager (SAM) to query the Security Accounts Database (SAD). This is a comparison query to verify that the user does have a valid logon ID and that the ID and password match the data contained in the SAD.

If the ID and password do not match an existing SAD entry, then the SAM reports the failure to logon, and the user is notified to either try again or seek administrator help.

If there is a match with the SAD data, then access is authorized, and the Local Security Authority (LSA) is notified by SAM that there is a match. The LSA creates an access token, which contains an encrypted copy of the user's Security ID or SID, password, group IDs, and access rights.

To specify a computer other than the local workstation, the user must choose that computer using the From list box, and the LSA from the specified computer will process the logon. If the computer is part of a domain, the domain's PDC will validate the user ID and password from the centralized domain accounts database. Users can also logon at a computer located in a trusted domain. For security reasons, the From list box entry only lists the servers that can authenticate the user. The user cannot add a new location to specify another domain name.

After the logon process, a copy of the resulting access token is kept at both the local and remote domain servers to regulate the user access to resources. Whenever a resource request comes in from the user, the access token identifies the user to the server process. The access token is compared against both local and remote access control lists (ACLs) to verify a user's rights and access permissions. An ACL is normally associated with an object. When a user attempts to access a secured object, his access token is checked against the object's ACL. The access token's SID is compared with the ACL, and the LSA knows what rights the user has.

User privileges are encoded in the access token. To know if a user is allowed a privilege, the security subsystem only has to examine the access token. No comparison with a database is needed. This information is derived from the users group membership. On a given system, a group is allowed certain privileges. If the user is a member of the group, he may execute those privileges.

# Object Security

As I have stated previously, NT security is object oriented. What this really means is that every time you access a file or run an applications program, you force NT to access and manipulate objects. Remember that accessing and manipulating require security and permissions. Therefore, NT is constantly checking permissions and access rights as it executes your commands. Even though the mechanisms to accomplish this are hidden from view, they play an important role, so we have to be aware of the process. These next sections describe how NT conducts object access, manipulation, and security checking.

Security requires the ability to control access to operating system resources, such as files, memory, and devices. From NT's standpoint, all resources are objects. Each object contains both the data and control functions that you can use to manipulate that object. Any access to objects is overseen by the Windows NT security system, and because the object can only be accessed by the object's functions, NT maintains access security on these functions.

An example object is a printer. View any printer under NT 4, and you will see a number of operations that you can perform and parameters you can change. Each printer has a Properties function that allows you access to the printer's next level of configuration. In reality, you do not see the internal workings of the printer. You only see what Microsoft or the printer's manufacturer wants you to see. You are shown only those controls that they allow you to change. The Properties function places limits around each object, creating an inherent security mechanism.

Access to objects is controlled by requiring a program or user to request NT to perform an object operation. These operations are based on the functions that the object exposes to the world, and even these can be controlled. Certain functions can only be accessed by specific users with the proper rights and privileges. This enables NT to quickly verify if a program or user can access an object simply by checking for the necessary permissions.

NT treats all resources as objects, including the most common:

- *File Objects*—Includes data, operating system, and application program files.

- *Window Objects*—Includes NT's default windows, as well as windows created by application programs.

- *Peripheral Objects*—Includes printers, video displays, keyboards, compact disks, and disk drives.

- *Process Objects*—Includes all executable programs—each program contains one or more threads and occupies memory space.

- *Thread Objects*—Includes all threads associated with all programs, along with their individual operating system priorities.

- *Synchronization Objects*—Includes all types of synchronization objects that are used to synchronize data transfer between processes and threads.

Each object and object type includes functions that are unique.

Under NT, objects are accessed using an open-access-close scheme. Before you can access any object, you must first open a handle to that object. A handle is a token that is returned by Windows NT to your program and uniquely identifies your connection to the object.

Accessing the object allows you to perform whatever functions are exposed by the object type using the object's handle. There are no limitations on the number of times you can access the object. However, you must only use the functions associated with the object, or NT will see the attempt as an access violation. Remember, NT creates an access token when you logon. That token plays an important role in determining if it will allow you to access the object. Closing the handle lets NT know you're finished with the object.

Let's look at this process in a little more detail.

## *Opening an Object*

To access an existing object, a process must first open the object's handle. The process of opening the handle is something like this: A process calls a function to open the file. The function call contains the file name and the file access type required. These are the requested rights.

The Kernel mode Object Manager asks the security reference monitor to compare the process access token with the file's ACL to determine if the requested rights can be granted. If the security reference monitor agrees, then the requested rights become granted access rights. If the rights are not granted, the access fails and the Object Manager returns an error message—the all too often seen "Access Denied."

You're not in the clear yet, because the Object Manager must also determine if the system can support the memory and resources associated with using the object. If you do not have sufficient resource memory remaining, the Object Manager returns an error message and shuts down the access attempt.

If you have sufficient memory and resources, the Object Manager passes the object's handle to the process through the function call. The handle and the granted access rights are placed in the object table for that process.

## *Accessing an Object*

After the table entry, when the process again attempts to access that object, the Object Manager checks to see whether the action is among the granted access rights associated with the object's handle. It merely checks the table, and, if the requested action is among the granted access rights, the access is permitted. Otherwise, the Object Manager returns an error.

ACLs are *not* checked for every access. NT checks the ACL only when a process first opens the object. Every future access is checked against the granted access rights from the object table, which results in increased access speed.

After being granted, the process retains the rights until the object is closed. If an object's security descriptor is made more restrictive, the change does not affect the rights of a process to access the object using existing open handles because the granted access rights are already in the table. Any security changes cannot take effect until the object is once again reopened. You cannot effectively limit someone's access after the initial granted access rights are stored. Only new object access may be prevented.

### Closing an Object

When a process is done using an object, it closes the object using a close function call. The Object Manager removes the handle and associated granted access rights from the object table. This handle can no longer be used to access the object.

When a process ends, all of its objects are automatically closed and properly cleaned up. This is one way NT ensures that failed processes do not affect memory or open objects. Good programming practice dictates explicitly closing all handles to all open objects to speed cleanup.

## Memory Protection

Under NT, no process, other than the operating system itself, can access the code or data memory of another process. Any process trying to violate kernel memory security is prevented by the Central Processing Unit (CPU). Any attempts to violate kernel security result in the immediate termination of the offending process.

### Separate Memory for Each Process

In previous versions of Windows, memory was allocated as a "Global Heap." The Global Heap was shared by all of the 16-bit applications that were running. While this design made it very simple to pass data between applications, it did little to aid the applications' security. And, if a program failed, it could disrupt other executing processes. Also, by being able to access all process memory, the Global Heap remained susceptible to virus infections.

With the advent of NT and the WIN32 API, memory was allocated on a process-by-process basis. Each process ran as well, or as poorly, in its own memory space without affecting the operation of other processes. If an application crashed, it was cleaned up by NT and order was restored.

# Conclusion

Throughout this chapter, we've discussed NT network security and why it is important to you. We also discussed the mechanisms behind NT security for the local workstation and the network. To make an effective use of security, you must understand what features can be used to best meet your needs. Your system may be a simple workstation that uses security only to prevent virus infection. Or, your needs may be far more complex, with multiple domains and thousands of users. Microsoft has designed each aspect of security with an attention to lessons learned from mistakes made in past versions of Windows.

As a review, let's take a look at how NT meets the threats we outlined at the beginning of this chapter.

*The Virus Threat*—NT security provides two effective mechanisms for defeating viruses. The first is the object security that protects file objects from being deleted by processes that do not have sufficient privilege. The second is the memory management function that prevents one program from impinging on the memory and resources of another program. Undoubtedly, viruses will still be designed to infect the NT operating system. But, at least for now, we do have these two protections.

*Unauthorized Access*—NT file and directory permissions effectively keep out the unauthorized user. Whether local or network, a user must gain access to the workstation or server through the normal logon process. Then, assuming he makes it this far, he must have not only logon rights, but rights to each file and directory that he wishes to access. If the user doesn't possess the proper permissions, files and directories cannot even be listed.

*Operator Error*—An operator can make a mistake and delete a file that he has ownership to. However, under NTFS, he cannot delete files that he doesn't have permission to delete. Many administrators only logon to NT as Administrator to perform operating system functions. They employ a User or Power User account to perform daily operator tasks. If, for any reason, they make a mistake, the reduced permission set limits the incurred damage.

*Unauthorized Changes*—NT security prevents users in groups other than the Administrators group from making changes to the operating system (see Table 4.4). The use of group memberships also prevents access to NTFS files and directories that have been secured by either their owner or a member of the Administrators group.

*Data Movement*—We have seen how copying and moving files security is structured within a computer. Data movement over the network is either through data communications or, generally, through shared resources. NT places security restrictions on both methods. Shared drives must first be created and then managed by allowing only certain user groups to gain access. Using the secure communications channel, passwords and sensitive token information are encrypted, thereby preventing line monitors from picking up passwords and user IDs.

*Object Monopolization*—All objects are under the control of NT security. Ownership of a monopolized object can be taken over by an administrator at any time. Administrators have the right to change execution priority scheduling and to load and unload device drivers. These rights are vital to restricting use of objects and preventing an errant process from monopolizing the computer.

*Erratic Program Execution*—The changes to Windows' design from the Global Heap to the separate memory space for each process drastically reduces the affect that one process can have on another. Previously, an erratic program could hang the computer or destroy data in memory that belongs to another process. Under NT's design, each process is isolated and any problems with an individual process is handled by NT.

PART

2

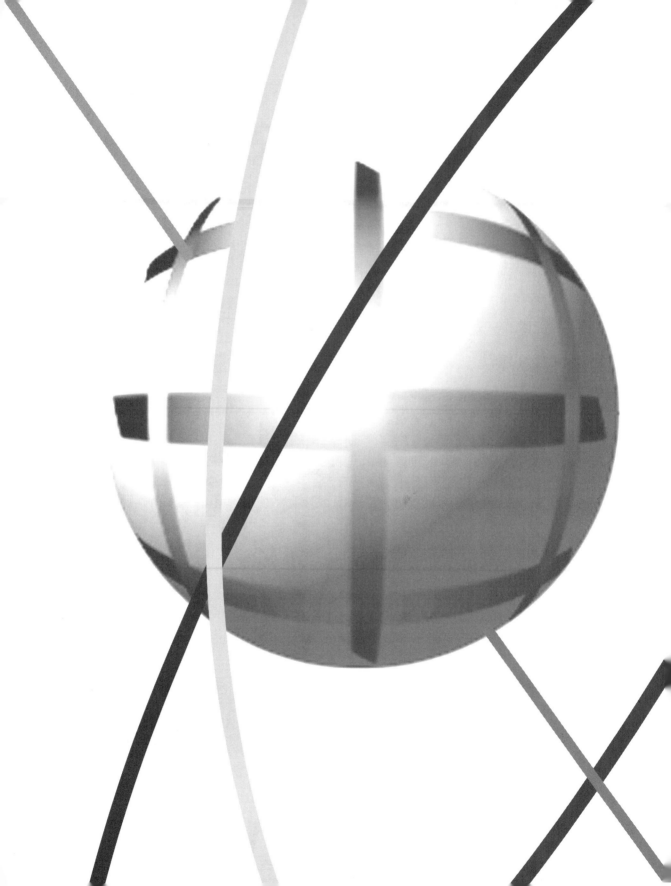

# Remote Networking

In this chapter, I will be describing a typical NT workstation and server from the standpoint of the remote user—you. As we all know, the need to keep in touch with, and stay up to date on, current projects is vital to good business (and your continued employment). Now, through the use of laptop computers and remote workstations, you can continue to productively communicate with NT networks, network servers, or your own desktop workstation, even though you may be out of the building—or even the state. Downtime, due to physical location or travel, has now become a relic of the past. Also, NT is designed to promote remote access while staying within its boundaries as a "Secure Operating System."

In this chapter, I think it is important that you progress with your understanding of both NT workstations and servers. Why, you're asking? Well, in addition to simple file access, servers often require the remote user (you) to govern NT by adding or removing users, overseeing performance, or managing a server-based application. Luckily, NT supplies remote management access tools that enable a LAN or NT Administrator to monitor and manage NT workstations and servers from remote locations, even using low-speed telephone lines.

# Remote User Requirements

Most mobile or remote computing users share a common set of requirements. One that comes immediately to mind is when you are working at home and you need to access the office computer. Or, you could be a thousand miles away on another LAN when you need to download database files. Either way, you need a software package to link your remote computer with home base.

In this section, I will review a set of requirements that can be addressed by a standard NT 4 application. In Table 5.1, you can see the major user requirements covering remote access. Keep in mind that not everyone needs to meet all of these requirements all of the time. Although, knowing what is standard with NT and where it is located can often be an advantage. The NT features described in the table can be found in one of the following three sources:

- The NT 4 Workstation CD-ROM

- The NT 4 Server CD-ROM

- The NT Resource Kit

# Remote Node Vs. Remote Control Applications

You might be confused between a remote node and a remote control application, and the differences are quite important. NT 4 does not include a standard remote control application as part of its release package (you can, however, purchase one from a third-party vendor), but it does come with a remote node application called Remote Access Service (RAS). As with any software, remote nodes and remote control each have their own benefits and drawbacks. I will be describing RAS in detail, but first, let's spend a few minutes discussing remote control.

## *Remote Control*

Essentially, remote control software is an application that turns your workstation or laptop into a dumb terminal. Remote control enables you to have full access to all your LAN-based workstation's resources, including its hard drive and NIC card.

**Table 5.1    Remote User Requirements (Matrix)**

| Remote Requirements | NT's Features |
| --- | --- |
| Logon to a desktop workstation | Using NT's Remote Access Server (RAS), you can logon to any NT system, workstation, or server on which you have an account and security authorization. RAS can be installed using the NT 4 Control Panel located on either the NT 4 Workstation CD or the NT 4 Server CD. |
| Obtain files from the desktop workstation | RAS enables you to copy files from any NT workstation or server from which you have the appropriate permissions. |
| Gain LAN network access from a remote site | RAS can connect a Windows for Workgroups, MS-DOS, Windows NT, LAN MANAGER, or Point-to-Point Protocol client to an NT workstation or server. |
| Execute application programs located on your desktop workstation | RAS connects the remote client to network resources. Any applications that support remote execution can be run on the remote client's computer. |
| Connect as a remote client using IP, IPX, or NetBEUI | RAS acts as a gateway to allow access to network resources using these protocols. |
| Remotely execute application programs located on your home LAN | RAS is a remote node which supports software applications that are remotely executable. This means that the application is executed on the remote client workstation. |
| Query database application servers located on your home LAN | There is no Standard NT application. To query databases remotely, you must have the remote application installed on the remote computer. |
| Administer a LAN-based server from a remote site | SRVMGR.EXE is stored in the \CLIENTS subdirectory on the NT 4 Server CD. |
| Monitor events on LAN-based servers from a remote site | The standard Windows NT 4 Event Viewer can be used, in conjunction with a RAS connection, to manage and monitor an NT server or workstation's System, Security, and Applications event logs. NT provides an additional Event Viewer in its Windows 95 Client section, located on the NT 4 Server CD. |

*continued)*

**Table 5.1  Remote User Requirements (Matrix)** *(continued)*

| Remote Requirements | NT's Features |
| --- | --- |
| Add or delete users from LAN-based servers or Primary Domain Controllers from a remote site | USRMGR.EXE is stored in the \CLIENTS subdirectory on the NT 4 Server CD. |
| Remotely administer a Dynamic Host Configuration Protocol (DHCP) LAN-based server | DHCPADMN.EXE is stored in the \CLIENTS subdirectory on the NT 4 Server CD. |
| Administer a LAN-based Windows Internet Naming Server (WINS) from a remote site | WINSADMN.EXE is stored in the \CLIENTS subdirectory on the NT 4 Server CD. By using WINSDMP.EXE, you can dump the records contained in a WINS database into an Excel compatible CSV file. |
| Reboot LAN-based workstations from a remote site | RPLMGR.EXE is stored in the \CLIENTS subdirectory on the NT 4 Server CD. |
| Remotely control a LAN-based desktop workstation or server | RAS does not enable a user to remotely control an NT workstation or server. RAS is a "Remote Node" application, not a "Remote Control" application. |
| Remotely change registry entries in a LAN-based server or workstation | The REGEDIT32.EXE utility is a Registry Editor that already exists on your NT workstation and can be used to remotely change registry settings on network servers and workstations. |

Let's assume that you and your trusty laptop are a thousand miles away from home, and you need to access your home workstation. You might also want to run a few applications, or even copy several files. Before you do anything, let's first take a look at the important elements of the remote control application:

- The remote control software consists of two applications: the client and the host. The client application runs on the remote client workstation, and the host application runs on the host workstation.

- The remote client workstation can be a laptop, desktop, or any other computer capable of running the client portion of the selected remote control software application.

- You will need two modems, either of which can be internal or external. They should be both fast and compatible with the remote control application.

- The host workstation can also be a laptop, desktop, or any other computer capable of running the host portion of the selected remote control software application.

- Last, but not least, you will need a standard analog (or modem-compatible) telephone line.

For the sake of our discussion, we're going to assume that you have already installed a remote control software client on your laptop and a remote control host on your desktop computer. Both your laptop and desktop computers are equipped with modems. As with virtually all other packages, the modems should support as fast baud rates as possible; remote control packages use the modems to transmit and receive graphic screens and text and are bandwidth intensive. Before you leave, you must set your desktop host to automatically answer incoming calls. Now, you're ready to communicate.

The client application acts as a console to the host application. For purposes of this discussion, I am considering a console to be limited to the human interface mechanisms, such as a monitor, keyboard, and mouse. Some remote control packages enable you to map client drives to be able to transfer files between the client's disks and the host. This allows you to upload local files to the host and, subsequently, the network.

When using remote control software, you must understand a few things:

- The only application running on the client is the remote control software.

- Applications that appear to be executing on the client are actually executing on the host.

- The client simply transmits your keystrokes and mouse movements through the modem to your desktop host.

- The client will display the same information and screens as the host.

- The applications running on the host performs as if the keystrokes are from its own local keyboard.

- Some remote control applications allow you to print remotely, at the host site.

- In most remote control applications, you have LAN access, assuming the host is attached to a LAN.

- Many remote control applications do not allow you to execute applications located on your laptop.

- Usually, the data passed between the client and the host are limited to keyboard, mouse, and screen updates. Searching databases and tasks moving large blocks of data are executed locally at the host, eliminating the extensive overhead of low-speed communication.

- While a single remote control host can support many remote clients, only one client can be connected at one time.

- In most remote control applications, the client must enter a user ID and password. Most remote control programs now support NT's network security and allow management of those resources deemed accessible based on the user ID.

- Many remote control applications provide you with the ability to call into a host, start an operation, and then disconnect. The host continues working on the operation you started once you disconnect. Depending on the choice of the application, you can call back to check on its progress.

As you may have noticed in the preceding list, I used terms like "most" and "many." Because NT does not come with standard remote control applications software, you will have to check on the features of the software that you have purchased. Remote control applications for NT are available from third-party independent software vendors.

## Remote Access Service

As I mentioned earlier, NT includes a remote node application in the standard product. This application is known as the Remote Access Service or, simply, RAS. In this section, I will describe RAS and note any differences between it and other remote node software applications.

Some client applications require direct network attachment. This is true for applications running on the remote client that must have complete data access, for example, word processing, spreadsheets, and databases. Remember, remote communication is not strictly limited to a laptop sitting in your hotel room. You may be located in another office across the country or at home, using your home PC. For these applications, you may need a remote node application, such as RAS. A remote node simply routes traffic between a low-speed link, such as a modem, and a higher-speed LAN.

Let's look at what makes up the remote node application:

- The elements consist of a client, host, router, two modems, and RAS. What's this about a router? A remote node access requires a router in order to route traffic from the incoming modem to the LAN. You can configure NT to route both multiple modems and connections between multiple LANs. When used on either an NT 4 server or workstation, RAS becomes the router.

- The host workstation can be a laptop, desktop, or any other computer capable of running the host portion of the selected remote control software application. Because RAS is part of NT, the host must be capable of supporting an NT 4 workstation or server.

- The client workstation can be a laptop, desktop, or any other computer capable of running the client portion of the selected remote control software application. The client must be capable of supporting MS-DOS, Windows for Workgroups, NT Workstation, or LAN Manager RAS clients.

- Both modems can be either internal or external and should be at least 28.8 Kbps or faster. Your host modem must be compatible with the Microsoft-published Hardware Compatibility List (HCL), available from Microsoft's FTP site at **ftp://ftp.microsoft.com**.

- Last, but not least, you will need a standard analog (or modem-compatible) telephone line.

RAS access attaches your client PC through a server to a local LAN as a network node. The only difference between a remote and local node is the speed of the connection. Virtually any task you can do or access from a local networked workstation can be done using RAS.

RAS connections are inexpensive. By adding the proper hardware (see the NT HCL), NT 4 RAS can support up to 256 simultaneous remote clients. However, the higher the number of simultaneous connections, the slower the file server response. This is why, when supporting more than a few clients, you will be required to dedicate a server to supporting RAS.

RAS users can benefit from NT's implementation of TCP/IP networking, including access to the WINS and DHCP. RAS users on client computers can dial in to remotely access their networks for services, such as file and printer sharing, electronic mail, scheduling, and SQL Server database access.

RAS connections can use IP routing to a RAS server and provide RAS clients access to TCP/IP networks. RAS also works with IPX routing for clients that use NetWare networks. Windows NT uses the industry standard Point-to-Point Protocol (PPP). This standard ensures that Windows NT is operative with third-party remote access servers and client software. RAS clients use DNS and WINS for name resolution services, and can create TCP sessions with systems on the local network.

NT 4 RAS configurations include the following components and specifications:

- Remote access client software for support of Windows NT, Windows for Workgroups, MS-DOS, and LAN Manager RAS clients. Note that MS-DOS users must have Microsoft's network client software installed to be compatible with RAS.

- Windows NT 4 RAS servers must support PPP. PPP is an encapsulating protocol that allows any client to use TCP/IP, IPX, or NetBEUI. IP protocol support permits accessing a TCP/IP network or the Internet. The IPX protocol supports remote client access to NetWare printers and servers. For more information on PPP, see the next section.

- Clients can dial in using standard telephone lines and a modem or network modem pool. Being a remote LAN node is fine, but to access any data on the LAN, you need to process a great deal of data. That data must all come across the modem's low-speed connection. Faster links are possible using ISDN. ISDN typically runs at 128 Kbps. This will provide transfer of approximately 13 Kbps as opposed to the approximately 3 Kbps you can expect over a modem. You can also connect RAS clients to RAS servers using X.25 or an RS-232C null modem.

- Windows NT logon and domain security also work with RAS. These require the user to logon by supplying a valid user ID and password before gaining access to the LAN. RAS also supports data encryption and callback mechanisms to provide secure network access. The RAS server can be configured to provide access to an entire network or to restrict access to only the RAS server.

- The NT 4 workstation and server both permit up to 256 RAS clients to dial in. This is a big change from previous versions of Windows NT in which the workstation only permitted dial-in access to one remote client. NT 4 has lifted that limitation in order to allow the NT workstation to be more adaptable to the Internet.

## POINT-TO-POINT PROTOCOL

The Point-to-Point Protocol (PPP) is a method for transmitting and receiving serial datagrams over point-to-point links. RAS uses PPP as its protocol between the remote client and the server. NT 4 only uses the PPP for the following reasons:

- *User Acceptance*—PPP is a standard, widely known protocol used by Internet Service Providers.

- *Multiprotocol*—PPP can transport IP, IPX, and NetBEUI data traffic. PPP can support all of these protocols simultaneously on one connection.

- *Security*—PPP provides two methods—Password Authentication Protocol (PAP) and Challenge Handshake Authentication Protocol (CHAP)—which allow logons to be automated. Each method provides an automated mechanism for sending your logon information to the remote system. Once the logon information has been received, the negotiation between the client and the server can be conducted. If the logon data is correct, RAS authorizes the client. If the data is not correct, the client's admission is denied. These steps take place inside PPP. Your

only requirement is to know your user ID, password, and the server's telephone number. RAS, using PPP, can then dial-up and automate the connection with no further user interaction.

- *Proven Technology*—PPP uses an old industry standard, High Level Data Link Control (HDLC), as a basis for encapsulating and communicating its datagrams.

- *Robust Communication*—PPP uses an extensible Link Control Protocol (LCP) to establish, configure, and test the data-link connection. The key word is extensible, which means that the protocol can be extended to incorporate future changes and to expand as circumstances dictate.

- *Matches NT's Networking Architecture*—PPP uses a group of Network Control Protocols (NCP) for communicating with different network-layer protocols. Using NCP allows PPP to support the simultaneous use of multiple network-layer protocols.

After initial connection to a remote PPP server, PPP uses the following protocols to negotiate a PPP connection:

- *Negotiate Link Control Protocols (LCP)*—PPP uses the LCP to create and configure link and framing parameters.

- *Negotiate Authentication Protocols*—PPP uses authentication protocols— either PAP or CHAP—to define the level of security validation the remote access server can perform, and what is required by the server. CHAP uses a challenge response with an encrypted response. PAP uses clear text passwords and is typically used if either the workstation or server cannot CHAP. CHAP is extensible and allows different types of encryption algorithms to be used, including the DES encryption and MD5 encryption.

- *Negotiate Network Control Protocols (NCP)*—PPP uses NCPs to define the different network protocol parameters for IP, IPX, and NetBEUI, including the Van Jacobson (VJ) header compression. PPP uses Internet Protocol Control Protocol (IPCP) for negotiating parameters for IP, Internet Packet eXchange Control Protocol (IPXCP) for negotiating parameters for IPX, and NetBIOS Frames Control Protocol (NBFCP) for negotiating parameters for NetBEUI.

## ISDN CLIENTS

For stationary RAS remote sites, much higher communications speeds can be obtained by using Integrated Services Digital Network (ISDN). Standard phone lines typically communicate at 28.8 Kbps. ISDN typically communicates at speeds of (half speed) 64 or (full speed) 128 Kbps. This provides a byte traffic increase of between two and four times.

If available in your area, an ISDN line, both client and server ends, must be installed by the phone company. In both the client and server, an ISDN modem must be used instead of the standard analog modem. While costs for ISDN equipment and lines are higher than for analog serial communication, the increased communication speed can improve performance, reduce other overhead costs, and reduce costs incurred by toll charges.

How does it work? An ISDN connection uses two B channels to transmit data at 64 Kbps and one D signaling channel transmitting data at 16 Kbps. The B channels can be configured to operate as one or more ports. RAS drivers allow you to combine the B channels to act as a single port. Combining the channels results in an aggregate line speed of 2 x 64 Kbps or 128 Kbps. The D channel remains at 16 Kbps and is not available for aggregation. Multiport or two 64 Kbps channels can service two customers at better than twice the speed that you can obtain from the current industry de facto standard of 28.8 Kbps.

To set up and install ISDN cards, you must install one on the server and one on each client. Follow the instructions associated with the ISDN board, and then configure each B channel to act as a port. Or, configure all B channels to act as a single port.

## X.25 CLIENTS

An X.25 network transmits and receives data using a packet-switching protocol, the X.25 protocol. The X.25 protocol relies on a global network of packet-forwarding nodes that cooperatively coexist to deliver an X.25 packet between its source and destination addresses. An X.25 network uses the packet-switching protocol and global network to bypass frequently noisy telephone lines. NT 4 RAS supports the X.25 standard using Packet Assemblers and Disassemblers (PADs), and X.25 smart cards. RAS clients can also use a modem and special dial-up X.25 carriers in place of a PAD or smart card.

## INTEGRATED DOMAIN SECURITY WITH RAS

After passing RAS authentication and establishing the RAS connection, users must logon to Windows NT. RAS uses the same account database as a Windows NT Server. This provides for easier administration because all users use the same accounts as direct connections. All authentication and logon information is encrypted when transmitted over the phone lines.

To validate a RAS session, there are six logon security steps:

1.  Once a phone connection is made, the RAS server transmits a challenge to the remote RAS client.

2.  The RAS client responds by sending an encrypted response back to the RAS server.

3.  The RAS server validates the response using its local or domain security database.

4.  If the validation is successful, the RAS client is connected. If the validation fails, the RAS connection is dropped, and the connection is denied.

5.  A security token is created using the RAS client logon entries for use in determining what resources or services the RAS client is entitled to.

6.  If a call back option is specified, the RAS server will disconnect and dial the RAS client using a predefined phone number. The call back option is designed to prevent an unwanted user gaining access by virtue of knowing a valid user ID and password. That user must also have access to, and be able to answer, the call back telephone number.

**TIP** Use the Call Back feature when traveling to charge the call to your work number. You can change the Call Back telephone number using the RAS Administrator from your remote site.

## *Installing Windows NT RAS*

Now that we've covered an overview of the technical aspects of RAS, let's install the service. Perform the following procedures to initially install RAS:

1.  Open the Windows NT Control Panel, and click on the Network option.

2.  Click on the Add Software option to display the Add Network Software screen.

3.  Select the Remote Access Service from the drop-down list. Then, click on Continue.

4.  When prompted by Setup, enter the location of the NT 4 CD-ROM. Because the default location is not always correct, check to see if the text box contains the CD-ROM's correct drive letter. Click on Continue once you've entered the correct location. The Remote Access Setup screen will then display a message telling you that RAS is now installed, but not started.

That was easy, wasn't it? But you're not through, yet. Like everything in NT, there are a few more steps that you need to complete, including a detailed setup, before RAS will work.

## CONFIGURING WINDOWS NT RAS FOR PPP AND IP CONNECTIVITY

Once you have installed RAS, you must perform the following procedures to configure the server.

1.  Install all modems you wish to use with RAS. Then, open the Control Panel, and click on the Modems option.

2.  Click on Add New Modem. This will bring up the Install New Modem Wizard, shown in Figure 5.1.

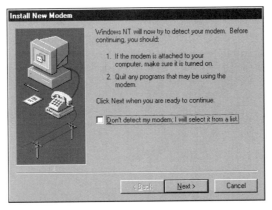

**Figure 5.1**   The Install New Modem Wizard will automatically detect your modem.

3.  NT will automatically detect and select your modem, assuming that it is connected. If your modem is not connected, or it is not listed in NT 4's Hardware Compatibility List (HCL), then check the "Don't detect my modem, I will select it from a list" check box. NT 4 will then display a list of modems contained in the MODEMS.INF file. Otherwise, check the control, and let NT detect the modem. This may take several minutes.

4.  Click on File Properties to display the menu shown in Figure 5.2. Use this screen to add, remove, and change the properties for all the modems you intend to attach to NT.

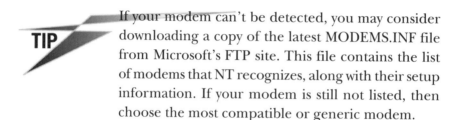

> **TIP** If your modem can't be detected, you may consider downloading a copy of the latest MODEMS.INF file from Microsoft's FTP site. This file contains the list of modems that NT recognizes, along with their setup information. If your modem is still not listed, then choose the most compatible or generic modem.

5.  Once you have installed all of the modems that RAS will use, open the Control Panel, and click on the Network option to configure RAS.

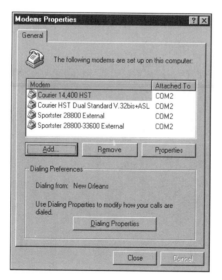

**Figure 5.2**   The Modems Properties menu enables you to manage modems and their associated properties.

6. Choose Remote Access Service from the list of installed Network Services, then select Properties. A menu similar to the one shown in Figure 5.3 will appear. Click on Add to add a port to the list.

7. If you have added a port, highlight the port entry on the list. Then, click on Configure.

8. You can now specify and configure the modems that RAS will use. Click on Add, and NT will display the menu shown in Figure 5.4.

9. Specify which of the installed modems RAS will be using by highlighting a modem and then clicking on OK. If a modem is not present, you may install a new modem by clicking on the Install Modem button. The subsequent menus are the same menus used to initially install your modems.

10. You must configure the Port Usage section to dial out and receive calls. Highlight a modem, and click on the Configure button to display the menu shown in Figure 5.5. Choose the type of port usage required. Note that these controls are radio buttons, and you may only choose one. "Dial out only" means that the selected modem can only be used to dial out or as a RAS client. "Receive calls only" means that the selected modem will only be used as a RAS host. The "Dial out and Receive calls" is the typical response. This option allows RAS to use the highlighted modem as both a client and a server.

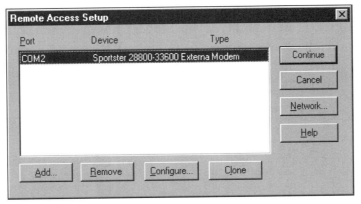

**Figure 5.3**   The Remote Access Setup menu provides the controls to configure the RAS on your computer.

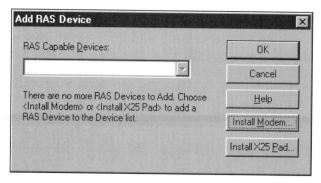

**Figure 5.4**   The Add RAS Device menu allows you to choose which of the modems RAS will use.

If you are planning to install multiport RAS service to more than four ports, you must first have the appropriate multiport serial communications card installed in your server. To identify an NT compatible multiport serial communications card, or any NT compatible communications device, first refer to the Windows NT 4 Hardware Compatibility List. Because this document changes constantly, it is in your best interest to obtain a fresh copy from time to time. It can be found at **ftp://ftp.microsoft.com**.

11.  Click on Network to display the Network Configuration screen. The Network Configuration screen shows three dial out protocol choices: NetBEUI, TCP/IP, and IPX. The Server Choices section of this screen contains check box options to configure RAS to accept incoming cli-

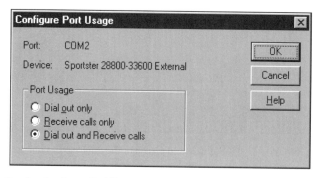

**Figure 5.5**   Use the Configure Port Usage menu to define how RAS will use a particular port.

ents running one or more of these same protocols. This means that an incoming NetBEUI client with the proper permissions can communicate across the server to a LAN using NetBEUI, TCP/IP, or IPX.

12. Select which protocols RAS can use to both dial out to LAN resources and to connect to remote clients. You must also configure parameters for each of the protocols being supported.

13. Select the type of authentication RAS will use for connecting remote clients. As shown in Figure 5.6, you have several choices for authentication, including the "Allow authentication including clear text" option, which permits connections using any authentication requested by the client, including CHAP and PAP. This option can be useful if your RAS clients are using various client software packages. Choose the "Require encrypted authentication" option to permit connection to any client authentication except PAP. All client connections would require encrypted passwords. Choose the "Require Microsoft encrypted authentication" option to permit connection using only the CHAP authentication. If you choose the "Require data encryption" check box, you ensure that all data is encrypted. NT 4 RAS incorporates the RSA Data Security Incorporated RC4 data encryption algorithm.

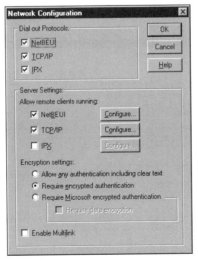

**Figure 5.6** The Network Configuration menu provides the controls to configure RAS for incoming clients and protocol LAN interfaces.

14. Select the Dial-Up Networking Multilink. This option combines multiple physical links into a logical "bundle." The PPP Multilink Protocol can provide up to 128 Kbps on one ISDN line. As we discussed, under ISDN, this is accomplished by combining ISDN's two B channels, where each B channel runs at 64 Kbps. The Multilink effectively doubles your bandwidth. In order to work, Multilink must be enabled on both the clients and server. This check box is only valid on NT 4 servers.

15. Select the configuration control next to the NetBEUI protocol to display the menu shown in Figure 5.7. You may allow remote clients connecting to the RAS using NetBEUI to either be routed or not routed through the server to the network. Clicking on the "Entire network" control will enable NetBEUI to be routed through the server. Selecting "This computer only" will force NT to limit the client's access to this server only. Click on OK to complete the configuration and return to the Network Configuration screen.

16. Click on TCP/IP to display the menu shown in Figure 5.8. This menu contains the controls needed to determine client network access, DHCP addresses, static address pool, or to allow a client to specify an IP address.

17. Click on either the "entire network" or "this computer only" option to allow an incoming client access to either the entire network or only the RAS server.

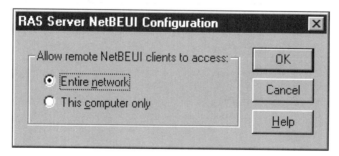

**Figure 5.7**   Use the RAS Server NetBEUI Configuration menu to determine how NT will support the incoming NetBEUI client.

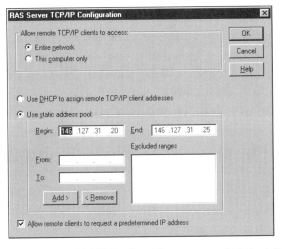

**Figure 5.8**   Use the RAS Server TCP/IP Configuration menu controls to define how NT will connect to TCP/IP clients.

18. You have three choices for providing a client with an IP address. If you have chosen to allow the client access to the entire network, this step becomes very important. The first choice is to use DHCP to assign the IP address. Use this option only if you have configured DHCP addressing in the network setup and are currently using a DHCP server. The second choice is the "Use static address pool" option. To specify a static address pool, you have two choices. The first allows you to specify a contiguous block of IP addresses from which NT will pick an appropriate address for your client. To do this, you must choose a Begin address and an End address specifying the block. There must be at least two addresses in this block. This also means that you must own those addresses when you configure this server. You may also choose a block of non-contiguous addresses by adding addresses into the Begin and End fields. Then, enter exception address ranges into the From and To fields, and click on Add. The "Excluded ranges" list will contain these entries. NT will then use this information to pick incoming addresses within the Begin and End range that are not excluded. The third choice for providing a client with an IP address is to select the "Allow remote clients to request a predetermined IP address" option.

19. Click on OK to exit the TCP/IP Configuration menu once you have specified all your selections.

20. Choose IPX from the Network Configuration menu to specify how RAS will configure incoming IPX clients. The menu shown in Figure 5.9 will be displayed. This menu contains controls that allow you to specify whether a client will be allowed access to the network. You may also specify if IPX network numbers will be automatically allocated by NT to incoming clients. Choosing the "Allocate Network numbers" radio button illuminates the From and To text boxes. Use these controls to specify the beginning and ending network numbers for a contiguous list of numbers to be allocated to incoming clients. For a single installation, you can choose the "Assign same network number to all IPX clients" option. Naturally, you can use this option only when one client at a time can gain access to the server. You can also choose the "Allow remote clients to request IXP node number" option for clients already connected to a remote LAN. Click on OK to return to the Network Configuration menu.

21. Click on OK to exit Network Configuration.

## USING THE REMOTE ACCESS ADMIN UTILITY

After you install RAS, you must grant users permission to use a RAS account. This can be done through the Remote Access Administrator utility. The RAS Admin utility, which is part of the standard server and workstation software, is one of NT 4's controls that can be used either locally or

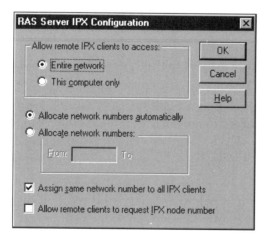

**Figure 5.9**    Use the RAS Server IPX Configuration menu controls to specify how NT will configure incoming IPX clients.

remotely by an administrator. The RAS Admin user can remotely access a server or workstation through either the resources of a LAN or as a remote dial-in client.

1. Select the NT 4 Start bar, and then choose Programs|Administrative Tools.

2. Select the Remote Access Admin icon to start the utilities. Notice that following the "Remote Access Admin" title at the top of Figure 5.10, the name of the current server is displayed. In this case, the server's name is CCNTMONITOR. Any changes made by you while in this utility will affect the operation of this server. If you choose the File menu, you will see a menu item named "Select Domain or server." This means that the Remote Access Admin utility can be used either as a local utility or to remotely configure another RAS server. Always make sure that you are configuring the correct server.

3. Select Users and Permissions to display the menu shown in Figure 5.11. This menu lists all the authorized NT users and provides the controls to enable or disable each user to access an NT workstation or server through a low-speed modem connection.

4. The Users list box contains all of the authorized users. As you highlight each user, the "Grant dialin permission to user" check box will be blank or will display a check, depending on whether that specific account can or cannot dial-in remotely. You can change the account

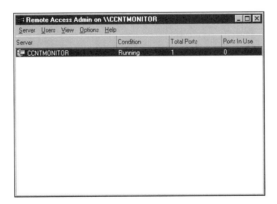

**Figure 5.10**   The Remote Access Admin main menu contains the controls to start and stop RAS, and assign user permissions.

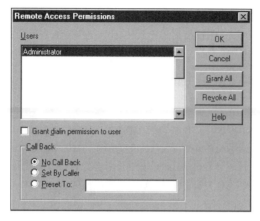

**Figure 5.11**    The Remote Access Permissions menu shows a list of users and provides the tools needed for users to access NT remotely.

privilege by checking the box for all appropriate users. If you want to grant or revoke privileges for all users, you can use the Grant All or Revoke All buttons.

5.  The Call Back controls enable you to specify that a user may or may not be called back, once he has properly logged into NT. There are three options to consider. The No Call Back control specifies that NT will not call the user back. The Set By Caller option allows a user to specify a phone number for NT to dial to call back. This option is important for users who travel and can't maintain a set calling number. The third option, Preset To, specifies that NT will call back the user at a set telephone number. In the event of no answer, NT will not continue the logon process.

6.  Another option you need to consider is the administrator's ability to remotely browse user permissions. Because browsing for user permissions over a low-speed line is time consuming, you may choose to turn browsing off as a default. Select Options|Low Speed Connection to turn browsing off. This option is a *toggle* so the same action turns browsing back on.

7.  To grant or revoke dial-in permission, select Users|Permissions to display the Remote Access Permissions—Low Speed Mode dialog box, as shown in Figure 5.12. This dialog box only shows one user at a

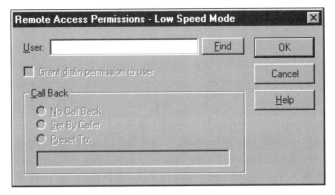

**Figure 5.12**   The Low Speed Mode menu allows an administrator to set client permissions to dial in across low-speed lines and automatically turn off browsing.

time. The Find option allows you to type in a user's ID so that NT can find the user. The Call Back options and the "Grant dialin permission to user" option operate the same with the higher-speed connection.

The RAS Admin utility has several other features that are very useful for managing one or more active RAS users:

1.   Select Server|Communication Ports to display the Communication Ports menu, shown in Figure 5.13. This menu contains the controls to disconnect a current user, send a message to a specific user, send a message to all users, and initiate the display of the Port Status screen.

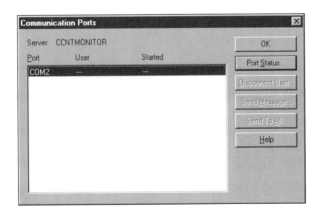

**Figure 5.13**   The Communication Ports menu displays a list of NT's RAS configured ports, along with the current users.

This menu becomes extremely important if your NT 4 server is supporting multiple ports and users.

2.  Click on the Port Status button to display the Port Status screen, shown in Figure 5.14. This screen contains the latest statistics and status for the currently selected port. NT automatically updates this screen as it services the port. Notice that the displayed information contains a list of common serial communication errors. The Port Status screen also shows the client usage of the three protocols, along with the client workstation's name. A control is provided to allow the administrator to reset the displayed statistics.

3.  Click on OK to close the window.

4.  Select Users|Active Users to display the screen shown in Figure 5.15. The Remote Access Users screen lists each user, a server name, and when the connection was started. In addition to displaying information, the screen contains a set of controls to communicate with one or all users, read a user's account, and disconnect a user.

5.  Highlight a specific user, and then click on User Account. A small screen will appear showing the details of the selected user's name— when his password was last changed, when his password expires, his privilege level, and his call back requirement.

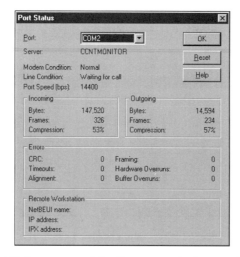

**Figure 5.14**   The Port Status menu contains the communications statistics for the currently selected port.

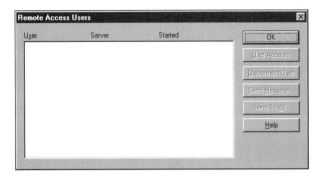

**Figure 5.15**  The Remote Access Users screen displays a list of currently attached users, along with the controls to manage and communicate with them.

For test purposes, be sure to try this next step only on a friend.

6.  Highlight a user, then click on Disconnect User. The user will receive a message that he has been disconnected by the server and that the RAS session is terminated. However, before you disconnect the user, make certain that you note his user account information. Disconnecting a user does not prevent him from re-establishing the RAS session. To prevent a user from reattaching to the server, you must change the user's account to withdraw dial-in privileges. This change should be done prior to disconnecting the user to prevent any possibility of re-entry.

7.  To send a message to a single user, highlight the user, and click on Send Message. A small screen will be displayed that will allow you to send a message to the selected user.

8.  To send a message to all users, click on Send To All. The same screen will be displayed to allow you to enter a message; only this time, the message will be sent to all of the currently attached users.

9.  Click on OK to exit the Remote Access Users menu. Then, select File|Exit to close the Remote Access Admin utility.

## CONFIGURING THE RAS PHONEBOOK

Assuming that you are configured to support both dial-in and dial-out RAS, you will want to set up your phonebook to allow you to dial out. NT 4 treats the RAS client as part of its Dial-up Networking. Follow these steps to configure the RAS phonebook:

1. Double click on the My Computer icon to display the disk drive icons and the Dialup Networking icon. Click on the Dialup Networking icon to display the first dial-out account name and phone number.

2. Click on the New control button to add a new entry to the phone-book, as shown in Figure 5.16.

3. You can use the tabs on the New Phonebook Entry screen to configure a dial-out account. In the Basic tab, enter a dial-out account name and phone number, and identify the modem to be used for this account.

4. In the Server entry tab, shown in Figure 5.17, enter the type of server to be dialed into. Choose one of the standard server types from the pull-down list.

5. Select the protocols to be used to communicate to the selected server (you can pick more than one). Remember, PPP can encapsulate these protocols and extract them on the other end. This will allow you to communicate using any or all of the three at the dial-in server's LAN.

Use care in selecting the next two configuration items. Not all servers will be compatible with this newer technology. Be sure to completely test the connection with and without these items selected before assuming that the dial-out account's installation is completed.

6. Choose "Enable software compression" to implement the VJ header compression. RAS uses the Van Jacobson Compressed TCP/IP head-

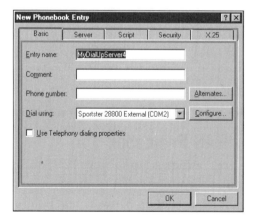

**Figure 5.16**   The New Phonebook Entry tabbed menu provides the controls to configure RAS dial-out accounts.

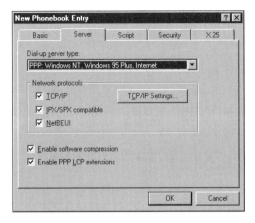

**Figure 5.17**    The Server tab allows you to specify the type of server and the protocols to
be used.

ers to negotiate IP addresses. If you are connected to a PPP server
and the TCP/IP utilities refuse to work, try turning off the VJ header
compression.

7.  Choose "Enable PPP LCP extensions" to implement the Link Control Protocol (LCP). LCP is used by RAS for establishing, configuring, and testing the data-link connection. If you cannot connect to a
server using PPP, or the remote computer terminates your connection, the server may not support LCP extensions. Try clearing the
Request LCP Extensions check box and reattaching to the server.

8.  If the dial-out account is a standard point-to-point with no intermedi-
aries, then choose None in the "After dialing (login)" group.

9.  For those users familiar with Telnet, select the "Pop up a terminal
window" option to display a terminal screen that allows you to manually navigate the intermediary devices.

10.  Scripts, shown in Figure 5.18, are command, or batch, files that control how RAS will handle any intermediary device or service that it
might encounter in setting up this dial-out connection. An intermediary device may be a service provider, an electronic switchboard, or
a security monitor, that will answer the call before the RAS connection on the other end. Scripts are contained within the SWITCH.INF
file. To use a script, you must first create it and then store it within the

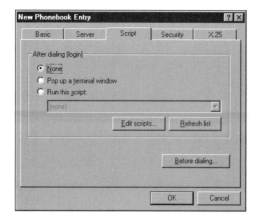

**Figure 5.18** The Script tab provides controls to specify what steps RAS will take to bypass intermediate devices.

SWITCH.INF file. You can also edit one of the existing scripts stored in the file. When you're finished, specify the desired script by using the pull-down list control and highlighting the desired script. Once you have selected a script, then select the "Run this script" radio button.

11. The Security tab, shown in Figure 5.19, allows you to specify what security settings are in effect at the destination server. Configure the appropriate security features for the destination server. Once you have chosen either clear text, encrypted, or Microsoft encrypted authenti-

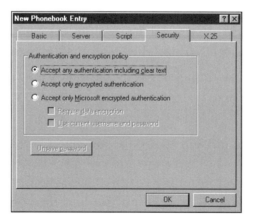

**Figure 5.19** The Security tab allows RAS to match the security requirements found on the destination server.

cation, then test the connection to verify that your logon is acceptable to the destination server. If you encounter problems connecting due to security access violations, contact the administrator of the destination server to obtain additional help.

12. The Security tab also allows you to specify secure communications by choosing the "Require date encryption" option. This is useful for communicating sensitive information, such as financial or personnel records. Remember, communication links can be monitored. If information is unsecured, it can be captured.

13. The "Use current username and password" check box allows you to specify that your current security identification information will be used to logon to the destination server. The "Unsave password" button allows you to specify a new password for each logon. This will prevent anyone with access to your computer from making use of this connection under your logon ID.

14. The X.25 tab allows you to specify an X.25 network provider and address.

## RAS AUTODIAL

A new feature of NT 4's RAS is AutoDial, which converts network addresses to RAS phonebook entries. The addresses are saved or "learned" by AutoDial so that when a remote network connection is specified, it will remember the appropriate phone number, security, and protocol settings to reconnect to the remote server. The server can be located on the Internet, any IP or NetBIOS server.

AutoDial monitors and learns every RAS connection for automatic reconnection later. If a RAS link is disconnected from a network during a program execution, AutoDial will attempt to automatically reconnect whenever the program references the remote connection.

To test AutoDial's directory and the locations it is listing, enter *C:\rasautou -s* at the command prompt. The resulting list will contain a description of the network card bindings and the current connections that AutoDial maintains.

## RAS CLIENT INTERFACE

The RAS client interface consists of Windows-based (NT, Windows 95, Windows for Workgroups clients) or character-based (MS-DOS clients) utilities that provide RAS users with the ability to connect, disconnect, and report the status of the RAS connection.

# Remote NT Server Management

You're at home, and you receive a telephone call. One of your NT 4 servers is not working. Don't bother getting dressed and driving in. With NT's remote server management tools, you now have an alternative. Remote server management tools allow you to manage remote servers across a phone line from home or across a WAN or LAN. In this section, I will be discussing the remote tools running on a Windows NT 4 server and workstation. Some tools available on the server do not come standard on the NT workstation. I will also be discussing the tools available to run on Windows 95 that allow you to monitor and control NT 4 servers.

These tools, which are available as Client-Based Network Administration Tools from the Windows NT Server disk in the \clients\srvtools\winnt\i386 directory (for an Intel-based machine), are shown in Table 5.2. There are also tools available for Alpha, MIPS, and PowerPC machines. To install the server tools to a client NT 4 workstation, run the SETUP.BAT file, located in the directory\clients\srvtools\winnt. SETUP.BAT will copy the files from the server CD to your client. SETUP.BAT doesn't create icons or a program group, so you will have to create these yourself. In fact, SETUP.BAT doesn't even tell you where it installs these files. The files are installed to the \%systemroot%\system32 directory.

**Table 5.2   Remote Server Tools for the NT 4 Workstation**

| File | Purpose |
| --- | --- |
| DHCPADMN.EXE | The DHCP Manager allows you to remotely manage a DHCP server |
| WINSADMN.EXE | The WINS Manager allows you to remotely manage a WINS server |

*(continued)*

**Table 5.2    Remote Server Tools for the NT 4 Workstation *(continued)***

| File | Purpose |
|------|---------|
| USRMGR.EXE | The User Manager for Domains allows you to add, delete, and modify user entries in the PDC and on individual servers |
| UPEDIT.EXE | The User Profile Editor allows you to create custom user profiles which can be remotely read and stored |
| RASADMIN.EXE | The Remote Access Server Administrator provides you with the resources to manage RAS remotely |
| EVENTVWR.EXE | This is another copy of the standard NT Event Log Viewer |
| RPLMGR.EXE | The Remote Reboot RPL Manager utility |
| SHUTGUI.EXE | This utility allows you to remotely shutdown and reboot you server or workstation |
| SRVMGR.EXE | A Server Manager that allows you to monitor and manage server resources remotely |

I will cover each of the files shown in Table 5.2 in the rest of this chapter. In addition to these files, there are two other sources of remote management files available for you to use. These additional files can be found on the NT workstation itself and in the Windows NT Resource Kit, available from Microsoft.

## DHCP Manager

The DHCPADMN.EXE is a client utility that you can use to remotely monitor and manage DHCP servers from your Windows NT 4 workstation. In order to use the utility, you must first logon to your workstation using an ID and password that has administrator's account privileges on all of the DHCP servers that you wish to manage.

Using the DHCPADMN.EXE, a LAN administrator can specify and manage global and subnet-specific DHCP servers anywhere on the LAN. Remember the description of DHCP in Chapter 3? A Dynamic Host Configuration Protocol server dynamically allocates IP addresses for networked computers. Rather than static IP addresses, these servers usually lease addresses for fixed periods of time to the network workstations. DHCP manages its workstations by segregating the network into scopes.

A DHCP scope is a group of workstations running the DHCP client service in a subnet. Each scope is controlled by a DHCP server. The servers may be located locally or across the country. This means that someone has to either manage these servers locally or, using this utility, manage them all from a central point.

The DHCP Manager window, shown in Figure 5.20, contains the controls to remotely manage a DHCP server. These controls provide you with the ability to remotely:

- Add DHCP servers to the server list

- Specify each DHCP server by name

- Remove selected DHCP servers from your servers management list

- Create a DHCP Scope

- Change the address pool for a scope

- Activate and deactivate lease recall on a scope

- Manage IP address reservation options

## WINS Administration

The WINSADMIN.EXE, shown in Figure 5.21, is a client utility that you can use to remotely manage WINS (Windows Internet Naming Service) servers from your Windows NT 4 workstation. This utility provides the con-

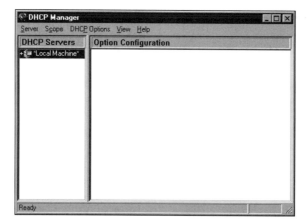

**Figure 5.20**  The DHCP Manager contains the controls required to manage multiple remote DHCP servers.

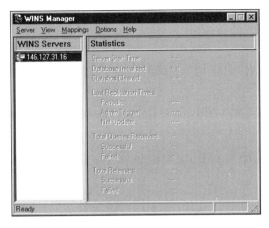

**Figure 5.21** The WINS Manager provides the controls to manage WINS servers across a network.

trols to enable you to attach to any WINS server that you have access rights to. In order to connect to a WINS server, you must first be logged onto your workstation using the same user ID and password that entitles you to administrator's rights on any of the WINS servers that you wish to manage.

A WINS server maintains a database of IP addresses and network computer names. The WINS service uses this database to map network names to their appropriate IP addresses. One of the features of WINS servers is their ability to operate distributed databases located across many different servers. This distributed database capability requires that many different WINS servers, often in different locations, be monitored and maintained. This requirement can be addressed by the WINS Administration utility. Using this utility, you have the ability to change configuration, specify options, manage backup replications, and monitor statistics for any WINS server on the network.

The WINSADMIN.EXE utility gives you all the flexibility you need to perform the following management functions:

- Scavenge addresses to identify which addresses should be overwritten or changed

- Obtain detailed statistics from any accessible WINS server

- Identify and purge the database of incorrect addresses or computer names that have been relocated into other WINS databases

- Change replication partners and start or stop database replications with existing partners

- Set the backup and restore WINS database folders; WINS will backup these folders every three hours

- Manage the WINS logging function

**TIP** Use the WINSDMP.EXE to dump the contents of a WINS database into a CSV file, which can be read by both Excel and Access. The WINSDMP.EXE is an NT Resource Kit utility that can save you time and effort, especially if you frequently work from home. The dumps generated by the WINSDMP.EXE utility are useful in maintaining a current listing of WINS server addresses. These can aid you in troubleshooting problems because finding specific addresses can sometimes be difficult and time consuming using the WINSADMIN.EXE utility.

## Server Manager

SRVMGR.EXE is included in the clients/i386 toolkit and can be run on the NT 4 workstation. This file is the same tool that is available on the NT server for use in managing NT 4 domains. In order to use this utility, you must first be logged on to a domain server or workstation using a valid Administrator, Domain Administrator, or Server Operator account. You must also have at your disposal the tools to change whatever activities you feel are adversely affecting your domain.

Managing the domain involves the ability to:

- Know which users are attached to your computer

- Control user activities by disconnecting errant users

- Protect resources from user-caused or accidental damage by replicating directories to other servers or workstations

- Stay informed, by managing who receives alerts from domain servers or workstations

- Convert a backup domain controller to the primary role

- Manage the services running on each domain server or workstation

The administrator may want to know who is attached to a network computer and what shares they are accessing. The shared resources information can be obtained using the Server Manager, which simply means running the SRVMGR.EXE file. The Server Manager menu lists the servers and workstations currently attached to your domain.

## MANAGE CONNECTED USERS

To monitor and control users that are attached to a computer, find the computer in the displayed list, and then select File|Properties. The menu shown in Figure 5.22 will now be displayed. This menu provides the controls necessary for you to monitor user and shared directories. Clicking on the User button displays the current user sessions. Clicking on the Share button displays the same information from the perspective of the shared directory. The In Use button displays a menu that shows you the users and lists the number of open resources, along with any locks they may have. The summary information lists the number of users, file locks, open files, and named pipes being used.

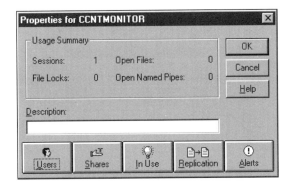

**Figure 5.22** The Properties menu provides a summary of user activity, as well as the controls to manage users, shares, replications, and alerts.

Click on Users to display the User Sessions menu shown in Figure 5.23. This menu lists who, by user name, is attached to your computer and what resources they are using. Move the cursor down the list and the menu will show what each user is connected to. Two control options are available. These options are to either disconnect one user or all the users from their shared resources.

Click on Close to return to the Properties menu, and then click on Shares. The Shared Resources menu is shown in Figure 5.24, and lists your computer's shared resources and which users are attached. This menu also provides you with the controls to disconnect one user or all users.

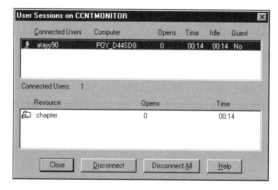

**Figure 5.23**  The User Sessions menu shows the currently attached users and provides the controls required to disconnect one or all users.

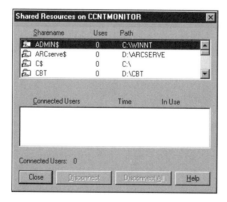

**Figure 5.24**  The Shared Resources menu shows the currently configured shared directories along with their attached users.

Click on the In Use control from the Properties menu. The Open Resources menu, shown in Figure 5.25, shows a list of the currently connected users and the resources they are using. The type of resources NT lists are:

- Files

- Print Jobs

- Named Pipes

For all other categories, NT designates unknown resources.

You have the option to close a selected resource or close all resources. Closing a resource is almost the same as disconnecting users. However, closing a resource will only affect the user's current use of that particular resource. Disconnecting the user affects everything he is doing on the server.

## REPLICATION

Certain resources—such as files, directories, and databases—are critical to server operation. They may also represent a significant investment in time, labor, and dollars. The Server Manager supplies the tools needed to replicate directories and their contents to other servers and workstations. Replication involves a partnership between two computers for the purpose of sharing directories on an automatic timetable. In a replication partnership, one server establishes a replication link with another computer. Once the partnership has been made, the server periodically sends the files contained in specified directories to its partner.

From the Properties menu, click on Replication to display the Directory Replication menu, as shown in Figure 5.26. The Directory Replication menu

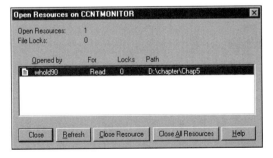

**Figure 5.25**    The Open Resources menu shows the currently shared resources, along with the attached users.

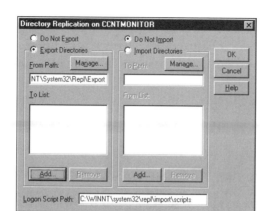

**Figure 5.26**    The Directory Replication menu provides the controls required to create and manage import and export directories.

is used to create, manage, and dissolve directory replication partnerships. An import directory contains files that are periodically copied from another server. The default directory on your NT 4 server is C:\WINNT\ System32\Repl\Import. However, you may add multiple directories to the import list.

An export directory contains files that you are saving on a replication partner workstation or server. The default export directory is, of course, C:\WINNT\System32\Repl\Export. Again, you may specify other directories to be exported, as required.

Clicking the Manage control on the Directory Replication menu brings up the Manage Exported Directories menu. The Manage Exported Directories menu, shown in Figure 5.27, is used to suspend or allow importing

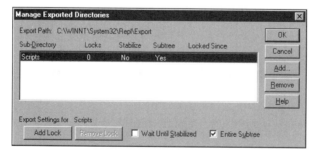

**Figure 5.27**    The Manage Exported Directories menu provides the controls necessary to add or delete subdirectories, locks, and file stabilization.

or exporting of files. You may lock one or more directories to prevent them from being replicated. Selecting the Wait until Stabilized control tells NT to wait until the contents of all of the directories have gone unchanged for at least two minutes. The Subtree control, if checked, allows you to specify that NT will replicate each directory and all subdirectories listed. If unchecked, only the first-level directories will be replicated.

## ALERTS CONTROL

Clicking on the Alerts button on the Properties menu displays the menu shown in Figure 5.28. The Alerts menu is used to view and manage which users and computers are notified in the advent of administrative alerts occurring on the selected computer. Administrative alerts are generated by NT when there are problems associated with server and resource use. Alerts can be generated by security problems, user problems, UPS server shutdown, and printer malfunctions.

To manage the alerts, simply add the name of a computer or user to be the destination for any alerts messages. This menu only provides controls for adding or removing the alerts destinations.

## DOMAIN CONTROL

In the event that you might wish to take the primary domain controller (PDC) offline, you can promote a backup domain controller (BDC) to become the PDC. From the main Server Manager menu, select one of the servers listed. Then select File|Promote to Primary Domain Controller. This will cause the selected server to assume the PDC's responsibilities and cause the PDC to become the BDC.

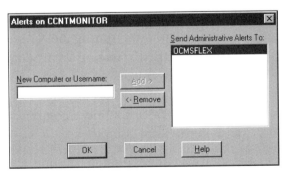

**Figure 5.28**  The Alerts menu is used to specify which users or computers will receive administrative alerts.

During normal maintenance, you will take servers and workstations offline. Once you return these computers to service, you should resynchronize the network. You can do this from the main Server Manager menu by choosing File|Synchronize with Primary Domain Controller. This will cause the domain directory database to be replicated from the PDC to all domain servers.

An NT PDC automatically synchronizes the domain. But, if the domain directory database is different between the PDC and either the BDC or the other domain servers, you may experience difficulty with user logons and access to shared directories.

**TIP** On a large LAN, use the Synchronize with Primary Domain Controller feature only when absolutely necessary. It places additional load on the network and could take hours to complete. Synchronization generates a substantial influx of network traffic as each server seeks to resynchronize with the PDC.

## SERVICES CONTROL

Services are programs that can be automatically started or stopped on the NT operating system. These services range from the Alerter service to the TCP/IP network services. A service is designed to perform some basic operational function, such as maintaining the computer's time, providing a network protocol, or providing an access to the clipboard. Each service has two basic parameters: the service's method of starting and the services operational status.

A service can be automatically started, manually started, or disabled. If a service is automatically started, it will start during the NT bootup sequence. A manual service is started by manually issuing a start command from either the Server Manager or the Control Panel's Services applet. The advantage in using the Server Manager to start and manage services is that you can use it to manage both local and remote computers. The Control Panel applet is only valid on the local computer.

A service's operational status is either running, starting, stopping, paused, or stopped. A running service is operational and able to perform its programmatic functions. A starting or stopping service is in a transitional state and, therefore, not functional. A paused service is temporarily stopped, but can be continued quickly. A stopped service is stopped and unable to function.

To configure services, first select the network computer to be configured. Then, select File|Services from the Server Manager's main menu. NT will display the screen shown in Figure 5.29. The services menu shows a list box with all the services that are currently configured on that computer. Each service's operational status is shown to the right of the service name. The menu offers you seven controls that allow you to perform the following actions:

- Close the Services menu.

- Start a selected service that is currently stopped.

- Stop a selected service that is currently running.

- Pause a selected service that is currently running.

- Continue a selected service that was paused.

- Set the startup method—Automatic, Manual, or Disabled—that NT will use to start the service. Startup can also be set to run using either a system account or a specific user security account.

- Combine a particular service with a hardware configuration profile. You may give this profile a meaningful name to designate its function.

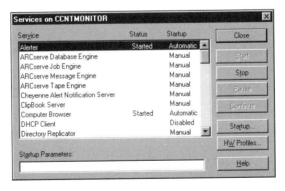

**Figure 5.29**   The Services menu is used to monitor and control the services available on the selected computer.

A common example is changing your laptop's networking configuration depending on whether the computer is docked or not docked. One profile may be named "docked". The other profile could be named "undocked". The docked profile includes an NT configuration using networked drivers. The undocked profile does not configure NT with network drivers, as the laptop is mobile and will normally not be connected to a network.

The Services menu also includes a Startup parameters field to enter a specific set of startup parameters to be used in conjunction with the service's startup.

## User Manager for Domains

You now have tools to administer the LAN, the domain controller, and the server from your NT 4 workstation. Next, you need to administer user accounts. To logon to the NT domain, you must have a valid user account on the PDC or server. To remotely change, add, delete, and monitor user accounts, NT provides the User Manager for domains called the USRMGR.EXE. You will find this file located in the \clients\srvtools directory on the NT server disk. The User Manager is designed as a tool to administer security on the PDC, BDC, servers, and workstations. With User Manager for Domains, you can perform the following administrative tasks:

- Select the domain or networked computer to be managed

- Create and manage user groups

- Administer the security policies for the domain or server

- Create user logon accounts

- Change user logon accounts and logon scripts

- Disable user logon accounts

This utility performs the same function as the NT User Manager utility, which is a standard tool on the NT 4 server.

Notice that in Figure 5.30 the User Manager utility's main menu is separated in two. The top portion of the menu contains a list of existing user accounts. The lower portion of the menu contains a list of existing group accounts.

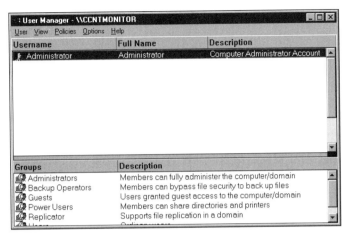

**Figure 5.30**    The User Manager provides the controls to allow the administrator to manage domain security.

# Event Viewer

NT 4 uses an event log to record significant system events. Event logs are located on every NT computer, server, and workstation in the domain. The problem is this: How can you remotely read the events contained in these logs? Do you need a special utility to run on your workstation in order to access and manage these logs? The answer is no, you already have an excellent tool as part of every NT system, EVENTVWR.EXE, the Event Log Viewer.

Every NT 4 event log is really three separate logs: Application, Security, and System. The Application log records application errors, significant application events, and other application-specific diagnostic messages. The Security log records the results of security audits throughout the system. In Chapter 4, we discussed that you have the ability to control the audit policy for any NT 4 workstation or server. The Security log captures the audit trail for user accounts and user resource access. The System log records NT system-specific messages, including service start-up failures and system-level errors detected during normal operation.

The standard NT 4 event log, located in the Administrative Tools group, is network friendly and can read event logs across the network or a RAS connection. The only requirement is that you are logged into your workstation or server as a member of the administrator's or domain administrator's group. Once you are properly logged in, select File|Select Computer. The resulting screens allow you to select one computer at a time from a list of Microsoft Network or NetWare networked computers.

Once you have attached to the remote computer's event log, you may perform the following major actions:

- Read the System, Application, and Security event logs

- Clear the remote system's event logs

- Archive or save the remote computer's event logs into an .EVT file

- Administer the logs by clearing, saving, and specifying log operations, such as log file size, overwrites, and the number of days before a log can overwrite itself

The Event Log Viewer is a useful tool for diagnosing potential long-term problems or problems associated with failed components. This event log is unique among remote server management tools in that it is stored on, and updated by, individual network computers. Most of the remote server tools only work when you are connected to a computer over the network. The event log updates continue regardless of remote connections. Your only role in interacting with the logs on the networked computers is to read and modify their operation.

## RPL Manager

The RPL Manager, RPLMGR.EXE, is an NT 4 workstation (or server) utility that can be used to remotely reboot networked Windows diskless workstations. If your network includes diskless workstations—workstations that are not equipped with hard or floppy disk drives—what happens at reboot time? Each workstation must be equipped with a network adapter that is configured with a Remote Initial Program Load (RPL) Read Only Memory (ROM) chip. At bootup, the ROM is used to start the workstation and configure the necessary network software in order to communicate with the server.

When you start, or boot, a computer, the operating system is loaded into its memory. The RPL manager loads MS-DOS and Windows workstations with software from a server's hard disk instead of from a workstation's hard disk.

The use of the RPL Manager service and diskless workstations has the following advantages:

- Because the operating software running on the workstation is physically located on the server, upgrading and revision control of the software applications and operating systems can be managed centrally.

- Because the only software that can be run on the workstation must come from the server, a more secure workstation environment is created. This prevents infections by many types of viruses.

- Diskless workstations initially cost less and are less prone to hardware malfunctions.

- The remote boot offers a greater level of control for the network administrator.

You and I will delve deeper into the concept of diskless workstations in Chapter 6.

## REGEDIT32.EXE

As with previous versions of NT, the NT 4 registry database contains information specific to the computer hardware, NT operating system services, and software applications. Each computer in your network has its own customized copy of the registry database. The problem is how to access and manage the many registry databases contained on these network computers. As with the Event Log Viewer, we go back to the basic NT operating system utilities. In this case, it is the REGEDIT32.EXE or the Registry Editor that already exists on either the NT 4 workstation or server. The Registry Editor can be used to read and manage the registry database located not only on your local computer but on any of the networked computers to which you have administrator account privileges.

The Registry Editor allows you to read, modify, and archive the registry database on another computer, as long as the server service on the remote computer has been started. The remote computer's operating system can be NT Server or Workstation.

To access a remote computer's registry database:

1. Start the REGEDIT32.EXE file on your local computer.

2. Select File|Select Computer to display the Select Computer menu.

3. Enter the name of the target network computer.

4. Click on OK.

The REGEDIT32 application will append two of the remote computer's Registry keys—HKEY_USERS and HKEY_LOCAL_MACHINE. The HKEY_USERS window contains all user profiles on the remote computer. The HKEY_LOCAL_MACHINE window contains the remote computer's configuration information.

Two additional windows (remote computer screens) appear on your Registry Editor screen in addition to the four from your local computer. Shrink down all the local screens, leaving only the two remote computer screens visible on your desktop. If you make any changes to the remote computer's registry, make sure that you are using the correct screen.

 If you make a change to the Registry and the change doesn't work, reboot NT, and use the Last Known Good Configuration selection shown during startup. This will reverse any changes.

## Remote Shutdown Manager

In the Windows NT Resource Kit you will find the file SHUTGUI.EXE. The file location is in the \%ResourcekitRoot%\i386\netadmin directory. This utility is an NT shutdown manager that enables a LAN or Server administrator to remotely shutdown and restart an NT server. SHUTGUI.EXE can run on either a local or remotely networked client or server.

The Shutdown Manager menu, shown in Figure 5.31, allows you to perform the following actions:

• Select a network computer to shutdown

• Kill applications without saving data to prevent restart hangups by trying to save data from a hung application

• Reboot after shutdown, which enables you continue managing the computer from a remote location

**Figure 5.31**  The Shutdown Manager contains the controls to remotely shut down an NT server or workstation and automatically restart it.

- Send a message to notify local operators of the impending shutdown

- Set a delay time to allow local operators to read the message; the delay is in seconds and defaults to 30

- Abort the shutdown during the delay period

The shutdown manager requires that you be logged on to the network, local or remote, as a user with administrator privileges and that the Remote Boot service be running on the computer to be shutdown. This is a powerful utility that could be used inappropriately and is an excellent case for carefully managing the administrator's logon ID and password. Once the NT computer reboots, you should use the Event Log Viewer to determine if all the services started and the operating system is operational.

# Conclusion

In the first part of the chapter, we reviewed a set of requirements for remotely accessing network computers from Windows NT 4. We then learned about and installed the Remote Access Server (RAS). In the second half of the chapter, we explored the principal tools available for remotely managing network servers and workstations. Because we've covered quite a bit of information, let's take one more quick look.

# RAS

RAS is NT's standard method of remotely connecting to either the server or workstation. Using RAS, you can logon, move files, access software applications on the remote computer, and remotely manage the network computer. RAS is a remote node type application that treats connections to a networked computer as standard nodes located on the remote network. A client connecting to RAS may access other computers throughout a LAN, assuming that the client has the proper group membership.

Client RAS accounts can be connected using MS-DOS (with Microsoft networking installed), Windows for Workgroups 3.11, Windows 95, and Windows NT (versions 3.1, 3.5, 3.51, and 4.0) workstations and servers. Using RAS to remotely connect to a workstation or server enables you to send and retrieve data to the host computer, or across the LAN to other computers allowing you logon privileges. RAS also enables you to use the server tools we have presented to monitor and manage the computer. In Chapter 9, we will discuss the RAS service across the Internet.

# Remote Server Tools

The server tools allow a LAN or server administrator to see inside a network computer from either a local network or a remote location. These tools can be used on the NT 4 workstation or server. Similar tools are available for Windows 95. These tools are especially useful if you travel or work from home. The selections of remote server tools shows you the wide range of remote services available to LAN, server, and workstation administrators.

The tools described in this chapter empower you to perform the following management functions:

- *Manage a DHCP Server*—The DHCPADMIN.EXE utility allows you to remotely make changes to DHCP leasing, scopes, and IP address pools.

- *Manage a WINS Server*—The WINSADMIN.EXE utility enables you to make changes to your WINS server database to update the entries and modify its operation.

- *Manage Your Network Servers*—Using the SRVMGR.EXE utility enables you to see which users are connected, manage replication, disconnect users, direct alerts, promote BDC to PDC status, start or stop services, and add or remove computers from your domain.

- *Manage User Accounts*—Using the USRMGR.EXE utility, you can add new users, suspend or delete existing users, move users to different groups, and change passwords.

- *View the Event Logs*—The EVENTVWR.EXE utility allows you to remotely read NT's event logs, make changes to log operation, and clear full logs.

- *Remotely Reboot Diskless Workstations*—The RPLMGR.EXE utility can be used to remotely reboot workstations that obtain their operating system and applications software from a server, over the LAN.

- *Manage the Computer Registry Database*—The REGEDIT32.EXE utility enables you to remotely connect to a computer and change its registry settings in order to modify the settings controlling software applications.

- *Remotely Reboot a Server or Workstation*—The SHUTGUI.EXE utility allows you to remotely shut down and reboot you server or workstation, either over a RAS connection or from another network computer.

In Chapters 7, 8, and 11, I will be discussing additional maintenance features that you can perform remotely, such as remote monitoring, performance logging, and Alerts management. Windows NT 4 has a powerful set of remote tools that can be very useful to you, whether you are the LAN administrator or simply want to better manage your desktop workstation.

CHAPTER

6

# Network Planning

In this chapter, I will describe the detailed analysis needed to design and install a modern local area network (LAN). Because *detail* is the truly operative word for a successful installation, please try to stay patient through all of the minutiae. Just knowing which questions to ask, and how far down the organizational chart you go to ask them, can make the difference between a valuable transition into the computer age and a dismal, expensive failure. For our discussion, I will be using the NT 4 Workstation and Server, and the Microsoft Network. I am also using NT and Microsoft's Backoffice suite as a fundamental part of our LAN design.

To better understand our needs, and arrive at a requirement-supported network, I am using a six-step approach to network planning and design. These steps are:

1. Establishing requirements based on business and user needs
2. Understanding the technical requirements
3. Choosing the best technological solution
4. Designing the network
5. Installing the network
6. Maintaining the network

# Project Goals

The goal of this project is to install a corporate-wide local and wide area network for our fictitious company, B&L Enterprises. Their network must meet the following goals:

- The network must increase efficiency at the department and division level.

- The network must reduce the company's recurring operating costs.

- The network must enable the corporation to expand their business using the same manpower.

These typical all-encompassing goals are set to help prioritize any technological decisions. Because you will have different alternatives, with different costs, try to keep these goals in mind to aid in your selection.

# Establishing Requirements Based on Business and User Needs

Now, let's get down to those details. B&L Enterprises employs 256 people in three divisions. The three divisions are physically located in three different states. Two B&L departments (one division), Sales and Advertising, have just been purchased from another corporation and were absorbed into the existing B&L company. They are the only division currently connected to a network and have been for five years. The other two sites both have well-entrenched paper systems and little or no understanding of computers and networking.

## Enterprise Design

First, you must understand and document the needs of those people who will use the network. This information is vital to the successful completion of any network installation. If people feel they've been consulted, and their requirements addressed, they will be more likely to support the network.

The first step is to identify B&L's internal departments and their functions. First, we need to determine the department's locations, information needs, business goals, and any other requirements. As I mentioned a moment ago, B&L has three divisions: Executive, Sales, and Purchasing. The three divisions are located in Georgia, North Carolina, and Virginia, respectively, as shown in Figure 6.1.

We must carefully review B&L's current network configuration for any communications bottlenecks. Talk to people who are using the system, and look for areas where personnel feel there are problems. In this project analysis, you must take into consideration the effects on the corporation during the transitional period—as networks are put in place—as well as the long-term forecast of any new application that will increase the network load. And you must remember that the majority of B&L's personnel are not familiar with any network or modern software applications.

## *Overall Business Review*

B&L considers itself to be a modern mail-order retail firm that specializes in selling clothing and outdoor equipment. The company publishes a mail-order catalog and has a Web page on the Internet. Its main customers are impulse buyers.

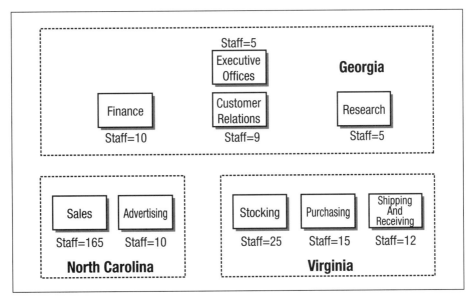

**Figure 6.1** The B&L company's divisions are located in three states: Georgia, North Carolina, and Virginia.

B&L has limited the use of computers and networking in their company because past management felt that people were only playing games on the company's computers. They also felt that the Web server and other existing tools were "necessary evils." However, B&L has revamped their management by hiring a new president, vice president, and two new division heads (Sales and Purchasing).

## SALES

Sales consists of 165 people broken into three groups: 135 people are in telephone sales, 25 are sales support, and 5 are sales administrators. Both Sales' and Advertising's personnel use workstations connected to an existing LAN. This LAN is operating at 60 percent of its maximum data transfer capability. All of the workstations in this department can be upgraded to install a new operating system. They are all 486/66 MHz machines with 8 MB of memory and a 500 MB hard disk.

The Sales department also manages a Web server, which is run on an older system and written using a Web server proprietary software application. The company retains a consultant to load its new catalog using Hypertext Markup Language (HTML). This consultant costs the company $75,000 annually.

Each telephone salesperson logs a customer's name, telephone number, and order into a ledger as they are talking on the phone. The sales support personnel then enter these ledgers into a custom-designed database application every day; the telephone sales personnel aren't able to review database entries until the next day. The support personnel also enter information from the shipping department that is faxed in daily. Shipping data is entered into a second database of shipped orders.

The major problems, as seen by Sales personnel, are the other divisions' existing paper-reporting systems, slow access to sales information, even slower shipping reports, and their outdated workstation/LAN hardware.

## ADVERTISING

The Advertising department, which is located in the same plant as the Sales personnel, consists of 10 people. Advertising is responsible for creating the company's paper catalog and the product listing shown on the

Web page. All of the workstations in this department can also be upgraded. Each workstation is a 486/66 MHz system with 8 MB of memory and a 500 MB hard drive.

Five people in this department are graphics design personnel who use an outdated networked CAD system to create the catalog and Web page illustrations. The annual graphics design man-hours required to update four new catalogs averages 2,000. The remaining five personnel are writers who use an outdated word processor package to create advertising copy for the new catalogs, mail-out brochures, and the Web page. Every catalog update requires an additional 500 man-hours for research, editing, and distribution.

The advertising copy is sent to a print shop, which lays out the final copy and prints the catalog. The Web page is outsourced to another consultant who updates the Web page every week. The consultant charges B&L $500 per week.

Five years ago, the company's catalog consisted of 50 pages. The latest catalog has 300 pages and weighs four pounds. The company mails a new catalog to every customer once each quarter. It also sends a copy of the latest catalog to each new customer as they become listed in the database. The latest price of printing each catalog is $15. The print shop's setup cost for each catalog edition is $25,000.

The major problems seen by Advertising personnel are the slow CAD package and the time it takes for the printer to create a new catalog: six weeks. This long lead time means that some of the catalog products become obsolete or replaced before the B&L catalog is in the customers' hands.

## STOCKING

There are 25 personnel working in the Stocking department. Twenty-two people are stock clerks involved in stocking new products and sending items to the Shipping department. Two people are planners, responsible for daily reports. One manager is responsible for the Stocking department's performance.

The Stocking department uses a paper planning system to inventory stock. The paper reports are physically distributed to the clerks every morning by the planners.

Most of the Stocking personnel feel that they could use a modern quality system for reporting problems found in incoming inspection. However, computers are suspect by the personnel as potentially causing layoffs.

## PURCHASING

There are 15 people in the Purchasing department, 10 are buyers and 5 are buyer support personnel who do research, evaluate bids, and maintain a modest quality system. Many of these people travel frequently to visit vendor companies. Ninety percent of this travel is in the U.S.

The Purchasing department is tasked with the job of buying finished goods from approximately 500 clothing and outdoor products firms. The annual purchases amount to $8 million. The Purchasing department does use computers to communicate with vendors. But, these systems are now five years old. The software applications are proprietary and are very costly to upgrade.

Purchasing relies on timely reports from Shipping and Receiving, and Sales; however, the information they get is one- to two-days old. This delay is due to the division's paper-based reporting system The two-day turnaround results in at least a one-day delay built into the Shipping schedule for getting the product to the customer.

## SHIPPING AND RECEIVING

The Shipping and Receiving department employs 12 people, including 1 supervisor, 2 freight specialists, 2 inspectors, and 7 shippers. The Shipping department's job is to:

- Receive incoming vendor goods

- Inspect for quality

- Send to the Stocking department

- Receive ordered material from the Stocking department

- Ship products directly to the end customer

The total annual incoming inventory items average 50,000 pieces. The total annual shipping items average 45,000 pieces. The Shipping and Receiving department is paper-based, including the quality system.

This department sees little need to change their existing procedures and feels that any changes may result in layoffs.

## EXECUTIVE OFFICES

The Executive offices consist of five people: one president, two vice presidents, and two secretaries. The Executive office personnel oversee all operations for the three divisions, including monitoring costs, profits, and quality. Many of these personnel travel extensively. Each of the five employees has a new workstation and the latest office software applications. However, they are currently primarily paper-based, receiving daily reports by fax or phone from the other two divisions.

The personnel see their problems as slow reporting and too many mistakes.

## FINANCE

The Finance department consists of 10 people: 1 Chief Financial Officer, 6 accountants, and 3 assistants. The department is responsible for reporting to the President the daily financial health of the company. Also, they produce the quarterly reports and yearly shareholders reports.

The personnel see their major problems as mistakes in reporting data and incomplete or too slow reporting.

## CUSTOMER RELATIONS

The Customer Relations department employs nine people, including one department head and eight customer specialists. The customer specialists are on the phone up to seven hours a day. They each use a word processor to prepare reports, which are hand delivered to the Executive offices and faxed to the Purchasing, Sales, and Shipping departments.

The department is responsible for the following:

- Monitoring customer satisfaction with the delivered products
- Resolving customer complaints
- Identifying future customer needs to the Sales department
- Reporting product quality complaints to the Purchasing and Shipping departments

The Customer Relations personnel see their problem as lack of communication between the different departments they have to deal with on behalf of their customers.

## RESEARCH

The Research department consists of five people, including one department head and four researchers. The department is responsible for researching new products and customer buying trends, and identifying quality or performance problems with the existing vendor materials. These personnel use word processor and spreadsheet programs to record and report their findings. These findings are then faxed to the Sales and Purchasing departments.

The Research personnel believe they receive little or no feedback from the other departments.

## *Locations*

Three buildings house B&L's divisions. All three buildings are owned by the company and are relatively modern. Only the Executive offices building was built to house office space; the other two buildings are upgraded factory space with brick walls and cement floors. All three locations are subject to random power loss. Two of the three buildings, the Executive offices and the Sales and Advertising buildings, are equipped with modern phone systems. The Purchasing building's phone system is scheduled to be upgraded in the next year. In Figure 6.2, we see that all three divisions use a fax machine as their principal method of sending documents. This figure also shows that the only division with an existing network is the Sales division. The other two divisions utilize hand-carried paper documents extensively.

## *Corporate Business Goals*

B&L Enterprises has defined its market profile as a fast conveyer of quality products to the young to middle-aged upscale consumer. It currently has a gross margin of 25 percent, eroded down from 32 percent over the past five years. The company wants to increase its profit back to the high of 32 percent within the next two years.

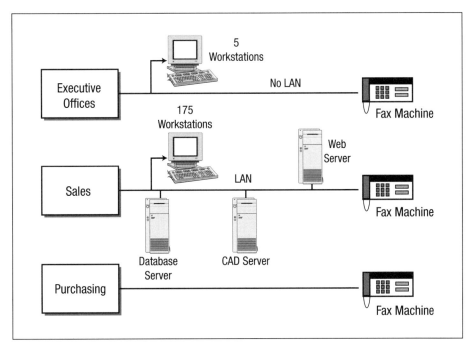

**Figure 6.2**   A look at the current B&L communications network.

Management feels it must show a significantly higher growth to increase investor confidence. These problems are offset by B&L's market prospects, which are currently considered very high, because B&L is in a retail revolution and a growth segment of the home shopping market.

The time has come for B&L to modernize its business processes by upgrading its relatively poor use of computer technology. Unfortunately, these changes are supported by only the top echelon of the company. Everyone is used to, and comfortable with, the existing paper systems. One major problem to be faced by the company is the employees' fear that computers will make many of their jobs obsolete.

In order to meet its business goals, B&L has set the goal for every department to be completely computerized within 18 months. The president's final schedule shows that the network must be in place and operational within a 12-month period, starting now.

## Security

The two primary areas requiring security are the Finance department and the Executive department. These two groups are responsible for payroll and financial results. The next requirement for security is in the Research department. This department is aware of the need for security, but doesn't currently employ any type of security system. Finally, the Sales department needs a firewall to prevent hacking into the company's catalog and sales databases.

## User Requirements

As you can see, a lot of in-depth research goes into network planning. User requirements have to be carefully extracted from the information gained by interviewing personnel from each division. This includes interviews with all working levels within the company. This information will then be prioritized by meeting with management personnel starting with the B&L President. An important analysis is the interdepartmental flow of information. An example of this analysis is shown in Figure 6.3.

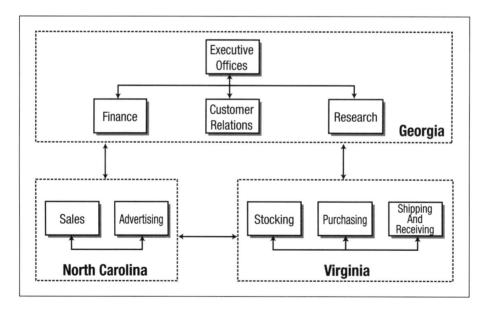

**Figure 6.3** B&L's current flow of interdepartmental communications.

## REQUIREMENTS ANALYSIS

The problems cited in department interviews are summarized in Table 6.1. Most of these problems can be addressed by a properly designed network coupled with department staff that are properly trained to use the new resources.

Each of the departments cited problems with the existing communications methods or computer resources. This information forms the basis for our technical solution.

- Communications problems describe the lack of direct data communications between two groups. Many of the departments interviewed only communicate by voice, telephone, or fax. Fax communication works well for read-only type material, but many of the faxed documents require someone to type in the data on the transmitting end and again on the receiving end. Figure 6.3 shows the existing lines of communication between the three divisions. The majority of this communications traffic is through the desktop telephone or fax machines.

- Structured data problems are associated with the lack of structure or raw data coming from one group to another. Associated problems are

**Table 6.1   User Problem Matrix**

| Department | Communications Problems | Structured Data Problems | Workstation Problems | Software Application Problems | Timely Data Problems | Data Accuracy |
|---|---|---|---|---|---|---|
| Executive Offices | Yes | Yes | No | No | Yes | Yes |
| Finance | Yes | Yes | Yes | No | Yes | Yes |
| Customer Relations | Yes | Yes | Yes | Yes | Yes | No |
| Research | Yes | Yes | Yes | No | No | No |
| Sales | Yes | Yes | Yes | Yes | Yes | No |
| Advertising | No | No | Yes | Yes | No | No |
| Stocking | Yes | Yes | Yes | Yes | Yes | Yes |
| Procurement | Yes | Yes | Yes | Yes | Yes | Yes |
| Shipping and Receiving | Yes | Yes | Yes | Yes | Yes | Yes |

incorrect or misinterpreted information. The user on the receiving end is burdened with putting structure to the data and then interpreting the results, oftentimes without being able to verify conclusions.

- Workstation problems are associated with the lack of modern computer equipment or equipment that is not equipped to support newer software applications.

- Software application problems are found in proprietary applications that were written to meet a narrow range of requirements and are not capable of being expanded. Many of these applications cannot share data as the data is neither structured nor even in a known format.

- Timely data problems relate to data that is not received when needed. As cited in the interviews, late data can result in adding at least one day in shipping products to the customer. Other symptoms of this problem are late reports and lost orders due to sales being unable to verify that a product is in stock.

- Data accuracy problems usually result from operator error, misinterpreted handwritten entries, or misentry on the receiving end. The results of these types of errors can be incorrect products being shipped, incorrect financial results, and incorrect stockholder reporting.

Each of the problems cited in Table 6.1 were identified from personnel experience. Often, problems recognized in one department may also exist in other departments but are not cited for varying reasons. Many people fear job loss as a result of increasing computer capabilities.

Until now, I have avoided listing some common problems, such as higher costs and time delays. But, unfortunately, the B&L company does suffer from higher costs resulting from inefficient operations. The cost of printing their quarterly catalog is too high, as is the cost of making updates to their Web server. The time it takes for a customer to receive his order is too long by at least one to two days. All of these problems are very common and can have a serious effect on cash flow.

## *Addressing User Problems*

The problems cited by the different departments can be grouped into possible solution categories. The original problem matrix can be further broken down into categories where similarities suggest possible technology, as shown in Table 6.2. This table shows where a network solution, coupled with new application and database software, can resolve many departmental problems. Care must be taken not to implement a technology just because it's the newest whiz-bang available. The newest technology changes virtually every year and upgrades should be planned rather than implemented on a whim.

## EMAIL

If all departments are connected by a universal email application, communication between departments and individuals is greatly enhanced. Email doesn't fix all problems, but it does boost communications speed. Email that uses a standard Messaging Application Programming Interface (MAPI) makes creating standard software considerably easier as each new application must conform to the email standard.

## LAN/WAN NETWORK CONNECTION

The combination of LAN connections enables departments located in the same plant to be able to communicate with each other faster and cheaper. WAN (Wide Area Network) connectivity allows each plant to communicate with the other plants with almost the same speed as between departments at the same location. Email and standard applications can be used across both the LAN and WAN networks to speed up reporting and database applications.

**Table 6.2    Departmental Problems VS. Possible Technology Fixes**

| Problem | Email | LAN/WAN Network Connection | New Hardware | Network Servers | Standard Software Applications | Central Data Storage | Standard Database Design |
|---|---|---|---|---|---|---|---|
| Communications | Yes | Yes | Yes | Yes | Yes | Yes | Yes |
| Structured Data | No | No | No | Yes | Yes | Yes | Yes |
| Workstation | No | Yes | Yes | No | Yes | Yes | No |
| Software Application | No | Yes | Yes | Yes | Yes | Yes | Yes |
| Timely Data | Yes | Yes | Yes | Yes | Yes | Yes | Yes |
| Data Accuracy | No | No | No | Yes | Yes | Yes | Yes |

## NEW HARDWARE

Every department, with the exception of the Executive offices, is running on outmoded workstations. Many of the departments are not even equipped with personal workstations. New workstations should be placed in these departments to allow the personnel to make use of the LAN/WAN connectivity and email. Other new hardware will be needed to support LAN and WAN connectivity, including routers, hubs, external communications equipment, and cabling.

## NETWORK SERVERS

Network servers, located in each department, can be used to run desktop software applications, database applications, email transfer across the WAN, and file storage. Servers can also be used to run the network domain security as PDCs and BDCs. Server-based applications can be shared among all LAN users and can be better managed because software application upgrades are made to only one machine. You will always have a trade-off between common applications, such as word processor, spreadsheet, and office graphics programs. If these are installed on an applications server, you can significantly increase network traffic. If they are installed on individual workstations, this means that upgrades, when made, must occur at each workstation. This is one reason to use the Microsoft Systems Management Server software application to automate workstation upgrades.

## STANDARD SOFTWARE APPLICATIONS

In the past, B&L hired a consultant to develop applications to meet one department's needs without regard to other departments or standards. Once a network is in place, different departments can make use of existing applications.

## CENTRAL DATA STORAGE

Centralized data storage has the following advantages:

- Data can be accessed by the entire company using one software application interface.

- Data can be better protected by security.

- When data is changed, the change is reflected everywhere.

- Data integrity is increased automatically, as each entry is only made once.

- Data is safer because backups occur at only one site.

- Further safety can be ensured using replication between one server and another.

## STANDARD DATABASE DESIGN

Good database design can greatly reduce the frequency and extent of incorrect operator entries. Using one database development package enables a designer to apply a common set of rules and procedures to all of the departments. In addition, training different users that have different levels of computer skills is made easier if the database design adheres to common standards.

## *Justification*

As a result of meetings with B&L employees and management, three areas have been identified that everyone agrees need attention. The first is that on the few existing systems that they currently have, response time is unacceptable, sometimes taking longer than a minute. Therefore, application response times is a major factor. Second is the ability of the employees to have quick and easy access to the Internet. Even though the company's Web page catalog is readily available to the public, many of the employees have never seen the catalog. The third priority is print services. Many of the employees do not feel comfortable with documentation that appears only on computer screens. They want paper documents. The old systems provided only three printers, one in each division. Any system being implemented must have printers available for general use. But, the need for printers may decrease in the future as personnel become more familiar with online documentation.

## CUSTOMER BENEFIT

B&L is a market-driven company. Therefore, customer benefit should be considered as part of the network design. Customer input has shown that often Sales or Customer Relations personnel are not familiar with the B&L Web page. Another complaint is that the Web page is slow to load and even slower to use. Network design must consider faster Web server response times for the customer. The design must also enhance the ability for Sales to review the Web page while on the phone to the customer. Customer ordering from the Web page must be revamped to be as fast and as error free as possible.

## B&L's Legacy Systems

The existing, or legacy, systems at the different B&L divisions are minimal. Most of the workstations, software applications, and network hardware are obsolete. B&L has never made a significant investment in networked computers.

### WORKSTATIONS

The five new workstations are located in the Executive offices. The 175 workstations in the Sales and Advertising department must be upgraded to run new operating system software. The CAD, Web, and database servers in these departments can be upgraded and converted to workstations. The Shipping, Purchasing, and Stocking departments currently have no workstations.

### EXISTING NETWORKS

There is only one existing, although outdated, network located in the Sales and Advertising division. This 4 MB network is currently being over utilized. Frequent network slowdowns are noticed because the CAD systems also use this network to run their applications. Adding additional use to this network will only increase user wait time and network communication delays.

### IDENTIFY APPLICATIONS

Currently, three proprietary applications are being used at B&L. All three are located in the Sales division:

- The customer database application allows telephone sales personnel to review their customer information. This data is no more recent than one day.

- The database application contains manually entered shipping, purchasing, and stock information. The data is used by the telephone sales personnel to identify later shipments and to inform customers of currently stocked items.

- The Web page application is written by an outside consultant. This application uses artwork and graphics supplied by the advertising group. The Web page can also accept orders from Internet customers which are then placed in a flat text file for use by sales support personnel to enter orders.

## EXISTING SERVERS

Only two servers exist and are located at the Sales division. One is used for CAD, while the other is used to run the sales databases. Both servers are also being used by these departments as file servers. These two servers could now be converted into personal workstations without the need for any additional upgrades. Because they don't support adequate disk storage, neither will remain in service as network servers.

## EMAIL APPLICATIONS

No legacy email applications exist.

## INTERNET SERVER APPLICATION

The existing Web server was designed two years ago and is slow, out of date, and costly to maintain. The current Web page is at the mercy of an outside consultant. Any change, either complex or simple, incurs a higher than normal cost. Customer data is difficult to recover from the Web server and the input screens are not as user-friendly as customers would like. Often, they prefer to call in their order rather than enter orders using the Web site's order entry screens. This requires additional time by sales personnel to take the orders.

## SPECIAL INTERFACES TO OTHER SYSTEMS

No special interfaces are required.

## EXISTING DATABASES

Three databases are currently being used: previous day sales data, shipping data, and the customer database. The shipping database contains a day-old list of items shipped to customers, items in stock, and purchased item delivery dates. Unfortunately, these database designs are proprietary. This means that the data cannot be easily exported to other applications.

## PROJECT DOCUMENTATION

Project documentation can make or break a network design. This is especially true at B&L because most of the company's employees, management and workers, are not highly trained computer experts. Although most have used computers and have a fundamental understanding of networks, their experiences have been limited to using application software and CAD packages. I recommend a standard five section documentation package.

Your first section should be the analysis of the user needs and requirements. This is the first place to catch any mistakes made during personnel interviews. The second section should contain a conceptual design of the network with particular attention to the details of what software will be used on what hardware platform.

The third section should contain a detailed design of the network, showing locations, bandwidths, hardware, software, and any new features, such as servers, remote dial-in servers, and routers. It is essential that all proposed network designs be diagrammed and made available for review. These diagrams must contain the network specifics at all three sites. Efforts should be made to obtain input from the users as to which applications and utilities should be installed.

The fourth section should contain a detailed list of the hardware and software to be purchased, along with their estimated cost. The fifth section should contain a detailed test plan, along with a maintenance plan detailing the number of personnel and types of services to be performed by each.

# Understanding the Technical Requirements

The cost of the new network must be justified as benefiting the employees and customers, as well as B&L. The justification should show, in measurable terms, that the employees' efficiency will be increased and that mistakes and inherent time delays can be resolved in a productive manner. Many companies base their expenditures for new equipment on a threshold return on investment (ROI). A typical ROI is the time it takes to return the investment to the company. Therefore, when developing a new network design, you should always calculate an ROI.

Here is an example: A new program will save the worker 10 minutes an hour over the current procedure, or 80 minutes a day. This means that an employee earning \$10/hour, will be more productive by 80 minutes a day or, calculating the ROI: (80*(\$10/60))=\$13.33 per day per employee. If you have 10 people using the software, you save \$133.33 per day total. This means that an investment of \$30,000 in software application expenses can see an ROI of (30,000/133.33)=225 days. A reasonable ROI is considered to be 6 to 18 months.

## Cost as a Design Element

The cost of installing a network and upgrading user workstations and software applications should be treated as an element of the design. Very few times do you have the luxury to "spare no expense." More realistically, you will probably have a tight budget, or you must create an estimated budget as part of the network planning process. Frequently, management will base their budget decisions on those tangible items such as ROI or a Cost Benefits Analysis, where you must justify the costs based on the benefits gained by the company.

To prepare a network budget, you must give careful consideration to the costs, not only of hardware and software, but also to the estimated employee cost. This number should include the time required for training. It must also include an estimate of the number of employees that must be hired to maintain the network. A network project cost estimate must include the entire network deployment process, beginning with the planning phase, through training and the final release to maintenance.

In our example, B&L is sensitive to costs and the budget will be tied to an ROI of 12 months. This may mean that the network will be phased into the divisions.

## Email Requirements

Workstation email requires that client software be installed on every workstation. It also requires that email server software be installed on any server that will become a post office or Mail Transfer Authority (MTA). The cost of email is based on the number of clients and servers being installed.

Both client and server email software requires a password entered separately from the NT logon. Server software requires a post office administrator password. At the server, an administrator may either add, change, or delete names and passwords of employees who can use the post office.

Since B&L is focusing much of its sales efforts toward the Internet, the company's email system must support a gateway to the Internet. The gateway must be a Simple Mail Transfer Protocol (SMTP) gateway that supports both the X.400 standard for messaging and the X.500 standard for addressing. To send email over the Internet, the user must access this gateway and type in the user's address on the Internet; for example, xyz@abccompany.com.

The email software selected for B&L must allow the sender to specify priority for each message. In addition, it must allow them to request a return receipt. A return receipt sends a message to the sender that contains the time and date that the message was delivered to the recipient's server. Specifying a "When Read" results in another message returned that contains the time and date of when the message was read by the recipient.

When a message is sent, it travels directly to the network post office. If the recipient is on the local LAN, then the post office sends the message directly to his inbox. It will be received by him the next time he logs onto his email account. If the recipient is not on the local LAN, the post office must forward the message across a WAN to a post office on another server that services the recipient. This function is usually named a Mail Transfer Authority (MTA). It is responsible for periodically sending message traffic out on the WAN to other post offices on other LANs. A post office administrator sets the frequency of the mail transfer. Depending on the volume of mail being sent and the message priority, the mail transfer is usually specified to occur anywhere from every 10 minutes to 4 times a day.

Once the message is delivered, the recipient must be able to perform the following functions:

- Read the message
- Save the message

- Delete the message

- Reply to the message

- Separate and save any attached files

- Forward the message to other email accounts

The email syetem selected for B&L must also be capable of automatically saving a sent message into a log file. This enables users to resend the mail message in case it was not received or was garbled in transmission. It is also a record of what was sent and when.

Because no email systems currently exist at B&L, a new email system can be purchased and installed without considering how to transfer existing data files. The new email system must be capable of meeting the needs of all three divisions—a system that is capable of supporting at least 300 users. And because the three divisions communicate over a WAN, at least three post offices and MTAs (one per division) must be installed.

## Server Requirements

As I stated at the start of this chapter, we will use the NT 4 Server as the operating system for all of our servers. In the B&L network, we see the need for servers that will perform the following functions:

- Mail server

- CAD applications server

- Database applications server

- Web server

- Primary domain controller server

- Print server

- Software distribution server

- Network administration server

While some of these functions can be combined into one hardware platform, many will require that dedicated servers be located at each B&L site.

## Workstation Requirements

As we also stated in the beginning of this chapter, we will use NT 4 Workstation as the operating system for each of the employees. While many of the people who will use these workstations could also be supported by either Windows 95 or Windows for Workgroups, these choices would incur additional costs in maintaining and updating several operating systems.

At B&L, only five workstations are configured to support NT 4 Workstation. This means that 178 existing workstations must be upgraded, and 74 workstations must be purchased. An additional five workstations should be purchased for spares. These are the reasons for selecting Windows NT 4 Workstation:

- The B&L selection must have the ability to run the various application software packages needed by the different divisions.

- The operating system (OS) must be able to execute MS-DOS applications. While most applications will be Windows compatible and use graphics rather than text operator screens, certain diagnostics and system recovery applications will be MS-DOS based.

- The workstation OS must possess the ability to implement and interact with domain level security.

- The workstation OS must be capable of running 32-bit applications.

- Many users at B&L expressed a desire to communicate, using a peer-to-peer connection, with other computers. They expect to frequently share files. The workstation OS must be capable of supporting multiple peer-to-peer connections.

- A single workstation OS reduces training and support costs because only one set of training is required for both user and LAN administration.

## Network Requirements

The B&L network doesn't include linking to other corporate networks. The new network will completely replace the one existing sales and administration network. This approach is both a help and a source of risk. The analysis shows that a 4 MB network is taxed at 60 percent. Therefore, you should make a more detailed analysis of the current network to avoid the mistake of under-specifying the required bandwidth. Currently, two databases and one CAD application use the network. The new network will support essentially the same traffic, and add email and file transfers.

## Product Availability

When a selection is made for either hardware or software vendor products, the product's availability is a major question. The products must first be available before they can be applied.

Also, many designers do not like to break new ground. Before you select a product or service, you will want to evaluate the proposed product, review benchmark results, and talk to previous customers.

In addition to products, any services that may be needed, such as cable plant installation, must be available to meet your installation schedule. Talk to your proposed vendors. If they plan to outsource any part of their work, then the subcontractor must be contacted to verify their availability to meet the installation schedule. If possible, you should consider using additional resources that can be employed in the event of schedule slippage or personnel unavailability.

## Equipment Availability within the Network

We must now look at another consideration for the success of the network. This would be the workstation, server, and software availability. It is important that you specify the standard usage of these facilities. For example, a workstation may only need to be available eight hours a day, five days a week. But, a server must be available 24 hours a day, 7 days a week. Planning backups, maintenance, available spare parts, and maintenance outages for the two types of computers is very different. A network plan for each server or workstation should include the following:

- User workstations should be backed up at least once a week.

- File and application servers should be backed up once a day.

- Failed workstations will be returned to service by substituting a spare device.

- Failed servers will be returned to service using spare parts.

- Servers should be configured using a fault tolerant disk system, such as RAID 5. RAID is an abbreviation for Redundant Array of Inexpensive Disks. There are six levels of RAID, from RAID 0 to RAID 5. Version 5 is the most cost efficient and offers the best protection from disk crashes. Many servers now sell RAID 5 as a standard disk configuration in servers. RAID 5 requires at least three disks of the same size. Any disk failure can be corrected by simply replacing the failed item with a spare. The RAID 5 hardware automatically reloads the new disk with files and applications. Many implementations of RAID 5 support a hot swappable spare disk drive that will be automatically started in the event of a disk failure. This reduces the need for maintaining shelf spares because a substitute is already in place—simply remove the failed component and mail it off for a quick replacement. Once a new disk is installed in the system, the spare drive once again becomes the hot swappable spare and the new disk is reloaded.

- Many servers are sold as Symmetric Multiprocessors (SMP). This means that a server may have from one to four microprocessors running the NT operating system. In the event of a processor failure, you simply remove the defective processor and replace it with a spare or restart the server to run, albeit more slowly. Newer servers will be capable of being configured with eight or more processors.

## Network Maintenance

During the planning stage, you must consider who will maintain the network after it is installed. Your plan should also include what tools will be needed. Too often, maintenance is not adequate due to money either not being budgeted or maintenance funding being used to offset cost overruns in other areas.

You should create a preliminary maintenance plan that will address the issues of spares, diagnostic software, and hardware that will be needed in the event of failure. You must assume that hardware will fail. Under this assumption, you can plan a strategy to rectify the failures:

- When a failure is discovered, what diagnostic tools will be available?

- If a component fails, what part of the network will be affected? A workstation failure may only affect the workstation's user, but a server failure may affect everyone.

- How fast must each component be repaired? Answering this question will help you determine which hardware spares will be required and what outside vendor maintenance contracts may be needed.

- Carefully consider warranty terms and limitations before purchasing hardware and software. The majority of vendors warranty their products for a period of time. What is the length of a warranty contract? Does the vendor include, or charge extra for, on-site support? What is the time window from a service call until someone shows up to repair an item?

- Many software vendors support users by posting fixes, patches, and new drivers on their Web pages. Do your selected vendors do this? If not, what are their policies for maintenance?

While manufacturers can assist in the support of their products, they often have a limited ability to support mixed-product environments.

Include schedule items for hardware and software burn-in. This period should be at least a week to identify and resolve hardware infant mortality or software incompatibility. This period should also include running the complete suite of diagnostics and performing the test plan.

## Risk Assessment

Figuring risk into your network planning is extremely important, because the areas of risk should be very carefully scheduled. For example, in the B&L network, the major risk is user acceptance. Many of the workers expressed deep misgivings due to their fear of possible job loss. Does this mean that they will not use the system or possibly work against a successful installation? Should security be increased to prevent intrusion and infections by viruses? Will the workers use the system to do their work? Will there be complaints that the system is too slow? Will they feel comfortable with workstation software? Will they back up files frequently? Any number of possibilities can be imagined. Management must be encouraged to support the project and encourage workers to use the network and workstations.

Include a Risk Assessment section in your network planning documentation. This approach will accomplish two things. First, you will be informing management that areas exist where they may be able to participate in order to try and alleviate unfounded employee fears. Second, you will be helping all personnel to understand that installing a new network is not simply a process of connecting a few wires and throwing a switch, but of coming together as a company in order to keep up with competition.

# Designing the Network

Once you've sorted out the user requirements, problems, and expectations, it's time to begin designing the network. Several alternative technologies can be used effectively at B&L. The basic design criteria is to purchase the best network service available within the allowed project budget. The next sections explore the various technologies and provide a brief explanation of each.

## *Network Topology*

A *network topology* refers to the cable plant design used to link the various network workstations, servers, hubs, and routers. The three most common cable topologies are the star, ring, and bus topologies.

A network topology is designed to meet the current network needs and also includes planning for both future enterprise growth and advances in technology. Designing the network around a well-designed cable plant will dictate how NT 4 will manage both workstations and the network's information flow. A well-designed cable plant also can influence network fault tolerance.

### STAR TOPOLOGY

The star topology, shown in Figure 6.4, is today's most commonly used network configuration. This type of LAN consists of cables radiating out in a star pattern from a central hub to every workstation or server in the network. This setup also includes printers and any other network peripherals.

The star topology is the most fault-tolerant design. A fault-tolerant design seeks a way around a failure in the network. The cable layout of the star makes it simple to upgrade equipment and to add new clients. The star is also the simplest way to manage and monitor network performance. If a workstation is unable to communicate, it can easily be switched to a new port, or a separate hub, for testing.

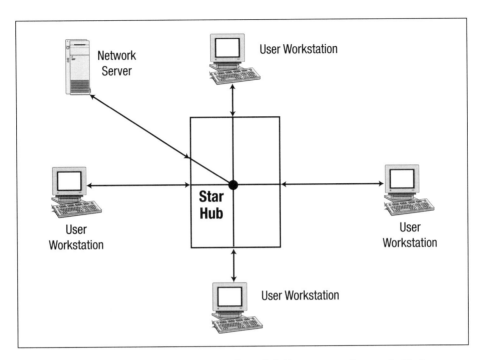

**Figure 6.4** The star topology connects each workstation or server to a central hub.

The star topology has one significant drawback, though. Because a separate cable must be run from each workstation and server to a hub, resulting cable costs are more expensive.

## TOKEN RING TOPOLOGY

The token ring is a true ring with a connection at each workstation client or server network interface card (NIC), as shown in Figure 6.5. Using this topology, a token is passed between the network clients, which allows them to talk to, or answer a query from, another network device. If a workstation or server fails, the network uses hardware relays to switch out the failed node. Some token ring networks are not configured with relays. So, if one workstation goes down, the entire network fails until that component is fixed. In this configuration, network failures are difficult to isolate. The token ring costs more than the star or bus topology.

## BUS TOPOLOGY

The bus topology comes in several flavors. The Ethernet thinwire media connects a coaxial cable between each network node, as shown in Figure 6.6.

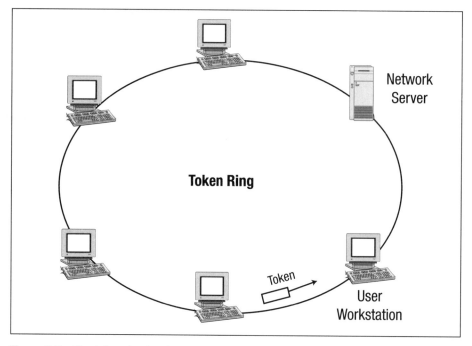

**Figure 6.5** The token ring topology connects each workstation or server to a ring.

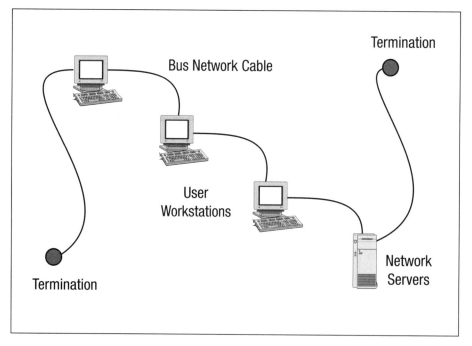

**Figure 6.6** The bus topology connects each workstation or server to a parallel bus.

Another coaxial cable connects to the next node, and so forth. The thickwire media uses a single, heavily shielded cable that runs throughout the facility. Each network node attaches to this single cable using a vampire tap. This is simply a clamping mechanism with sharp teeth that is used to pierce the cable's insulation and shielding.

The good news is that the bus is simple to use. The thinwire version is easy to install and requires less cable than either the star or ring topologies. The bus is easy to extend and terminate. However, network problems are hard to isolate and, by using the bus topology, network traffic tends to see more pronounced slowdowns during periods of heavy activity.

## *Cable Plant*

The cable plant forms the backbone of the network. The most efficient operating system in the world cannot overcome a poorly designed cable plant. This section describes several optional cable types and the differences among them.

## UTP

Unshielded Twisted Pair, or UTP, is the most commonly used cable because it is thin, flexible, and easy to handle. UTP cable can be efficiently installed behind plasterwall in offices and run in small conduit to cross open spaces. It's made from insulated strands of wire twisted together inside a plastic sheath. UTP cable is also called 10BaseT because it has typically been used in networks operating at 10 Mbps. UTP is designed to carry an unaided signal 300 feet. UTP cable is usually run between a patch panel and a wall plug.

To connect between the wall plug and the computer, a jumper cable terminated by two RJ 45 connectors is used. Each connector is slightly larger than a phone jack. UTP cable adds to the network fault tolerance. Unlike thinwire Ethernet, if a UTP cable breaks, it only affects the workstation, not the entire network. UTP cable is also much less expensive than coaxial cable.

UTP cable is rated as Cat 5, or category 5, and must comply with a separate standard, 568B. The 568B standard is widely used and specifies the following:

- Establishes a minimum set of cabling requirements to be used within an office environment. These requirements specify that all connectors and components must be tested and certified to the 568B standard.

- UTP cable is constructed using two pairs of insulated wire that are twisted together and bundled within an insulating plastic outer casing. Cat 3 and Cat 5 UTP are the two cable types typically used in LAN environments. Make sure the entire cable plant conforms to Cat 5 ratings, to ensure that the network can later be upgraded without replacing a majority of its physical plant cable and connector components.

Cat 5 cabling has a minimum of eight twists per foot and uses insulation that, when combined with the twist count, ensures higher speed performance.

The maximum allowable length for Cat 5 cabling used at the top network speed (155 Mbps) is 100 meters (approximately 300 feet). This length includes the total length of the cabling between the hub and the workstation, including patch cords.

## Fiber

Fiber cable comes in three different styles: single-mode, multi-mode, and composite. Fiber cable can support much faster network speeds than wire cable, but is also more expensive.

Single-mode fiber is created using 12 strand, 8.3 micron, loose-buffered fiber optic cable. It is recommended for all exterior segments. Multi-mode fiber is constructed using 4 strand, 62.5 micron, 125 mm fiber optic cable. This fiber will be connected to power drops. Multi-mode is essentially interior fiber cable. Composite fiber, as you may have guessed, is created using both single- and multi-mode fiber bundles. These bundles are combined in a plastic casing. The type of casing dictates whether the cable can be used as an interior or exterior cable.

For the B&L network, fiber is too expensive. It offers much better performance, but higher than average performance is not a prerequisite for this application. The network only requires standard 10 Mbps UTP.

## *Access Methods*

In any network, many will use resources across the network at the same time. LAN access is governed by widely accepted standards. These standards define how to send signals and regulate network traffic to reduce wait times and network congestion. Access methods are programmed into both the network and client operating systems. Every NIC has a specified access method built into the card. Some cards use daughterboards to give the cards different personalities and enable them to attach to LANs using different access methods. A daughterboard is a second printed circuit board that is connected to the first by either a cable or plug connector. You can exchange daughterboards to adapt the NIC to various networks.

The two access methods that we will consider are the token ring and Ethernet. The reason for these choices is that either method adapts well to the office environment with standard UTP wiring.

As we discussed earlier, the mechanism that gives the token ring network its name is a token, which is nothing more than a digital message that continually circulates in one direction around a physical network ring. If a token is passed to a workstation, and that workstation has a write queued, then its data is sent to its network destination.

On an Ethernet network, each network node monitors the network for traffic. If no traffic is currently using the network, then a node can use the network to transmit data. But, if two nodes try to transmit information at the same time, they each see a collision. If a collision occurs, then both nodes stop transmitting and wait for a statistically determined period of time before monitoring the network and retransmitting. On a heavily used network, collisions occur frequently. On long networks, a collision can even occur beyond the start of transmission. This is known as a late collision and is a result of the time electrons take to move down the LAN cable. At the moment that one node begins transmitting, the network is inactive. But, another node has actually already sent data. When that late data is received, you have a collision and, again, both nodes stop transmitting and wait. Collisions occur naturally and increase with network traffic. Ethernet is also known as CSMA-CD (Carrier Sense Multiple Access-Collision Detect).

Ethernet is currently the most popular access method. Cable plants running Ethernet can be constructed using thickwire, thinwire coaxial cable, or UTP cable.

Ethernet networks typically run at transmit rates of 10 Mbps, but newer installation can install a fast Ethernet that runs at 100 Mbps. Either speed can be used with a bus or star cable plant. Ethernet is the cheaper of the two access methods and the one I have chosen to install at B&L. We will use Ethernet running on a star topology, as shown in Figures 6.7, 6.8, and 6.9.

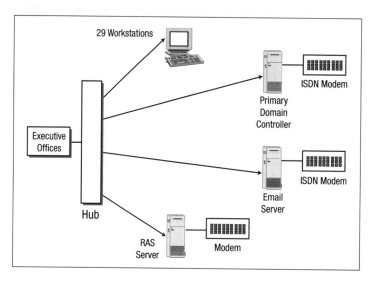

**Figure 6.7**  The Executive office's network connects 29 workstations to 3 networked servers.

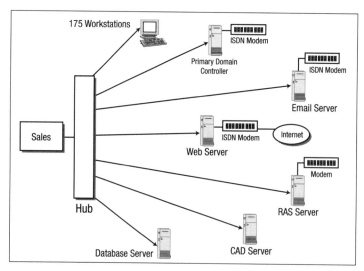

**Figure 6.8**  The Sales division's network design connects 175 workstations to 6 networked servers.

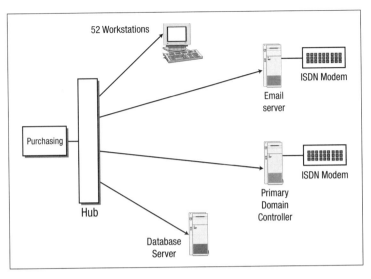

**Figure 6.9**   The Purchasing division's network design connects 52 workstations to 3 networked servers.

# Network Elements

A network consists of more than just servers and workstations. Many different elements are included as an outgrowth of the network design. This section expands the previous section to include active network elements.

## SERVERS

For each of the divisions, I have chosen a minimum of three NT 4 Servers to perform the following functions:

- An email server will be used as the local post office. All network users will be connected in order to receive email services. The email server will also communicate over an ISDN b line to the email servers located at the two other divisions.

- A primary domain controller (PDC) server will contain the security databases and be responsible for logging on any users attaching to the network either locally, over a RAS connection, or from one of the other two divisions using an ISDN communications line. The PDC is configured to perform the task of IP routing for the network. In the future expansion, a dedicated router will be used. The cost of using individual dedicated routers is too cost prohibitive for the initial stage.

- A RAS server will manage the remote users who dial into the server using a standard telephone line. Initially, this server will support five standard 28.8 Kbps modems. At a later time, the server will grow to support a modem bank of between 15 to 20 modems.

The Purchasing and Sales divisions will include an additional database server attached to the network to provide a platform for new database software applications. These applications are server-based and will be accessible by all network users.

The Sales division will also have a CAD server to supply an improved CAD application package to the Advertising department. This is an upgraded server and application package.

## HUBS

Hubs will be used at each site in order to connect the network in a star configuration. The Sales division will use several hubs to attach the larger number of connections. I've decided on a hub that has at least a 50 percent expansion capability to allow for future growth. When expansion time comes, B&L will simply plug new boards into the hub chassis and attach additional cabling.

## MODEMS

Modems will be used to perform the following tasks at B&L:

- The Executive and Sales divisions will use standard 28.8 Kbps telephone line modems to communicate between personnel traveling and the home division. Both divisions cited the need for frequent travel, with the traveler needing access to personal files and email.

- Each of the three divisions' email and PDC servers will use ISDN modems to communicate interdivisional network traffic. The email server regularly dials out to download stored email to the other divisions. The PDC uses the ISDN modem to allow personnel in the other divisions to logon and access files located in their respective domains. The domain security is designed using the Master Domain model. The executive office is the master domain and has established trust relationships with the two domains located at the Sales and Purchasing divisions.

The ISDN lines were selected based on the expected network traffic and cost. An alternative would be to install dedicated communications lines. Because the distances between divisions are significant, the ISDN solution is forecasted to satisfy network demands for the next three to five years.

- The Sales division will include an ISDN modem to connect the company's Web server to a local Internet provider. ISDN is configured to combine both b channels giving the Internet link a 128 Kbps rate. This setup will be adequate for the next three years.

## WORKSTATIONS

The 486/66 MHz workstations that are currently located in the Sales division will be upgraded to 16 MB of RAM with 1 GB hard drives, and each will be configured with a new 16-bit Ethernet NIC.

The five Pentium workstations at the Executive offices will be upgraded with 16-bit NICs. These workstations are more than adequate to run the NT 4 workstation operating system. The remainder of the B&L personnel will be supplied with new 100 MHz Pentium workstations that are configured at the factory. They will come standard with 16 MB of RAM and 1.6 GB hard drives.

The new configurations will be adequate to support Windows NT 4 Workstation through future corporate growth.

## PRINTERS

High-speed printers are attached to the PDC in every division. The Sales division will be configured with five printers to service sales and sales support personnel. The Purchasing division will be configured with three printers for use by the shipping and purchasing personnel. The Executive offices will be configured with two printers.

# Protocols

I decided on the TCP/IP protocol to be the standard network protocol at B&L because:

- TCP/IP was developed as a routable protocol. It serves as the standard for wide area networks and for access to the Internet.

- B&L is already connected to the Internet. Initially, only the personnel in the Sales division will have the necessary hardware and software resources to be able to connect to the Internet as clients.

- TCP/IP should provide the most flexible transport, no matter how large B&L's network grows.

- The Sales division's Web server will be assigned a specific Internet address by their selected Internet Service Provider.

## Laptop Portable Computers

Laptop computers are chosen as the platform for traveling B&L employees. The laptops chosen were 486/66 MHz computers with 16 MB of RAM and 1 GB hard drives. Each unit comes standard with an internal 28.8 Kbps modem, which is required for B&L dial-up networking. In addition, a pluggable LAN connector is included to allow the laptop computers to be able to connect to the local LAN while the user is in the office. These units connect to either the serial or parallel ports on the laptop and accept an RJ45 patch cord to connect to the LAN. The pluggable connectors are often slower than a standard NIC, but they double the usefulness of the user's laptop computer.

## LAN Management

Implementing a new LAN at B&L requires a dedicated staff of personnel to oversee and manage the installations at each of the three company divisions. The LAN staff, which will be comprised of two employee at each site, will be dedicated to the following tasks:

- Administer security on the primary domain controllers. This task requires a security administrator to coordinate user names and passwords between the system and the users. The security administrator is also responsible for establishing a security policy specifying the assignment of user rights to NT objects and resources, including remote dial-in capability.

- Manage the domain post offices. This task includes monitoring post office operations, troubleshooting problems, and verifying that mail is being regularly sent to, and received by, the other post offices. In addition, the post office manager must establish rules and regulations governing how long email will be maintained on the server and each workstation.

- Manage server-based applications and their client connections. This process includes verifying that new applications are compatible with existing operating systems and user workstations, maintaining current software revision levels, assisting users with software problems, and monitoring server usage.

## *Domain Security Design*

In this section, we'll discuss the design of the domain security. We'll take a look at each of the domain configurations and an example of each, expanding on our discussion in Chapter 4.

### TRUSTED DOMAINS

B&L is aware of the need for security and will benefit greatly by using the Master Domain model to administer domain security. The Master Domain model will be used to allow the overall network security to be administered from the Executive offices. As illustrated in Figure 6.10, the Sales and Pur-

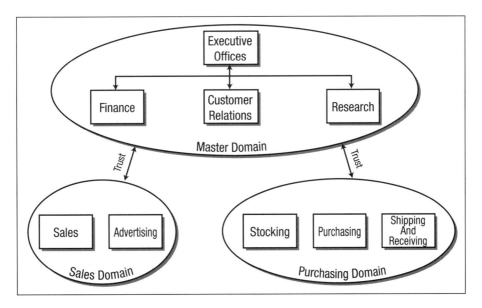

**Figure 6.10** Domain design includes trust relationships between Sales, Purchasing, and the master domain.

chasing domains have established bi-directional trusted relationships with the Executive offices' master domain. This allows all three divisions to intercommunicate for email and file transfer. An employee who normally works in the master domain may logon to a workstation at either of the trusted domains.

## SECURITY

Security is critical to managing B&L's network applications and internal, sensitive company data. Securing networked resources involves preventing unauthorized access to the networked system and resources, regardless of whether the jeopardy comes from internal user systems on your own network, or from remote systems.

I considered three primary factors when designing the B&L network security:

- The prevention of unauthorized access to the systems on the B&L network is accomplished by combining a heightened user security awareness with a well-managed security policy.

- Network security awareness begins with educating the B&L employees regarding the moral obligation each user has to protect both company and personal data. This includes protecting other employees' data from unauthorized access. A clear policy must be created that explains the differences between publicly available network resources and proprietary resources.

- Another important aspect of security education is an explanation to users of the role played by passwords (both to their accounts and to other restricted resources on the network). A surprising number of security breaches are the result of poor password selection and control. Adequate password security should include cautioning users to never give their passwords to others. They should be required to select passwords that are not tied directly to them, for example they should not use birthdates, spouse names, or other important (and well known) factors in their lives. Under NT 4 Server or Workstation, the User Manager for Domains enables the LAN administrator to manage passwords by requiring that all users change their password on the first logon attempt. This prevents anyone from accessing their account through the use of a default password. The LAN administrator should also enforce regular password changes. While many users do not welcome this policy, it definitely prevents use of your account by other people who temporarily know your password.

As we all know, networked information is not totally immune to unauthorized access. Whether the potential threat originates from a user at a system physically located on the network, or from a user at a remote Internet system, there are measures that B&L can take to minimize the likelihood that unauthorized intrusions will occur.

One step toward protecting systems is to compartmentalize access to data files on network workstations. This means that the security at B&L must restrict sensitive files from both unauthorized B&L company employees and outside users. NT 4 Servers and Workstations allow you to place restrictions on your individual files and applications. By using NTFS formatted drives, you can restrict or allow various levels of access. For example, you may specify that a file can only be modified by you, the owner, while allowing other user groups to only read it. Even further restrictions can prevent others from reading the file. B&L decided that the overall network security policy be established by the security administrator. The responsibility for restricting access to workstation files is the responsibility of every user.

Physically configuring the network in a manner that restricts access is a popular way to protect sensitive data on a network. This is typically accomplished by using a dedicated software application to perform data packet filtering. These applications are commonly known as *firewalls*. The firewall acts as a filter to permit only desired traffic to cross, while preventing undesired traffic. A firewall can be constructed to allow B&L employees to have full access to the Internet, while making the B&L divisions unavailable to unauthorized Internet users.

Another solution to ensure privacy of information is encryption. Encryption is the scrambling of binary data through either a hardware or software algorithm. The information passes through the network in this encrypted form and is decrypted via a similar mechanism once it arrives at its designated destination. This is similar to the encrypting done on cellular phones to prevent unauthorized eavesdropping by outsiders.

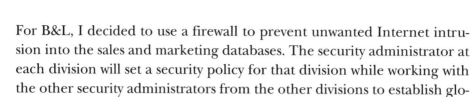

For B&L, I decided to use a firewall to prevent unwanted Internet intrusion into the sales and marketing databases. The security administrator at each division will set a security policy for that division while working with the other security administrators from the other divisions to establish global requirements and policies.

## Recovery Planning

Data backups and disaster recovery are a fundamental part of LAN design and management. Information is being created, sent, and received at B&L daily. While the value of this information may vary with time, you must design a backup and recovery system that will maintain the data in a recoverable state until its deletion is authorized. A well-maintained LAN must be equipped with regularly scheduled backups of critical data and files. Backups refer to copying files to a mass storage, usually removable disk or magnetic tape, that can be stored safely for a period of time. The primary backup is digital magnetic tape that can contain 20 to 30 GB of data in a single cartridge. Recovery is, for the lack of a snappier description, the process of recovering the stored data and restoring it to active use.

These considerations are important to backup and recovery operations:

*   *Backup Operations Schedule*—Backups to a storage media must occur on a regular basis. This process usually occurs at night, because backups require a large portion of the network's bandwidth, up to 60 to 70 percent. The hours of midnight to 5 AM are traditionally set aside to conduct automated backups.

*   *Backup Servers*—B&L will include a backup server as one of the standard three servers at each site. The server will be configured with a backup device—a Digital Linear Tape, or DLT, which holds 30 GB of compressed data. The other alternative, is Digital Analog Tapes (DAT), which are often prone to tape stretching and limits the life of each tape cassette. The server will also be equipped with a software application that will collect and move the backup files from their network locations to the tape. NT 4 has a built-in backup application. Other more sophisticated applications are available from independent software vendors (ISVs). The server loads the tape and then checks the contents against the source files. Finally, the server reports on the

backup job's status. In the B&L design, the email server will perform this role at all three divisions.

- *Replication between Servers*—Replication enables NT to automatically back up important files between a replication export server and a replication import server. The replication technique was first introduced on NT as the method that a primary domain controller copies user account information to the backup domain controller. In the B&L LAN, I use replication to move security data and critical data files between the PDC and the BDC. In this case, the BDC is also configured as the email server.

## Naming Services

The B&L network is considered to be a small network with the largest segment being no bigger than 135 users. However, even this size network requires that each workstation or server can find the address of a destination network device. This is why naming services were created. A naming service translates a network computer's name into an IP address and vice versa. In the B&L LAN, a Windows Internet Naming Service (WINS) is used to perform this function. The WINS service is installed on each network's PDC. In the B&L design, the WINS databases are replicated to the BDC, which, in the event of a PDC failure, will be promoted to become the domain's PDC.

# Installing the Network

The network installation phase is the point where planning and real-world equipment come together. The better the planning, the easier the installation, and the more frequently the job is delivered at or below budget.

## Cable Plant Installation

The cable plant is usually the first part of the network to be installed. Running cable, drilling through walls, installing conduit, and installing hubs and servers are time-consuming tasks. It is often very disruptive to the personnel working in the building. At B&L, the cable installers were assigned to a later shift to minimize interference with office personnel. This, coupled with careful attention to cleanliness, is important in developing user confidence. If the employee comes in and finds his desk littered with wall particle or insulation from the ceiling, support for the network will be undermined.

Cable plants are often run from the individual wall outlets into a room that is dedicated to housing the head end. A head end is the point where the individual UTP cables are terminated into a patch panel. The head end room at B&L also contains the hub, all servers, all modems, and the terminating point of outside telephone communications lines.

Cables are attached to punch down blocks in the patch panel. A punch down block is simply a jack that terminates the cable running from the wall socket. From the patch panel, they are connected to the hub via short patch cables. The reason for using a patch panel is to allow maintenance personnel to isolate problems by unplugging and switching patch cables between hub ports. It also provides an easy way to activate and deactivate the various office wall plugs.

Both workstations and network servers are connected to the patch panels and, subsequently, to hub ports, as shown in Figure 6.11. If a failure is

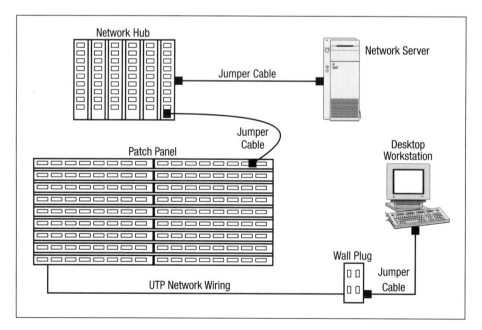

**Figure 6.11**    The cable plant connects desktop workstations through the patch panel to the network hub.

found at a wall plug, the cable installers can readily test the integrity of the patch panel, wall plug, and interconnecting cable runs.

## Personnel Training

All B&L users must be adequately trained in the use of both workstation hardware and software. In addition to the support from network administrators, training classes and Computer Based Training (CBT) courses are also encouraged. CBT training is an interactive course that runs on a computer workstation. CBT courses step users through an overview, a question and answer period, and a detailed information curriculum. They also provide the employees with reference and review information.

CBT courses can be installed on the employees' workstations to maintain their skill level long after the training courses have been completed. Another benefit of CBT courses is that they can be used to train new employees to a minimum skill level, until they can be scheduled for classes.

## Installation Testing

At the beginning of this effort, we created a detailed plan to install, configure, and test the network hardware and software. We must be certain to follow the plan and test each item as it is added to the network. This will help to avoid having to troubleshoot the overall network if a problem develops. Once the network is running, it is often difficult to isolate problems.

We need to run each part of the test plan until we are satisfied that the network components are performing to specification, paying special attention to the network security. We must make certain that each user can logon to the network quickly. Security problems are often among the worst problems to isolate and correct.

## Microsoft's SMS

The Systems Management Server (SMS) is a member of Microsoft's Backoffice solution. SMS runs on an NT Domain Controller platform and enables the LAN administrator to monitor, configure, and maintain software on the various servers and workstations attached to the LAN.

SMS is a Windows NT Server-based product that provides the LAN administrator the ability to manage software distribution, inventory hardware and software, and provide remote control capabilities. Using SMS empowers the LAN administrator with the following tools:

- *Software Distribution*—SMS allows software updates to be loaded to servers and workstations from a central location. This prevents the need for LAN personnel to physically install new software at each workstation every time there is a software update or new release. SMS software updates can be automated to occur after normal working hours to prevent excessive network traffic during the work day, which can slow down system response time.

- *Network Monitoring*—SMS includes the Network Monitor, which is a tool to capture and view network traffic. Using this tool, LAN technicians can diagnose network problems on either servers or workstations and monitor software updates to prevent possible workstation update problems. We'll cover the Network Monitor in more detail in Chapter 8.

- *Hardware and Software Inventory*—SMS provides an inventory of what software is loaded on which workstations and servers. This data enables the LAN administrator to accurately determine LAN requirements when purchasing new software updates or new software applications. The inventory of both hardware and software reduces problems associated with new software running on incompatible hardware platforms.

## Installation Documentation

Once the installation has been completed, there are basically two items we'll need to deliver to the B&L company. The first is a properly functioning network. The second item is the documentation library that records the network's planning, design, and installation. The final set of documentation will remain with the network and be used by future network administrators.

Items included in the documentation library are:

- A complete list of hardware, along with specification sheets for each item.

- Software manuals and documentation for each application and operating system installed on the network's workstations and servers.

- Paper and electronically created diagrams of the network topology.

- Workstation hardware and software configurations. This information should also be contained in the SMS server.

- Server hardware and software configurations. This information should also be contained in the SMS server.

- Security policies and a list of users.

- Planning documentation created during the project's planning stage.

- The test plan and a step-by-step record of the test plan's execution, including any problems found and resolutions implemented.

- An "As-Built" drawing of the final installed layout of the network physical components, including wiring, hubs, workstations, and servers.

- The selection criteria and any testing results associated with selecting the installed network hardware.

- The selection criteria and testing results made during the selection of all network software. This should include a location of servers or workstations on which the software is installed.

- A security policy, which is the record of what security decisions were made and which servers and workstations are affected by these policies.

- Documentation of the decisions behind making the choices for network design. This document includes any cost or performance records discovered during the design process.

## Maintaining the Network

The final phase of the project is the maintenance phase. At this point, the network equipment is bought and installed. The cable plant is installed and tested. The employees are using workstations and server applications through the network. Is this the end of the project? No, the project will continue until the daily list of problems is reduced to virtually zero. At

B&L, the maintenance personnel continue testing the network, actively looking for problems. They are tasked with answering user questions on a wide range of topics, from how to set the screen on the NT 4 Workstation to, "Why can't I get my mail?"

## Support Planning

The next step in network installation is to implement the network support plan that we prepared at the beginning of the project. A support plan simply assigns responsibilities for supporting the network—tasks and re-sponsibilities assigned to both in-house and third-party service companies. All support plans should cover the following situations:

- *Phone Support*—Phone support should be available during working hours. At B&L, these hours are 8:00 AM to 4:30 PM.

- *On-site Support*—Who is responsible for troubleshooting and repairing network equipment during normal working hours? What is their esti-mated time to respond to calls? Are there different levels of service, such as normal, high, and critical?

- *Spare Support*—B&L chose to buy additional workstations to allow net-work support personnel to replace failed workstations with spares. Several of the spare workstations have sufficient hardware to be able to operate as servers. Therefore, the servers, if regularly backed up, can also be replaced by the spare workstations. Spare parts represent a costly decision. But, if the system is not growing rapidly, judiciously selected spare parts and spare systems are effective in maintaining net-work components.

- *Off-hours Support*—You're working late in the evening to provide the boss with a badly needed report, and your workstation crashes. What do you do? Who do you call? Who is responsible? These are all ques-tions that every user should be able to answer. B&L has chosen a third-party support vendor to service off-hour calls. The third-party vendor has offices near B&L's in all three states. The name and phone num-ber of the vendor is taped to every workstation in all three divisions.

- *Emergency Server Support*—When a workstation fails, only one person is dropped from the network. When a server is down, many people are dropped. Therefore, many companies have special agreements with third-party repair vendors that require their personnel to be on site within 2 hours and have spare parts available and installed within 12 hours. This requirement puts the burden of stocking spares on the third-party vendor.

Each of these tasks is in response to failures that might occur once a month or, maybe, once every six months. However often, when they do occur, a fast response time to bring the network back up is critical.

## DEFINE THE SUPPORT OBJECTIVES

Establish support objectives from an end-user perspective and with consideration toward the company's organizational culture. Establish reasonable expectations and assure that processes are in place to achieve them. Include components for:

- End-user support

- Flow of information to user support engineers

- Support for end-user support engineers

- Response time

- Accountability

- Service levels

- Escalation paths

## The Role of Network Maintenance Personnel

Support personnel must be adequately trained in the technologies present in the new network. If the new network is to be considered a success, the employees must feel that it is an improvement over the old system. At B&L, only the Sales personnel have any direct experience with computers and a network. Their perception of how well the network meets their needs is often defined by their relationships with the maintenance personnel. Judgment is often based on how fast their problems get solved and how well their questions are answered. Network user confidence is also based on how well they have been trained to use application software. A majority of the maintenance personnel time can be reduced if users really understand, and are comfortable with, the software applications on their workstations.

Network technicians must be able to use the tools provided with the NT 4 standard release. We cover these tools in Chapter 7. NT 4 has an excellent set of tools to be used to diagnose both software and hardware failures. The tools also enable a technician to monitor the network for upcoming operation problems, such as slowdowns and impending hardware failures. Sometimes, parts fail with no warning. Usually, though, an NT 4-knowledgeable technician can spot a future problem days before it actually occurs.

## The Role of the Help Desk

Following the network installation, designated service personnel will be responsible for maintenance. Many organizations use service personnel to staff a "Help Desk" where a user may call in with a problem and one of the service personnel will answer questions about the user's problem. If a problem is determined to exist, then a serviceperson is dispatched to the user's location to fix the problem. The help desk may consist of two or three people, or it may be constructed in layers. The first layer answers the user phone calls and, through a scripted question-and-answer session, determines if the problem is real or caused by the user. If the problem is determined to be real the user is passed to the second help desk layer. The second layer is responsible for more detailed analysis of the complaint and, if unable to fix the problem, a serviceperson is dispatched to the user. Some companies have two or three layers, with each layer being more and more specialized.

## The Training Plan

The training plan should be based on the following:

- Amount of training time and budget available for each student

- The relative skill level that each student needs to acquire

- The relative level of experience and skill that each student has before training

- The availability of computer training equipment and classroom space

Many outstanding courses are available from external sources and third-party training vendors who conduct regular classes in specific locations.

Many of these training vendors will conduct an on-site class based on a minimum number of students who will attend.

## Conclusion

In this chapter, we discussed one approach to network planning based on several years of personal experience installing networks. The six basic steps to network planning should always begin by first talking to the users. The success or failure of any network project begins with how comfortable the employees will feel about using the new network technology. Proper planning always helps to make the users more comfortable. If a plan is drawn up that clearly itemizes the tasks, project goals, and features that the network will have, then the installation and maintenance phases will go more smoothly. If planning and user requirements are forfeited in lieu of installing only the newest technology, no one will be satisfied. NT 4 is a versatile part of the network that, if properly used, can reduce network costs and increase overall network performance.

PART

3

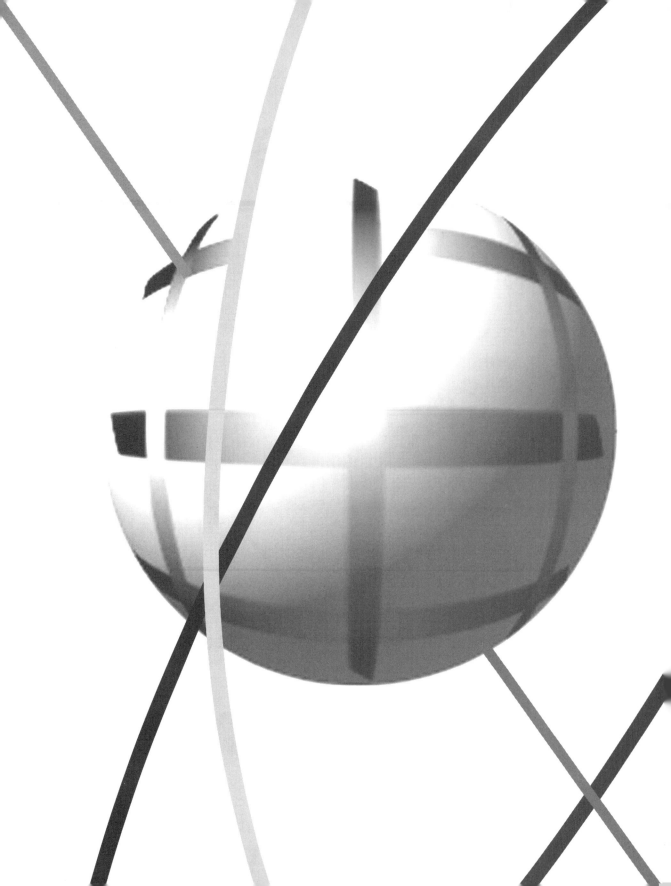

# Built-In Maintenance

**M**aintenance. I can't stress it enough. Even those of you who are new to networking know that maintenance is the key to a long and productive network life. As you know quite well by now, NT 4 contains a wealth of features and capabilities. However, when one of the features or capabilities doesn't work, or is improperly configured, it is often difficult to detect the problem, let alone find the cause.

In this chapter, we are going to examine four of NT 4's maintenance tools. These tools, which come standard with NT 4, are useful for identifying, diagnosing, testing, and verifying problems you might be experiencing with your system's performance and operation:

- Performance Monitor (also called Perfmon) comes standard with all NT 4 workstations and servers. Performance Monitor is available in the Start|Programs|Administrative tools directory.

- Network Monitor (also called Netmon) is available in the Start|Programs|Network Monitoring directory of the NT 4 server.

- Microsoft NT Diagnostics is available in the Start|Programs| Administrative tools directory of both NT 4 Server and Workstation.

- NT 4 Task Manager (also called Taskman) is accessible by using the Ctrl+Alt+Delete keys and then clicking on the Task Manager control button on the resulting screen.

Each of these tools is designed to provide an insight into NT 4's operation but from different perspectives.

# The Performance Monitor

The Performance Monitor, which has been included with NT since its first release (3.1), is very useful in diagnosing both local and network NT operational problems through the use of monitoring objects. Each object's performance, which is determined by a number of variables, is captured in a Registry counter and made available to the Performance Monitor user.

The Performance Monitor can also be used to measure network traffic and actual performance, and to identify bottlenecks.

Performance Monitor is not a single utility. It is really four utilities combined under one name:

- *Charting Utility*—Displays multiple performance variables in either a line or bar chart format. The line chart automatically includes a history of the object over a configurable period of time. The bar chart shows the object's performance captured in an instance of time.

- *Alerting Utility*—Monitors a configurable set of variables and tests each variable against a threshold value. If the variable's value either exceeds or falls below a threshold, Performance Monitor displays the alert on the screen and can run an executable program, if one is configured.

- *Logging Utility*—Captures and logs the values for one or more objects. (Remember, each object contains multiple variables.) The logging function captures this data at configurable intervals of time. The captured data is then automatically saved into a specified log. When the logging is completed, the contents of the log can be charted using the charting utility.

- *Reporting Utility*—Can be configured to display object variables captured at specified time intervals. This utility only reports an instantaneous value for each variable.

These utilities, which I'll describe in detail in the following sections, are all selectable from the initial Performance Monitor display screen. Each utility displays its own unique screen and set of configurations. All of the configurations can be saved and reused later.

Performance Monitor also accepts (in any of the four utilities) configured objects and their variables from multiple computers over the network. This is a very useful feature because, many times, abnormal activity in one of the network computer can be the source of problems. To discover this type of problem, you may have to compare the level or volume of activity to diagnose which computer is causing the problems.

Performance Monitor allows you to specify a sampling period—from 1 to 9999 seconds—for each of the utilities to collect data. Performance Monitor internally counts down the sampling and, once it reaches zero, captures the variable data. After the sample data has been acquired, the timer is reset to the configured value. Of course, Performance Monitor's sampling accuracy is a function of the number and location (local or network) of the computers being sampled. I have found it to be accurate within a scale of +/- one minute for multiple variables from network computers. To increase the sampling accuracy, run Performance Monitor only on the local computer and limit the number of variables being sampled.

Performance Monitor also allows you to export the sampled data as either TSV (Tabbed Separated Variable) or CSV (Comma Separated Variable) ASCII files. Both the TSV and CSV formats can be imported into a spreadsheet or database. In this format, the data is stored in a flat file with each data variable being separated by either a tab or a comma. The end of a sample is terminated by a carriage return (hex 0d). Exported files contain a date and time stamp associated with each of the data samples. This stamp shows exactly when the sample was taken. Other information contained in the exported file includes the source computer, object, and data variable contained in each sample.

**TIP** If you regularly transfer exported Performance Monitor files to a database, such as Access or Paradox, you can develop database reports, which you can use to characterize a computer's or network's operational performance over a period of time. The only limitation is the amount of storage that you can allocate to the database. You can use changes to the computer's performance profile to support the need for expansion, indicate growth, or serve as an early warning of a developing problem.

## Charting Utility

The Performance Monitor charting utility is used to graph—as a line chart or a histogram chart—specified NT object variables. Let's look at the line chart first. This chart can simultaneously display many variables over a configurable period of time. Using the line chart enables you to observe the behavior of a variable as a function of time. In other words, the line chart is a historical view of the variable. The variable's history becomes important when you are looking at repetitive behavior. As an example, let's suppose that every night your system experiences a flood of broadcast messages. By using the Performance Monitor line chart, you can identify, in realtime, when these messages occur and for how long a period they last. Another feature of the charting utility is the ability to configure the chart to accept data from a source other than NT. The charting utility can then display the data stored in a Performance Monitor log. I'll discuss this aspect later in the chapter.

The second type of graph is the histogram chart, which is a comparison chart that displays instantaneous values of one or more selected variables. Each variable is displayed as a bar in the histogram. Although this type of chart contains no history, it does allow you to measure the relative activity from more than one computer. We'll continue with our broadcast message example. You have identified the time period when the broadcast message traffic starts. To discover which of the network computers is contributing to the broadcast traffic at the time indicated by the line chart, activate the charting utility (we'll talk about how to do this later in the chapter) and configure the chart to display a histogram. Next, select the network segment object from each of the suspect computers. Finally, monitor each one for the number of broadcast packets during that time period. The histogram will show an increase in their relative activity and then identify one or more of the computers as the prime suspect. I'll cover these types of problems in more detail later in Chapter 8, *Testing and Trouble-shooting the NT Network.*

## CHARTING OPTIONS

To use the Performance Monitor charting utility, you must first configure the chart options shown in Figure 7.1. This menu contains the following user-selectable options:

- *Legend*—Specifies whether a list of variables will be shown at the bottom of the chart's screen.

- *Value Bar*—Displays a selected variable's last, average, min, max, and graph time values, beginning with the first sample. The status also shows the chart's displayable time period. This value equals the sample rate of the chart multiplied by the number of the chart time periods (which is 100). The time period shown on a chart with a sample frequency of 300 seconds is 30000 (the equivalent of 500 minutes or 8.33 hours).

- *Vertical Grid and Horizontal Grid*—Displays a grid on the chart.

- *Vertical Maximum*—A configurable setting for scaling a chart. The default range for a chart is 0 to 100. Each variable chosen has an individual default scaling value that can also be configured. These two features allow you to see the details for all the variables at the selected

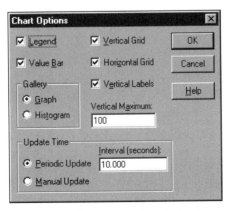

**Figure 7.1**  Use this menu to specify Performance Monitor's chart options.

scale. Only the maximum is shown because the minimum is always zero. The vertical maximum default is 100.

- *Vertical Labels*—Displays the vertical scale on the left side of the chart. The scale that is shown always starts at zero and extends to the selected vertical maximum.

- *Gallery box*—Contains two radio buttons to specify the type of graph desired: line chart or histogram.

- *Update Time box*—Contains two radio buttons that specify when charted variables are updated. The Periodic radio button specifies that the charted variables are to be sampled at the period specified in the Interval text box. The text box value is always in seconds. The Manual radio button indicates that the variables are updated manually by selecting the camera icon on the tool bar.

## LINE CHART

Let's take a look at a sample line chart. Figure 7.2 shows the minimum and maximum percentage variable sampled manually over a five-minute period. The variable shown at the bottom of Figure 7.2 contains the following elements:

- Name of the variable (minimum and maximum percentage)

- Scale (1)

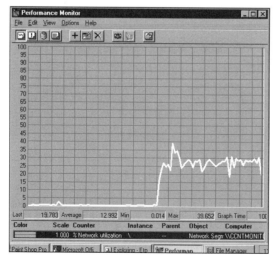

**Figure 7.2** A network utilization sampled manually over a five-minute time period.

- Counter name, which is contained in the Registry (network utilization)

- Instance (1)

- Parent (none)

- Object (the network segment)

- Source computer (CCNTMONITOR)

Each variable is shown in a different color and line type. To distinguish a specific variable, use the backspace key on your keyboard. The selected variable's color will change to white. I have not yet found a limit to the number of variables that can be simultaneously configured, but an upper limit must exist. However, a practical limit exists for displaying variables. When too many variables are added to a chart, the chart becomes over-crowded and the important variables lose their significance.

## HISTOGRAM

Figure 7.3 shows a histogram chart comparing the percentage capacities for the four different processors contained in CCNTMONITOR. Although Performance Monitor doesn't label the individual bars on the graph, the bar on the left is processor 0 and the bar on the right is processor 3. The chart indicates that processor 0 is performing at 25 percent of its rated

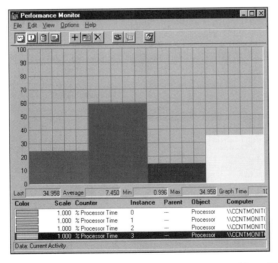

**Figure 7.3** This histogram displays the current percentage capacities of the processors in CCNTMONITOR.

capacity to execute the current work load, processor 1 is running at about 60 percent of its rated capacity, processor 2 is running at 15 percent, and processor 3 is running at 35 percent capacity.

## ADDING VARIABLES TO THE CHART

Figure 7.4 shows the menu for adding variables to a chart. To add a variable, you must complete the following steps:

1. Choose which computer to add to the graph.

2. Select an object that is supported on that computer.

3. Select which variable(s) or counter(s) contained within that object should be displayed.

   Appendix B contains a complete list of NT 4's objects and variables. You can also use the Performance Monitor context-specific help screen, shown in Figure 7.4, to better understand the NT variable represented by the selected counter.

4. Choose which instance of that variable is to be used.

5. Choose the color that Performance Monitor will use to display that variable.

6. Choose the scale that Performance Monitor will use on the chart.

7. Choose the width of the line displaying that variable.

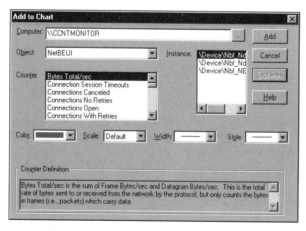

**Figure 7.4**    Use the Add to Chart menu to specify which variables should be added to create a new chart or to append to an existing chart.

8. Choose the line style to be used.

9. Save the chart's configurations and settings by selecting File|Save.

*Instance* is the only item that we haven't discussed. Performance Monitor differentiates between the instance of each variable you select. For example, the histogram shown in Figure 7.3 displays four instances (0 through 3) of the same variable. Each instance represents one variable out of several that can be displayed.

**TIP**

To choose which instance to display, add the four to a chart and observe their individual behavior. Then, choose which instance best describes the variable that you wish to monitor.

## *Alerting Utility*

Alerts allow you to maintain constant surveillance parameters. Each alert measures a variable's captured value against a predefined alert threshold. Alerts are useful to you in several ways. First, they can be used to start a program to control NT or one of its tasks in the event that a major variable exceeds a threshold. Another use involves starting a second instance of Performance Monitor in order to capture data at a different frequency. Remember our broadcast message problem? Once the network utilization exceeds a threshold, say 40 percent, another instance of Performance Monitor's logging utility can be started to collect broadcast message traffic at a faster rate. For example, while the alerting utility is running at a 5-minute sampling rate, the logging utility can log these values at a 10-second sampling rate. This provides for a more detailed analysis of the problem without adding to the broadcast traffic.

Figure 7.5 shows the alert configuration menu that provides the controls needed to configure each alert.

### ADDING AND CONFIGURING AN ALERT

To configure alerts, perform the following steps:

1. Choose which computer to add to the alert.

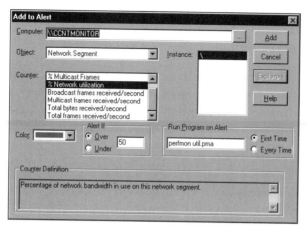

**Figure 7.5**   Configuring an alert includes a mandatory variable choice and alert threshold.

2.  Select an object supported on that computer.

3.  Select which variable(s) or counter(s) contained within the object is to be included in the alert.

4.  Choose which instance of that variable is to be measured against the threshold.

5.  Choose the color that Performance Monitor will use to display that variable on the alert screen.

6.  Choose the threshold value that Performance Monitor will compare against the variable's value.

7.  Choose the "Alert if" value for Performance Monitor to use in comparing the value and threshold, such as *if the variable reads >50 (%) then alert* or *if the variable's reading is <50 (%) then alert.* To specify the variable's range (upper and lower threshold), two alerts must be used to correctly specify the variable.

8.  If required, choose a program to be run in the event that the variable exceeds the configured threshold.

9.  Choose whether this program will run every time the threshold is exceeded, or only the first time.

10. Save the alert settings, including the variables and their thresholds, by selecting File|Save.

As in the chart configuration screen, the individual variables are defined in Performance Monitor's context-sensitive help.

The alert screen, shown in Figure 7.6, shows the date and time that a sample was taken, the sampled value of the variable, the threshold, the name of the variable, and the name of the computer from which it was sampled.

## Logging Utility

Performance Monitor's logging utility samples data from a set of configurable objects and stores their values in a log file. The logging utility captures an entire Performance Monitor object, including all of its variables, at a user-configured sampling rate. The log file itself has virtually no user interface. You must configure the charting utility to display the captured log by specifying that the chart will read from a log file. To do this, select Options|Data from the Perfmon pull-down menu. A screen appears allowing you to enter the location and name of the log file. Once the log is selected, the chart allows you to specify one or more objects and variables from the limited list contained in the log file. The data can then be exported to either a TSV or CSV file.

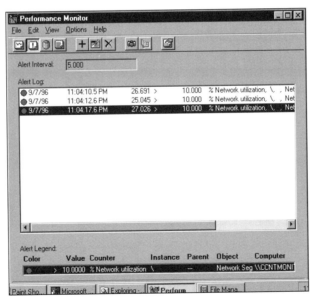

**Figure 7.6** The alert screen shows that the alert variable has exceeded its alert threshold.

You may include as many objects as you wish in the log file. The major limitation is the storage required by the log file. The amount of space is a function of the log's sampling frequency and the number of objects being logged. Once you have configured a log file, click on Performance Monitor's camera icon. The logging screen will show the log file's size jumping from zero to a higher value. The amount first shown in the file size data box is the amount of disk space that each subsequent sample will take up. For example, if the file size is 1000 K, and the sampling frequency is set at 10 seconds, the file will grow by 1000 K every 10 seconds. Whether or not these numbers become significant to you will depend on the amount of disk space you have available to store the log file.

## CONFIGURING A LOG FILE

To configure a log file, perform the following steps:

1. Using the chart's configuration menu, select which computer(s) will be sampled to the log file.

2. Once all of the computers have been selected, select View|Log from the pull-down menu. A screen similar to the one shown in Figure 7.7 will appear.

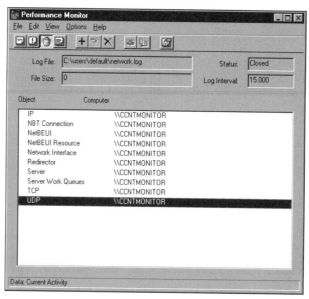

**Figure 7.7** The logging utility's main screen shows the log specifications.

3. Click on the + toolbar button to add an object. A menu similar to the one shown in Figure 7.4 will appear. This menu will allow you to choose objects from one of the computers previously attached to Perfmon.

4. Select the computers and their associated objects that will be logged. Again, the individual variables are defined in Performance Monitor's context-sensitive help. Once the computers and their associated objects have been specified, you must configure the log options.

5. Click on the options button (the right-most control showing a hand pointing to a page) on the toolbar. The log options menu will appear.

6. Enter the directory that will be used to store the log file in the Save in text box.

7. Enter the name of the log file in the File name text box.

8. Select either the Manual or Periodic update radio button from the Update Time box. If you select Periodic, be sure to enter the number of seconds between each sample in the Interval text box.

9. Click on Start Log to begin logging.

10. Click on Save to save the log file.

11. After leaving the log options menu, select File|Save to save the log's configuration into a PML file.

Once you've finished entering the settings, minimize the Perfmon logging screen (Figure 7.7) to continue logging. If you choose to close the log, you will automatically stop the logging function. The log file will then remain unchanged until it is reopened.

The log may be read at any time with another instance of the charting utility.

## *Reporting Utility*

The Performance Monitor reporting utility displays sampled data in a report format. This report shows you the last scanned value for each variable. A report is most useful as a follow-up reading of the variables following an alert or to combine data from a selected set of variables on the same display.

## Configuring the Reporting Utility

To create a report, perform the following steps:

1. Using the chart's configuration menu, select which computer(s) will be sampled to the log file.

2. Click on the + button on the toolbar to add objects to the report.

3. From the resulting menu, choose objects from one of the computers you previously attached to Performance Monitor in Step 1.

4. Select which computers and their associated objects will be included in the report. Once the computers and their associated objects have been specified, you must then configure the report options.

5. Click on the options button (the right-most control showing a hand pointing to a page) on the toolbar. A menu will appear that contains options to control updates and the sampling frequency, as shown in Figure 7.8. I recommend selecting the Manual update option, as the report continuously changes with each sample taken.

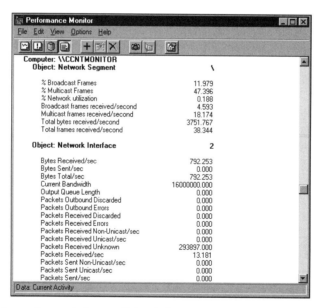

**Figure 7.8** A sample report shows a Network Segment object and a Network Interface Object.

6. Save the report configuration by selecting File|Save. The report configurations are saved as a PMR file.

# The Network Monitor

Network Monitor is a network diagnostic tool that is included with NT 4 Server. The first release of Network Monitor was included in the release of Microsoft's Systems Management Server (SMS). Network Monitor performs many of the same functions as a third-party network analyzer. As shown in Table 7.1, a network analyzer is a dedicated hardware tool that is easily adaptable to multiple types of networks, physical cable plants, large capture buffers, and higher speed operations. Although Network Monitor is limited by the computer host it runs on for its network access and speed, it is easy to operate and can be quickly configured and set to capture data.

**Table 7.1  A Comparison of a Typical Network Analyzer and Microsoft's Network Monitor Software**

| Analyzer | Network Monitor |
| --- | --- |
| Captures network traffic to a large memory file | Captures network traffic to a memory file; the size of the memory file is dependent upon its host computer's memory configuration |
| Displays the data capture file to the screen | Displays the data capture file to the host computer's screens |
| Data is time stamped | Data is time stamped |
| Data contains protocol information | Data contains protocol information |
| Data contains header information | Data contains header information |
| Data contains protocol flags | Data contains protocol flags |
| Data can be displayed as hexadecimal or ASCII data | Data can be displayed as hexadecimal or ASCII data |
| Captured data includes packet errors and error types | Captured data includes packet errors and error types |

*(continued)*

**Table 7.1    A Comparison of a Typical Network Analyzer and Microsoft's Network Monitor Software (continued)**

| Analyzer | Network Monitor |
|---|---|
| Easily adaptable to multiple physical networks, such as Fiber optic, 10 baseT, thin | Uses the network and protocols configured to its host computer; to use another physical network type, another NIC must be installed in the host |
| Configurable capture filters | Supports a limited set of capture filters |
| Configurable display filters | Supports a large set of display filters |
| Easily adaptable to many network speeds | Depends on its host computer's NICs speed |
| Configurable trigger settings | Supports a limited set of trigger settings |

Network Monitor operates under the NT 4 operating system and will run with either Server or Workstation. To operate Network Monitor correctly, the computer platform it is running on should contain at least 32 MB of RAM. This is due to the memory capture file. Once a capture file fills up, it will overwrite the existing data (with a subsequent loss of data). Network Monitoring requires a substantial capture file to allow it to capture a broad spectrum of network traffic. The bigger the capture file, the bigger the memory must be in the computer that is running Network Monitor.

Network Monitor can run on one or more NT workstations or servers. It must be able to cross the network to obtain data from network computers. This is accomplished by installing a Network Monitor agent on any computer to be interfaced to Network Monitor. Network Monitor directly interfaces across the network with monitoring agents installed in the NT protocol stack of the network computers. Network Monitor and the networked agents interact to capture network traffic monitored at the local (Network Monitor) computer or at any of the network computers.

Network Monitor's main screen is comprised of the four tiled windows shown in Figure 7.9:

- Network Graph

- Session Statistics

- Station Statistics

- Total Statistics

Each of these windows can be displayed individually or collectively by checking the appropriate settings in the Window pull-down menu.

## *The Network Graph Pane*

The Network Graph pane, shown in Figure 7.10, contains five bar graphs. Each bar graph displays an instantaneous reading of a single value. These are:

- *% of Network Utilization* —This value describes the amount of network bandwidth currently being consumed. Remember, a network's real-world limitation is always lower than its published specifications.

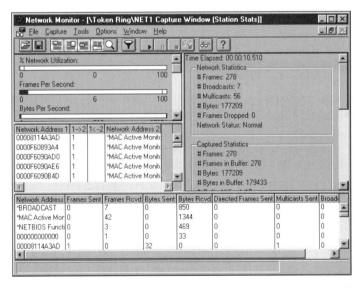

**Figure 7.9**   The main Network Monitor display screen shows network traffic in four separate panes.

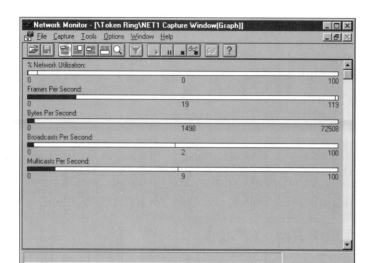

**Figure 7.10**    The Network Graph pane displays a set of instantaneous statistics, presenting an overview of current network traffic.

- *Frames Per Second*—The number of frames being transmitted on the network.

- *Bytes Per Second*—The number of 8-bit bytes being counted on the network in one second.

- *Broadcasts Per Second*—The number of broadcast packets Network Monitor has counted on the network in one second.

- *Multicasts Per Second*—The number of multicast packets counted on the network in one second.

The Network Graph pane provides a quick look at the network. The principal points of interest on the graph are the % of Network Utilization and the number of Broadcasts and Multicasts being captured. If these values are high, your network may be supporting too much nonessential traffic.

One nice feature of the Network Graph pane is the sliding line that defines the highest reading captured on each scale (such as the Broadcasts Per Second scale, which defines values from 0 to 100). The current value is 2, and the sliding bar indicates that a reading of approximately 50 was taken since the start of Network Monitor operation.

## The Session Statistics Pane

The Session Statistics pane displays a summary listing of the conversations between various hosts. The hosts are listed as 1 and 2. The heading 1>2 shows how many bytes are being sent by host 1 (the column on the left), to host 2 (the column on the right). The heading 1<2 shows the reverse—host 2 sending data to host 1. In Figure 7.11, the hosts on the left are transmitting traffic, and the hosts on the right are not responding. This is an indication that this traffic is either UDP or consists of broadcasts and multicast transmissions.

The Session Statistics pane is useful in detecting a host that is dominating the network. Figure 7.11 shows an undominated network where no single host is transmitting large blocks of data.

## The Station Statistics Pane

The Station Statistics pane, shown in Figure 7.12, displays a summary of the total number of frames started by each host shown in the Network Address column. The host transmissions are shown with the number of frames, bytes sent and received, and the number of broadcast and multicast frames started.

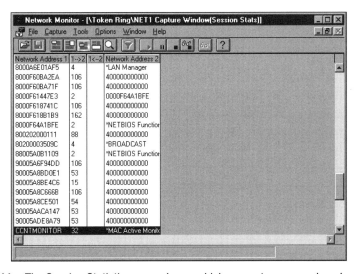

**Figure 7.11**  The Session Statistics pane shows which computers are exchanging data, each shown by its MAC address.

| Network Monitor - [\Token Ring\NET1 Capture Window(Station Stats)] |
| --- |
| File   Capture   Tools   Options   Window   Help |

| Network Address | Frames Sent | Frames Rcvd | Bytes Sent | Bytes Rcvd | Directed Frames Sent | Multicasts Sent | Broadcas |
| --- | --- | --- | --- | --- | --- | --- | --- |
| *BROADCAST | 0 | 2356 | 0 | 795012 | 0 | 0 | 0 |
| *LAN Manager | 0 | 47 | 0 | 2815 | 0 | 0 | 0 |
| *MAC Active Mor | 0 | 1591 | 0 | 50912 | 0 | 0 | 0 |
| *NETBIOS Functi | 0 | 391 | 0 | 94846 | 0 | 0 | 0 |
| 00008114A3AD | 37 | 0 | 1184 | 0 | 0 | 37 | 0 |
| 0000F60893A4 | 38 | 1 | 1233 | 49 | 1 | 37 | 0 |
| 0000F6090652 | 59 | 11 | 3652 | 1040 | 19 | 37 | 3 |
| 0000F60908EA | 100 | 62 | 5847 | 9176 | 61 | 37 | 2 |
| 0000F6090AD0 | 158 | 122 | 9917 | 12233 | 118 | 37 | 3 |
| 0000F6090AE6 | 39 | 2 | 1300 | 112 | 1 | 37 | 1 |
| 0000F6090B4D | 44 | 0 | 1520 | 0 | 0 | 44 | 0 |
| 0000F6090C7E | 37 | 0 | 1184 | 0 | 0 | 37 | 0 |
| 0000F609126D | 38 | 2 | 1243 | 114 | 0 | 37 | 1 |
| 0000F609150D | 79 | 41 | 34382 | 41429 | 39 | 37 | 3 |
| 0000F6093711 | 37 | 0 | 1184 | 0 | 0 | 37 | 0 |
| 0000F6093A1D | 42 | 5 | 1505 | 314 | 3 | 37 | 2 |
| 0000F6093B22 | 1064 | 487 | 269837 | 59734 | 619 | 37 | 408 |
| 0000F6093E06 | 41 | 4 | 1432 | 236 | 3 | 37 | 1 |

**Figure 7.12**   The Station Statistics pane shows an overview of the network traffic, including frames, bytes, and broadcast transmissions.

The Station Statistics pane is useful for comparing the number of bytes transmitted and received by each host. Again, if a single host is dominant on the network, its byte counts will drive up the network's percentage utilization. In Figure 7.10, the % Network Utilization graph shows only a small (<10%) use of the network, indicating that the dominant host is not a problem.

## The Total Statistics Pane

Figure 7.13 shows the Total Statistics pane. This pane displays statistics describing the traffic detected on the network, including frames captured, per second utilization statistics, network adapter card statistics, and the number of frames currently in the Network Monitor capture buffer. These statistics are captured as a function of time. In the upper-left corner of Figure 7.13, Network Monitor shows the Time Elapsed value: 2 minutes, 35.739 seconds. Network Monitor is reasonably accurate to the millisecond.

The Total Statistics pane is useful for overall monitoring of network activity, managing the capture file, and spotting errors.

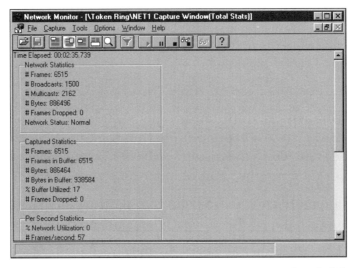

**Figure 7.13** The Total Statistics pane shows an instantaneous overview of all the network's traffic.

## Installing the Network Monitoring Agent

Before the Network Monitor can sample data from an NT 4 workstation or server, you must install the Network Monitoring agent as part of that computer's network protocol stack. To install the agent, follow these steps:

1. Select the Network icon from the Control Panel, and then select the Services tab.

2. Click on Add, then select the Network Monitor agent from the scroll down list. NT will add the agent to the computer's protocol stack.

3. Shut down and reboot the computer.

Once it has restarted, the Network Monitor will be able to capture information from the agent.

## Creating a Capture Filter

From virtually any viewpoint, network data appears to come and go at random, with many protocols mixing with multiple sources, destination addresses, and message types. Network Monitor is designed to help you differentiate between the seemingly random data passing over the network.

Network Monitor can capture traffic by:

- Capturing all of the network data and using a display filter to sort out which packets are meaningful.

- Limiting its capture to data defined by a capture filter.

- Capturing network traffic until a specific trigger event occurs. You can create a custom capture trigger to stop capturing data after a specific event. Once the trigger has been identified, Network Monitor will shut down the capture mode and await operator action.

To create a capture filter, select Capture|Filter from the menu. Network Monitor will then display the capture filter configuration screen.

In Network Monitor, you can determine the direction that data takes as it crosses the network. This means that the filters you create can specify whether data flowing into or out of a specific device will be captured. The data direction can also be set to capture packets that are being either transmitted to or from a specific address. The data direction enables you to see just the data coming into your computer, without having to capture all the data being transmitted on the network.

The capture filter can be thought of as a mask that uses four configurable parameters—network addresses, protocols, patterns, and direction—to sort network traffic. Let's look at these in more detail:

- *Network Addresses*—If addresses are configured in the capture filter, Network Monitor will test each network packet for the appropriate MAC address. If the traffic contains the appropriate addresses, it is then collected in the capture buffer.

- *Capture Protocol*—Capture filters can be configured to capture only packets that match specified protocols.

- *Capture Patterns*—Capture filters can be created to match packet data against a specific pattern found inside the packet.

- *Direction*—Network Monitor can see the packet's direction, whether it is being transmitted to or from a network computer. This feature allows you to isolate a particular workstation by either address, protocol, patterns, or direction in order to observe only the data flowing into or out of that computer.

Now, let's look at what we have to do to create these filter settings.

## ADDING CAPTURE ADDRESSES

You can design a capture filter to specify frames that are sent to or from a desired address. All of the computers that you have included in your filter are listed on the line in the Capture Filter decision tree that begins with INCLUDE. When two computers are included in the decision tree and a relational operator appears between them, they become an *address pair*. For example, the line ABC → ANY in a capture filter tells Network Monitor to capture all packets that the ABC computer sends to any other network computer.

To add a capture filter address, follow these steps:

1. On the toolbar, click on the Filter button (the button that resembles a funnel).

2. Under Add, click on Address to display the Address Expression menu. The Address Expression menu displays the list of computer addresses that are currently stored in the Network Monitor's address database.

3. In the Station 1 box, select either a computer address or the word ANY. ANY translates to any address seen in Station 1 as being acceptable to the capture filter.

4. In the Station 2 box, select the second computer that you want to include in the filter. You may again choose ANY.

5. In the Direction box, select the direction of data traffic that you want to monitor. Select the right and left arrow to specify frames that travel in either direction between the addresses specified in the Station 1 and Station 2 boxes. Select the right arrow to capture frames that travel in only one direction between the computers specified in the Station 1 and Station 2 boxes.

6. Click on the Include button if you accept the addresses and direction specified. Click on the Exclude button if you want the filter to ignore data from the specified addresses and direction.

7. Click on Edit to change the addresses in either the Station 1 or Station 2 boxes. Network Monitor will display the Address Database to allow you to add, change, or delete one or more addresses contained in that database.

8. Click on OK to complete the capture filter.

 **TIP** If a capture filter contains an EXCLUDE statement, it will nullify an INCLUDE statement. This simply means that if a packet meets the capture filter's EXCLUDE requirements, Network Monitor will not capture the packet, even though the packet may also meet the requirements of one or more INCLUDE statements.

## ADDING CAPTURE PROTOCOLS

You can use a capture filter to specify only network frames using the protocols that you specify. All protocols that you include in your filter are listed on the line in the Capture Filter decision tree that begins with SAP/ETYPE=.

To enable or disable a protocol, follow these steps:

1. On the toolbar, click on the Filter button (remember, it resembles a funnel).

2. Highlight the line that begins SAP/ETYPE, and then select Line from the Edit box.

   The Capture Filter Protocol menu appears. This menu displays two boxes. The top box contains all of the enabled protocols. The bottom box contains only disabled protocols. The filter default enables all protocols.

3. To disable a protocol, select an enabled protocol, and then click on the Disable button. To disable more than one protocol, hold down the Ctrl key and click on all the protocols you want to disable. Then click on the Disable button. To disable all protocols, click on the Disable All button. Click on OK to return to the Capture Filter menu.

4. To enable a protocol, select a disabled protocol, and click on the Enable button. To select more than one protocol to enable, hold down

the Ctrl key while selecting the protocols protocol, and click on Enable. To enable all protocols, click on the Enable All button. Click on the OK button to return to the Capture Filter menu.

5. Verify that you have made the appropriate changes to the filter.

## ADDING CAPTURE PATTERNS

Capture patterns limit Network Monitor to saving only those frames that contain a specific pattern of data. To add a capture pattern, follow these steps:

1. On the toolbar, click on the Filter button.

2. Highlight the Pattern Matches line, and then select Line from the Edit box.

3. Enter a hexadecimal number in the Offset box to specify how many bytes into the frame the pattern must occur. To start the search for the pattern at the beginning of the frame, select From Start of Frame. To start the search for the pattern beyond the topology header, select the From End of Topology header.

**TIP** If you have as much of a problem with hexadecimal data as I do, remember that you can use NT 4's calculator in the scientific mode to convert decimal to hexadecimal and vice versa.

4. In the Pattern box, type the pattern that you want to match. You can enter the pattern in either Hex or ASCII. Be sure to select the appropriate Hex or ASCII control on the menu.

5. Click on the OK button to return to the Capture Filter menu. Verify that the patterns line has been changed to reflect your configuration.

## *Setting a Capture Trigger*

A trigger is an action that is carried out when a specified set of conditions is met. Before using Network Monitor to capture data from the network, you can set a trigger to either stop the capture or to execute a command file. If you use the Network Monitor agent to capture remotely, you can set a trigger on the remote system. If this trigger involves the execution of a program or batch file, the execution will be invisible to users of the remote system. Execute triggers that you set on a remote capture always execute on the remote system.

## CREATING A CAPTURE TRIGGER

Lets begin by creating a trigger:

1. Select Capture|Trigger to display the Capture Trigger menu, which is shown in Figure 7.14.

2. To initiate a trigger for a particular pattern, select Pattern Match. To create the pattern match, use the procedure shown in *Adding Capture Patterns.*

3. To initiate a trigger when a specified percentage of the capture buffer is filled, select Buffer Space. In the Buffer Space group box, enter the maximum percentage of the capture buffer that must be filled before initiating the trigger.

   You may create a trigger that combines events, such as selecting Pattern Match and Buffer Space. This combined trigger will cause Network Monitor to continue looking for a specified pattern until the capture buffer is filled to your specified level. Once filled, it will stop capturing data.

4. Specify the action to be taken by Network Monitor once the trigger has been matched. To do this, enter a trigger action in the Trigger Action group box. The default is No Action. If you only want to stop

**Figure 7.14**    The Capture Trigger menu contains the controls needed to configure a Network Monitor capture trigger.

the capture, choose Stop Capture. If you wish to execute a file, select Execute, and enter the path to the executable file.

5. Click on OK.

An excellent use of the trigger feature is to stop a Performance Monitor capture log when an event has occurred. Performance Monitor can log data to a recoverable file for a much longer period of time than the Network Monitor can update a capture file. The Network Monitor's capture file is located in RAM, whereas the Performance Monitor's log file is located on a hard drive. A very handy feature of Performance Monitor is that it can store a log file on either a local or remote drive. The cooperation between Network Monitor and Performance Monitor can be extremely helpful when troubleshooting random errors or a flawed sequence of events.

## CAPTURING DATA

Data capture with Network Monitor is fast and easy. Just follow the steps shown here:

1. Create your capture filter.

2. Create a capture trigger, choosing 100%. This value will stop the data from overwriting itself in the capture buffer.

3. Select Capture|Start to begin the capture process. You can also depress the F10 function key to start the capture.

4. Capture statistics will appear in each of the four capture window panes.

5. To stop a Network Monitor capture file, press Shift+F10.

6. To stop the capture process and view the data from the capture buffer, select Capture|Stop and View. This will stop the capture and immediately display the capture buffer on the screen.

 The Network Monitor's capture buffer is located in RAM for purposes of speed. Select the computer containing the most RAM to run Network Monitor and increase the buffer size beyond its default setting of 1 MB.

## Buffer Settings

The amount of data that Network Monitor can capture is dependent on the size of the capture buffer. When you start the Network Monitor, its default buffer size is 1 MB. A good working buffer size is 10 MB or, if possible, even higher. The Microsoft NT Diagnostics Resources tab (Administrative Tools|NT Diagnostics|Resources|Memory) allows you to view the amount of available memory. Use this information to determine the capture buffer size. The Memory tab contains a detailed account of how NT is using both the physical RAM and the virtual memory. The key decision is to provide Network Monitor with as large a capture buffer as possible, without causing NT 4 to page out the memory. If paging starts, you will lose captured frames.

The number of data bytes that are captured per frame is strictly dependent on the problem you are trying to solve. If your problem involves data corruption or a specific data sequence, then you must try to capture as much data as possible. Many network problems are a function of protocols or specific addresses. For these types of problems, you should limit the amount of data captured to protocol information.

### CONFIGURING THE CAPTURE BUFFER AND CAPTURE DATA BYTES

To configure the capture buffer, follow these steps:

1. Select Capture|Buffer Settings to display the Capture Buffer Settings menu.

2. Modify the capture buffer by entering a new (hopefully higher) buffer size in the Buffer Size box. Be careful! If you set the buffer size to exceed the amount of physical RAM, frames will be dropped due to swapping RAM memory to the page file.

3. To change the number of data bytes captured per frame, select a frame size from the Frame Size box.

4. Click on OK to finish the settings and return to the main Network Monitor menu.

## Saving Data

If you want to save the captured data, choose File|Save. A Save Data As dialog box will appear allowing you to select which drive and directory to use for saving the data. Using this same dialog box, you will also name the captured data file. The capture file's default extension is .CAP. I recommend keeping the default. If you change it, you will need to reassociate the new extension with the Network Monitor.

## Printing Captured Data

While the saved capture files are useful, you can only load them into the Network Monitor. If you wish, you can export the captured buffer data into a text file. Once it is in the text file, you are free to apply formatting and use the advanced tools available in your word processor. You can also print all or part of the captured data. Perform the following steps to print the captured data buffer to a text file:

1. Display the capture file in the Frame Viewer window. (For instructions on how to do this, see *Working with Captured Data* later in the chapter).

2. Select File|Print from the Network Monitor's pull-down menu to display the Print menu, which is shown in Figure 7.15.

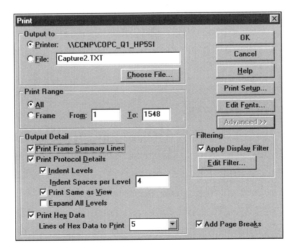

**Figure 7.15**    The Print menu contains the controls needed to print all or part of the captured file to a printer.

3. Specify the destination for printed output into the Output box.

4. If you choose the Printer radio button, the printout will be sent to your default printer.

5. Choose File|Print to display the Get Print Filename menu. From this menu, select the desired print file.

6. Under Print Range, enter how many captured frames are to be printed.

7. Choose All to print the entire capture file, or choose Frame to print a range of captured frames. For the latter, you must enter the starting frame number in the From box and the ending frame number in the To box.

8. Configure your printer's settings, and pick the fonts that will be used.

9. Click on the Advanced button to set printing options, including applying the current Display Filter to the capture buffer that is being printed.

10. Click on OK.

## Exporting Captured Data

To save the captured frames to a text file, follow these steps:

1. Select File|Save As.

2. Enter the file name and choose the Text File (TXT) format to export the capture file. Apply the existing display filter to save a selected subset of the capture file.

3. Click on OK.

## Setting Display Filters

Once you've captured network data, you might want to search through the capture file for specific addresses, protocols, and properties. The bad news is that a capture file can contain thousands of captured frames. The big question is *how do we find the correct set of desired frames?* Well, as you know, Network Monitor uses a capture filter to specify which frames to capture. The good news is that it also uses a display filter to select which frames to display. The Create Display Filter menu is very similar to the Capture Filter menu.

You can specify a range of addresses, protocols, and/or patterns to sort out the captured data. To create a display filter, use the same techniques that we used to create a capture filter.

## Working with Captured Data

You use the Frame Viewer window to display captured information. You can display the Frame Viewer window by following these steps:

1. Select Capture|Stop and View.

2. On the toolbar, click on the Display Captured Data button to display the Frame Viewer window, as shown in Figure 7.16.

This window contains three panes: Summary, Detail, and Data. The Summary pane displays a row and column listing of the data contained in the buffer. This information includes names, MAC addresses, IP addresses, and the protocol for each frame. The Detail pane contains a detailed listing of a specific packet (or frame). The packet's internal envelope detail is segmented into an information tree. The branches of the tree are dependent on the type of protocol that the packet uses. The Detail and Data panes are linked to the Summary pane. When you are working in the Summary pane, you use the cursor control keys to move through the listing,

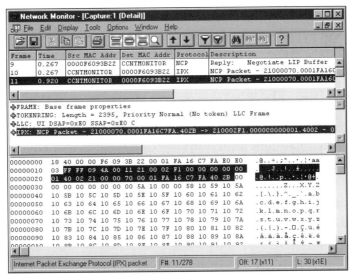

**Figure 7.16** The Frame Viewer window contains three panes, each presenting a view of the data contained in the capture buffer.

row by row. As you select each row, the displayed information changes in the Detail and Data panes. This design allows you to stay coordinated and easily step through the buffer in order to access all of the information contained in any of the panes.

The Data pane contains a listing of the data contained in the packet (in both hexadecimal and ASCII). The Data pane is also linked to the Detail pane. As you move through the Detail pane, the data associated with the protocol is automatically highlighted.

The Frame Viewer window is an excellent way to review the contents of the capture buffer. However, you can also export the data to a text file and use a word processor to find specific data.

# Microsoft NT Diagnostics

The NT Diagnostics application is a standard part of the NT Toolkit. To start the NT Diagnostics application, select the Administrative Tools|NT Diagnostics. The diagnostics package will collect data as it loads. This means that the various tabs will contain up-to-date information when you open them. NT Diagnostics' predecessor, Microsoft System Diagnostics (MSD), was first introduced in Windows 3.1. In that operating system, the MSD was little more than a tool to verify configuration. With each new release of 16-bit Windows and NT, the diagnostics became more sophisticated. The new Microsoft NT Diagnostics release, in addition to showing the system configuration, also provides an excellent view of operational statistics. The network statistics are quick to use and comprehensively describe the system's network health. Performance Monitor's reporting utility serves the same function.

NT Diagnostics has built-in networking capability. Select File|Select Computer to display a dialog box that allows you to enter any of the network workstations or servers on which you have administrative privileges. This means that from your desktop NT 4 workstation, you can observe the configuration and statistics for any of the NT 4 computers on your network. As you can see, this is a very powerful feature.

The diagnostics package contains nine tabs. Because we are talking about networks, I will be discussing just two of the tabs: Network and Resources. They are the principal screens associated with network operation.

## *The Network Tab*

The Network tab contains the following four screens:

- *General Screen*—Contains an overview of your computer's network security.

- *Transport Screen*—Contains a list of your transport interface cards with their MAC addresses.

- *Settings Screen*—Contains a list of the current network options from the NT Registry, as shown in Figure 7.17. This list is not complete; in order to see the complete list, you must use the scroll bar or print the Settings screen by clicking on the Print button.

- *Statistics Screen*—Contains a continuously updating list of NT 4's network statistics, as shown in Figure 7.18. Again, the list shown is not complete. You must scroll the list because it contains several screens of data. In this screen, pay particular attention to the error codes. While the number of bytes sent and received are important numbers, the error counts will identify a potential network problem quickly. Because the NT Diagnostics utility is network compliant, use it to trace inter-computer communications problems.

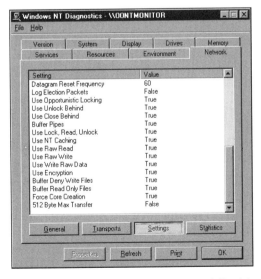

**Figure 7.17**   The Settings screen contains the current network Registry settings for the selected NT 4 computer.

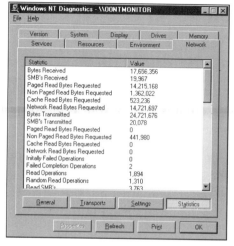

**Figure 7.18**   The Statistics screen shows a continuously updated list of the network indicators for the selected computer.

## The Resources Tab

While the Resources tab does not directly present network information, it does show the internal workings of the NT 4 operating system. As shown in Figure 7.19, you can use this tab to check on the basic operation of each

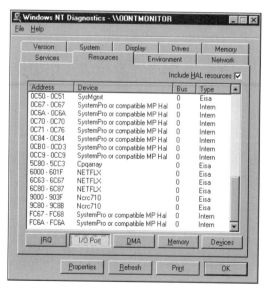

**Figure 7.19**   The Resources tab shows an overview of the internal connections for the various system and I/O components.

network computer. The Resources tab provides several control buttons that present various views of NT 4's internal resources:

- IRQ, or Interrupt Request, control produces a list of the system components and their individual interrupt levels.

- DMA, or Direct Memory Access, control lists those components that are using DMA to transfer data to and from memory.

- Memory control shows the amount of physical RAM currently configured by NT 4. This screen also lists the amount of virtual memory available and its current size.

- Devices control shows which devices are connected to the computer and their current operating status, such as running, stopped, etc.

# The NT 4 Task Manager

The Task Manager, another of NT's maintenance tools, allows you to manage the applications, processes, and general performance of a particular computer. You access the Task Manager by simultaneously depressing Ctrl+Alt+Del and clicking on the Task Manager option. The Task Manager contains three tabs: Applications, Processes, and Performance. Let's take a brief look at each of these tabs.

## The Applications Tab

The Applications tab displays a list of the currently loaded applications. As shown in Figure 7.20, the computer has four applications loaded: File Manager, NT Explorer, Paint Shop Pro, and the Microsoft Office Shortcut Bar. All four of these applications are Running, as opposed to Stalled or Stopped. This tab also contains three controls buttons—End Task, Switch To, and New Task—which enable you to manage your currently running tasks and/or start new tasks.

## The Processes Tab

The Processes tab displays a list of all the processes that are currently running on your machine, as shown in Figure 7.21. The processes shown include all of the background tasks and services that NT is operating.

**Figure 7.20**   The Applications tab lists the tasks that are currently loaded.

**Figure 7.21**   The Processes tab displays a list of executing processes and a summary of the resources they are using.

In addition to the name of the process, this tab contains the following information:

- A process's identification (PID).

- The percentage of the central processing unit (CPU) that each processor is currently using.

- The total amount of CPU time that each process has used since the computer was restarted.

- The current memory usage of each task. This information is useful in spotting processes that continue to occupy more and more memory. These are commonly known as memory leaks. A memory leak is created by a process that increasingly demands more memory resources without ever returning the memory to the operating system. I will discuss memory leaks in more detail in Chapter 8.

## The Performance Tab

The Performance tab contains several graphs that show the current and historical use of your CPU memory resources. In addition to the graphs, the tab includes four boxes containing summaries of process information and various views of NT 4 memory. In Figure 7.22, the system shown is using few CPU and memory resources.

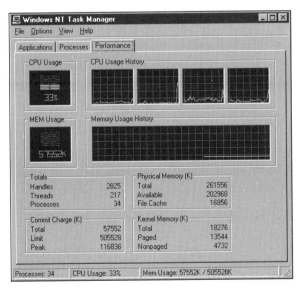

**Figure 7.22**   The Performance tab displays up-to-date operating system information in a graphical format.

# Conclusion

NT 4 comes standard with many diagnostic and performance monitoring tools. The NT Resource kit includes additional tools and utilities. In this chapter, I have described four tools that come standard with either NT 4 Workstation or Server.

We have reviewed Performance Monitor, a utility that can monitor NT 4's internal and network operation. Performance Monitor should be actively used when the network, servers, and workstations are performing normally. During this time, you will learn to understand what a normal operation really looks like. This knowledge is extremely helpful when problems occur.

We also reviewed the Network Monitor, which is a utility that helps you to make sense out of the apparently random network traffic. You can trap specific events and monitor the network traffic into and out of individual network computers. This tool can be extremely helpful when troubleshooting random network problems, such as bad Network Interface Cards or routers.

The Microsoft NT Diagnostic utility is a quick-look utility that provides an immediate array of information concerning system and network operation. The utility is network friendly, meaning that it can connect to any computer running the NT 4 network operating system, anywhere on the network.

The NT 4 Task Manager is a built-in utility that shows you precisely what applications and processes are running on a computer. Using the Task Manager, you can monitor network processes to view their operation and consumption of computer resources.

These tools are important because they offer a way to see inside your computer's operation. They will monitor, test, and verify NT 4's operation. Without such tools, you would have to resort to the old trial-and-error approach to fixing problems. While this approach might be credible for a single computer, it would become impossible when troubleshooting hundreds of computers, routers, bridges, and other components on a network.

# 8

# Testing and Troubleshooting
# the NT Network

In Chapter 7, I introduced you to several of the many tools that are built into NT 4. In this chapter, we'll concentrate on using these tools, plus a few others, to diagnose typical network problems. But first, let's cover some basic troubleshooting philosophy.

Although the network is running, it may not be running at its optimal performance level. Is that so important? Not if you are satisfied with the performance and your network customers aren't complaining. If a network is operating to everyone's satisfaction, why bother investigating it? Well, for one, if you don't monitor and understand the network's normal performance, how will you ever know when it's working correctly? Too many LANs are run on the firefighting principle where a day with no complaints is a day of sunshine. Preventative troubleshooting requires that you get to know your network's performance and be able to quickly detect any change in its operation.

There are two types of troubleshooting: hard breakdowns and soft breakdowns. The first type involves finding and fixing a hard component breakdown, such as a server that will not respond to the network. The second type, the soft breakdown, is exhibited when a component does not perform to its specification, such as an Ethernet LAN that exhibits too many late collisions. We will cover both types of troubleshooting in this chapter.

One major observation has been voiced in the network industry concerning network problems: Today's networks have become more complex and, proportionally, so have their problems. It has never been easy to track down communications problems because there are so many variables. But when you extend those networks across the country or around the world, problems can become a virtual nightmare (pun intended).

In this chapter, I will concentrate more on network troubleshooting philosophy than on solving actual problems. I'll provide a number of generic troubleshooting examples for us to examine. Unfortunately, I have had the misfortune of experiencing *all* of the examples shown in this chapter while using NT during production LAN operation. Production LAN operation occurs when the LAN is being accessed during the normal work day to access file servers, applications servers, and transport files during three daily production shifts.

# Identifying Network Performance Bottlenecks

Network bottlenecks are often hard to detect and can affect network operations in subtle ways. The approach I recommend is to break the network problem into its component parts. Assume that any network client/server problem has three parts: the client, the network, and the server. Any of the three can be either a cause or an effect of a bottleneck. In the first example, I will show you a network problem that required a review of all three parts. In the second and third examples, I'll cover other potential bottlenecks.

## Case History #1: A Limited Network Slowdown

We'll begin with an example of a common network problem. A single client communicates daily with a server and experiences slow network response while using his server-based application. He began experiencing this problem two weeks ago, and it occurs seven days a week. The slowdown occurs only during the early afternoon, never in the morning or after 4:00 PM.

This section includes three theories on the cause of the slowdown. The order of these theories is based on what I consider to be the most logical approach to the problem, checking the probable causes in order. Of course, because this problem started two weeks ago, the absolute first thing to do is to check the records for any changes that were made at that time, to the workstation, server, or the network. Unfortunately, no such changes are documented. (Nothing comes easy!)

Let's look at a detailed analysis of this problem.

## THEORY #1: I BET IT'S A NETWORK PROBLEM

Because the network traffic is higher in the afternoon than in the morning, the user may be experiencing normal *out of bandwidth* delays. If Theory #1 is true, the first place to start is to monitor the network's utilization during the afternoon. Use Performance Monitor, and view the Network Segment object. Be sure that you include all of the counters contained in the object. The counter that is the best indicator of network over-utilization is the *% of Network Utilization*. The other counters in this object provide you with an overview of what traffic is utilizing the network. Performance Monitor's objects are contained in Appendix B of this book. You may find it helpful to review the objects as you follow along.

In this case, the network utilization is less than 15 percent during the afternoon. This means that (% * bandwidth(bps)/# of average bits per byte = (0.15 * 10,000,000)/10 = 150,000 bytes per second are crossing the network. The Network Segment object reports that the *Bytes/Second* counter shows the byte traffic during the user's slowdown is 148,000. That's close enough to conclude that Theory #1 is not the likely problem.

## THEORY #2: MAYBE IT'S A CLIENT WORKSTATION PROBLEM

The client's workstation may be the source of the problem since he is the only one reporting the difficulty. An investigation into his workstation can be conducted by both Performance Monitor and Network Monitor from anywhere in the network. Configure Performance Monitor using the System object, Memory object, and Network Interface object to monitor and collect data from his workstation. You should also include the Network Segment objects from another network computer that is functioning properly. This approach will provide a means of comparison.

Using the Performance Monitor logging utility, you can monitor these events for a single day or an entire week. The objects selected will allow you to see NT 4's CPU and systems operation right at the client's workstation. You will also be able to see any possible memory problems, along with any network traffic generated by or to his workstation. The chart in Figure 8.1 shows the results of the workstation monitoring. Specifically, the workstation is idling, with a CPU utilization of less than 15 percent. Network traffic generated by the workstation is very minimal (<100 bytes per second), and the total network utilization is again less than 15 percent. The workstation's virtual memory remains relatively constant throughout the day. The paging file does not appear to be abnormal, with paging occurring at a one page per second rate.

With the information gathered thus far, it doesn't appear that the slowdown is related to the workstation being overused. Since the client is able to use the network without any problems during other times of the day, it looks like Theory #2 is ruled out.

## Theory #3: It Could Even Be a Server Problem

By looking at the data that was gathered and ruling out Theories #1 and #2, there is only one part left to explore. The problem has to be with the

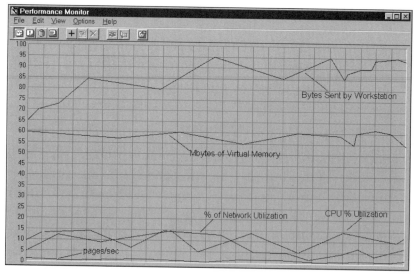

**Figure 8.1** Performance monitoring chart of the client's workstation for the entire day (24-hour period).

server. But the applications server supports 15 users during a 24-hour period. Only three of these users (one on each of the three shifts) are clients for the application that was reported as being too slow. The other 12 users randomly access the server during the period of time that the problem occurs. So, there appears to be no more than a single user connected to the server during the problem period.

At this point, even the server doesn't appear to be a promising candidate for the problem. As you know, though, appearances often can be deceiving. So, let's configure both Network Monitor and Performance Monitor to the server and log the results for a full day.

During the 2:00 PM time frame, using the Network Monitor, we find very little network traffic being sent to or from the server. We log the server's internal operation through the System object, Server object, Network object, and Memory object.

During the day, the server's CPU utilization from the System object fluctuates between 5 percent and 70 percent, with the peak percentage occurring in the early afternoon. During the time period between 12:00 PM and 3:00 PM, the server's memory begins paging at a rate of 25 and peaks at 125 pages per second. The Server object's bytes total/second, for both of the servers, transmit and receive traffic at 200 bytes/second. During the period when the CPU utilization is highest, the network traffic at the server decreases. This indicates a possible slowdown in service during this period.

From these readings, we can assume that the server's resources are being used by one or more internal processes starting around 12:00 PM. Checking the services that are running, we find that the schedule service is working properly. Next, we must investigate the WinAT GUI, which schedules timed processes, command files, and events to occur at different times. The schedule service has no process starting at 12:00 PM. The only WinAT scheduled activities are three application processes that start at 12:00 AM.

From our command console, we review the event log for the two-week period and find no red stop events. But we do discover yellow cautions every day for the last two weeks. This tells us that the Timeservice was not able to reach the Timeservice server. Therefore, the server's time of day has not been updated for at least two weeks. We next check the time of day on the server and find that it is 12 hours off.

We restore the server to the correct time of day and restart the Timeservice. The user does not experience any further slowdowns while using the application. We've solved the problem.

OK, you're probably thinking that this was a relatively easy problem. But it does point out several items of importance:

- Don't depend too heavily on automation software to discover hidden problems. The NT 4 event log did its job by presenting a cautionary alert that the Timeservice was no longer able to receive an updated time. This was missed because, in the past, a small application program was used to scan only for critical (red) alerts in the log.

- Check the server's operation daily, or at least weekly, to catch impending problems before they begin to affect network operations. Because the network disruption wasn't severe and only affected one user during specific times of the day, the error could be a simple problem with the user's workstation. The network utilization during the problem period was low. The server's offset time over utilization posed only a temporary slowdown and wasn't noticed. This shows how easy it is to be lulled into a period of complacency by making incorrect assumptions.

- We need to update the event log scanner program and configure the Performance Monitor Alert utility to check the CPU utilization and Memory paging on all servers around the clock. This way, if any server's level of activity exceeds a threshold, an immediate alert is received.

This problem is an example of how to apply the necessary tools, along with a systematic approach to solving network problems. In this example, the bottleneck was the server's resources.

## Case History #2: The Intermittent NIC

A network running eight production application servers is running slowly. During the nightly backups to tape, the servers intermittently fail to answer the software application that monitors their operation at one-minute intervals. There are no user complaints that the network is running too slowly.

This time, I'll provide two theories to account for the problem. Again, the order of these theories is based on what I consider to be the most logical approach to the problem.

## THEORY #1: AN INCREASE IN NETWORK UTILIZATION

The first thing that comes to mind is that the network is experiencing delays due to higher than normal traffic.

We check the traffic logs for the last month and find that during the backup period (3:00 AM to 6:00 AM) there is high usage when the backup server downloads the files to tape. We connect Performance Monitor to the network and log several 24-hour periods using the Network Segment object. While the nightly traffic is showing a high percentage of utilization during the early morning hours, the *Bytes/Second* variable averages only 625,000, or approximately a 63 percent utilization. In the past, the percent of utilization has shown a peak of 71 percent. However, we see that the length of the backups has now been extended to 7:30 AM, an extension of 90 minutes. We review the backup tapes to see if there is more data being transferred. There is a 2 percent increase, 350 MB, in the amount of data. So, the extra 90 minute period is simply an extension of the time required to complete the backup, with no apparent reason.

We now know that while the percent of network utilization is down, it takes longer to move the same amount of data. If Theory #1 was true, we would see either an increase in the utilization or an extension of time. Only the increase in time is seen during testing. So, Theory #1 is only partially right.

## THEORY #2: THE NETWORK'S BANDWIDTH HAS BEEN REDUCED

If it takes longer to send the same amount of data over a network with a fixed 10 Mbps, the network's true bandwidth must be lower than 10 Mbps.

During the night, when traffic is very low, we perform a quick check of the bandwidth by sending a large, fixed-size file (500 MB) across the network that has a previously recorded transfer time. We configure Performance Monitor's logging utility at a 60 second update rate, monitor the *bytes/second* and start the transfer. The result of this test shows that the time to transfer the test file is 18 minutes. Previous transfer tests on this file showed that it would transfer during periods of light network traffic in 12 to 14 minutes. This is a 45 to 50 percent increase in transfer time. This increase indicates a resulting reduction in our network's true bandwidth from 750,000 bytes per second to a range between 350,000 to 400,000 bytes per second. Why did this occur?

We review the logged information and find that the number of bytes being transferred on the network during this period of time was much higher than 500 MB. It was actually 720 MB. When we check the other Network Segment object's variable counters, we find that the broadcast traffic reports that 200 MB were sent during the transfer time period. So, our extra traffic is beginning to have a face: broadcast traffic.

Our next test is to isolate the subnetwork to just the eight servers and one NT 4 workstation monitor. We run the test file across the network to obtain comparable results. At last, we are beginning to make progress. We find that a broadcast source on the server subnetwork is broadcasting the extra traffic. In this situation, the level of broadcast traffic is far too high. The question now is which server, and why? Our next step will be to locate those devices on the subnetwork that are contributing to the problem.

We can use Performance Monitor's Network Interface object from each of the servers to identify those servers transmitting broadcast packets on the network. We can also use Network Monitor to sample the network and identify the broadcast traffic's source. I will show examples of both.

To test Theory #2, we must configure Performance Monitor to log the Network Segment object from one server and the Network Interface object for all servers. The *Total Bytes/Sec, Multicast Bytes/Sec,* and the *Broadcast Bytes/ Sec* variables in the Network Segment object providethe total number of broadcast and multicast bytes on the network The *Packets Sent Non-Unicast/ Sec* variable from the Network Interface object identifies the number of broadcast and multicast packets being sent by each server.

Performance Monitor's results show the culprit. One of the application servers is transmitting the extra 225 MB during the network transmission of the test file. We now know who is creating the extra traffic. The question is, however, why is it being sent? For the answer, we will use Network Monitor to capture any traffic being sent by the errant server.

We configure Network Monitor with a capture filter specifying any bytes being transmitted by the suspect server to any network device. We transfer the test file across the network again between two other servers. After the test, we notice that the capture buffer is full.

So, let's stop for a minute and view the capture buffer. It contains the data that was sent by the suspect server. We find that it contains all hexadecimal FFFFFFFFF, or, simply put, noise. Once the suspect server's NIC sees a large transmission taking place, it sends noise packets at the rate of one for every two good data packets being seen on the network. Our next step is to replace the NIC and rerun the test. The new test now shows that the network bandwidth has been restored. The culprit has been found.

An alternative to the procedure that I just described is to use only Network Monitor to view the data on the network and look through the capture file for flawed data, such as the hexadecimal FFFFFFF. However, this approach may require you to sift through thousands of captured frames before you find a bad packet. To do this effectively, you must have some idea of what the extra packets look like. In certain cases, they may simply be a repeat of the data being sent on the network, which would make it more difficult to find.

## Case History # 3: The Reluctant Backup Server

A network is running 15 application servers. During the nightly backups to tape, all of the servers intermittently fail to answer a ping application that monitors their connection at one-minute intervals. Once the servers log five failures to respond, the monitoring program issues an alarm that pages the primary and secondary LAN administrators.

There are no user complaints that the network is running too slowly. However, there aren't too many users on the network at 3:00 AM. The backup files are tested and can be restored, and there are apparently no data errors. While everything appears to be working normally, the loss of connection is still a mystery.

Although this situation doesn't really disrupt anything, it is important to investigate in more detail. Performance Monitor and Network Monitor are both started. Performance Monitor is started on each of the 15 application servers and the backup server. The Network Segment object, Network Interface object, and System object will be logged by each server's Performance Monitor with a data collection rate set to five-minute intervals.

Network Monitor is configured with a capture filter set to use each server's MAC address. The filter is also configured to monitor only the ICMP protocol, which is responsible for answering the ping transmission.

The tests are logged for a 72-hour period. Network Monitor shows that during the 72 hours, each of the servers failed to respond at least five times a night. This loss of response occurred during the period of time that each server was downloading files to the backup server. The application creating the ping commands is also running on the backup server.

Let's take a look at my three theories on this problem.

## THEORY #1: THE BACKUP SERVER

The backup server is losing the ping echoes from the application servers. My first guess is that the ping echo could be dropped because it is a low priority message. The backup server's Performance Monitor is started, and the ICMP object is logged. A ping log is started to record the exact time each ping occurs, along with the status of the response. As each ping is transmitted, the log will note the time to the millisecond. As the echo is returned, that time is also recorded. If a ping is not returned, the log lists the occurrence as an error.

A further test is run for two nights. The ICMP object contains some counters that are of special interest:

- *Message Sent/Second*—Shows the rate of ping messages being sent.

- *Message Outbound Errors*—Counts the number of errors that were not sent because of a backup server problem, such as the lack of available buffers.

- *Messages Received Errors*—Counts the number of error messages received that are defective, such as bad or missing checksums or partial messages.

- *Receive Time Exceeded*—Counts the number of times exceeded messages are received.

Following the test, the Performance Monitor log is attached to the Performance Monitor chart in order to review each of these variables. The ping log and the Performance Monitor graph are compared using a spreadsheet program. Performance Monitor shows normal operation until an error is found in the ping log. The number of Receive Time Exceeded errors (timeouts) correspond to increases in the ping log.

This means that pings are being sent to the servers. But for some reason, the backup server is receiving a timeout error from each server while receiving the server's file data. This information decreases the probability that the problem is being caused by the backup server.

## THEORY #2: THE APPLICATION SERVERS

The backup server communicates with 15 servers running on a special high-speed server subnet. A problem at the server-level would have to be present in each server. This occurrence would be highly unlikely.

But, there is one common denominator: the servers' subnet. The backup server is located on one subnet that is separated from a high-speed LAN by a router. The application servers are also isolated by another router on their own subnet. This means that two routers are located between the backup server and the application servers, with every packet and ping having to pass through each router.

The servers are eliminated from the list of possible problems because of their shared problem.

## THEORY # 3: THE ROUTERS

Either one, or both, of the routers could be causing the error; each is heavily loaded during the backup process. Ping applications are started on two servers and two workstations in the backup server's subnet.

Four continuous ping sources are started using the NT 4 TCP/IP PING network utility (see Table 8.1). The two routers are pinged by each of the four applications. Ping logs are created for each ping application.

The overnight tests are run again, and the results are tallied. The results are as follows:

- Both routers respond to the pings during periods of normal network traffic. Once the backups begin, the router on the backup server's subnet fails to pass the ICMP traffic to the application server transmitting the most data. This is why the application server being backed up appears to fail the ping test during its backup.

**Table 8.1  TCP/IP Network Utilities**

| Utility | Description |
| --- | --- |
| NETSTAT | Displays protocol statistics and current TCP/IP network connections. |
| HOSTNAME | Prints the name of the current host. |
| NBTSTAT | Displays protocol statistics and current TCP/IP connections using NetBIOS over TCP/IP. The command will also purge and reload the LMHosts file to update any changes. |
| ROUTE | Manipulates network routing tables. |
| TRACERT | Documents the route from your computer across the network to a remote computer. TRACERT sends ICMP echo packets to the remote computer using several Time-To-Live (TTL) periods. As each router between your local computer and the remote computer receives the packet, they decrease the TTL by at least one, then forward the packet, making the TTL a router or hop count. |
| PING | Verifies network continuity between your computer and remote network computers. The ping command sends ICMP echo packets across the network to the host and waits for the return of the echo packets. The ping command can be modified to send packets continuously, allowing you to troubleshoot the network structure between the two computers. |
| ARP | Displays and modifies the IP physical address translation tables that are used by the Address Resolution Protocol (ARP). These tables allow you to identify IP addresses from physical (MAC) addresses or vice versa. |
| FINGER | Displays user connectivity information on a destination system that is also running the Finger service. |
| IPCONFIG | Displays your current TCP/IP network configuration values, including the DHCP addresses. If no parameters are included, IPCONFIG lists all of the current TCP/IP configuration, subnet mask, and WINS and DNS configuration. |

- Following the backups, the router passes the ping ICMP traffic correctly. The source of the problem is located, and the router is repaired, eliminating the problem.

The lesson found in this case is that even simple command-line tools can be effectively used to troubleshoot complicated problems. The NT 4 TCP/IP PING utility is both simple and effective in diagnosing a LAN connection problems.

# Using TCP/IP Command-Line Network Utilities

NT 4's implementation of the TCP/IP protocol includes a set of utility routines that you can use at the command line to perform the following functions:

- Monitor network operations

- Trace a network path, including each router, from one network device to another

- Purge and reload the LMHosts file

- Change the network routing tables

- Identify the current IP configuration and settings

- Test network connections

## Case History # 4: An Unreachable Host

Frequently, you will be called upon to verify that a remote network device is attached to a network. This situation often arises during the installation of new equipment on the network. You try to attach to a remote device using the NT 4 File Manager, or Explorer, only to have NT 4 inform you that the device cannot be found. So, what do you do?

The first step is to check your addressing service(s). These services can consist of one or all of the following:

- Windows Internet Naming Service (WINS)

- Domain Naming Service (DNS)

- LMHosts file

To keep things interesting, I've decided that you have all three services configured on your local NT 4 computer. You must now check each service to verify that the remote destination name is properly entered and that the associated IP address is correct.

While checking, you find that NT 4 is using only the LMHosts file to resolve network names. After reading the LMHosts file, you find that the remote host's IP address is incorrect. What do you do now? Do you fix the file, then shut down and restart the machine? Or is there an easier set of steps that will also resolve this problem?

Remember, there are TCP/IP utilities that you can use to solve problems like this. But, while you remember their names, you don't remember their command strings. Now what?

1. Select Start|Programs|MS-DOS Prompt to get to the command line.

2. Enter one of the names listed in Table 8.1, followed by the "?" parameter (for example, PING /?).

3. NT 4 will then return a complete list of PING's command options, along with some examples.

4. Enter PING, followed by the IP address of the remote host that you cannot reach, and press Enter.

5. PING will send ICMP packets to the designated host and wait for a reply. If no reply is received, PING will display the message *Request Timed Out*. If a reply is received from the remote host, PING will then display, in milliseconds, the time it took the remote host to reply.

6. Once you have established that the host is on the network and responding, you must provide NT 4 with a means to resolve the remote host's name into the IP address that you just entered. Because you have changed the LMHosts file, you must save it back to its directory \%system root%\system32\drivers\etc.

7. Enter NBTSTAT /? at the command line. This command will reload the LMHosts file without requiring NT 4 to be rebooted. NT 4 now displays the NBTSTAT options. Notice the -R option which first purges

and then reloads the LMHosts file. Enter NBTSTAT -R and NT 4 will then display the message that it has purged and reloaded the address table. This table is the NBT remote cache table, which, in this case, NT 4 uses to resolve network names into IP addresses.

8. Now your system can recognize the remote host's name and couple it with an IP address. Next, you will need to see the remote host and identify which shared directories you are able to access. This step requires NET VIEW utility, which is discussed in Table 8.2. Enter NET VIEW \\host name, and press Enter. For the host name, use the same name that you entered into the LMHosts file. NT 4 will return the remote host's name, MAC address, and the names of all shared directories that you are able to access.

9. Next, you may now attach one or more of the shared drives to your local computer by using either File Manager, Explorer, or the NET USE command-line utility. The NET USE command allows you to cite a specific drive letter, such as G:. You may also use a * in the command line to allow NT 4 to pick the next available drive letter. If you have trouble remembering the command-line format and switches, enter NET USE /? to display the help screen shown in Figure 8.2. If you need more detailed help that will explain the meaning and options for each switch and option, enter NET HELP USE to display the screen shown in Figure 8.3.

```
Command Prompt

C:\users\default>net use /?
The syntax of this command is:


NET USE [devicename | *] [\\computername\sharename[\volume] [password | *]]
        [/USER:[domainname\]username]
        [[/DELETE] | [/PERSISTENT:(YES | NO}]]

NET USE [devicename | *] [password | *]] [/HOME]

NET USE [/PERSISTENT:(YES | NO}]
```

**Figure 8.2**   The NET USE  screen provides a summary explanation of the command switches and modifiers.

```
NET USE [devicename| *] [\\computername\sharename[\volume] [password| *]]
[/USER:[domainname\]username] [[/DELETE] | [/PERSISTENT:{YES | NO}]]

NET USE [devicename| *] [password| *]] [/HOME]

NET USE [/PERSISTENT:{YES | NO}]

NET USE  connects a computer to a shared resource or disconnects a computer from a shared resource.
         When used without options, it lists the computer's connections.

Devicename  Assigns a name to connect to the resource or specifies the device to be disconnected. There
         are two kinds of devicenames: disk drives (D: through Z:) and printers (LPT1: through LPT3:).
         Type an asterisk instead of a specific devicename to assign the next available devicename.

\\computername  Is the name of the computer controlling the shared resource. If the computername
         contains blank characters, enclose the double backslash (\\) and the computername in quotation
         marks (" "). The computername may be from 1 to 15 characters long.

\sharename  Is the network name of the shared resource.

volume  Specifies a NetWare volume on the server. You must have Client Services for Netware
         (Windows NT Workstations) or Gateway Service for Netware (Windows NT Server) installed and
         running to connect to NetWare servers.

password  Is the password needed to access the shared resource.

*  Produces a prompt for the password. The password is not displayed when you type it at the password
         prompt.

/USER  Specifies a different username with which the connection is made.

domainname  Specifies another domain. If domain is omitted, the current logged on domain is used.

username  Specifies the username with which to logon.

/HOME  Connects a user to their home directory.

/DELETE  Cancels a network connection and removes the connection from the list of persistent
         connections.

/PERSISTENT  Controls the use of persistent network connections. The default is the setting used last.

YES  Saves connections as they are made, and restores them at next logon.

NO  Does not save the connection being made or subsequent connections; existing connections will be
         restored at next logon. Use the /DELETE switch to remove persistent connections.
```

**Figure 8.3**   The NET HELP USE screen provides a more detailed explanation of the command switches and modifiers.

### Table 8.2   Network Command Line Utilities

| Utility | Description |
| --- | --- |
| NET CONFIG | Lists the current workgroup settings. |
| NET DIAG | Runs network diagnostics to test the connection between two computers. The command reports the diagnostic results of the computer specified in the /STATUS switch. |
| NET INIT | Loads protocols and network adapter-drivers without first binding them to Protocol Manager. This technique is often useful for troubleshooting network software without committing any changes to NT 4's network protocol stack. |

*(continued)*

**Table 8.2 Network Command Line Utilities *(continued)***

| Utility | Description |
|---|---|
| NET LOGOFF | Terminates the connection between your computer and the shared resource on another computer. |
| NET LOCALGROUP | Identifies you as a member of a group. |
| NET ACCOUNTS | Updates the user accounts database. The command utility also modifies password and logon requirements for all records. |
| NET COMPUTER | Adds or deletes computers from a domain database. This command is available for use with NT 4 servers only. |
| NET CONFIG, NET CONFIG SERVER, and NET CONFIG WORKSTATION | Displays configuration information of the Workstation or Server service. When NET CONFIG is used without the SERVER or WORKSTATION switch, it displaysa list of configurable services. When you add the SERVER option, NET CONFIG displays or allows you to make changes to Server service settings. When you add the WORKSTATION option, NET CONFIG displays or allows you to make changes to the Workstation service settings. |
| NET CONTINUE SERVICE | Restarts an NT 4 service that has been suspended by NET PAUSE. |
| NET FILE | Closes shared files and eliminates any file locks. To list open server files, use the NET FILE command without options. |
| NET GROUP | Displays server group names, or modifies a server's global groups. |
| NET HELPMSG | Provides a fast, effective way to look up help message numbers. When NT 4 generates a network diagnostic message, use this command to ask NT for additional information. |
| NET LOCALGROUP | Displays an NT 4 computer's local groups. The command can also beused to modify the local groups already configured on the computer. |
| NET NAME | Displays, creates, or drops a computer's messaging (alias)name. |
| NET PAUSE | The NET PAUSE command is used to pause or suspend an NT 4 service or resource. |

*(continued)*

**Table 8.2   Network Command Line Utilities** *(continued)*

| Utility | Description |
|---|---|
| NET PRINT | Shows the current status of print jobs and printer queues. The command results in display of the queued print jobs, their sizes, and their status. |
| NET SEND | Works with the NT 4 Messaging service to send messages to other network users. |
| NET SESSION | Lists, displays session information, and disconnect sessions between two or more NT 4 servers. |
| NET SHARE | Lists all shared resources on a network computer. |
| NET START | Lists or starts NT 4 or third-party network services. |
| NET STATISTICS, NET STATISTICS SERVER, and NET STATISTICS WORKSTATION | The NET STATISTICS command Lists the contents of the statistics log for either a local workstation or server. When the SERVER modifier is added, the command lists the current Server service statistics. When the WORKSTATION modifier is added, the command lists the current Workstation service statistics. |
| NET STOP SERVICE | Stops an NT 4 or third-party service. To execute this command, you must be a member of the Administrator's group. |
| NET TIME | Allows your computer tocross the network and obtain time-of-day and dateinformation from the local TOD (Time-of-Day) server. |
| NET USE | Attaches a shared drive to a network source. |
| NET USER | Lists, modifies, or creates user accounts on NT 4 servers. |
| NET VIEW | Shows a list of shared resources on a network computer. |

# Third-Party Network Management Tools

In the previous sections, I've shown you how to monitor and troubleshoot software and network communications problems. But what happens when workstation hardware fails? What should you do when a server shuts down in a remote network location? How do you monitor and maintain the network hardware, as well as the software? For larger networks, you can purchase enterprise network monitoring packages that allow you to see and command any network device, even those that are located at the farthest extent of the WAN. Two of the better known enterprise packages are IBM's Net View 6000 and Hewlett-Packard's Open View.

But what about medium to smaller networks? It is difficult to justify spending $20,000 to $30,000 for software to manage a network with 400 workstations and servers. This means that you must consider either limiting the scope of management or adapt less-expensive software to fit your needs. In the past few years, independent software vendors (ISVs) have discovered this market.

Another source of medium to smaller network-management tools involves companies that add such packages to their hardware or software offerings at a reasonable price. I call these packages add-on management software products.

The package included in the following discussion is the Compaq Insight Manager, or CIM. CIM was designed to aid the medium to smaller LAN administrator who is unable to employ an enterprise-type solution. CIM was designed to readily attach to an enterprise network solution by incorporating into their product the interfaces necessary to communicate with the larger monitoring packages. This product is not part of NT 4. It is available for purchase from Compaq or Compaq's third-party sales.

## What Does a Network-Management Package Do?

Management packages vary widely in use and performance. Many packages are oriented to monitoring SNMP parameters of servers, workstations, and network routers. These packages work from a chart, or map, that graphically describes your network in terms of the devices located on it. You can superimpose these maps with overlays that relate to location or management of the network nodes. The software communicates with the mapped network devices on a regular basis, such as every five minutes.

These communications often consist of a server that is designated to run the package, a common software front-end, and specialized software modules that are created to interrogate a specific network device. For example, you may have five different routers and three different workstation operating systems. In the past, for each of these different devices you would have to develop or purchase proprietary software just to communicate over the network. Now, these packages include specific code in a more general purpose format called the Management Information Base (MIB).

MIBs consist of a set of objects that represent a device's software structures, which contain the existing set of information about that device. An MIB is used by a network manager to monitor and manage one or more network devices. These devices can often use the same MIB. This is done by adding a unique set of parameters for an object that is specific to a particular model or brand of product. These objects can be different types of either devices or protocols, with each object exposing a unique set of interface data to the management system.

The Compaq Insight Manager is dedicated to monitoring Compaq hardware using its network interface. Compaq's philosophy is that they will do everything they can to prevent a component, server, or workstation failure. If a device's failure can be predicted, then the imminent failure is forecast to the LAN administrator as soon as possible.

CIM regularly monitors the operation of the servers on its monitor list. Each server is queried concerning its overall health and status. In addition to the graphical displays, you can configure CIM to prepare regular reports on the attached servers. These reports are also configurable and can contain a wealth of information concerning the server's operational health and performance.

CIM can be used in a standalone configuration, where it is the only network management software on the network, but it will also interface with most of the larger network management packages. This flexibility allows you to expand your network, from one or two servers to a large network, without wasting your software investment.

CIM can also run on non-Compaq workstations, but will provide full monitoring only to Compaq network servers. CIM is capable of generating a pager output in the event of a server fault or loss of network access.

## Configuring CIM

CIM can be configured to support any network that contains one or more Compaq servers. The server list, shown in Figure 8.4, displays nine servers, each with a differing operational status. Each server is shown with its operation condition displayed next to it. The black ball indicates that this server is currently offline. The red ball indicates that the server has one or more defective components. The green ball indicates that the server is fully functional and successfully communicating with CIM. In the example shown in Figure 8.4, the majority of balls are green.

A yellow ball, which is not shown in the figure, indicates that the server has recently recovered from a fault. This status ball will remain yellow until the fault indicator has been deleted by service personnel. The status count, located at the bottom of Figure 8.4, shows a count of the server's status categories. For a small LAN, such as this one, these lights are not important. However, when connected to a larger LAN, with 50 to 100 servers, these lights provide a quick look at the overall status of your network.

CIM will work well in both small and large LANs due to the manageable design. The Servers and No Filtering pull-down windows, located at the top of Figure 8.4, are used to specify which subset of servers are selected to

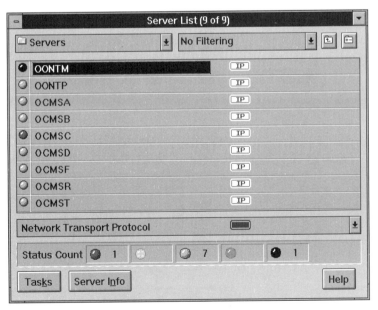

**Figure 8.4** The Server List displays all of the all monitored Compaq servers.

be displayed. You should apply these filters to the entire list of servers. Depending on which filter is chosen, the appropriate screens will be displayed. The server list is only the tip of the iceberg. Double click on one of the servers and a small help menu appears to allow you to select the Server screen.

## The Server Screen

The Server screen displays the next level of detail for a specific server. A typical server, CCNTP, is shown in Figure 8.5. CIM shows the type and model of the server. In this case, the server is a Compaq 5000 in a rack-mounted case.

You can click on the buttons surrounding the server's picture to show a further breakdown of the server's internal configuration and performance. Clicking on the Configuration button creates a detailed listing of the server's hardware and firmware configuration. This information is often useful when you are troubleshooting the server with help from either Compaq or a third party.

Clicking the Recovery button shows a screen that contains the latest system problems, alerts, and shutdown status. A green box around the button indicates that the server is enjoying good health.

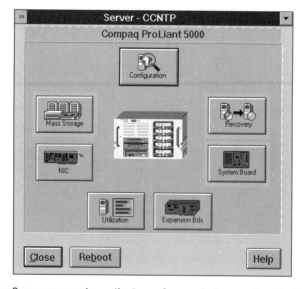

**Figure 8.5** The Server screen shows the type of server being monitored, along with buttons to access more detailed internal server information.

Clicking on the System Board button enables you to review the configuration and status of the server's motherboard, as shown in Figure 8.6. This information is useful for verifying configuration information or troubleshooting a possible motherboard problem. The System Board screen displays your current CPU and memory configuration. In Figure 8.6, the server shown is configured with four Pentium Pro processors operating with a 200 MHz clock. From this display, you can branch down to view the correctable memory log or the currently configured Input/Output (I/O) devices. The  System Board screen shows the physical memory contained within this server. The server shown has a 640 K base memory and a total memory configuration of 1 GB.

The Expansion button enables you to access information on any expansion boards that have been added to your server. CIM provides information and status for these boards.

The Utilization button enables you to monitor the server's bus and CPU utilization for periods of 1 minute, 5 minutes, 30 minutes, and 1 hour. This information is useful for capacity planning and monitoring. An over-taxed server will not serve a robust application environment.

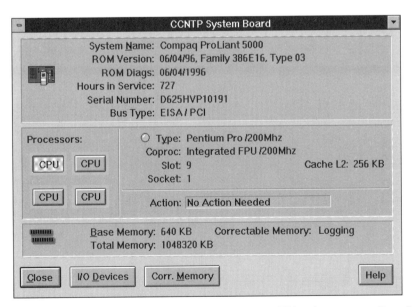

**Figure 8.6**    The System Board screen displays the server's CPU and memory configuration.

The NIC button provides access to the server's network communications status, as shown in Figure 8.7. The NIC card is a fundamental part of any server with operation and functionality being critical to the successful operation of the LAN. The data presented on the NIC-Ethernet Statistics screen is useful for monitoring the server's network transmit and receive errors. In Figure 8.7, the NIC card is experiencing more transmit errors than receive errors. In this case, the card is experiencing high collision rates and deferred transmissions. These problems are usually caused by overuse of a network's bandwidth.

Clicking on the Mass Storage button opens the Smart Logical Drives screen, shown in Figure 8.8. This screen provides a quick look at the configuration and status of the mass storage system attached to the server. The Smart Logical Drives screen shows two hard disk storage containers. The hard drives operate in a RAID 5 configuration.

You can display more detailed information by selecting one of the two logical drive controls located at the top-left corner of the screen. Use these buttons to select between the two cabinets. Double clicking on any one of the hard disks shown in the cabinets will result in another screen showing

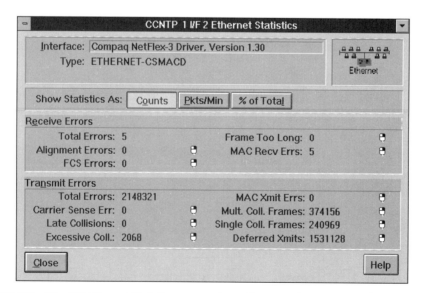

**Figure 8.7** The NIC-Ethernet Statistics screen shows the current error status of the Ethernet CSMACD card, including both transmit and receive errors.

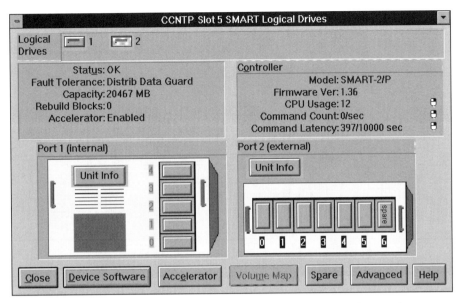

**Figure 8.8** The Smart Logical Drives screen displays the servers current mass storage configuration.

the detailed statistics of one hard drive, including errors and operational characteristics.

## Troubleshooting a Server Problem

CIM is an excellent example of a management tool. But how well does it support you when a failure occurs? To answer that question, let's look at the anatomy of a component failure through the eyes of CIM.

In this example, CIM has paged the LAN administrator with a hardware problem on the OCMSC server. Because CIM is portable, it can be used throughout the network, including your desk at home, to view reported problems. The LAN administrator has configured CIM on his console and has enlarged the CIM application screen, shown in Figure 8.9. The server shown appears to have a mass storage problem. This type of problem is extremely dangerous because the database and files stored on the mass storage system could be in jeopardy.

Double click on the Mass Storage system (currently enclosed in a red box), to display the next level screen. In this screen, you have two choices: SCSI-1 and SCSI-2. SCSI-1 is also currently surrounded by a red box. Double

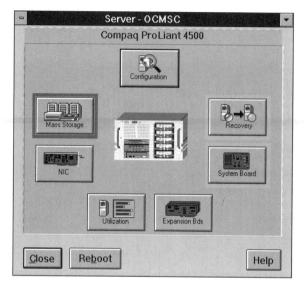

**Figure 8.9**   The Server-OCMSC screen shows a Compaq 4500 server with a mass storage problem.

clicking the SCSI-1 button will display the screen shown in Figure 8.10. At this point, we are down to the fourth level of information. This level allows you to view the server's internal components, along with their respective status.

In Figure 8.10, under the SCSI Devices heading, the failed component is shown to be item 6. In this case, item 6 is a DLT tape drive. The hard resets represent the number of times that the Compaq management subsystem has issued resets to the failed device. There was 1 soft reset and 1850 hard resets made during this attempt. This screen clearly indicates the source of the server failure.

This, of course, is a simplistic example, but it is indicative of the type of tools that are available from both hardware and software vendors. Each of the vendors has a vested interest in your satisfaction of their product. Failures occur all the time, but the better the tools you have at your disposal, the quicker you can diagnose, repair, and restore your network service.

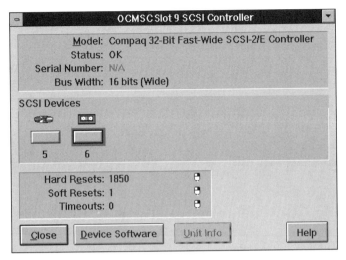

**Figure 8.10**   The SCSI Controller screen graphically shows the defective part, outlined in red.

# Conclusion

In this chapter, I presented several network problems, including the steps taken to troubleshoot them and the solutions that were found. I've tried to show you that the important issues aren't the solutions but the tools and procedures used to find them. The tools discussed in Chapter 7, along with some command-line utilities described in this chapter, were used to troubleshoot these problems. The NT 4 release CD and the NT Resource Kit contain many additional utilities that can be very helpful and informative to your understanding of NT's operation. More importantly, these utilities will help you find the solution to many different types of problems.

While the NT 4 operating system is complex, it is an excellent operating system. Unfortunately, NT'scomplexity can often mask or hide network problems. It pays to learn how to use all of the tools that Microsoft and third-party vendors offer. You never know when you may have to use them to repair a critical problem.

PART

4

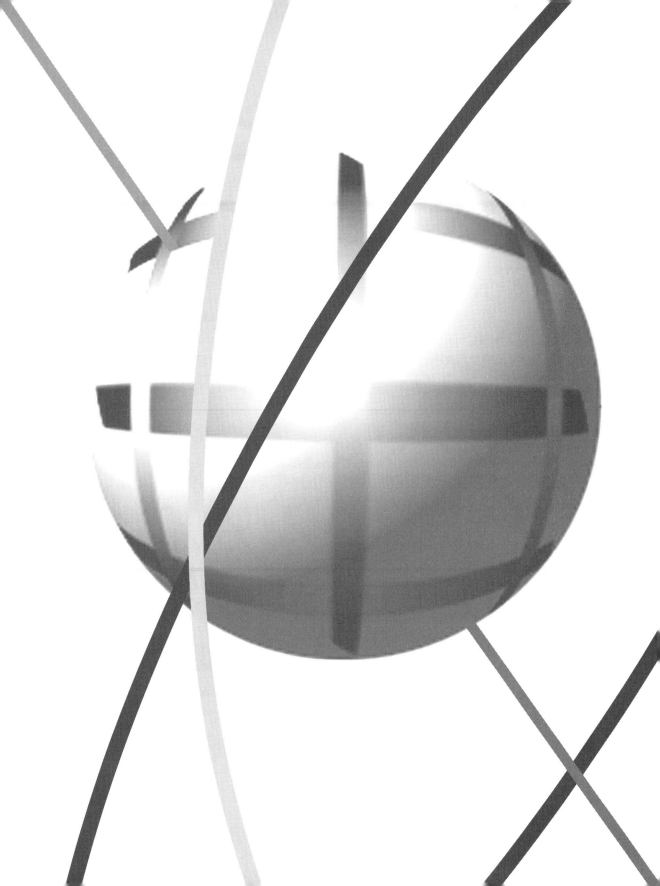

# Configuring NT for the Internet

**A** few years ago, the primary function of an operating system was to manage the hardware resources of a computer. Time has changed this situation quite dramatically. Now, a good interface to the Internet has become a major factor in survival of all operating systems for the next century.

Microsoft's Windows NT can be used as both an Internet client and a server. Microsoft is taking a comprehensive package approach, providing customers with products like Internet Information Server, Internet Explorer, and FrontPage, working side by side with Windows NT to surf the Net efficiently.

In this chapter, we will discuss how the different functions provided by Windows NT can be employed effectively to interface your system to the Internet and an intranet. First, we'll walk through some of the basic terminology and the technology available for use on the Internet. Then, I will go into detail to help you understand Microsoft's Internet Information Server, which is integrated into Windows NT 4 Server, and how it allows us to manage an organization's Internet server. I will also cover security, performance issues, and several add-ons like FrontPage and Catapult.

# Understanding the Basics

There are a number of protocols and services available with Windows NT to set up your Internet connection. But, before we explore these services and protocols, you first have to understand the basics. If you are familiar with these basic concepts, feel free to skip to the next section, *Internet Connectivity*.

## What Is the Internet?

The *Internet* is a global network of computers that can communicate with each other by using a common language. The Internet refers to a specific collection of networks around the world, linked together using the Transport Control Protocol/Interface Protocol(TCP/IP) protocol suite.

The Internet began in the late 1960s as a research project sponsored by the U.S. government through DARPA, the Defense Advanced Research Projects Agency. Today, the Internet has grown to more than 2 million *hosts* (computers connected directly to Internet "cloud") in over 130 countries. In addition to DARPANeT, the U.S. portion of the Internet includes the Military Network (MilNet), NASA Science Internet (NSI), and the largest of these networks, NSFNet (National Science Foundation Network). It is safe to say that the Internet is the fastest growing computing transformation ever.

## What Is an Intranet?

An *intranet* refers to any TCP/IP network that is not connected to the Internet. The term *private network* is often used to indicate an intranet, a corporate network, or an internal network.

An intranet takes the World Wide Web model, which allows companies to communicate with the marketplace via the Internet, and adapts it to the specific boundaries of an organization. This allows certain information to remain accessible only to its employees, and not the Internet public. An intranet allows an organization to share internal information with its employees by using any Web browser on any computer platform.

## What Is the World Wide Web?

The World Wide Web, commonly known as the Web, is a unique way to view information on the Internet. The Web is an Internet service, based on the *Hypertext Transport Protocol (HTTP)*, that delivers multimedia objects (text, sound, video, images, database access, and interactive applications, for example) to your computer. These objects are grouped together into *pages* using a scripting language called *Hypertext Markup Language (HTML)*. To view a Web page, you use a *browser*. A browser is an application, such as Netscape Navigator or Microsoft Internet Explorer, that requests a page on the Web using HTTP, then displays the page on your screen. HTML pages are text files that include special codes called *tags*. These tags control text formatting, the placement of objects on the page, and hyperlinks. You click a hyperlink to jump from one Web page to another.

The content for the Web is created and maintained on computers that are configured to act as Web sites. A Web site responds to requests from browsers and returns HTML pages. Web sites are typically maintained by organizations. Individuals sometimes run their own Web sites, or they create HTML pages and load them onto public sites.

The content of the Web is dynamic. It changes daily, and in many cases, hourly. The number of Web sites, as well as the scope and richness of their contents, is growing astronomically. The Web offers business information, online shopping, and searchable databases.

## Telnet

*Telnet* allows you to remotely log in to other computers and can give you access to databases and many information services. Telnet service is slowly diminishing, and a lot of today's systems do not offer this service any longer. However, this is sometimes the only way that you can access information from someone who does not provide an online interface.

## FTP

*FTP* stands for *File Transfer Protocol*. It allows you to transfer documents and programs all over the place. You can FTP to any "anonymous" site in the world using this hypertext interface. FTP is the most extensive tool for transferring files from one computer to another. In fact, I use FTP to transfer the chapters for this book to my publisher.

## *Gopher*

*Gopher* is a distributed document search and retrieval system that allows users to view and obtain all sorts of files, programs, and software. Internet Gopher was developed by the University of Minnesota in April 1991 to help their campus find answers to computer-related questions. It has since grown into a full-fledged worldwide information system used by a large number of sites in the world. To find more information on Gopher go to **gopher://boombox.micro.umn.edu/11/gopher.**

# Internet Connectivity

The Web and other Internet services, like Gopher and FTP, need a method to connect to the Internet. A number of methods are available to connect, including ISDN, ADSL, T3, and T1. In this section, I will describe these methods in a little more detail.

## *The Internet through Windows NT ISDN*

*Integrated Services Digital Network (ISDN)* is a high-speed, full-digital telephone service. Just as compact discs have taken recorded music to digital quality levels, ISDN upgrades today's analog telephone network to a conditioned, digital system. ISDN can operate at speeds up to 128 Kbps, which is five times faster than today's analog modems. ISDN can dramatically speed up the transfer of information over the Internet or over a remote LAN connection, especially rich multimedia graphics, audio, video, and similar applications that normally run at LAN speeds.

Windows NT operating system offers native, built-in ISDN support that is well-integrated with the networking and communications subsystems. The result is high performance and excellent interoperability with a broad range of ISDN equipment. Check Microsoft's HCL (hardware compatibility list) for equipment compatibility. Use the Remote Access Service (RAS) in Windows NT to connect an ISDN service to your system. Figures 9.1 and 9.2 show how the RAS connection is set up. Click on the Add button in Figure 9.1, and then select Remote Access Service, as shown in Figure 9.2. For more information on RAS, see Chapter 5.

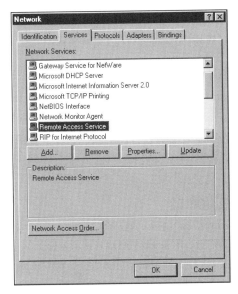

**Figure 9.1**    You can set up an NT ISDN connection with RAS.

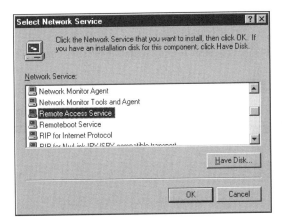

**Figure 9.2**    NT ISDN connection installation.

## INTERNET SOFTWARE FOR ISDN

Microsoft's Internet Explorer has been extensively tested for use with ISDN on Windows NT. An add-on, Get ISDN, is another product from Microsoft that allows users to check whether ISDN service is available in their immediate area. This software allows you to choose a continent, a region from the continent, and then prompts you to fill out the state and phone number. When you press Next, the query displays the results for the location, as shown in Figure 9.3. To find out more about this service, go to **http:// www.microsoft.com/isapi/windows/provider.exe**.

## Internet Connection Types

Now that we have looked at ISDN, let's compare it to some of the other connection choices. Table 9.1 represents typical levels of service for full Internet connections in North America. The Internet services offered through Internet Service Providers (ISPs) in other countries may differ significantly.

### COMMUNICATIONS CHOICES

*Asymmetric Digital Subscriber Line (ADSL)*, created by Analog Devices and Partner Aware, Inc., is the first chipset that conforms to the new standard (ANSI T1.413 category 1). ADSL provides local telephone companies a way to take advantage of the "Information Superhighway" without investing in fiber-optic cable.

The chipset can move data downstream (network to home) as fast as 8 Mbps and can achieve interactive rates as high as 500 Kbps. The 8 Mbps can support several digital video channels, while the interactive rate can

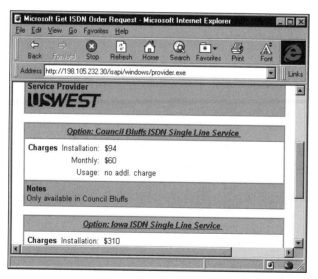

**Figure 9.3**  Get ISDN gives you the information for the services in the area.

**Table 9.1   Connection types**

| Connection | Maximum BPS | Maximum Bytes | Simultaneous Users Supported |
|---|---|---|---|
| Frame Relay | 56,000 | 56,000 | 10-20 |
| ISDN | 128,000 | 12,800 | 10-50 |
| Fractional T1 | — | varies as needed | varies as needed |
| T1 | 1,500,000 | 150,000 | 100-500 |
| T3 | 45,000,000 | 4,500,000 | 5000+ |
| ADSL | 8 Mbps | 500 Kbps | — |

handle two-way teleconferencing, high-speed Internet surfing, and LAN access. ADSL furnishes telephone companies with access to next-generation multimedia communication, allowing them to compete with hybrid-fiber-coax (HFC) technology from cable television suppliers.

Still, critics contend that ADSL is merely an interim solution that Fiber-To-The-Curb (FTTC) installation will soon render obsolete. Other industry insiders are not so sure. This is a new technology still under test.

The type of connection needed depends on the server traffic. A light-duty server can use Frame Relay or ISDN. A server with moderate traffic might have a T1 line or some fraction of a T1 line installed. Large businesses that expect heavy Internet traffic may need a fractional T1, a full T1, multiple T1 lines, or possibly a T3 service in order to handle thousands of users.

Modem connections to the Internet are available, but are typically used for individual client browsing and are not recommended for servers. A connection to the Internet using a phone line and modem can service only two or three simultaneous users. (Modem connections might be used for text-only Internet servers with only a small number of potential users.) Modem connections are "slow links" because data is transmitted at the speed of the modem, typically from 300 to 28,800 bps, far too slow for efficient operation of a Web server.

# Internet Protocols

After you have made a decision about the connection method, you will need to choose an Internet protocol for your system. In this section, I will show you how to install and implement different Internet protocols.

## *The Internet through Windows NT PPP*

*Point-to-Point Protocol* (*PPP*) is a protocol for exchanging IP (Internet Protocol) packets and other frames over serial communications lines. It is capable of escaping control characters, so the line doesn't need to be totally 8-bit clean (as opposed to SLIP/CSLIP, which require a totally clean line). However, even PPP doesn't work over 7-bit lines. Eight data bits are always needed. If you have a 7-bit line, or if some other characters than the control characters ASCII 0 to ASCII 31 need escaping, you could try using Twinsock or Virtual TCP (for Windows) or Term (for Unix).

These steps show the procedure for setting up a PPP link:

1. To set up PPP under Windows NT, go to Accessories, and click on Dial-up Networking.

2. Enter a name for your connection.

3. Enter the phone number that you will be dialing.

4. Select either PPP or SLIP through the response window screen, as shown in Figure 9.4.

5. After selecting the option for interactive text login, enter your system's IP address.

6. Enter the DNS or WIN server IP address (the IP address of the remote system).

7. Click on Finish. Your connection name appears in the box. It is saved for your PPP connection use.

## *The Internet through Windows NT SLIP*

*Serial Line Internet Protocol* (*SLIP*) is specific to TCP/IP networks. The SLIP connection setup with Windows NT is exactly the same as the PPP setup explained previously. NT can be set up to dial into a SLIP server, but

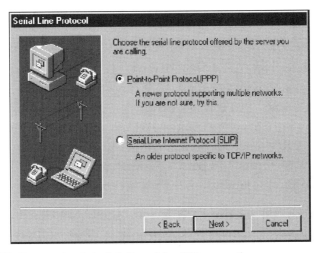

**Figure 9.4**   NT allows a simple installation of the PPP connection.

NT 4 cannot be configured with standard software to be a SLIP server. To set up NT to dial into a SLIP server, simply select SLIP at Step 4 in the previous section.

## *The Internet through Windows NT PPTP*

Windows NT 4's RAS allows remote users to access their network via the Internet by using *Point-to-Point Tunneling Protocol* (*PPTP*). PPTP is a new networking technology integrated with RAS that supports multiprotocol *Virtual Private Networks* (*VPN*). PPTP uses the Internet as the transfer mechanism instead of long-distance telephone lines or a toll-free service, greatly reducing transmission costs.

PPTP enables remote users to access their networks securely across the Internet in two ways: by dialing into an ISP or by connecting directly to the Internet. In either case, PPTP provides one essential benefit: secure over-the-Internet data transfer. In addition, PPTP works with IP, IPX, NetBEUI, and other mainstream protocols.

PPTP enables modems and ISDN cards to be separated from the company's RAS server. They can now be located at an ISP's modem bank or a *Front-End Processor* (*FEP*). This approach greatly reduces costs because modems and ISDN cards are loaded on the ISP's server, not the company's server. PPTP means less administrative overhead because the ISP, rather than the network administrator, manages the connection hardware. PPTP requires no changes to your existing client software.

PPTP encrypts and encapsulates PPP packets on top of TCP/IP. The specification outlines how to handle data packets and remote connections to Microsoft NT's RAS. PPTP relies on the security routines supported by RAS, including the Challenge Handshake Authentication Protocol (CHAP) and 40-bit RSA RC4 encryption algorithms. This makes sure the user has authorized access to the company's network and scrambles any data sent through the tunnel so unauthorized users can't understand it.

For technical details on the PPTP go to **http://129.13.170.142/intdev/inttech/pptp.htm**. To get a look as Digital's PPTP software, check out **http://www.digital.com/info/Internet**.

No matter what communication method and protocol you use to make the connection, you need some tool to manage the system where all the information resides. Let's explore in detail how Microsoft Internet Information Server is set up under Windows NT 4 for Internet access.

# Exploring the Integration of IIS and NT Server 4.0 Setup

Miscrosoft's Internet Information Server (v2.0) is fully integrated into the Windows NT Server (v4.0) setup, allowing you to set up Internet services on your organization's server while installing Windows NT Server. However, IIS can also be installed separately later. (See *The Internet Information Server Installation* section for more details.)

Microsoft Internet Information Server (IIS) is a network file and application server that transmits and receives information in HTML pages using HTTP. The Internet Information Server, shown in Figure 9.5, includes the following components:

- Internet Information Server services (Web, FTP, and Gopher)

- Internet Service Manager (the tool for monitoring the Internet Information Server)

**Figure 9.5** Microsoft's Internet Information Server.

We've pretty much covered the bases on the standard IIS services (see the *Understanding the Basics* section for more details), so let's move right along with the IIS installation and then the Internet Service Manager.

## The Internet Information Server Installation

If you installed NT 4.0 without installing Microsoft Internet Information Server, you can install IIS now by following these steps:

1. Run Setup. IIS will display the screen shown in Figure 9.6. Select the services you want to install. At this time, you can also change the directory location where your files will be installed.

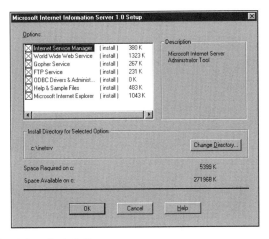

**Figure 9.6** IIS standalone installation.

2. Select the option you want, and click on OK.

You will see the installation being processed and then Web, Gopher, and FTP services started.

> *Note: If IIS is already installed, running the setup will give you three options—Add/Remove, Reinstall, and Remove, as shown in Figure 9.7. If you are reinstalling the software, follow the steps for a first time installation.*

After the setup is successfully completed, you can configure IIS. We will learn about configuring IIS in the next sections.

## *The Internet Service Manager*

Internet Service Manager provides three views—Report, Servers, and Services—to help you enhance the performance of your NT-based server. Let's look at these in a little more detail.

### REPORT VIEW

Report view, shown in Figure 9.8, is the default view. Report view is useful for sites with only one or two computers running Internet Information Server. Report view alphabetically lists the selected computers, with each

**Figure 9.7**  IIS installation options if the service is already installed.

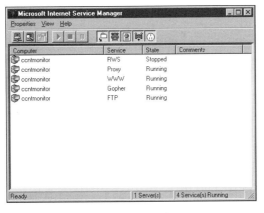

**Figure 9.8** The Internet Service Manager's Report view.

installed service shown on a separate line. Click on the column headings to alphabetically sort the entire list.

## SERVERS VIEW

The Servers view, shown in Figure 9.9, displays the services running on network servers by computer name. Click on the plus symbol next to a server name to see which services that server is running. Double click on a service name to see its property sheets. The Servers view is most useful for sites running multiple computers because it allows you to see the status of the services installed on a specific computer.

**Figure 9.9** The Internet Service Manager's Servers view.

## Services View

The Services view, shown in Figure 9.10, lists the services on every selected computer, grouped by service name. Click on the plus symbol next to a service name to see the servers running that service. Double click on the computer name under a service to see the property sheets for the service running on that computer. Services view is most useful for sites with widely distributed servers because it allows you to see which computers are running a particular service.

## *Connecting to a Server*

You can use two methods to connect to a server:

1. In the Internet Service Manager, select Properties|Connect to Server. In the Server Name box, type the server's host name, IP address, or NetBIOS name.

   *Or*

1. In the Internet Services Manager, select Properties|Find All Servers to display a list of servers.

2. Double click on the server you want to connect to.

Once you've connected to a server, you may need to start, stop, or pause a service. These steps show you how:

**Figure 9.10**   The Internet Service Manager's Services view.

1. In the Internet Service Manager, select the service you want to start, stop, or pause.

2. Select Properties|Start Service, Stop Service, or Pause Service.

## Property Sheets

The Internet Service Manager property sheets allow you to configure and manage the Web and other services. To modify the settings on a property sheet, follow these steps:

1. In Internet Service Manager, double click on the desired server or service name to display its property sheets.

2. Click on the tab at the top of each property sheet to display the properties for that category.

3. Adjust the properties for the service, then click on OK to return to the Internet Service Manager.

   *Note: In special instances, like configuring virtual servers, you may need to use the Registry Editor (Regedt32.exe) to configure IIS or Windows NT Server.*

Let's take a look at the property sheets in more detail.

### THE SERVICE PROPERTY SHEET

The Service property sheet, shown in Figure 9.11, is used to control who can use your server and to specify the account used for anonymous (or Guest) client requests to log on to the computer. Most Internet sites allow anonymous logons. If you allow anonymous logons, then all user permissions, such as permission to access information, will use the IUSR_*computername* account. In order to use your current security system to control information access, change the anonymous logon account to an existing account (or accounts) on your network.

### THE DIRECTORIES PROPERTY SHEET

The Directories property sheet, shown in Figure 9.12, lists the directories available to users, with some possible exceptions, such as protected files or system files, which they will not be able to access.

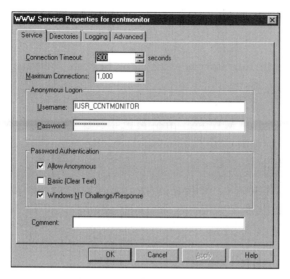

**Figure 9.11** The Service property sheet allows you to control who can use your server.

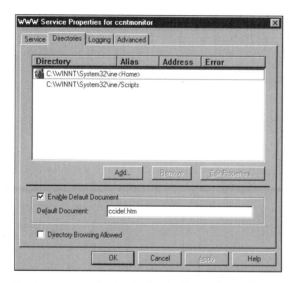

**Figure 9.12** The Directories property sheet lists the directories available to users.

IIS provides \Wwwroot, \Gophroot, and \Ftproot as the default home directories for each service. The files that you place in the home directory of IIS and its subdirectories are available to remote browsers.

You can add other directories outside the home directory that will appear to browsers as subdirectories of the home directory. This means that you can publish Web pages from other directories and have those directories appear to reside within the home directory. Such directories are called *virtual directories*. We will talk about how to set up virtual directories in a later section.

The published directories can be located on local or network drives. If the virtual directory is a network drive, be sure to provide a user name and password with access to that network drive. If you specify a user name and password, all IIS access to that directory will use that user name and password. Be extra careful when using Universal Naming Convention (UNC) connections to network drives to prevent possible security breaches.

## THE LOGGING PROPERTY SHEET

The logging property sheet, shown in Figure 9.13, allows the administrator to log the server activity. The server activity can be logged to a file or to

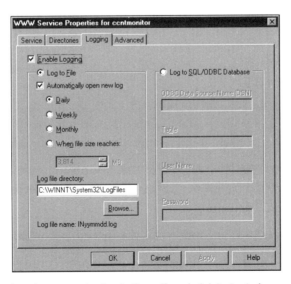

**Figure 9.13**  The Logging property sheet allows the administrator to log server activity.

an ODBC-supported database. If the server activity is logged to a file, the administrator can specify how often to create new logs and which directory these logs should go to. However, if the log is going to the ODBC Data Source Name (DSN) table, you must supply a valid user name and password to the database.

## *Logging Server Activity with IIS*

Microsoft IIS automatically logs all activity on your server, including who has been using the server and how many times your online information was accessed. This information is helpful to analyze traffic at your site and identify possible problems. To set up logging actvities:

1. In the Internet Service Manager, double click on the service to display its property sheets.

2. Select the Logging property sheet.

3. Determine in which directory the logs will be stored.

4. Specify how often logs are to be collected (every day, every week, every month, and so on).

5. Select the log tools (such as NT Performance Monitor or Insight Manager) you want to use to analyze the logs your server collects.

As we discussed earlier, this property sheet allows you to log information to a file or to a database. Let's look at each of these options in more detail.

### LOGGING TO A FILE

When logging to a file, the maximum total log line is 1200 bytes. Each field is limited to 150 bytes. The Logging property sheet provides several more options that you will need to specify when you choose to log to a file:

- *Automatically Open New Log*—Use this option to generate new logs using the specified frequency. If this option is not selected, the same log file will grow indefinitely.

- *Log File Directory*—This option sets the directory containing the log file.

- *Filename*—Lists the file name used for logging. If multiple services are configured to log to the same directory, they will use the same file.

Let's set up logging to save to a file. Follow these steps:

1.  In the Logging property sheet, select the Enable Logging check box.

2.  Select Log to File.

3.  To create a new log file when certain conditions are met, select the "Automatically open new log" check box. This option tells the service to close the log file and create a new one with a different name in the same directory when the appropriate interval or file size is reached.

The file names generated for log files depend on the options you select. If the "Automatically open new log" option is selected, the file name will be *SLOG*. If the "file size reaches" option is selected, the file name will be S*nnn*.LOG (where *nnn* is a sequentially increasing number for each log recorded). If either the Daily, Weekly, or Monthly option is selected, the file name will be *mmddyy*.LOG (where *mmddyy* is the month, day, and year when the log file was created).

For the Daily, Weekly, or Monthly option, the log file is closed the first time a log record is generated after midnight on the last day of the current log file. The new log file name will include the date of the first day in the log file.

## Logging to an SQL/ODBC Database

Logging to a file is the default method of logging when IIS is installed. If you prefer to collect logs in a database, you must install ODBC (v2.5 or later). You should then use the sample HTML pages installed with IIS to set up logging to a database. To access the pages, ensure that the Web service is running, then in the Internet Explorer, or another browser, type the local computer name.

For the best results, log to a Microsoft SQL Server database (v6.0 or later). If you do not want to log to a database or use the Internet Database Connector on a Web server, do not install any ODBC drivers. Choose Log to SQL/ODBC Database to log activity information to any ODBC-compliant data source. Set the Data Source Name (DSN) table, and specify the user name and password to use when logging to the database.

## THE ADVANCED PROPERTY SHEET

You can use Internet Service Manager's Advanced property sheet, shown in Figure 9.14, to control access to your server and to set the maximum network bandwidth for outbound traffic.

You have several choices when it comes to access: You can specify the IP address of the computers to be granted or denied access, you can grant access to all users, or you can deny access to all users. If you choose to grant access to all users by default, you can then specify the computers to be denied access. Conversely, if you choose to deny access to all users by default, you can then specify which computers will be allowed access.

You can also use the Advanced property sheet to limit the network bandwidth allowed for all of the Internet services on the server. Limiting the amount of bandwidth dedicated to users of IIS is a handy feature if your Internet line has multiple purposes. Limiting bandwidth will then allow other operations (such as email and remote logins) to use the same line without being slowed down by too much activity on the Internet server. To change the bandwidth, follow these steps:

1. In Internet Service Manager, double click the service for which you want to change the bandwidth usage.

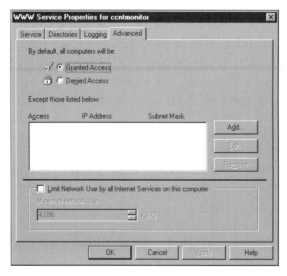

**Figure 9.14** The Advanced property sheet offers options for controlling rights and network traffic.

2. Click on the Advanced tab.

3. Select "Limit Network Use by all Internet Services on this computer," then select the number of kilobytes per second you want to allow for Internet services.

4. Click on Apply, and then click on OK.

As long as the actual bandwidth being used remains below the level you set, the read, write, and transfer functions are enabled. If actual bandwidth approximates the value you set, reads are blocked. If actual bandwidth exceeds the level you set, reads are rejected, and file transfers are blocked until bandwidth equals or falls below the set value.

# Using Other Windows NT Tools

The Internet Service Manager can be configured, controlled, and monitored by using the Windows NT utilities that directly affect your IIS. This section explains how you can use other Windows NT utilities to monitor or enhance your IIS site.

## *The Network Applet*

The Network applet in the Control Panel allows you to configure TCP/IP settings, including IP address, subnet mask, and default gateway. Double click on TCP/IP Protocol in the Installed Network Software listing to display the TCP/IP Configuration dialog box.

To set Domain Name System (DNS) settings, click on the DNS tab and set hostname, domain names, and DNS servers to resolve names.

## *The Services Applet*

You can use the Services applet as an alternative to the Internet Services Manager to start, stop, and pause Web, Gopher, and/or FTP services.

Once you start the applet, click on the Startup button to display the Log On As dialog box. You use this dialog box to configure how a service starts when you boot the computer. You can also use this dialog box to override the Web service account setting in the Service property sheet of Internet Service Manager. You should only change this setting if it is part of your security strategy; otherwise, stick with the default settings.

### The ODBC Applet

The Open Database Connectivity (ODBC) applet allows you to set up data query connectivity between databases created using different applications and formats.

### Setting File Access

Use Windows NT Explorer to set directory and file permissions on Windows NT File System (NTFS) drives. Click the right mouse button on the file name, click on the Security tab, and then click on Permissions.

### Setting User Access

User Manager for Domains, in the Administrative Tools program group, is a tool that you can use to manage security for a Windows NT server computer. With User Manager you can:

- Create and manage user accounts

- Create and manage groups

- Manage security policies

# Security with Internet Information Server

Connecting computers to the Internet is not only useful, it is very powerful. Within hours, it becomes possible to communicate with millions of people and companies worldwide. This broad flexibility imposes a degree of risk—not only can you communicate with people and other systems, it is also possible for users to attempt to initiate communication with your system. Although connecting to servers on the Internet is generally done with good intentions, there are always those few malicious individuals, with entirely too much time on their hands, who will attempt to infiltrate internal networks via your Internet server system. The Windows NT operating system is designed to help you secure your systems and information against intruders.

Your security configuration is crucial for safe operation of your server on the Internet. Although it is unlikely that your site will be maliciously tampered with, Internet servers are available to the general public, and there may be some degree of public intrusion.

This section will help you effectively use both Windows NT Server and Internet Information Server security at your site. You should understand all of the information in this section before connecting your computer to a public network. If you do not understand the information, you should consult the available Windows NT Server and Internet Information Server documentation, an authorized Microsoft Solution Provider, or another reliable source before installing your site on the Internet.

You can use the following topics as a checklist to ensure you have effectively secured your Windows NT server system. Additionally, you can prevent security breaches by properly configuring the services running on your computer.

## Preventing Intrusion by Setting Up User Accounts

Windows NT Server security helps you protect your computer and its resources by requiring assigned user accounts. You can control access to all computer resources by limiting the user rights of these accounts.

Every operation on a computer running Windows NT identifies who is doing the operation. For example, the user name and password that you use to log on to Windows NT 4 Server identifies who you are and defines what you are authorized to do on that computer.

You configure user rights in the User Manager. Simply select Policies|User Rights, and then choose the appropriate rights for the account. One specific right of note is "Log on Locally," which is required for users to use Internet Information Server services.

## Preventing Intrusion by Allowing Anonymous Access

When a client request does not contain a user name and password, such as an anonymous FTP connection or a Gopher request, an anonymous connection is processed. This approach prevents hackers from attempting to gain access to sensitive information with fraudulent or illegally obtained passwords.

Each Internet service maintains a Windows NT user name and password to be used for the processing of anonymous requests. When an anonymous request is received, the service "impersonates" the user configured as the anonymous logon user. The request will succeed if the anonymous logon user has permission to access the requested resource, as determined by the resource's Access Control List (ACL).

**TIP** If the user does not have permission to access the resource, the response returned to the client contains a list of supported authentication schemes for gaining access to the resource, based on server configuration.

You can modify the anonymous logon user account on the Service property sheet of the Internet Service Manager. For instance, you can set multiple IIS services running on the same computer to use the same anonymous logon user accounts. And including the anonymous logon user account in file or directory ACLs allows for precise control of the resources available to anonymous clients.

The anonymous logon user account specified must be a valid Windows NT user account on the server computer, and the password specified must match the password for this user in that computer's user database. As I mentioned in the previous section, you set up user accounts and passwords with the Windows NT User Manager. Keep in mind that the anonymous logon user account, like all user accounts, must have the right to log on locally (in the User Manager, select Policies|User Rights, and then choose "Log on Locally").

The IUSR_*computername* account (the anonymous access account) is created during Microsoft Internet Information Server set up. If the computer name is Sales1, then the anonymous access account name is IUSR_Sales1. By default, all Microsoft Internet Information Server client requests use this account. In other words, IIS clients are logged on to the computer using the IUSR_*computername* account. The IUSR_*computername* account is permitted *only* to log on locally; no network rights are granted that could allow an unauthorized user to damage your server or its files.

The IUSR_*computername* account is also added to the group Guests. If you have changed the settings for the Guests group, those changes also apply to the IUSR_*computername* account. You should review the settings for the Guests group to ensure that they are also appropriate for the IUSR_*computername* account.

A randomly generated password is created by the system for the IUSR_*computername* account. For maximum convenience and security, I suggest that you change the password. To do this, you must specify the new password for the account in the User Manager and on the Service property sheet of the Internet Service Manager for each Internet Information Server service installed.

When you install IIS on a PDC or BDC, the anonymous logon user account is created in the user account database of the domain. When you install IIS on a domain member server or a standalone server, the account is created on the local computer. If you install IIS on multiple domain controllers of the same domain, a separate user account is created in the domain user database for each Internet server system. This setup does not cause any conflicts because each user name is unique, containing the name of the associated computer. However, you may find it more convenient to create a single anonymous logon user account in the domain to use for all IIS domain controllers in the domain. This approach can simplify administration of ACLs. To create a single anonymous account, follow these steps:

1. In the User Manager, create a new anonymous logon user account in the domain. Be sure that this account is made a member of appropriate groups, given a secure password, and given the right to log on locally (select Policies|User Rights, and then choose "Log on Locally").

2. On the Service property sheet of the Internet Service Manager, specify the new anonymous logon user name and password. You must do this for each Internet Information Server service running on all PDCs and BDCs in the domain. Figures 9.15, 9.16, and 9.17 show each Internet service (Web, Gopher, and FTP) with the anonymous logon and password.

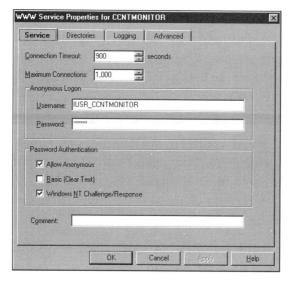

**Figure 9.15**  Web Service tab with Anonymous Logon setup.

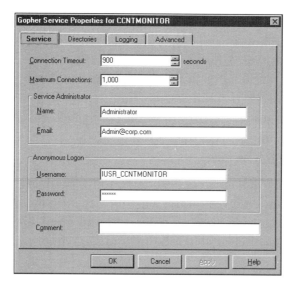

**Figure 9.16**  Gopher Service tab with Anonymous Logon setup.

3.  When you install Internet Information Server on other domain con-
    trollers in the domain, be sure to use the Internet Service Manager to
    modify the anonymous logon user name and password to match those
    created with the User Manager. Do this for each Internet Informa-
    tion Server service you install.

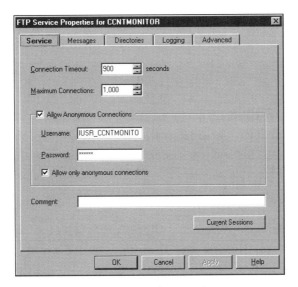

**Figure 9.17**    FTP Service tab with Anonymous Logon setup.

If you allow remote access only through the IUSR_*computername* account, remote users will not need to provide a user name and password, but they will have only the permissions assigned to that account. For some situations, you will find that this approach provides the best security.

## Preventing Intrusion by Requiring a User Name and Password

If you require authenticated clients, users must supply a valid Windows NT user name and password to access the system. Basic authentication does not encrypt your user name and password before transmission, it simply encodes the information using UUEncode. Unfortunately, anyone with access to your network, or to a segment of the Internet that transfers your packets, can easily decode this information.

The Web service also supports the Windows NT Challenge/Response encrypted password transmission. Microsoft recommends using only the Windows NT Challenge/Response method of password authentication. Unfortunately, only Internet Explorer version 2.0 or later supports this type of authentication.

Password authentication is useful if you want only authorized individuals to use your server or specific portions controlled by NTFS. You can have both IUSR_*computername* access and authenticated access enabled at the same time.

## SETTING THE OPTIONS

You set authentication options on the Service property sheet of Internet Service Manager. This section details the options you can select for both the Web and FTP services.

For the Web service:

- *Allow Anonymous*—When this check box is selected, anonymous connections are processed and the anonymous logon user name and password are used for these connections. When this check box is cleared, all anonymous connections are rejected, and basic or Windows NT Challenge/Response authentication protocol is required to access content.

- *Basic*—When this check box is selected, the Web service will process requests using basic authentication. Basic authentication sends Windows NT user names and passwords across the network without encryption. This check box is cleared by default for security reasons.

- *Windows NT Challenge/Response*—When this check box is selected, the service will honor requests by clients to send user account information using the Windows NT Challenge/Response authentication protocol.

If the Basic and Windows NT Challenge/Response check boxes are both cleared (and the Allow Anonymous check box is selected), all client requests are processed as anonymous requests. In this case, if the client supplies a user name and password in the request, they are ignored by the Web service, and the anonymous logon user account will be used to process the request instead.

For the FTP service:

- *Allow Anonymous Connection*—When this check box is selected, FTP logons with a user name of anonymous will be processed. These anonymous connections will be processed on behalf of the Windows NT user account specified on the Service property sheet. When this check box is cleared, users will be required to enter valid Windows NT user names and passwords to log on to the FTP service.

- *Allow Only Anonymous Connections*—When this check box is selected, user logons with a user name other than anonymous will be rejected.

- *Windows NT Challenge/Response*—FTP user names and passwords are sent across the network in clear text. When this check box is cleared, Windows NT passwords will be sent to the server without encryption. This check box is selected (enabled) by default for security reasons.

## Client Requests Containing Credentials

Some servers need to provide for requests containing credentials (a user name and password). When a client sends a request containing credentials, it is in one of the following situations:

- An FTP client logs on with a valid Windows NT user name and password. This requires that the FTP service "Allow only anonymous connections" check box be cleared. FTP sends passwords across the network in clear text.

- A Web (HTTP) request's headers contain a user name and password (this is generally in response to an "access denied" response from a server). This is HTTP basic authentication. HTTP basic authentication sends passwords across the network in clear text.

- A Web browser supports Windows NT Challenge/Response authentication protocol, and an anonymous client request is denied access to a resource. In this case, the browser automatically sends the Windows client's user name and password to the Web server using the Windows NT Challenge/Response authentication protocol. In this release, the only browser that supports Windows NT Challenge/Response authentication protocol is Internet Explorer 2.0 or later.

When an IIS service receives a client request that contains credentials, the anonymous logon user account is not used in processing the request. Instead, the user name and password received by the client are used by the service. If the service is not granted permission to access the requested resource while using the specified user name and password, the request fails, and an error notification is returned to the client.

For the Web (HTTP) service only:

When an anonymous request fails because the anonymous logon user account does not have permission to access the desired resource, the response to the client indicates which authentication schemes the service supports. This is determined by the configuration of the Web service's authentication features. If the response indicates to the client that the service is configured to support HTTP basic authentication, most Web browsers will display a user name and password dialog box, and reissue the anonymous request as a request with credentials, including the user name and password entered by the user.

If a Web browser supports Windows NT Challenge/Response authentication protocol, and the Web service is configured to support this protocol, an anonymous Web request that fails due to inadequate permissions will result in automatic use of the Windows NT Challenge/Response authentication protocol. The browser will then send a user name and encrypted password from the client to the service. The client request will then be reprocessed, using the client's user information. The user account obtained from the client is the same account with which the user is logged on to the client computer. Because this account, including its Windows NT domain, must be a valid account on the Web server computer, Windows NT Challenge/Response authentication is very useful in an intranet environment, where the client and server computers are in the same, or trusted, domains.

Note that the FTP service supports Read and Write only; the Gopher service supports Read only, as shown in Figures 9.18 and 9.19.

## *Securely Configuring the Web Service*

In addition to implementing the suggestions in Chapter 4 on securing Windows NT server, you can further enhance your security by using Internet Service Manager to configure the Web service.

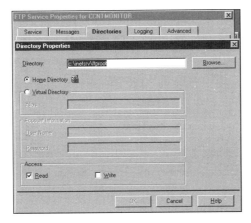

**Figure 9.18**   FTP Service with Read and Write directory access options.

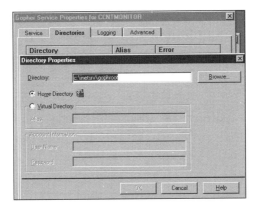

**Figure 9.19**   Gopher Service with directory access.

## CONTROLLING ACCESS BY USER NAME

To gain access to files, users must be identified with a valid user name and password. If you are allowing anonymous logon using the IUSR_*computername* account, you should first ensure that computer-wide User Rights (in the User Manager Policies menu) do not allow the IUSR_*computername* account, the Guests group, or the Everyone group any right other than "Log on Locally." Next, ensure that the file permissions set in the Windows NT File Manager are appropriate for all content directories used by Microsoft Internet Information Server.

If you allow basic or Windows NT Challenge/Response password authentication, users can supply a user name and password to gain access to areas that require specific authorization. The user name must be valid on the computer running IIS or in a Windows NT domain accessible from that computer.

To set user name and password security:

1. In the Internet Service Manager, double click on the service to display its property sheets, then click on the Service tab.

2. In the Anonymous Logon box, enter the user name and password to be used by the Web service when accessing resources on behalf of an anonymous client. This account must be a valid account in the Windows NT User Manager.

3. In the Password Authentication box, select the following options:

   - Allow Anonymous

   - Basic (clear text)

   - Windows NT Challenge/Response for encrypted authentication (remember, this option works only for clients using Internet Explorer version 2.0 or later)

4. Click on OK.

## IMPLEMENTING ACCESS BY IP ADDRESS

The source IP address of every packet received is checked against the Internet Information Server settings in the Advanced property sheet, which we discussed earlier in the chapter. As I pointed out in that section, if IIS is configured to allow access by all computers except those listed as exceptions to that rule, access is denied to any computer with an IP address included in that list. Conversely, if IIS is configured to deny all IP addresses, access is denied to all remote users except those whose IP addresses have been specifically granted access.

IP address security is probably most useful on the Internet to exclude everyone except known users. IP address security can also be used to exclude individuals or entire networks that you do not want to grant access to.

Let's take a moment to work through the different techniques you can use to grant or deny access to users.

To deny access to a specific computer or group of computers:

1. In the Advanced property sheet of Internet Service Manager, click on the Granted Access button.

2. Click on Add.

3. In the IP Address box, enter the IP address of the computer to be denied access to your site, or click on the button next to the IP Address box to use a DNS name, such as www.company.com.

4. To deny access to a group of computers, select Group of Computers. In the IP Address and Subnet Mask boxes, enter the IP address and the subnet mask for a group to be denied access.

5. Click on OK. Access will now be granted to all computers except the ones in the window with an Access status of Denied.

6. In the Advanced property sheet, click on OK.

To grant access to only a specific computer or group of computers:

1. In the Advanced property sheet of the Internet Service Manager, click on the Denied Access button to display the WWW Advanced tab, as shown in Figure 9.20.

2. Click on Add, which displays the Grant Access On dialog box shown in Figure 9.21.

3. In the IP Address field, enter the IP address of the computer to be granted access, or click on the button next to the IP Address box to use a DNS name, such as www.company.com.

4. To grant access to a specific group of computers, select Group of Computers. In the IP Address and Subnet Mask boxes, enter the IP address and the subnet mask for the group to be granted access to.

5. Click on OK. Access will be denied to all computers except those in the window with an Access status of Granted.

6. In the Advanced property sheet, click on OK.

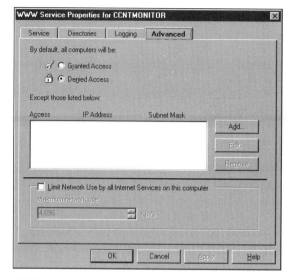

**Figure 9.20**   The WWW Service Properties Advanced tab.

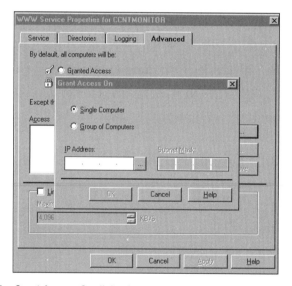

**Figure 9.21**   The Grant Access On dialog box.

## DISABLE DIRECTORY BROWSING

Unless it is part of your strategy, you should disable directory browsing on the Directories property sheet. If it is not configured correctly, directory browsing can expose the entire file structure. You run the risk of exposing program files or other files to unauthorized access.

## Interactive and Network Users

If you use the predefined Windows NT user accounts INTERACTIVE and NETWORK for access control, your use of these accounts may affect client access to some resources. In order for a file to be accessed by anonymous client requests or client requests using basic authentication, the requested file must be accessible by the INTERACTIVE user. In order for a file to be accessible by a client request using Windows NT Challenge/Response authentication protocol, the file must be accessible by the NETWORK user.

## Customized Authentication

If you need a Web request authentication scheme not supported by the service directly, obtain a copy of the Internet Server Application Programming Interface (ISAPI) Software Development Kit (SDK). Read the ISAPI Filters specification on how to develop user-written ISAPI Filter dynamic link libraries (DLLs) that handle request authentication. You can pick up your copy of the ISAPI SDK at **http://www.microsoft.com/intdev**.

## Setting Directory Access for the Web Service

When creating a Web publishing directory in the Internet Service Manager, you can set three access permissions in the Directories dialog box. The setting of these access permissions applies to the defined home directory or virtual directory (we'll discuss virtual directories in detail later in the chapter) and all of its subdirectories. Let's take a look at these permissions, which are shown in Figure 9.22.

### READ

In order for files stored in a directory (home directory or virtual directory) to be downloaded to a client, you must enable the directory's Read permission. If a client sends a request for a file that is in a directory without Read permission, the Web service will return an error. Directories containing information to publish (HTML files, for example) would typically have this permission enabled.

Directories containing Common Gateway Interface (CGI) applications and ISAPI DLLs would typically have this permission disabled, to prevent clients from downloading the application files.

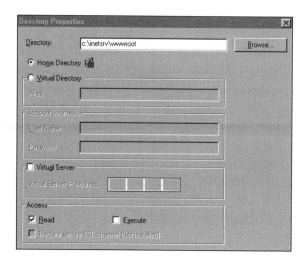

**Figure 9.22**   The Directory Properties dialog box.

## EXECUTE

A client request can invoke a CGI application or an ISAPI application in one of two ways. The file name of the CGI executable or the ISAPI DLL can be specified in the request (URL), as shown here:

```
http://inetsrvr.microsoft.com/scripts/httpodbc.dll/scripts/
pubs.idc?lname=Smith
```

For this request to be valid, the file httpodbc.dll must be stored somewhere in the Web publishing tree (in this example, /scripts), and the directory it is stored in must have the Execute permission selected. This way the administrator can permit applications (CGI or ISAPI) to be run from a small number of carefully monitored directories.

The other way to configure CGI and ISAPI applications is to use the Web File Extension Mapping feature, which allows your executables and DLLs to be stored somewhere other than the Web publishing tree. An example URL would be:

```
http://inetsrvr.microsoft.com/scripts/pubs.idc?lname=Smith
```

In this example, the script file is stored in a directory of the Web publishing tree that has the Execute permission enabled. The service, upon receiving the request, will use the file name extension mappings to determine where to find the application, which can be stored anywhere. This technique prevents users from invoking CGI and ISAPI applications directly by adding parameters in the URL. This is, therefore, a more secure mechanism and useful for all Web applications and scripts.

### REQUIRE SECURE SSL CHANNEL

This option must be selected to require encrypted communication for a directory.

## *NTFS File Security*

The Web, Gopher, and FTP services included with the Microsoft Internet Information Server are fully integrated with Windows NT Server user accounts and file access permissions.

Every access to a resource, such as a file, an HTML page, or an ISAPI, is done by the services on behalf of a Windows NT user. The service uses that user's user name and password in the attempt to read or execute the resource for the client.

In addition to user accounts, you should place your data files on an NTFS partition. NTFS provides security and access control for your data files. You can limit access to portions of your file system for specific users and services by using NTFS. In particular, it is a good idea to apply ACLs to your data files for any Internet publishing service.

# Running Other Network Services for the Internet

You should review all of the network services that you are using on any computer connected to the Internet.

The fewer services you are running on your system, the less likely you will make a mistake in administration that could be exploited. Use the Services applet in the Control Panel to disable any services not absolutely necessary on your Internet server.

## *Unbind Unnecessary Services from Your Internet Adapter Cards*

Use the Bindings feature in the Network applet to unbind any unnecessary services from any network adapter cards connected to the Internet. For example, you might use the Server service to copy new images and documents from computers in your internal network, but you might not want remote users to have direct access to the Server service from the Internet.

If you need to use the Server service on your private network, disable the Server service binding to any network adapter cards connected to the Internet. You can use the Windows NT server service over the Internet; however, you should fully understand the security implications and comply with Windows NT server licensing requirements issues. When you are using the Windows NT server service, you are using Microsoft Networking (the SMB protocol rather than the HTTP protocol) and all Windows NT Server licensing requirements still apply. HTTP connections do not apply to Windows NT server licensing requirements.

You should also disable the FTP server service included with Windows NT (this is required if the Microsoft Internet Information Server FTP service will be installed) or configure the service to ensure adequate security. Follow the directions on the Services tab, Messages tab, Directories tab, Logging tab, and the Advanced tab of the FTP service.

### CHECK PERMISSIONS ON NETWORK SHARES

If you are running the Server service on your Internet adapter cards, be sure to double check the permissions set on the shares you have created on the system. It is also wise to double check the permissions set on the files contained in the shares' directories to ensure that you have set them correctly.

# Securing Data Transmissions with Secure Sockets Layer (SSL)

Microsoft Internet Information Server offers a protocol for providing data security layered between its service protocols (HTTP) and TCP/IP. This security protocol, called Secure Sockets Layer (SSL), provides data encryption, server authentication, and message integrity for a TCP/IP connection. SSL is a protocol submitted to the W3C working group on security for consideration as a standard security approach for World Wide Web browsers and servers on the Internet.

SSL provides a security "handshake" that is used to initiate the TCP/IP connection. This handshake results in the client and server agreeing on the level of security that they will use, and fulfills any authentication requirements for the connection. Thereafter, SSL's only role is to encrypt and decrypt the byte stream of the application protocol being used (for example, HTTP). This means that all the information in both the HTTP request and the HTTP response are fully encrypted, including the URL the client is requesting, any submitted form contents (such as credit card numbers), any HTTP access authorization information (user names and passwords), and all the data returned from the server to the client.

An SSL-enabled server can send and receive private communication across the Internet to SSL-enabled clients (browsers), such as Microsoft Internet Explorer version 2.0 or later.

To enable SSL security on a Microsoft Internet Information Server, you'll need the help of the IIS Key Manager, which is shown in Figure 9.23. The

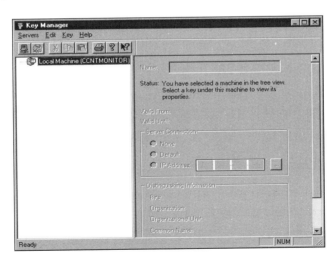

**Figure 9.23**  Internet Information Server Key Manager.

Key Manager allows you to define a key with distinguishing information—like organization name or country—and then use the key to view the machine and the properties.

Enabling SSL security requires that you complete these four steps: generating a key pair file and a requesting file, requesting a certificate from a certification authority, installing the certificate on your server, and activating SSL security on a Web service directory. We'll discuss these steps in more detail in a moment, but first, I want to list a few things you should keep in mind the when you enable SSL security:

- You can enable SSL security on the root of your Web home directory (\Wwwroot by default) or on one or more virtual directories.

- Once enabled and properly configured, only SSL-enabled clients will be able to communicate with the SSL-enabled Web directories.

- URLs that point to documents on an SSL-enabled Web directory must use "https://" instead of "http://" in the URL. Any links using "http://" in the URL will not work on a secure directory.

- SSL security is enabled and disabled by using the Internet Service Manager.

## *Acquiring an SSL Digital Certificate*

As part of the process of enabling Secure Sockets Layer (SSL) security on your Internet server, you need to generate a key pair and then acquire an SSL certificate. The new Key Manager application simplifies this procedure.

### GENERATING A KEY PAIR

Use Key Manager to create a key file containing the key pair and a certificate request file, as shown in Figure 9.24. Here's how you do it:

1.   In the Internet Server program group, click on Key Manager.

2.   Select Key|Create New Key.

3.   In the Create New Key and Certificate Request dialog box, fill in the requested information, as follows:

     - *Key Name*—Assign a name to the key you are creating.

     - *Password*—Specify a password to encrypt the private key and bits.

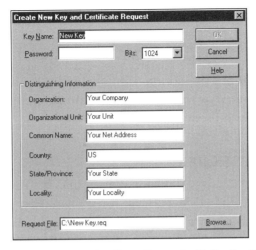

**Figure 9.24** Creating a new Key and Certificate Request with the Key Manager.

- *Bits*—By default, Key Manager generates a key pair 1024 bits long. To specify a key that is 512 or 768 bits long, make the proper selection in this box.

- *Organization*—An International Organization for Standardization (ISO) registered top-level organization or a company name.

- *Organizational Unit*—Your department within your company, such as Marketing.

- *Common Name*—The domain name of the server, for example, www.mycompany.com.

- *Country*—Two letter ISO country designation, for example, US, FR, AU, UK, and so on.

- *State/Province*—For example, Washington, Alberta, California, and so on. Do not abbreviate.

- *Locality*—The city where your company is located, such as Redmond or Toronto.

- *Request File*—Type the name of the request file that will be created.

4. Click on OK. When prompted, retype the password you typed in the form, and then click on OK again.

Your key will appear in the Key Manager window under the computer name.

**TIP**  Do not use commas in any field. Commas are interpreted as the end of that field and will generate an invalid request without warning.

## Acquiring a Certificate

The key generated by Key Manager is not valid for use on the Internet until you obtain a valid key certificate for it from a key authority, such as VeriSign (**www.verisign.com**). Send the certificate request file to your key authority service to obtain a valid certificate. Until you do so, the key will exist on its host computer, but cannot be used.

## Installing Your Certificate to Your Server

After you complete your certificate request, you will receive a signed certificate from the certification authority (consult your certification authority for complete details). It will look something like this:

```
—BEGIN CERTIFICATE—
JIEBSDSCEXoCHQEwLQMJSoZILvoNVQECSQAwcSETMRkOAMUTBhMuVrMmIoAnBdNVBAoTF1JTQS
BEYXRhIFN1Y3VyaXR5LCBJbmMuMRwwGgYDVQQLExNQZXJzb25hIEN1cnRpZm1jYXR1MSQwIgY
DVQQDExtPcGVuIE1hcmt1dCBUZXN0IFN1cnZ1ciAxMTAwHhcNOTUwNzE5MjAyNzMwWhcNOTYw
NTEOMjAyOTEwWjBzMQswCQYDVQQGEwJVUzEgMB4GA1UEChMXU1NBIERhdGEgU2VjdXJpdHksIEluYy
4xHDAaBgNVBAsTE1B1cnNvbmEgQ2VydGlmaWNhdGUxJDAiBgNVBAMTG09wZW4gTWFya2V0IFR
1c3QgU2VydmVyIDExMDBcMA0GCSqGSIb3DQEBAQUAA0sAMEgCQQDU/71rgR6vkVNX40BAq1po
GdSmGkD1iN3sEPfSTGxNJXY58XH3JoZ4nrF7mIfvpghNi1taYimvhbBPNqYe4yLPAgMBAAEwDQYJKoZIhvc
NAQECBQADQQBqyCpws9EaAjKKAefuNP+z+8NY8khckgyHN2LLpfhv+iP8m+bF66HNDUFz8ZrV
Ou3WQapgLPV90kIskNKXX3a
—END CERTIFICATE—
```

Copy and save the text to a file, using a tool such as Notepad, giving it a name you can remember (for example, certif.txt).

To install a certificate, start the Key Manager (see Step 1 in the previous exercise). Select Key|Install Key Certificate, and follow the on-screen instructions.

*Note: If you do not specify an IP address while installing your certificate, the same certificate will be applied to all virtual servers created on the system. If you are hosting multiple sites on a single server, you can specify that the certificate be used only for a given IP address by adding the IP address during installation.*

### CONFIGURING A DIRECTORY TO REQUIRE SSL

Once you have installed the certificate, you can enable SSL security from Internet Service Manager for the Web service. You can require SSL on any virtual directory available through the Internet server on the Directories section of the Service property sheet.

## *Additional SSL Suggestions*

Microsoft recommends that you use separate content directories for secure and public content (for example, C:\Inetsrv\Wwwroot\Secure-Content and C:\InetsrvWwwroot\Public-Content). It is also important to avoid having a server directory not protected by SSL as a parent for a secure directory.

I also suggest that you save your key file in a safe place in case you need it in the future. It is a good idea to store your key file on a floppy disk and remove it from the local system after completing all setup steps. *Don't forget the password you assigned to the key file.*

# Performance with NT and Internet Information Server

When you first start your Web service, performance will not be an issue. However, when your Web server is stabilized and you get up to speed with commercial implementations, the importance of performance increases. The factors that contribute to the performance of a server are:

* *Scalability*—Web servers should be easy to install and manage. They should also have the capability of handling the growth of the next-generation of dynamic sites. When setting up your server, be sure to leave enough memory for functions like database and mail server applications.

- *Dynamic Content*—As the Internet progresses to 3D, audio, video, and specialized Web pages, the power to support these functions also increases. Your Web server should be able to handle these demands.

- *Peak Planning*—The pattern of client access to Web servers can peak at levels higher than expected. A high-performance server allows a site to be better prepared for peaks.

## Performance Measurements

You can measure the performance of a Web server in many ways. The following are some of the performance metrics you should take into account:

- *Connections per Second*—This represents the sum of successful interactions across all the clients. An interaction is establishing a TCP/IP connection between the client and the server, sending a request from the client to the server over the connection, receiving the correct data from the request, and closing the TCP/IP connection.

- *Web Transactions per Second*—This is the number of client requests and responses per second.

- *Safety and Security*—As you know by now, security on the Internet is a very hot topic and figures heavily into the performance of your Web server. Internet Information Server uses the Windows NT directory services and brings requirements like user ID and password to the Internet. IIS is integrated with the Windows NT security model and built-in SSL.

- *Viewable by Everyone*—A server should be compatible with any browser.

- *Easy to Manage*—A Web server should provide monitoring, logging, and new user services. The IIS Internet Service Manager shows information graphically.

- *Designed for Network*—A Web server should be able to host multiple sites securely, and network managers should be able to host multiple sites easily on a single server. This approach optimizes hardware investment and simplifies systems management without compromising security.

As you configure Windows NT Server for the Web, keep these criteria in mind, and don't forget to allow for growth; 10 percent per year is used throughout the industry as a standard growth figure.

# Web Virtual Servers and Virtual Directories with IIS and NT

An Internet Information Server-based computer can have multiple domain names, which enables a single server to appear as several servers. These additional servers are called *virtual servers*. You can associate each content directory with a specific virtual server. This feature makes it possible to service Web requests for two domain names (such as http://www.company1.com and http://www.company2.com) from the same computer.

If the path for a virtual directory is a network drive, you must provide a user name and password with access to that network drive. If you have assigned more than one IP address to your server, when you create a directory, you must specify which IP address has access to that directory. If you don't specify an IP address, the directory will be visible to all virtual servers.

The default directories created during setup do not specify an IP address. You may need to specify IP addresses for the default directories when you add virtual servers. Let's explore and learn more about the concept of virtual servers and directories in detail.

# Creating and Configuring Virtual Servers

By convention, each domain name, such as www.company.com, represents an individual system. However, it is possible to use a single server system and make it appear to be not only a primary server (for example, named www.company.com), but also servers for different departments of your company (for example, marketing.company.com, sales.company.com, and so on). You do not need a different computer for each domain name.

To complete the exercise in this section, you must obtain IP addresses from your ISP for the primary server and for each virtual server you want to create. For example, you assign the first IP address in the Domain Name System (DNS) as www.company.com (your primary server) and assign C:\Wwwroot as its content home directory. You register the second IP address in the DNS as marketing.company.com and assign a different drive or directory as its content home directory. Thus, it appears to users on the Internet that there are two computers when, in fact, it is the same computer running one copy of the Web service. If you create a home directory without specifying an IP address, that home directory will be used for all requests containing server IP addresses not specified in other home directories.

These multiple IP addresses can be assigned to multiple network adapter cards or to a single card. You use the Network applet in the Windows NT Control Panel to bind the additional IP addresses to your network adapter card.

After you've assigned the IP address to the network adapter card, you must assign a home content directory to that IP address. In the Directories property sheet, select the Virtual Server box, and enter the home content directory's IP address. You can also restrict virtual directories (directories that are not home directories) to one virtual server by assigning an IP address to them, as well.

To create a virtual server, follow these step:

1. In the Internet Service Manager, double click on the Web service.

2. Click on the Directories tab.

3. Click on Add.

4. In the Directory box of the Directory Properties dialog box, select a directory by clicking the Browse button.

5. In the Alias box, enter the name you have chosen for your virtual server.

6. Select the Virtual Server check box.

7. Enter the IP address for the virtual server. This address is usually supplied by your ISP.

8.  Select the Execute option if you want to allow users to execute applications on your site.

9.  Click on OK.

**TIP**  To create more than five virtual servers, you must change a Windows NT Registry entry.

## Creating and Configuring Virtual Directories

Now, let's turn our attention to virtual directories. An Internet service can have one home directory and any number of other publishing directories. These other publishing directories are referred to as *virtual directories*. Each directory can be located on a local drive or across the network by specifying the directory with a Universal Naming Convention (UNC) name, and a user name and password to use for access permission. Virtual directories on network drives must be on computers in the same Windows NT domain as the Internet Information Server.

To simplify client URL addresses, the services present the entire set of publishing directories to clients as a single directory tree. The home directory is the root of this "virtual" directory tree, and each virtual directory is addressed as if it were a subdirectory of the home directory. Actual subdirectories of the virtual directories are available to clients, as well.

Virtual directories will not appear in directory listings (called *directory browsing* for the Web service). To access a virtual directory, users must know the virtual directory's *alias* (more on this concept in a moment) and enter the URL in the browser. To aid users in accessing the individual Internet services, you can also:

*   Create links in HTML pages (Web)

*   Create explicit links in tag files (Gopher)

*   List virtual directories by using directory annotations (FTP)

Directory browsing on the Web service is very similar to browsing in FTP. Directory browsing is useful if you have a lot of files that you want to share quickly without converting them to HTML format.

When a virtual directory is defined in the Internet Service Manager, an alias is associated with the virtual directory. The alias, as I mentioned a moment ago, is the subdirectory name that will be used by clients to access information in the virtual directory. If alias names for virtual directories are not specified by the administrator, an alias name is generated automatically by Internet Service Manager.

For example, suppose an administrator defines the following two directories for the Web service:

- C:\Inetsrv\Wwwroot <home directory>

- D:\Webdata Alias = data

If C:\Inetsrv\Wwwroot contains the subdirectory C:\Inetserv\Wwwroot\Scripts and D:\Webdata contains the subdirectory D:\Webdata\Images, the following URLs can be requested by a Web client:

- http://inetsrvr.cciinet.com/schedule.htm

- http://inetsrvr.cciinet.com/scripts/query1.htm

- http://inetsrvr.cciinet.com/data/stocks.htm

- http://inetsrvr.cciinet.com/data/images/graph1.htm

You can create an almost unlimited number of virtual directories for your service, although performance may suffer if you create too many of them. Use them only as required.

One of the directories listed on the Directories property sheet is marked as a home directory (sometimes referred to as a root directory). The path used in a client request to refer to the home directory is a forward slash (/). When a client request contains a path of /, or does not specify the path to a resource, the Internet server looks in the defined home directory for the resource. For example, all of the following URLs refer to the Web server's home directory:

- http://inetsrvr.cciinet.com

- http://inetsrvr.cciinet.com/

- http://inetsrvr.cciinet.com/content.htm

The action taken by the Web server for the first two URLs depends on the settings of the Default Document and Directory Browsing options (more on these options later) specified on the Service property sheet of Internet Service Manager. For the third example, the HTML file, content.htm, which is located in the home directory, is sent to the client. If a file by that name does not exist in the home directory, the server returns an error to the client. Other directories are not searched for such a file.

When a client logs on to the FTP service, the service looks for a subdirectory under the specified home directory with the name of the user logging on. For anonymous FTP logons, the service looks for a directory called "anonymous" under the home directory. If such a directory exists, the user will start the session with it as the current directory. If such a directory is not found, the current directory will be the home directory.

Subdirectories of the home directory are accessible to clients. For example, if a Web server is configured with a home directory of C:\Wwwroot, then the URL

```
http://inetsrvr.cciinet.com/data/content.htm
```

looks for a file by the name content.htm in the directory C:\Wwwroot\data. If the "data" subdirectory doesn't exist, or the file is not found in that directory, the server will return an error. The FTP service allows users to change the current directory to subdirectories of the home directory (by using the cd command), and Gopher selectors can refer to objects in subdirectories of the home directory.

Enough talk. Let's work through the steps to create a virtual directory:

1. In the Internet Service Manager, double click the service for which you want to add a virtual directory.

2. Click on the Directories tab, and click on Add.

3. Click on the Virtual Directory button, and enter the name of the virtual directory in the Alias box.

4. Set the Access permissions, using the following list as a guide:

   • *Read*—This option must be selected for content directories.

- *Write*—This option must be selected for directories that will accept data from users. Assign Write access cautiously to prevent unauthorized users from placing malicious files on your computer.

- *Execute*—This option must be selected for directories containing programs, scripts, and Internet Server API (ISAPI) applications. Make sure that directories with Execute enabled do not also have Write enabled; this will prevent programs (not necessarily of the friendly variety) from being copied to your server and then started, which could cause damage to your system. Also, make sure that directories with Execute enabled do not also have Read enabled; this will prevent users from seeing your interactive content files.

- *Require Secure SSL Channel*—This option must be selected to require encrypted communication for a directory.

5. Click on OK.

## Specifying Account Information

This entry applies only if the physical directory is listed by using a UNC path, such as \\Research4\Public\WWWfiles. If this is the case, enter a user name and password with permission to use the network directory share, then click on Apply and OK. Virtual directories on network drives must be on computers in the same Windows NT domain as the Internet Information Server.

## Setting the Directory

To specify the fully qualified path for the directory to use for the selected virtual server, click on the Add button, and enter the path in the Directory box of the Directory Properties dialog box, or use the Browse button to pick the directory to use.

## Specifying Your Home Directory

As we discussed earlier, each of the Internet services publishes information stored in one or more directories. The administrator specifies these publishing directories on the Directories property sheet of the Internet Service Manager. Adding a directory on this property sheet allows the respective service to make available to clients information stored in the specified directory and all of its subdirectories. Directories not listed on this property sheet are not available to clients.

Every server must have a home directory for content files. The home directory is the "root" directory for that service. A root directory does not have a name. By default, the home directory and all subdirectories are available to users.

If your HTML content files are contained under one directory tree, all you need to do is copy them to the default Web home directory (\Wwwroot) or change the home directory to refer to the location containing your files. However, if your files reside in multiple directories or on multiple computers on your network, you will need to create virtual directories to make those files available by following the steps in the *Creating and Configuring Content Directories* section.

To add a directory, follow these steps:

1. In the Internet Service Manager, double click on the service for which you want to add a directory.

2. Click on the Directories tab, and click on Add.

3. In the Directory box, enter the name of the new directory or select a new directory by using the Browse button.

4. In the Access box (if applicable), select the access you want to give users who connect to that directory.

5. Click on OK.

6. Click on Apply, and then click on OK.

To delete a directory, follow these steps:

1. In Internet Service Manager, double click on the service for which you want to delete a directory.

2. Click on the Directories tab.

3. In the Directory list, select the directory you want to delete.

4. Click on Remove.

5. Click on Apply, and then click on OK.

## Setting the Default Document

If a remote user sends a request without a specific file name (for example, http://www.cciinet.com), the Web service will return the specified default document, if it exists in that directory. You can place a file with the specified default document file name in each subdirectory. In the Directories property sheet for the Web service, change the Default Document entry to the default file name you will use on your system. Often, the default document is set to be an index file (for example, Index.htm) for the contents of that directory (or of the entire server).

If no default document is available, the server will return an error, unless directory browsing is enabled. If directory browsing is enabled, a directory listing containing links to the files and directories in that directory will appear.

# Publishing Information

Now that you have installed and configured Microsoft Internet Information Server and it is running, you are ready to publish on the Internet or your intranet. Providing information with Internet Information Server is easy. If your files are in HTML format, just add them to the appropriate home directory. For example, if you are using the Web service, place the files in the \Wwwroot directory.

## Using a Browser to Administer Internet Information Server

The HTML Administrator program can perform the same functions as the Internet Service Manager. You can use HTML Administrator with your Internet browser to administer IIS across the Internet. To use HTML Administrator, you must be logged on to a user account that has Administrator privileges on the computer being administered. Then, point your Internet browser to *computername*/htmla/htmla.htm. For example, if your workstation is named www.nt.org, you would point your browser to http://www.nt.org/htmla/htmla.htm.

If you are using a browser that is capable of Windows NT Challenge/ Response (NTLM) authentication (such as Microsoft Internet Explorer), you can use NTLM authentication. If you are not using a browser capable of NTLM authentication, then you must use basic authentication (although this is not recommended).

# Other Add-Ons with NT Server

In this section, we'll discuss some of the add-ons you can use with NT server, including the Catapult server, Merchant server, ActiveX controls, and FrontPage. Of course, I can't possibly cover all the bases; my choices represent the more popular products in an already flooded market. My goal is to make you aware of the technology that exists to help you understand how the various products can help to enhance your Internet or intranet system.

## *Catapult Server or Catapult Proxy Server*

Catapult server, which works hand-in-hand with IIS's Internet Service Manager, is a product that sends and receives a private network's Internet packets by *proxy*. Proxy is defined in general terms as "authority or power to act for another." In the context of network computing, a proxy service is a service provided by a computer that assumes authority and power to act for computers to which it is connected. Such a service is useful in situations that require computers on networks that are not directly connected to each other to exchange information. The proxy service allows information exchange while maintaining security for individual computers. By using a proxy server, a corporation can securely isolate its private intranet from the anarchy of the public Internet.

Proxy services are particularly appropriate for today's environment, in which the popularity and growth of the Internet has created a need for corporations, organizations, and schools to allow Internet access from client computers on their private networks. At the same time, these entities need to isolate their intranets from the Internet for a variety of reasons, including security, private addressing, and transport incompatibility. The Catapult server proxy service reconciles these potentially incompatible needs. By using a Catapult server, you are able to secure your network against intrusion. The computer running Catapult acts as a barrier that allows you to make requests to the Internet and receive information but does not allow access to your network by unauthorized users.

When a client application makes a request for an object on the Internet, Catapult server responds by translating the request and passing it to the Internet. When a computer on the Internet responds, Catapult server passes that response back to the client application on the computer that made the request.

Catapult supports the Remote Windows Sockets (RWS) service, shown in Figure 9.25. RWS enables any Windows client to route its HTTP requests through Catapult, even when those clients are on an IPX network. This feature is the major difference between Catapult and other proxy servers, like Netscape Proxy Server. Catapult can live on networks other than IP— including Novell's IPX.

The RWS service consists of server software that establishes a virtual connection between the client and the HTTP server, and forwards data once a connection has been established. A client DLL determines if a request needs to be remotely rerouted through Catapult.

According to Microsoft, this means that corporations can turn their old IPX networks (which account for about 60 percent of networks) into fashionable IP networks, where clients browse HTML documents residing on servers simply by adding a proxy server, as shown in Figure 9.26.

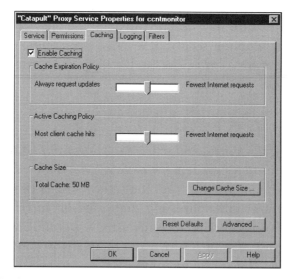

**Figure 9.25** The Catapult Server RWS service.

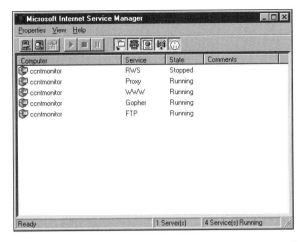

**Figure 9.26**　The Catapult Server Proxy service provides a private network client with access to the Internet.

RWS provides the following options:

- *Property Description Service*—Contains system information.

- *Permissions*—Grants or denies access to services.

- *Caching*—Stores copies of popular Internet objects locally to reduce bandwidth requirements.

- *Logging*—Records Internet transactions to text or to an ODBC/SQL-compliant database.

- *Filters*—Grants or denies access to sites on the Internet.

To run Catapult server, the gateway computer must have Windows NT 4 (or later) installed. A *gateway* refers to software, or a computer running software, that enables two different networks to communicate. You would configure Catapult server to enable your workstations to communicate with remote services on the Internet; then, you would select the appropriate hardware for a gateway computer, adequate bandwidth for the Internet connection, and the level of security for protecting your private network or intranet.

You would set up your computer with two network adapter cards. One card to connect the gateway computer running Catapult server to your intranet; the other card to connect your computer to the Internet.

Catapult server features include:

- Protection of private networks from Internet access

- The ability to control access by user, protocol, and domain

- Support for most Internet protocols and Windows Sockets applications

- Support for IPX/SPX or TCP/IP on private networks

- The ability to cache Internet resources

- User authentication

- Domain filter checking (controlling access to specific Internet sites)

- Remote Procedure Call administration

- Page caching, so that HTML pages are only downloaded once by the proxy server

Catapult server supports many Internet applications (Web, FTP, RealAudio, IRC, NNTP, SMTP/POP3, and Telnet) and includes user- and domain-level access control, as well as Internet resource caching. The server also supports HTTP, FTP Read, and Gopher for computers on your private network running TCP/IP.

Catapult Server also supports Windows Sockets protocols—such as Telnet and RealAudio—for computers on your private network running either TCP/IP or IPX/SPX.

## *Merchant Server*

Let's take a break from all this tough stuff and take a look at something more fun—like virtual shopping. All right, so it's not the same as "real" shopping, but we're moving into the 21st century here—gotta be progressive. Microsoft's Merchant server software provides all the components required for the electronic retail market. It includes an online store, a shopping user interface, order capture, processing and routing software, and merchandising tools, as shown in Figure 9.27.

From a retail perspective, the opportunity for growth in online shopping is huge. The U.S. retail market is a $2 trillion-per-year business. Direct mail accounts for $60 billion per year, and online sales account for

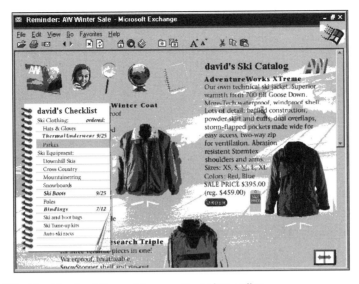

**Figure 9.27** The Merchant Server lets you set up shop online.

approximately $300 million (per Forester Research, Inc.). That's a relatively small market share. Why? Well, not only do online shoppers lose out on the richness of the shopping experience, but there are those nagging doubts about the security of online transactions.

Microsoft is working closely with the industry to create an electronic retailing solution that matches the business needs of merchants. Microsoft has analyzed the process of online retailing and broken it into the following steps:

1. Creating the online store.

2. Managing the online store.

3. Handling the purchase.

An online store is more than just a collection of HTML pages. The online store needs to be managed just like the retail store. Deciding how much shelf space should be allocated to each product and changing the store layout are familiar problems to merchants in the "real world," and the same issues exist, albeit in a modified form, in the online world.

Microsoft has provided *merchant services workbench*, which helps in managing the online store. This feature allows online merchants to:

- Track orders

- Manage returns

- Analyze customer behavior

- Manage virtual shelf space and layout

If virtual shopping is ever going to get a stong foothold, online stores need to be designed to follow traditional shopping patterns for customer convenience. Microsoft has pinpointed three major areas that must be addressed to make customers feel comfortable in an online store. Customers need:

- A way to collect the items they want—the digital equivalent of the shopping basket

- A secure place to store credit information—the digital equivalent of the wallet

- A purchase authorization—the digital equivalent of a credit card signature

Microsoft's *Internet Shopper* fills all three of these needs. The Internet Shopper resides on the client computer and allows customers to have a familiar interface for purchasing at a number of online stores. Customers won't have to learn their way around every store.

The interface also provides a safe, yet convenient, form of payment. Customers enter credit card information when they first use a card. This information is password protected. When customers make purchases, they simply use the password.

While the Internet Shopper provides customers with a friendly shopping environment that supports the traditional patterns of browsing and purchasing that customers use in retail stores, it also enables merchants to display their brands as part of a consistent, convenient, and secure customer experience.

The server component, which resides on the merchant's computer, has two parts. One handles order processing and financial transactions. The other handles Web page generation from a database. It even has an integration point for legacy systems.

For more information on the Merchant server, search the Web, or contact Microsoft at **merchsrv@microsoft.com**.

## ActiveX Technology/ActiveX Control Pad

Microsoft's ActiveX Control Pad is a tool that helps you to create Web pages that come alive by adding animation, 3D virtual reality, video, and other multimedia content to your Web site.

ActiveX Control Pad includes:

- A text editor for editing HTML documents

- An object editor for placing ActiveX controls directly into HTML documents

- A script Wizard for VBScript or JavaScript generation

- A WYSIWYG page editor for creating fixed, 2D layout regions for HTML documents with HTML layout control

- ActiveX controls that you can incorporate into your Web pages

The ActiveX Control Pad text editor, shown in Figure 9.28, allows you to edit raw HTML code. The Object Editor, shown in Figure 9.29, lets you

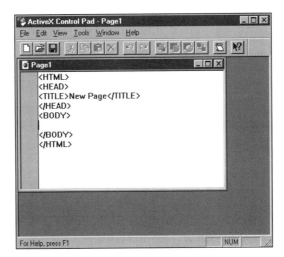

**Figure 9.28**   Microsoft ActiveX Control Pad—Text Editor.

**Figure 9.29**  Microsoft ActiveX Control Pad—Object Editor.

edit individual ActiveX objects in an HTML file using a visual interface similar to a Visual Basic form. The Object editor includes a modal form and a property table for inserting the control.

The Script Wizard, shown in Figure 9.30, allows you to add interactivity to Web pages. Script Wizard includes a user interface for easily connecting an event with an action. As you can see in the figure, all the events are displayed on the left, and the associated actions are displayed on the right.

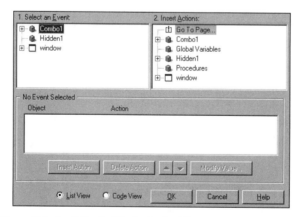

**Figure 9.30**  Microsoft ActiveX Control Pad—Script Wizard.

The user simply double clicks on an event to select an associated action in the right column. You can add multiple actions to a single event without any programming.

ActiveX is a new and exciting technology that is definitely worth further investigation. For more information on ActiveX Control Pad, check out Microsoft's Web site at **http://207.68.137.7/workshop/author/cpad**.

## FrontPage

Another Web tool, FrontPage, is a vendor-independent, cross-platform client/server authoring tool for Web sites.

As you can see from Figure 9.31, FrontPage has two components: the FrontPage client and the FrontPage server. The FrontPage client includes the FrontPage Explorer, FrontPage Editor, To Do List and Wizard, and templates for personal and business pages, and Web sites.

The FrontPage server includes the Personal Web Server, Server Extensions, and the Server Administrator. Figure 9.32 depicts the FrontPage architecture.

FrontPage technology includes the use of *WebBots*. A WebBot (or, simply, bot) is an active object that encapsulates interactive capabilities. Web page designers simply drop the bot on the Web page, and Voila! Instant

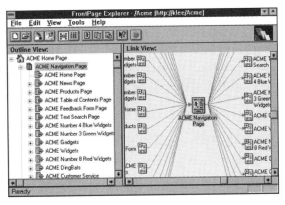

**Figure 9.31**    The Microsoft FrontPage consists of two components: the FrontPage client and the FrontPage server.

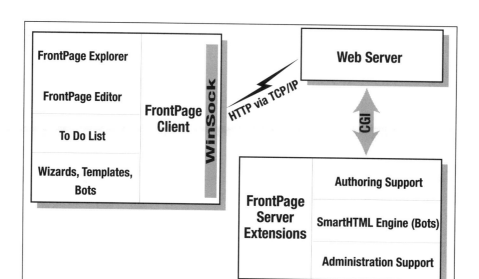

**Figure 9.32** Microsoft FrontPage architecture.

interactivity. Traditionally, such capabilities would require that custom programs be installed on the Web server using the CGI mechanism. Isn't technology grand!

FrontPage includes a number of standard bots that perform a variety of unique activities:

- *Search Bot*—Performs a full-text search across all pages in a Web site or across all messages in a discussion group.

- *Table of Contents Bot*—Displays a complete outline of all pages in the Web site, and (optionally) automatically updates that outline whenever any page is added, deleted, or renamed within the Web site.

- *Discussion Bot*—Creates a threaded discussion group.

- *Registration Bot*—Allows end-users to automatically add themselves to the list of users permitted to browse a protected Web site, with a user name and password.

- *Save Results Bot*—Allows the results of any HTML form to be appended to a file on the server, in any of eight formats (suitable for importing into databases, viewing in a text editor, or viewing in a Web browser).

- *Include Bot*—Includes a separate document, page fragment, or individual image onto another page (useful, for example, with a navigation bar which should reside in one place for easy maintenance, but may be included in many pages throughout the Web).

- *Scheduled Include Bot*—Is like an Include Bot, but the inclusion is only effective during a specified time period, before and after which the inclusion is automatically disabled.

- *Scheduled Image Bot*—Is like the Scheduled Include Bot, except that only a single image is included (useful for images such as "New", which should only appear for a specified period and then automatically be removed).

- *Timestamp Bot*—Indicates when a page was last edited by an author or (optionally) when it was last automatically updated, with various date and time formats available.

- *Substitution Bot*—Performs macro substitutions, allowing the values of various data items (such as the company address) to be centralized for easy updating.

- *Annotation Bot*—Records comments that are displayed in the page when viewed in the Microsoft FrontPage Editor but are not present in the HTML file actually viewed by an end user with a Web browser. This feature is similar to hidden text in a word processor and is particularly useful for instructions embedded in templates.

- *Confirmation Field Bot*—Allows a confirmation page to include values that were entered by the user on the original form that led to the confirmation page.

- *HTML Markup Bot*—Allows the author to enter (and preserve) HTML tags that are not yet recognized by the Microsoft FrontPage Editor.

For more information on FrontPage, go to **http://www.microsoft.com** and search the site. Take your time at this one; there's a lot to see.

# Conclusion

All around the world, people and businesses have invested in personal computers, networking, and training so that information can be created and shared easily. The Internet and intranets help organizations get more out of their information investments. By combining the best of the Web with the best creation, analysis, and collaboration tools, organizations will be able to reap the full rewards of an Internet and intranet connection. The new capabilities in Windows NT 4.0 build on the existing infrastructure, providing an evolutionary path for Internet solutions with revolutionary results.

In this chapter, you have learned how to configure NT for the Internet and how IIS works into the system to help with security and system administration. You've seen that NT, with Catapult server, can be used to make your intranets safe from intruders and how Merchant server can get your online retail business running smoothly. You've also previewed FrontPage and ActiveX Control Pad—some of the hottest technology on the Web today.

The basis of Microsoft's strategy is an open software platform, based on the Windows NT server and workstation operating systems, that will enable network managers to deploy high speed, multimedia, and video-enriched Internet solutions on existing network infrastructures. The deployment of open systems helps to increase options and reduce risk by allowing smooth transition to new technologies.

# 10

# NT 4 in the Multivendor Environment

In today's environment of interdepartmental, worldwide computing networks, the concept of a consistent, heterogeneous environment is not often achieved.

There exist many different networking standards, cables, protocols, and operating systems, very few of which readily integrate. Throw into the equation the issues of connectivity over public and private telephone networks, and it is understandable how many managers have lost their minds in the effort to integrate a company's systems.

Let's assume that any issues involving LAN access standards (for example, token ring and Ethernet) have been addressed, and that bridging/routing issues across the LAN and WAN have been resolved. Let's then think about some of the considerations in linking dissimilar systems:

- *Protocols*—Do the systems being integrated support the same networking protocols? If so, the process of getting these systems to talk is made simpler. If they do not, you may have to implement some type of gateway service to help bridge the gap between technologies.

- *What Is the Goal?*—What is the intended goal of the integration? Is it to meld the features of the systems? Or, is it part of a migration from one NOS to another?

- *Benefits*—What are my perceived results of performing this integration? Will the organization be able to share information more efficiently, or will my administration overhead increase dramatically?

In this chapter, I will discuss some of the methods being used to integrate NT with the most popular network operating systems and what advantages your company may gain by employing a multivendor environment (MVE).

# Mainframe Environments

The integration of a network operating system into the mainframe environment poses additional problems over the integration of network operating systems. The majority of mainframe systems were not designed to operate over LAN-type implementations.

Proprietary protocols are common in the mainframe environment, often with the use of dumb terminals and proprietary cable infrastructure. The integration with mainframe environments can therefore potentially require:

- The replacement of dumb terminals with PC type machines

- Terminal emulation software to connect clients with the mainframe

- A complete rewire of the cabling infrastructure

- The use of bridges or gateways to enable the clients operating on the LANs to be able to communicate with the mainframe over the mainframe's proprietary protocol

Two examples of proprietary mainframe protocols are IBM's SNA and Digital's DECNet. Microsoft provides support for SNA through the SNA Server product. This allows for NT server to function as a gateway between the LAN and mainframe environments.

We will not go into the details of integrating NT with mainframe environments in this chapter.

# MVE Vs. Open Systems

Is the MVE synonymous with open systems implementations? In a word, no. Open systems implies the seamless integration of operating systems and environments using a consistent set of standards; and as we will see in this chapter, integration is by no means seamless. Plenty of coaxing may be required in getting operating systems to talk. Then, making the features of the systems talk can involve more nursing.

The implementation of open systems is not only dependent on common networking protocols being implemented, but also, when the systems can communicate with each other, the services offered by the NOSes must also conform to agreed-upon standards. The problem is there are too many standards available, with new ones being offered all the time.

The method of integrating systems in the MVE is more often than not achieved by the NOS, or third-party vendors, providing additional services to connect to other environments. If these additional services were not provided, integration couldn't happen.

## Distributed Computing Environment

Now would be a good time to recap the subject of the Distributed Computing Environment (DCE). As you may recall, DCE is a method by which different network operating systems integrate seamlessly, without the need for additional services and gateway packages, and for the development, use, and maintenance of distributed applications. Because a DCE is designed to be operating system independent, it allows users access to applications and data from anywhere in the network while still protecting data with effective security.

This initiative has been tried in the past (for example, the OSI model was supposed to provide open systems connectivity) without much success. However, the current push to DCE is being driven by the Open Software Foundation (OSF) along with the support of some computer industry heavyweights. This gives DCE a chance of becoming a well-utilized standard; in fact, DCE compliant products are becoming available.

The architecture of the DCE model is a layered system, with the most basic services (called supplier services) residing at the operating system level, and the higher application levels (consumers of services). These services are organized in two categories: fundamental distributed services and data-sharing services.

Fundamental distributed services are designed to provide tools for developers to create end-user services which include:

- *Remote Procedure Call (RPC)*—Distributes application execution across computers in the network. RPC can be used as the basis of client/ server applications.

- *Directory Services*—Provides a single naming model throughout a distributed environment. Users are able to access resources, such as file and print services, without needing to know where the services reside on the network.

- *Time Services*—Regulates system clocks in a network to provide accurate scheduling of distributed applications, as well as maintaining accurate event sequencing.

- *Security Services*—Provides authentication, authorization, and user account management through secure communication methods.

- *Threads Services*—Allows an application to service many actions simultaneously.

Data-sharing services are services that are built on top of fundamental distribution services and are designed to facilitate better information use. These services include:

- *Distributed File System*—Utilizes the client/server model to join file systems of computers while providing a consistent interface.

- *Diskless Support*—Provides support for diskless workstations.

The OSF DCE is designed to be used over a variety of networks and operating systems. The environment is written in C, which makes use of standard interfaces to allow porting to different operating systems. System vendors are providing DCE products for Unix, Microsoft Windows, MVS, and OS/2.

Whether all implementations of DCE will be compatible with each other remains to be seen. In the past, vendors have provided "standard" products that users later discovered were adjusted slightly to fit their operating system. Will this happen with DCE?

# Protocols of NT in the MVE

Before we leap into the implementation of multivendor environments, it is important that you have an understanding of the underlying mechanisms involved in integrating unlike environments. These protocols are covered in more detail in Chapters 1 and 2, but I've included them here to touch on their application in the MVE.

## The OSI Reference Model

Introduced in 1978 by the International Organization for Standards (ISO), the Open Systems Interconnection (OSI) model provides a framework for the development of standards for computer-to-computer communications.

The model defines standards that allow for the flexible interconnection of systems using data communications facilities, and is concerned with the exchange of information between a pair of open systems. It is not concerned with the internal functions of individual systems.

The model divides the communication process into a hierarchy of seven interdependent functional layers, where each layer communicates with the same layer on the other system.

Here's a brief description of each layer:

- *Physical Layer*—Responsible for the transmission of bit streams across a particular physical transmission channel.

- *Data Link Layer*—Provides reliable data transmission from one device to another and shields higher layers from concerns regarding physical transmission channels.

- *Network Layer*—Concerned with routing data from one network device to another. Responsible for establishing, maintaining, and terminating the network connection between any number of devices for transferring data along that connection.

- *Transport Layer*—Provides data transfer between two users at an agreed-on quality of service.

- *Session Layer*—Provides the services used to organize and synchronize a given dialog occurring between devices and to manage the data exchange. Controls when devices in communications with each other can send and receive data.

- *Presentation Layer*—Responsible for the presentation of information in a way that is meaningful to the network devices.

- *Application Layer*—Provides a means for similar or dissimilar application processes to exchange information.

The purpose of the OSI model is to provide a framework for standardization, where, within the model, one or more protocol standards can be developed at each layer. Networking protocols normally operate at Layers 3 and 4 of the OSI model.

The model facilitates the standards-making process in two ways:

- The pace of standards development is made faster by the model. Functions at each layer are well-defined, allowing standards to be developed simultaneously for each layer.

- Introduction of new standards is simplified. Boundaries between layers are well-defined; a new standard in one layer need not affect any of the workings of the other layers.

Although the OSI model never produced a commercial protocol stack that is fully compliant with its standards, it has proven to be a good starting point for many of the commercial protocol stacks being used today.

## TCP/IP

The Transmission Control Protocol/Internet Protocol was created during the late 1970s and early 1980s to address network problems, and soon became the de facto standard for internetwork communications.

The development of TCP/IP began in 1969 when the Department of Defense's Advanced Research Projects Agency (DARPA) attempted to link three computers. In 1973, Bob Kahn and Vinton Cerf began development of TCP, which became an operational TCP/IP implementation in 1975. In 1978, TCP/IP was the preferred method for ARPANET traffic and eventually became the standard for sending traffic across what has come to be known as the Internet. TCP/IP is tightly integrated with Unix.

TCP/IP is composed of two interrelated protocols: TCP, which is connection oriented and works at layer 4 of the OSI model; and IP, which is connectionless and works at layer 3 of the OSI model.

TCP assures delivery of packets between two points, guarantees ordered delivery without error, and provides five services:

- *Acknowledgment* —Informing sender a packet has been received.

- *Checksumming*—Calculation of a control sum (checksum), which is used to detect transmission errors.

- *Flow Control*—Mechanism used to reduce the frequency of lost packets.

- *Retransmission*—Provision for the automatic retransmission of lost or defective packets.

- *Sequencing*—Uses packet numbers to verify that packets have been received in the order they were sent.

IP is responsible for delivering packets between two points, but does so without guarantees. Sending and receiving devices are responsible for sequencing and error detection. IP provides datagram services and transmits self-contained packets, but does not contribute the five services TCP provides.

Some application protocols that use TCP/IP are FTP, NFS, SMTP, SNMP, TELNET, UDP, DNS, and ARP. Windows NT 4 provides support for some TCP/IP applications through the Microsoft TCP/IP stack included in Windows NT 4.

# IPX/SPX

Internetwork Packet Exchange/Sequenced Packet Exchange is the network transport stack used by Novell for their NetWare operating systems. The stack is based on Xerox's XNS (Xerox Network System) and was designed at a time when few LAN-specific transport protocols existed. Today, IPX/SPX is in wide use as a routable networking protocol.

IPX/SPX is comprised of two network protocols:

- *IPX*—The primary means of providing services to the client devices in a NetWare environment. It is a connectionless datagram protocol. IPX is closely linked with NetWare Core Protocol (NCP), Service Advertising Protocol (SAP), and Routing Information Protocol (SIP).

- *SPX*—A connection-oriented communications protocol. SPX uses IPX to deliver messages, and guarantees packet delivery and retains packet sequence by maintaining a connection between the communicating devices.

Windows NT supports the IPX/SPX protocol stack, which provides NT with a base to integrate with NetWare environments. Microsoft networking clients can also access NT servers over IPX/SPX.

## NetWare Core Protocol (NCP)

NCP is the principal protocol for transmitting information between a NetWare server and its clients, and is carried in IPX frames. NCP provides:

- Login requests

- File access

- Access to printing services

- Resource allocation

- Network management and security

- Inter-server communications

# NT and Novell

The most common integration of network operating systems today exists between Windows NT and Novell NetWare. In the mid-1980s, Novell built a large user base of Novell-based networks, covering everything from the small office to large corporate enterprise networks.

Throughout this section, I will provide examples of how to use the features available when integrating NT 4 with NetWare servers. NT comes equipped with the tools necessary to integrate your Microsoft network with NetWare. These tools include:

- Gateway Services for NetWare

- Migration Tool for NetWare

## Gateway Services for NetWare

The Gateway Services for NetWare (GSNW) allows for the creation of a gateway through which Microsoft networking clients can gain access to Novell NetWare file and print resources.

By using the GSNW, clients can access utilities and NetWare-aware applications. Any Microsoft network client can access Novell NetWare resources via the GSNW, without the need to load additional NetWare network drivers on the clients. The services also allow the server on which the gateway is installed access to NetWare resources.

GSNW uses two of the NetWare compatibility features of Windows NT Server: the NWLink protocol and NWLink NetBIOS. NWLink is an implementation of the IPX/SPX transport protocols used by the NetWare network. NWLink NetBIOS is a Microsoft-enhanced implementation of Novell NetBIOS, and transmits Novell NetBIOS packets between a NetWare server running Novell NetBIOS and a Windows NT computer, or between two Windows NT computers.

The gateway services in NT 4 have been expanded to support Novell NetWare 4.x servers. This includes support for NetWare Directory Services (NDS).

See Chapter 3 for details on installing GSNW.

## Configuring the Gateway Service for NetWare

In order to activate the gateway and provide connectivity between the NT 4 and Novell servers, you must have a user account on the NetWare server with the necessary rights to the resources to be accessed. This account must be a member of a group NTGATEWAY on the NetWare server with the necessary access rights to the NetWare server. Bear in mind that to create the NTGATEWAY group and user account to activate the gateway, you must have a client with access to the Novell server so that you can actually create the user and group accounts.

Controlling the membership of the NTGATEWAY group can be used to determine what NT 4 servers can be gateways and what access users have to the resources. More than one user name can exist in the NTGATEWAY group.

The gateway service is configured from the GSNW program in the Control Panel, which is shown in Figure 10.1. To configure the gateway service:

1. If you are connecting to a Novell 3.x server, select the Preferred Server option and enter the name of the server you wish to connect to. This is the NetWare server queried for available resources on the NetWare network and login authentication.

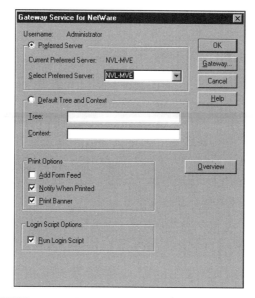

**Figure 10.1**    The GSNW program is used to configure your connection from the NT 4 server to the NetWare server.

If you are going to connect to a NetWare environment using Novell Directory Services (NDS), select the Default Tree and Context option and enter the NDS name and the position of the user name you will use to log in. You can then access all the resources in the default tree without the requirement for further password prompts.

2.  Select the desired print options.

3.  Select the Run Login Script option if you wish to process the NetWare login script for your user name.

TIP    Any changes you make to the gateway configuration apply only to the user currently logged on to the NT 4 server. This user name is displayed at the top of the gateway configuration window.

To activate the gateway service:

1.  From the GSNW, click on the Gateway button to launch the Configure Gateway window, shown in Figure 10.2.

2. Enter the gateway account user name, followed by the password with confirmation. This user name must exist in the NTGATEWAY group on the NetWare server.

The changes to the gateway configuration will not take place until you reboot the server.

## THE GATEWAY IN OPERATION

When the gateway is in operation, clients on the Microsoft network access the NetWare server via an NT 4 server, on which shares are created of volumes on the NetWare server. Adding shares has immediate effect and does not require a system reboot.

Shares are administered through the GSNW program in the Control Panel. The share function gives you the ability to add, remove, and configure permissions for shares. To add a share:

1. From the Gateway Configuration window, click on the Gateway button to launch the Configure Gateway window.

2. Click on the Add button.

3. Enter the name of the share, the network path of the share (in UNC format, for example, \\NVLSVR\SYS\LOGIN), any comments, and a drive on the NT 4 server that the share will be mapped to.

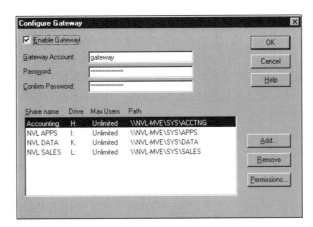

**Figure 10.2** The Configure Gateway window allows you to activate the gateway and configure shares to the NetWare server.

4. If required, specify the share user limit.

To remove a share:

1. From the Gateway Configuration window, click on the Gateway button to launch the Configure Gateway window.

2. Select the share from the share list you wish to remove.

3. Click on the Remove button.

**TIP** NT 4 does not inform you whether users are connected to a share when you attempt to remove it. It is, therefore, possible to remove a share that users are currently attached to.

Once you've created a share, you manage it through the Permissions options on the Configure Gateway window. You assign permissions in the same manner you assign shares to volumes on NT 4 servers. Access rights for Microsoft network clients to the NetWare server are managed from these shares, which allows users without NetWare accounts to access information stored on the NetWare server. Clients see the NetWare resources as shares on the NT 4 server. As long as the user has the correct rights to use the share, he can accesses the NetWare resources.

For example, assume there is an NT 4 server, NT-MVE, connected to a NetWare server NVL-MVE through the Gateway Service for NetWare. You wish to create a share to the SALES directory on the SYS volume and allow all members of the NT 4 global group REGION 1 SALES read access to the share. From the Configure Gateway window in the GSNW program, you would add a share called NWSALES and assign it to the network path \\NVL-MVE\SYS\SALES. You would then use the permissions option to allow REGION 1 SALES read access to the share. Microsoft network clients would access this NetWare resource through the share \\NT-MVE\NWSALES on the NT 4 server.

It's worth noting that clients accessing NetWare servers through the gateway service access the NetWare server slower than if they were running NetWare drivers. Therefore, if your clients are running operating systems that provide their own services for NetWare, such as Windows 95, you may wish to consider accessing the NetWare server directly from the client for a faster response time.

The file attributes used in NetWare are not the same as in NT 4, so when accessing files on a NetWare server through the gateway service, certain rights-mapping functions are applied. Table 10.1 describes these mappings. When copying a file from a Microsoft network client to a NetWare server via the gateway service, these attributes are preserved.

The gateway service does not support the NetWare file attributes RW (Read Write), S (Shareable), T (Transactional), P (Purge), Ra (Read Audit), Wa (Write Audit), and Ci (Copy Inhibit). However, it is possible to administer these rights from an NT 4 server running the gateway service (assuming the user name has the correct rights to do so) through the use of NetWare utilities such as filer and rights. NT 4 supports most of the other NetWare utilities, including fconsole, syscon, userlist, map, and chkvol.

Some, but not all, NetWare-aware applications can be run on NT 4 with the GSNW as if it were a NetWare server. To run NetWare-aware applications from your NT 4 computer, the NWIPXSPX.DLL, NETWARE.DRV, NWNETAPI.DLL, and NWCALLS.DLL files may need to be installed on the NT 4 computer.

NWIPXSPX.DLL provides support for 16-bit NetWare-aware applications and is available from Novell. If it does not already exist on your system, you should place the file in the \\*systemroot*\\ SYSTEM32 directory. Installing the file requires a system reboot for the changes to take effect. If you are running NT 4 on a MIPS or ALPHA AXP, you must place the file TBMI2.COM

**Table 10.1    File Rights Mappings**

| Windows NT File Attributes | NetWare File Attributes |
| --- | --- |
| R (Read Only) | Ro, Di (Delete Inhibit), Ri (Rename Inhibit) |
| A (Archive) | A |
| S (System) | Sy |
| H (Hidden) | H |

in the \*systemroot*\SYSTEM32 directory and add the following line after *vwipxspx* in AUTOEXEC.NT:

```
lh systemroot\system32\tbmi2.com
```

NetWare-aware programs that use the NetWare application programming interface to send and receive NCP packets may require NETWARE.DRV (which is installed when you install the GSNW program) and either NWNETAPI.DLL or NWCALLS.DLL. If your NT 4 computer does not already have either the NWNETAPI.DLL or NWCALLS.DLL file, you can get a copy from Novell and then place it in the \*systemroot*\SYSTEM32 directory.

## *Migration Tool for NetWare*

The Windows NT Server Migration Tool for NetWare enables the migration of user and group accounts, volumes, folders, and files from Novell NetWare servers to Windows NT servers. If the NT server is also running File and Print Services for NetWare (FPNW), users' login scripts can also be transferred.

The Migration Tool enables:

- Preservation of most user account information

- Control of the transfer of user and group names

- Setting of passwords for transferred accounts

- Control of the transfer of account restrictions and administrative rights

- Selection of the folders and files to transfer

- Selection of a destination for transferred folders and files

- Preservation of effective rights (the NetWare equivalent of permissions) on folders and files

- Performing trial migrations to test how current settings will actually transfer information

- Generation of comprehensive log files, detailing what happened during migration

The Migration Tool requires that the NT server to be migrated to is either a PDC or BDC running the NWLink protocol and GSNW. To preserve file and folder permissions, the NT server should have at least one volume formatted for NTFS. However, the actual Migration Tool can be run from a remote NT server or workstation.

When migrating from a NetWare environment to NT, you should consider the process required to upgrade your clients to Microsoft network clients. Alternatively, you could install the File and Print Services for NetWare (FPNW) on the NT server to allow the NT to appear as a NetWare server. Installing FPNW will also allow you to migrate login scripts from the NetWare server to NT.

Before performing your migration, consider the differences between the NetWare and NT enterprise structures and plan how your Novell servers will be migrated to NT servers. When migrating more than one server, it's best to migrate the largest NetWare server first. See Chapter 4 for a description of the NT domain model.

Accounts migrated to an NT domain are automatically created on the PDC, although the migration may be performed through a BDC, which will automatically migrate the account throughout the domain and PDC.

## NetWare Accounts Vs. NT Accounts

NetWare accounts and NT accounts both contain the same basic information, namely user name, password, and full user name. They also perform the same function of establishing a user's identity on the network.

In NetWare, default account restrictions are set using the Supervisor options and can be changed for individual user accounts. In NT, some restrictions are set individually, while others are set globally for all accounts in the domain. When accounts are transferred during a migration, individual restrictions that can be modified for each NT account are transferred individually for each NetWare account. For NT policy settings, you have two options: transfer the settings from the NetWare Supervisor account or retain the NT policies. Table 10.2 details the account restrictions when migrating from NetWare to NT.

**Table 10.2    Transferring Account Restrictions During a Migration**

| NetWare Account Restriction | Windows NT Equivalent | Method of Transfer |
| --- | --- | --- |
| Expiration Date | Expiration Date | By individual user account |
| Account Disabled | Account Disabled | By individual user account |
| Limit Concurrent Connections | None | Not transferred |
| Require Password | Permit Blank Password | As policy for all accounts |
| Minimum Password Length | Minimum Password Length | As policy for all accounts |
| Force Periodic Password Changes | Password Never Expires | By individual user account |
| Days Between Forced Changes | Maximum Password Age | As policy for all accounts |
| Grace Logins | None | Not transferred |
| Allow User to Change Password | User Cannot Change Password | By individual user account |
| Require Unique Password | Password Uniqueness | As policy for all accounts |
| Station Restrictions | None | Not transferred |
| Time Restrictions | Logon Hours | By individual user account |
| Intruder Detection/ Lockout | Account Lockout | As policy for all accounts |
| User Disk Volume Restrictions | None | Not transferred |

The NetWare Supervisor account has complete control over the NetWare network and can provide other users and groups with limited administration privileges. NT administration groups also have complete control over their networks and can provide other users with limited administration privileges through the use of built-in groups. The administration of NT is a domain-wide privilege, which negates the requirement for separate administration accounts for each server in any given domain. NetWare, however, provides Workgroup and User Account managers to administer individual servers. These account managers are added to administrator groups during a migration and are given administrator privileges.

The NetWare File Console Operator is similar to the Server Operator in NT. However, the Server Operator group has greater privileges, so File Console Operators are not automatically added to the Server Operators group as part of a migration.

Printer Server Operators and Print Queue Operators have the same combined equivalence of the NT Print Operator group. NetWare users who are Printer Server Operators and Print Queue Operators are added to the Print Operators group. Users who are Print Queue Operators only are not migrated to the Print Operator group.

## NETWARE FILES AND FOLDERS VS. NT FILES AND FOLDERS

Table 10.3 shows how the NetWare folder rights are mapped to NT server folder permissions, and Table 10.4 shows how the NetWare file rights are mapped to NT server file permissions. All files transferred as part of a migration are automatically owned by the Administrators group.

## STARTING THE MIGRATION TOOL

Only administrators can perform migrations. You can launch the Migration Tool from within the Administration Tools program group or by running the command line *nwconv*. To perform a migration, you must be attached to the NetWare server as Supervisor.

**Table 10.3    Mapping NetWare Folder Rights to NT Server Folder Permissions**

| NetWare Folder Rights | NT Server Folder Permissions |
|---|---|
| Supervisory (S) | (All) (All) |
| Read [R] | (RX) (RX) |
| Write (W) | (RWXD) (RWXD) |
| Create [C] | (WX) (not specified) |
| Erase (E) | (RWXD) (RWXD) |
| Modify (M) | (RWXD) (RWXD) |
| File Scan (F) | (RX) (not specified) |
| Access Control (A) | (P) (P) |

**Table 10.4  Mapping NetWare File Rights to NT Server File Permissions**

| NetWare File Rights | NT Server File Permissions |
| --- | --- |
| Supervisory (S) | (All) |
| Read [R] | (RX) |
| Write (W) | (RWXD) |
| Erase (E) | (RWXD) |
| Modify (M) | (RWXD) |
| File Scan (F) | N/A |
| Access Control (A) | (P) |

The Migration Tool, shown in Figure 10.3, allows you to:

- Indicate the NetWare server(s) to be migrated from and the NT server to be migrated to

- Select the users and groups to be migrated

- Select the files and folders to be migrated

- Perform a trial migration and generate log reports to analyze how the migration would perform; you can adjust the parameters and continue to perform trial migrations until the desired results are achieved

- Perform the actual migration

- Migrate users and groups separately

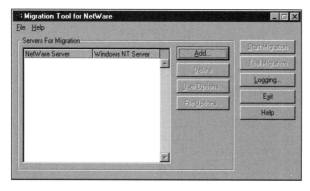

**Figure 10.3**  The Migration Tool for NetWare.

## CONFIGURING THE MIGRATION TOOL

You can configure the following options when migrating users and groups:

- *Password Options*—Because passwords on NetWare servers are encrypted, they can not be migrated to the NT server. The default option is to provide a null password for migrated users. You also have the option of either making the password the same as the user name, specifying a single password for all users, or use a mapping file to provide individual passwords for each user. It is also possible to specify if the user must change his password the first time he logs in to the NT network.

- *User Name Conflicts*—It is possible that the same user names exist on the NetWare and NT servers. This option specifies how to deal with this situation should it arise during a migration. The default option is to not transfer the conflicting user name from the NetWare server and then to write a record of the conflict to an error file. You also have the option of not transferring any account information, overwriting the existing account (which will negate any existing password), or creating a new account by adding a prefix to the user name.

- *Group Conflicts*—If a group exists on the NetWare and NT servers, the default option in the Migration Tool is to add the migrating users to the existing NT groups. The other options allow you to not move the group and then to write a record to the error log, create a new group by adding a prefix to its name, or use the mapping file to achieve complete control of the migration of each group.

- *Transfer Account Restrictions*—By default, the NetWare account restrictions contained in the Supervisor account become the new NT security policy. However, you can choose to override the default and retain the existing policy settings of the domain.

- *Transfer Administration Rights*—Users with Supervisor rights are not, by default, given administration privileges on the NT server. They can be added manually to the Administration groups.

When migrating files and folders, you can configure the following parameters:

- *Volumes to Transfer*—The default is to transfer all options; however, you can manually select volumes individually.

- *Destination Share*—Unless you specify otherwise, the share to be copied to will have the same name as the volume being copied from. Be sure to configure the permissions on this share before performing the migration. If you are migrating multiple NetWare servers to one NT server, you may wish to use separate share names for volumes that exist on more than one server to avoid files on a volume on one server being overwritten by files from another server.

- *File and Folders to Transfer*—Allows you to select which files and folders you wish to migrate. By default, everything except the \SYSTEM, \LOGIN, \MAIL, and \ETC folders is selected. To transfer hidden and system files, you must manually select them.

## THE MAPPING FILE

The mapping file provides you with increased control over how the migration of users and groups is performed. Although you can create the mapping file before running the Migration Tool, it is easier to let the Migration Tool create the mapping file for you because it places the relevant headers and all users and groups you wish to transfer in to the mapping file automatically. You can then edit the file manually (using a program such as Notepad) before performing the migration.

Select the Create option in the User and Group Options window to create the mapping file. Specify new user names and passwords for each user being transferred and new names for each group being transferred. All entries for users are listed under the [users] heading and have the format:

```
old_username, new_username, password
```

All entries for groups are under the [groups] heading and have the format:

```
old_group, new_group
```

## PERFORMING THE MIGRATION

As I mentioned earlier, you can perform a trial migration or an actual migration. I recommend that you always perform a trial migration and study the results carefully before performing an actual migration. Running a trial migration creates three log files:

- *LOGFILE.LOG*—Contains information on users, groups, files, folders, and the NetWare server to be used in the migration.

- *SUMMARY.LOG*—Provides an overview of the migration including names of servers, and number of users, groups, and files transferred.

- *ERROR.LOG*—Records any problems that occurred during the migration, as well as system errors that may have caused the migration to halt.

You can perform the trial migration as many times as you want, refining parameters as necessary until the migration will function as you require. Once you're satisfied, go ahead and perform the actual migration.

## EXAMPLE MIGRATION

Let's perform a sample migration of users and files from a NetWare server to a new NT PDC with very few existing users.

The NT server, NT-MVE, resides in the domain DOMAIN-1. The NetWare server, NVL-MVE, which is a 3.12 server, is to be connected to the NT server via the GSNW. The purpose of the migration is to eventually migrate away from the NetWare server and replace it with an NT domain. Initially, the NetWare users will be migrated to the NT server but will continue to access the data on the NetWare servers through shares configured in the GSNW. Then, the directories and files will be migrated to the NT server.

Prior to running the migration, we will assume, for the sake of this example, that the NWLink protocol on the NT server is configured, and that both the NT and the NetWare server are using the Ethernet 802.3 frame type.

To enable the gateway service, the NetWare Supervisor creates the NTGATEWAY group on NVL-MVE and adds the user GATEWAY, who has supervisor privileges, on the NetWare server. The NT administrator sets the preferred server to NVL-MVE in the GSNW and enables the gateway using the GATEWAY user name.

We are now ready to begin our migration process. But before we start, let's examine the user and directory configuration of NVL-MVE. Table 10.5 relates the users on NVL-MVE to the groups on the server. The administrator of the network realizes that the user names on the NetWare server are not particularly meaningful, so she's decided to use a mapping file during the migration to rename the users with more relevant names (the user names shown in parentheses).

**Table 10.5  Group Membership on NVL-MVE**

|  | Groups | | | | |
|---|---|---|---|---|---|
|  | **Accounting** | **Everyone** | **Management** | **NTGateway** | **Sales** |
| Acct1 (smithr) | X | X |  |  |  |
| Acct2 (orangej) | X | X |  |  |  |
| Acct3 (appleb) | X | X |  |  |  |
| Acct4 (jonesk) | X | X |  |  |  |
| Acctmng (marsb) | X | X | X |  |  |
| Administrator |  | X |  | X |  |
| CEO (simpsonh) |  | X | X |  |  |
| Guest | X |  |  |  |  |
| Mgt1 (coulderd) |  | X | X |  |  |
| Mgt2 (smithersf) |  | X | X |  |  |
| Sales1 (smitha) |  | X |  |  | X |
| Sales2 (mccoyz) |  | X |  |  | X |
| Sales3 (browng) |  | X |  |  | X |
| Sales4 (goodenk) |  | X |  |  | X |
| Salesmng (kingh) |  | X | X |  | X |
| Supervisor | X |  | X | X |  |

NVL-MVE is a relatively small server with one volume SYS. The directory structure of the SYS volume is shown in Figure 10.4.

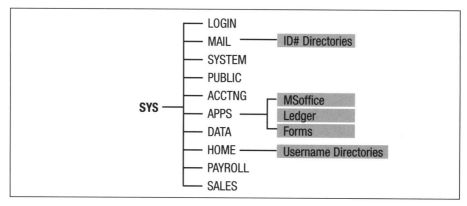

**Figure 10.4**  Directory structure of the SYS volume.

Each group has the following basic rights to the directory structure:

- Accounting has rights to the ACCTNG directory

- Everyone has access to APPS

- Mgmt and Sales has access to DATA

- Sales has access to SALES

We'll perform the migration of the users in three steps. First, we'll configure the Migration Tool, including the mapping file. Then, we'll do a trial migration. And finally, we'll perform the actual migration.

OK, let's configure the Migration Tool:

1. Start the Migration Tool for NetWare.

2. Select NVL-MVE for the NetWare Server and NT-MVE for the Windows NT Server, as shown in Figure 10.5.

3. Click on User Options.

4. Select Transfer Users and Groups and Use Mappings in File.

5. Enter the name of the mapping file (for example, example.map) and then edit the mapping file to replace the old user names with the more meaningful ones shown in Table 10.5.

6. In the Passwords tab, select the User Must Change Password option. When the user logs on to the Microsoft network for the first time after

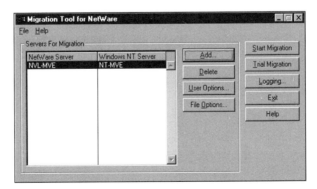

**Figure 10.5**  Adding the NVL-MVE and NT-MVE servers for migration.

the migration, he will have a new user name, the password will be blank, and he will be required to change his password.

7.  In the Defaults tab, select Use Supervisor Defaults and Add Supervisors to the Administrators Group.

8.  Click on OK.

We are now ready to perform the trial migration and review the log files. Figure 10.6 shows the trial migration in progress.

If everything looks okay, perform the actual migration by clicking on the Start Migration button. The results of the migration will be shown in the User Manager for Domains, as shown in Figure 10.7.

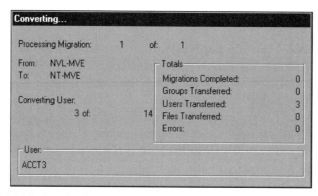

**Figure 10.6**    A trial migration in progress.

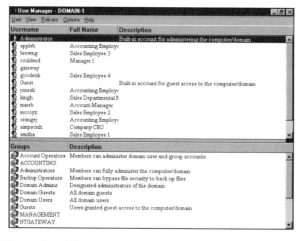

**Figure 10.7**    The results of the migration, as shown in the User Manager for Domains window.

As you can see, the users have been renamed and migrated from the NetWare server along with the NetWare groups.

Because we haven't migrated the files and directories from the NetWare server yet, we really should provide access to these files. We do this by providing shares to the NetWare server through the GSNW program.

1. Select the GSNW icon in Control Panel to start the Gateway Service for NetWare.

2. Click on the Gateway button.

Using the previously mentioned basic directory rights on the NetWare server, let's create the shares on the NT server, as shown in Figure 10.8.

Once a share has been created, you can then add the appropriate permissions to the share, as shown in Figure 10.9.

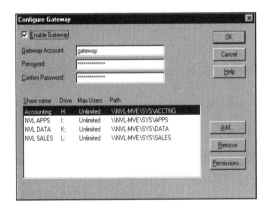

**Figure 10.8**  Creating shares to the NetWare server.

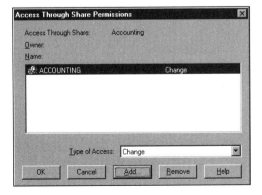

**Figure 10.9**  Adding permissions to a newly created share.

Now that the users have been successfully migrated to the NT server, and shares have been created to allow the Microsoft clients to access the NetWare files and directories, we need to move all files and directories on the NetWare server to a directory SYS on the NT server. Here's how it's done:

1. Start the Migration Tool for NetWare. The NetWare and NT server to be merged should still be displayed on the server list. Make sure that the Transfer Users and Groups option under User Options is not selected.

2. Click the File Options button, and select Transfer Files.

3. Click on the Modify button to confirm that the share name will be SYS and that the path of the share is C:\SYS, as shown in Figure 10.10.

4. Click on the File Options button. Notice that the \ETC, \LOGIN, \MAIL, and \SYSTEM folders are not selected, as shown in Figure 10.11.

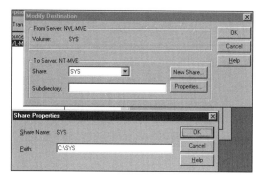

**Figure 10.10**    Confirming share name on the NT server.

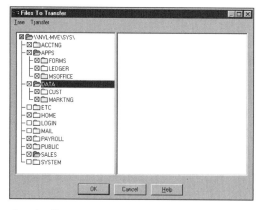

**Figure 10.11**    Selecting the files and directories to be migrated.

5. Perform a trial migration and review the log files. The results of the trial are shown in Figure 10.12.

6. If everything looks okay, perform the actual migration by clicking on the Start Migration button. The selected files will then be migrated form the NetWare server to the NT server.

## Client Services for NetWare

The Client Service for NetWare (CSNW) is similar in concept to the GSNW in that it provides Microsoft network clients with connectivity to NetWare resources. However, where the gateway service provides access to multiple users, the client service runs on an NT 4 workstation and provides access only to the user logged on to the workstation.

The Client Services for NetWare in NT 4 have been expanded to support Novell NetWare 4.x servers, which includes support for NetWare Directory Services (NDS). The new NDS client gives NT 4 workstation users the ability to use NetWare login scripts and access file and print services. Virtual Loadable Modules (VLM) support, however, is not included.

The CSNW uses two of the NetWare compatibility features of Windows NT Server: the NWLink protocol and NWLink NetBIOS. NWLink is an implementation of the IPX/SPX transport protocols used by the NetWare network. NWLink NetBIOS is a Microsoft-enhanced implementation of Novell NetBIOS, and transmits Novell NetBIOS packets between a NetWare server running Novell NetBIOS and a Windows NT computer, or between two Windows NT computers.

See Chapter 3 for details on installing the CSNW.

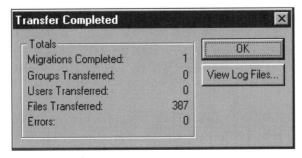

**Figure 10.12**   The results of a trial migration of files and directories.

## CONFIGURING THE CLIENT SERVICE FOR NETWARE

Once the service has been installed, you can administer it through the CSNW icon in Control Panel. To configure the client service:

1. If you are connecting to a Novell 3.x server, select the Preferred option, and enter the name of the server you wish to connect to. This is the NetWare server queried for available resources on the NetWare network and login authentication.

   If you are going to connect to an NDS environment, select the Default Tree and Context option and enter the NDS name and the position of the user name you will use to log in. You can then access all the resources in the default tree without the requirement for further password prompts.

2. Select the desired print options.

3. Select the Run Login Script option if you wish to process the NetWare login script for your user name.

## USING THE CLIENT SERVICE FOR NETWARE

After you have configured the client service, you can attach to NetWare resources through Network Neighborhood or Windows NT Explorer. When you attempt to attach to a NetWare resource, you are connected to the resource as the current user logged on to the NT workstation. If you wish to connect as a different user, enter the user name and password into the Connect As dialog box.

## *File and Print Services for NetWare*

The File and Print Services for NetWare (FPNW) for NT 4, which is available from Microsoft, allows a Windows NT server to appear as a Novell NetWare 3.12 server for file and print services, without installing additional drivers on the clients. Even though the NT server is acting as a Novell NetWare server, it will also continue to service requests from Microsoft network clients.

FPNW enables existing NetWare users to gain access to NT resources, share directories and printers for NT and NetWare users, allow NT administrators to manage NetWare printers, and make NetWare printers available to

Microsoft network clients. FPNW for NT 4 also contains a new version of the Migration Tool for NetWare (v1.1).

FPNW requires the Gateway Services for NetWare and NWLink protocol be installed on the NT server where FPNW is to be installed. FPNW understands the NCP and SMB protocols.

FPNW allows for the creation of NetWare-enabled NT user accounts, which are administered centrally from the NT domain. A separate database of NetWare and NT accounts is not required. FPNW supports:

- File management, including permissions for Server Manager, File Manager, and third-party tools

- Creation and management of user accounts through User Manager for Domains

- Management of printers and print queues

- Remote administration

- Secured logins

- Packet burst and Large Internal Packet (LIP)

- NetWare locking and synchronization of primitives

- Long file names compatible with OS/2 LFN support

FPNW does not support:

- Workgroup managers

- Accounting

- User disk volume restrictions

- Setting inherited rights masks

- NetWare Loadable Modules (NLM)

- Transaction tracking systems

## INSTALLING FILE AND PRINT SERVICES FOR NETWARE

The process of installing FPNW creates a share called SYSVOL on the NT server drive specified during the installation process. This drive should be a NTFS partition so file and folder permissions can be maintained. The structure of SYSVOL is very similar to the NetWare SYS volume, in that it creates the subdirectories \LOGIN, \MAIL, \PUBLIC, and \SYSTEM.

During the installation of FPNW, an FPNW service account is created, which is used to start the FPNW service. This service can be started on system startup or manually.

FPNW adds functionality to the File Manager, Server Manager, User Manager for Domains, and Control Panel applications. For File Manager and Server Manager, the FPNW adds a new menu item, FPNW, which provides the ability to create, manage, and delete volumes shared for NetWare clients. Server Manager is provided with the additional functionality of configuring server-specific settings for FPNW. User Manager for Domains is augmented with the ability to make NT accounts NetWare-enabled and manage the NetWare properties from an additional dialog box. Finally, an FPNW icon is added to Control Panel.

FPNW also installed several 16-bit utilities (*login, setpass, attach, logout, map, slist, capture,* and *endcap*) that can be used by MS-DOS clients to login and access the service provided by FPNW. More on these utilities later in the chapter.

NT workstations and servers not running FPNW have the option of installing the FPNW administration tools. These tools provide all the features added to the File Manager, User Manager for Domains, and Server Manager, except for the ability to create volume accounts on the local computers.

Let's install FPNW:

1. In Control Panel, start the Network program.

2. Click on the Add Service button.

3. Click on the Have Disk button.

4. Insert the FPNW CD-ROM into the drive, and enter the path to the CD-ROM drive and the path of the hardware platform (for example, e:\i386).

5. Select FPNW from the OEM list and click on OK. The Install File and Print Services for NetWare box will appear, as shown in Figure 10.13.

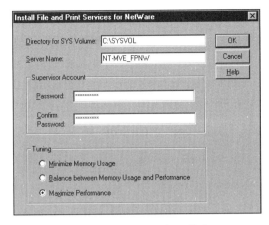

**Figure 10.13** Configuring the FPNW service during installation.

6. Enter the location for the SYSVOL directory (remember it should be on an NTFS drive) and the NetWare name of the NT server as it will appear to NetWare clients.

7. Enter the password for the Supervisor account.

8. Select the performance characteristic from the Tuning box.

9. If the service is being installed into a domain, you are prompted to enter the FPNW service account password.

10. Enter the password, and click on OK to perform the installation.

## CONFIGURING FPNW

Once the FPNW service is installed, you have the option of configuring the performance of the service, frame types, configuration startup, and changing the FPNW service account password.

FPNW supports three levels of performance tuning, which allows you to balance the amount of memory the server uses against how fast the server runs. The three levels are:

- *Minimize Memory Usage*—Decreases the amount of memory usage required to run FPNW. Choose this option if your server performs minimal file operations.

- *Balance between Memory Usage and Performance*—Provides higher performance than the previous option by balancing the amount of memory the server uses with the speed at which it will run. Use this option for machines that are used for sharing applications and providing file and print sharing services.

- *Maximize Performance* —Increases the speed at which the server will run; this option is used on servers that support heavy networking activity.

To adjust the performance configuration:

1.  Choose Control Panel|Network.

2.  Select the FPNW service.

3.  Click on the Properties button, and adjust the performance.

NetWare supports multiple frame types. You should be aware of the frame types being used on your NetWare network before installing FPNW to ensure that your FPNW server will be compatible with the NetWare network. If the NetWare network is running only one frame type, the FPNW service will automatically detect the frame type. If more than one frame type is being used, you will have to manually enter the frame types.

Frame type administration is performed through the Network icon in Control Panel:

1.  In Control Panel, start the Network program.

2.  Select the FPNW service.

3.  Click on the Properties button, then click on the Advanced button.

4.  Set the FPNW service to automatically detect the frame type to be used or manually enter the frame types, as shown in Figure 10.14. You can also specify the internal network number, which is an optional entry and is defaulted to 00000000.

The startup configuration of the FPNW service is configured in the same way as any other service in NT, through the Services icon in Control Panel.

The FPNW service account is the account that is used to start the FPNW service. I don't recommend that you make a habit of changing this password, because you will also have to change the local service account password on each server running FPNW in the domain.

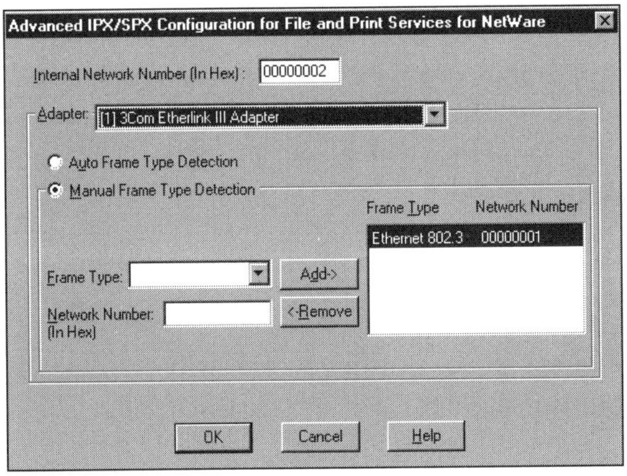

**Figure 10.14** Advanced configuration of FPNW.

# Managing User Accounts on an FPNW Server

You manage user accounts on an FPNW server the same way you would on a standard NT 4 server: through the User Manager for Domains, which has the additional capabilities on a FPNW server to create, configure, and modify NetWare client accounts.

To access NetWare resources, the NT user account must be NetWare-enabled. This allows the user to access an FPNW server without reconfiguring NetWare clients. To make an account NetWare-enabled, open the User Properties dialog box in the User Manager for Domains, and select the Enable NetWare Login option. Additionally, by adding NetWare-enabled accounts to the NT server built-in group accounts, the same supervisor privileges assigned on a NetWare network can be assigned to NetWare-enabled accounts. You can add NetWare-enabled accounts into the same global and local groups as standard NT accounts and provide them with the same rights that any other member of the groups has. However, you need to keep in mind, at all times, the domain model you are using and how these NetWare-enabled accounts could have access, through trust relationships, to servers running FPNW. Remember, NetWare clients will not be able to login to NT servers not running FPNW.

When creating a NetWare-enabled account, the passwords for the NT server account and NetWare account are synchronized. If you are enabling an existing NT server account to be used from a NetWare client, you will be prompted to enter a new password for the user. When you, as an administrator, need to change the password for NetWare-enabled accounts, use User Manager for Domains which will change both the NT server and FPNW user passwords.

NetWare-enabled user accounts can change their own passwords in three ways:

- Use the NetWare setpass utility, which will change the user's FPNW password, but not their NT server password.

- For an NT 4 workstation client, the user presses Ctrl+Alt+Del and selects the password option, which will update both the NT and NetWare passwords.

- For older Microsoft network clients, such as Windows for Workgroups, the user may change the password in the same manner as always. This change will only affect the user's NT password; the user will have to use the setpass utility to change the FPNW password. Alternatively, a user on a NetWare or NT client other than NT workstation can change both passwords by running the chgpass utility. In order to run this utility, the client must be running IPX/SPX protocol, and the PDC for the domain must be running FPNW and GSNW.

When you launch the User Manager for Domains from a FPNW server, you will notice two additional items: an Enable NetWare Login option (as previously described) and NW Compat button. Clicking on the NetWare Compat button displays the NetWare Compatible Properties dialog box, shown in Figure 10.15, from which you can set the NetWare-specific account information, such as:

- NetWare account expiration

- Number of grace logins

- Number of concurrent connections a user may have to a server

Additionally, the existing User Properties dialog box buttons have augmented functionality.

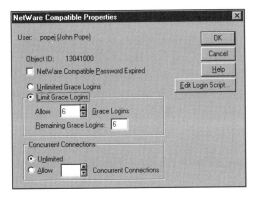

**Figure 10.15**    The NetWare Compatible Properties dialog box allows you to configure
NetWare-specific account information.

The User Profile Property dialog box has the option of specifying the location of the NetWare home directory relative path. This path is specific to users logged on as NetWare clients and is relative to the server's home root directory. The path is actually in two parts: the root of the home directory, which is specified on a per server basis, and the relative path, which is specified in the user's account.

It is possible for a NetWare-enabled account to possess two login scripts: one when connecting to the network as a Microsoft client and the other when connecting as a NetWare client. Additionally, when the user logs on as a NetWare client, if a system login script exists on the server, this will run before the user's personal login script. Each server can have only one system login script, which is stored as the file SYSNET$.DAT in the SYSVOL\PUBLIC directory. Personal login scripts for NetWare-enabled users are stored in the SYSVOL\MAIL directory contained in each user's own subdirectory in the file LOGIN.

The method by which NT and NetWare set login restrictions differs only in the restriction times—NetWare provides restriction times in 30-minute increments, and NT uses 60-minute increments. When using FPNW, NetWare login restrictions are rounded to the nearest hour, which allows more time for the user to login to the server. For example, if you specify a 7:30 A.M. starting time, the NetWare user will actually be able to login at 7:00 A.M. Consequently, if the ending time is specified for 4:30 P.M., the user will have access until 5:00 P.M.

The Logon To dialog box has been extended under FPNW to allow you to specify which NetWare clients a specific user can login through. You can allow the user to login via all NetWare clients by selecting the User May Log On From All NetWare Workstations. You can also limit access to specific clients by selecting the User May Log On From These NetWare Workstations and then selecting the Add button to add the network address and node number of the workstation. The node number is optional.

Managing the group membership of NetWare-enabled accounts requires special consideration. NetWare-enabled accounts can be placed in NT groups the same way as normal NT accounts; however, you must be aware of any trust relationships you may have between domains. Even if you place NetWare-enabled accounts into groups with permissions to access resources in other domains, the NetWare clients will not be able to access resources on servers that do not have FPNW installed.

## MANAGING VOLUMES AND FILES

FPNW allows you to manage and share the volumes to be used by both NetWare and Microsoft clients. These volumes are managed through extensions in the Server Manager and File Manager.

Using FPNW, you can share a directory on a server running FPNW as a volume that is accessible by NetWare clients. Existing shares used by Microsoft clients can also be shared out for NetWare clients, or shares can be created for access by NetWare clients only. When you share a directory as a NetWare volume, you can share it more than once with different names and permissions.

In conjunction with the NetWare Migration Tool, you can migrate NetWare volumes, files, and subdirectories to the FPNW server to allow access to the volumes by NetWare and Microsoft clients.

 Migrate NetWare volumes to NTFS partitions on FPNW servers. This will allow you to retain permissions and attributes assigned by the NetWare server.

To create and share a NetWare volume:

1. Create the directory if it has not already been created.

2. From the FPNW menu in File Manager (this menu is not implemented in the Windows NT Explorer), select Create Volume to display the Create Volume dialog box. You can also select the Shared Volumes command from the FPNW menu in Server Manager.

3. Enter the name of the volume, the path of the directory to be shared, and the user limit, if applicable.

4. Click on the Permissions button and set the permissions as you would with a standard NT server.

5. Click on OK to create the volume.

This process will create a share accessible by NetWare clients but not automatically for Microsoft clients.

Once a volume has been shared, you can select FPNW|Volume Properties in the File Manager to view the volume's properties, change the permissions to the volume, and change the number of users that can connect to a volume. To view all of the NetWare volumes and manage their properties, select FPNW|Manage Volumes. Figure 10.16 shows you the Manage Volumes command options.

## MANAGING PRINTERS

FPNW provides greater printer access to both NetWare and Microsoft clients. Using FPNW, NetWare clients can access print resources on Windows NT servers, and NT servers can assume the management of printers previously managed by NetWare print servers, including printers attached directly to the network through print server devices. See Chapter 3 for a description of the NT printing environment.

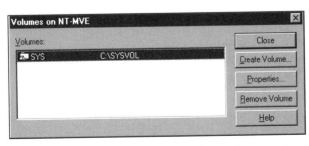

**Figure 10.16** From the Volumes dialog box, you can view and manage the status of all volumes on an FPNW server, as well as create and remove volumes.

When you create a share to a logical printer on an FPNW server, it can be made available to both NetWare and Microsoft clients. A printer connected directly to the NT server or through a network connection using the DLC protocol is shared by creating a logical printer in the Print Manager. NetWare clients access these printers by specifying the printer name in the queues option of the Capture command. Microsoft clients access these printers through the printer share.

To install a printer controlled by an FPNW server:

1. Use the Add Printer wizard.

2. Select the My Computer option.

3. Select the printer port.

4. Enter the printer name, driver, and description.

5. Select the "Share this printer on the network" option, and provide a name for the printer share.

To make printers controlled by NetWare print servers available to Microsoft clients, you must create a logical printer on the NT server and assign it to the special printer port

```
NetWareCompatiblePServern
```

where $n$ is a number. By default, two of these ports are available, but this number can be increased by modifying the HKEY_LOCAL_ MACHINE\SYSTEM\CurrentControlSet\Services\FPNW\Paramters key of the Registry. To associate NetWare print servers, attached printers, and print queues to the NT server printer, use the Print Servers command on the FPNW menu in the Server Manager. You can use the NT server to manage the following types of NetWare printers:

- Printers cabled directly to NetWare print servers.

- Printers attached directly to the network.

Selecting FPNW|Print Server in the Server Manager allows you to:

- View, add, and remove printers.

- Manage printers serviced by FPNW.

- Assign print server operators and users.

- Change the password for the print server.

- Change the file servers serviced by the print server.

- Configure the printer, determine who will be notified in the event of a printer error, and configure which print queues the print device will service *for each printer serviced by the print server.*

To set up a NetWare printer on the FPNW server, follow the standard procedures for creating a printer from the Add Printer wizard in the Printer group on the NT server. Then:

1. Assign the printer port to a NetWareCompatiblePServer$n$ port.

2. Create a share for the printer.

3. In the Server Manager, select FPNW|Print Servers.

4. Click on Add.

5. Enter the print server name, description, and password for the print server.

6. Click on OK to create the print server.

To add a printer to the print server:

1. In Server Manager, select FPNW|Print Servers to display the Print Servers dialog box, listing all the print servers defined for the FPNW server.

2. Choose the print server you wish to add a printer to.

3. Click on the Add button.

4. Enter the name of the printer and the number of the printer port.

5. Select the type of printer port.

6. Click on OK to add the printer.

If you are assigning a printer to more than one print server, you can define the printer's parameters once and then use the Defined Elsewhere parameter in the Type box on subsequent print servers.

Once the printer has been added, you can assign print queues to it. The print queue is assigned to the print device of the logical printer created in the Print Manager. You can also set the priority of the print queue. To select the print queues the printer will service:

1.  In Server Manager, select FPNW|Print Servers.

2.  Choose the print server whose print queues you want to set, and then click on the Printers button.

3.  Select the printer from the list of printers on the server, and choose the Queues button. A list of available print queues is displayed. You have the option of adding and removing print queues.

4.  Select the queue to be added, and click on the Add button. When adding a queue, the queue you select should be the logical printer you created using the Print Manager.

5.  Set the queue's priority. This is a value between 1 and 10, with 1 being the highest priority.

## Configuring Print Servers

After you have installed a print server, you can configure who has access to print to and manage the print server. You can also administer the printers attached to the print server. To configure the print server:

1.  In the Server Manager, select FPNW|Print Servers.

2.  From the Print Server list, select the print server to add users or groups that will be print-server operators for that print server.

3.  Click on the Operators button.

4.  From the list of Available Accounts, select the accounts you wish to be print-server operators, and click on the Add button.

From the Print Servers command, you can also remove printers attached to the print server, change a print server's name and password, add or remove servers that are serviced by the print server, and remove a print server from being serviced by a NetWare printer.

To set up print-server users:

1.  In the Server Manager, select FPNW|Print Servers.

2.  From the Print Server list, select the print server to add users or groups that will be print-server users for that print server.

3.  Click on the Users button.

4.  From the list of Available Accounts, select the accounts you wish to be print-server users, and click on the Add button.

## CONFIGURING PRINTERS SERVICED BY PRINT SERVERS

Once you have created a NetWare printer, you can modify its settings through the FPNW menu in the Server Manager. Configuring a printer allows you to:

- Specify the type of printer port, such as parallel, serial, or if the port is defined elsewhere

- Determine whether to use interrupts, and if so, what interrupts to use

- Configure the serial port characteristics

- Specify queue service mode

- Specify buffer size and starting form

To configure the printer:

1.  In the Server Manager, select FPNW|Printer Servers.

2.  From the Print Server list, select the print server whose printers you wish to configure, and then select the printer to configure from the list of printers.

3.  In the Printer box of the Configure Printer dialog box, type a name for the printer.

4.  Select the printer type.

5.  Click on OK when the printer is configured.

It is always helpful to users to be informed when a printer error occurs. To configure a printer to notify users of errors:

1.  In the Server Manager, select FPNW|Printer Servers.

2.  Select the print server whose printer you wish to configure for the error notification.

3. From the list of printers, select the printer to be configured.

4. Add the users or groups you want to be informed of error conditions. You can also remove exiting accounts if they are no longer to receive messages.

## MANAGING FILE AND PRINT SERVICES FOR NETWARE

You manage FPNW through the FPNW application in Control Panel. Using this tool will allow you to perform functions, such as:

• Managing FPNW properties

• Controlling user connections

• Managing volumes

• Sending messages

Managing FPNW properties allows you to configure:

• *The FPNW Server Name* —Specifies the name used by NetWare clients to identify the FPNW server. This name should be different from the NT name for the server. Changing the FPNW server name requires a system reboot to take effect.

• *Description for the Server* —A description for the server that may be used to easily identify it (for example, location within a building).

• *Home Directory Root Path* —This path is relative to the NetWare SYS volume, which by default is *drive*.\SYSVOL. Changing this value has immediate effect.

• *Default NetWare Queue* —Indicates the default printer queue for the server. Select the queue from the list of available print queues. This is the default print queue to which users print when running the *capture* utility.

• *Allowing New Users to Login* —Enables additional users to connect to the server.

• *Server Response* —Enables the server to respond when NetWare clients poll for the nearest server when they start.

Controlling users connections allows you, as an administrator, to disconnect users from the server and send messages to connected users. You administer user connections by clicking on the Users button from the FPNW Properties dialog box.

**TIP** It is wise to inform users when you are going to disconnect them from the server, otherwise they may lose data.

The Volumes button in the FPNW Properties dialog box allows you to view the volumes shared by a server and the users connected to those volumes. A user connected to a particular volume can be disconnected from the server by following these steps:

1. Select the volume the user is connected to.

2. Select the user from the list of users.

3. Click on Disconnect.

Alternatively, you can disconnect all users from a volume by selecting the volume and then clicking on the Disconnect All button.

The Files button in the FPNW Properties dialog box allows you to view the server files opened by NetWare clients and disconnect these clients from files when necessary. You can close the connection to a file by selecting the file from the list of opened files and then clicking on the Close File button. Alternatively, you can close all files by clicking on the Close All Files button.

As I mentioned earlier, FPNW provides some command-line utilities that are available for NetWare client users. The utilities are:

- *Attach*—Allows you to log in to another server running either NetWare or FPNW while remaining logged in to the current server. You must be logged in to at least one server before being able to run the *attach* command.

- *Capture*—Enables you to view print queues and printers, redirect a print job to another print queue, print from an application without exiting the application, and print multiple copies of a print job.

- *Endcap*—Ends a capture on one or more parallel printer ports. You can also use *endcap* to send data to local FPNW or NetWare network printers or files.

- *Login*—Starts a login script for a particular server and gains access to that server's resources as specified for the rights for that user. When using the login command, you must specify a valid user name and password.

- *Logout*—Enables you to log off from one or all servers you are attached to.

- *Map*—Displays current drive mappings and can also be used to create or change network drive mappings. All drive mappings are temporary.

- *Setpass*—Allows you to change your FPNW password on one or more FPNW or NetWare servers that you having an existing connection to.

- *Slist*—Lists all servers running NetWare or FPNW.

FPNW also provides an additional parameter to the *net user* command that allows you to make an account NetWare-enabled. You can also use the net user command to add new NetWare-enabled accounts and disable existing NetWare accounts. The syntax of the command is:

```
net user username [password | •] /fpnw[:yes | no]
```

## THE FPNW MIGRATION TOOL

The Migration Tool shipped with FPNW is essentially the same as the one provided with the Gateway Service for NetWare, with a couple of additional features. The main enhancement is that users' login scripts are also automatically migrated to the NT server during a migration. Migrated login scripts are stored in the SYSVOL\MAIL directory on the FPNW server. You may need to edit these login scripts to enable all mapping functions after the migration.

For more information on the Migration Tool, review the *Migration Tool for NetWare* section presented earlier in this chapter.

## *Microsoft Directory Service Manager for NetWare*

The Microsoft Directory Service Manager for NetWare (DSMN) enables the synchronization of user accounts between Windows NT server domains and servers running Novell NetWare version 3.x or 2.x. This is achieved without having to install additional drivers on Novell NetWare servers or clients.

DSMN extends the Windows NT server directory service features for user and group account management to NetWare servers. DSMN makes it possible to centrally manage user and group accounts that have access to servers running Windows NT server and servers running NetWare. Each user has just a single password to access multiple servers running either network operating system. This password stays automatically synchronized for all servers. DSMN requires that the GSNW service be installed.

**TIP** NetWare clients do not have access to NT resources. If you wish to allow NetWare users to access NT resources, use FPNW.

## How DSMN Works

When adding a NetWare server to a domain, you select which user and group accounts to move to the NT domain. Any accounts not moved cannot be maintained by NT but can be maintained by the traditional NetWare means, or even deleted. The accounts are copied to the PDC of the NT domain.

For NetWare accounts that are copied to NT, use only User Manager for Domains to manage them; otherwise, they will become unsynchronized and require manual maintenance.

After the accounts have been copied to the NT server, you need to select how the NT accounts will be propagated back to the NetWare server. A maximum of 2000 user and group accounts can be propagated. All members of propagated groups are distributed. Only copy accounts to a NetWare server that require access to that server. All propagated accounts are replicated to any BDCs in the domain.

## The Functionality of DSMN

A NetWare server added to an NT domain is administered through User Manager for Domains and changes are automatically propagated to NetWare servers. A NetWare server can exist in only one NT domain; however, multiple NetWare servers can be added to a single NT domain (32 is the recommended maximum).

**TIP** Modifying propagated user accounts through NetWare tools only makes changes to the NetWare copies of the accounts. Therefore, the account will become out-of-synch in the domain.

When adding new accounts, you must make them NetWare-enabled so they can be propagated to the NetWare server and be able to login to the NetWare server. You can also propagate existing NT accounts by making them NetWare-enabled.

You perform NetWare server administration in NT domains through the Synchronization Manager, which is added to the NT Administrative Tools when the DSMN service is installed. All administration of NetWare resources, except for account administration, is still performed by the NetWare management functions.

When adding multiple NetWare servers to an NT domain, be aware of the consequences of identical group and user accounts. Group accounts are effectively merged on the NT. It is also possible to force the service to merge accounts with different names. If there is a NetWare account with the same name as an existing NT account, the rights and permissions of the NetWare account are passed on to the NT account. If the existing account is NetWare-enabled, the account's existing password is used. Otherwise, a new password is given to enable it to be propagated to the NetWare servers.

When employing DSMN in a multidomain environment, it is important to note that DSMN does not operate across domains; accounts are only propagated onto NetWare servers in the domain that contains the accounts.

When you install DSMN, an account synchronization database is established on the domain's PDC. This database stores information on the users and groups being propagated to each NetWare server in the domain and the update status of all group and user accounts on each NetWare server. The update status tracks which updates to accounts have been propagated to the appropriate NetWare servers.

Before we go on, it is important that you understand how user and group accounts are propagated between NT and NetWare servers. Table 10.6 compares how NetWare account restrictions are mapped to the equivalent NT permissions.

**Table 10.6   Mapping NetWare Account Restrictions**

| NetWare Account Restriction | NT Equivalent | How Implemented |
|---|---|---|
| Account Expiration Date | Account Expiration Date | By individual user account; NetWare setting preserved |
| Account Disabled | Account Disabled | By individual user account; NetWare setting preserved |
| Limit Concurrent Connections | Limit Concurrent Connections | By individual user account; NetWare setting preserved |
| Require Password | Permit Blank Password | As policy for all accounts; NetWare setting discarded |
| Minimum Password Length | Minimum Password Length | As policy for all accounts; NetWare setting discarded |
| Force Periodic Password Changes | Password Never Changes | By individual user account; NetWare setting preserved |
| Days between Forced Changes | Maximum Password Age | As policy for all accounts; NetWare setting discarded |
| Require Unique Passwords | Password Uniqueness | As policy for all accounts; NetWare setting discarded |
| Allow User to Change Password | User Can Not Change Password | By individual user account; NetWare setting preserved |
| Grace Logins | Grace Logins (DSMN feature) | By individual user account; NetWare setting preserved |
| Station Restrictions | Logon Workstations | By individual user account; NetWare setting preserved |
| Time Restrictions | Logon Hours | By individual user account; NetWare setting preserved |

*(continued)*

**Table 10.6    Mapping NetWare Account Restrictions (continued)**

| NetWare Account Restriction | NT Equivalent | How Implemented |
|---|---|---|
| Intruder Detection/ Lockout | Account Lockout | As policy for all accounts; NetWare setting discarded |
| User Disk Volume Restrictions | None | Not Transferred |

Because NT and NetWare store passwords in an encrypted format, it is not possible to move the passwords from the NetWare server along with the accounts. Therefore, when a NetWare server is added for management, you have the following options to choose from to assign passwords to the accounts:

- Give each user a blank password

- Set each user's password to be the same as their user name

- Create a password that is assigned to all users

- Give each user a randomly assigned password

- Use a mapping file

The propagation of built-in NetWare users and groups requires special consideration when employing a DSMN solution. Groups and users that require special consideration include:

- *Supervisor*—The NetWare Supervisor account is equivalent to the NT Administrator. When adding a NetWare server to an NT domain through DSMN, you can choose whether to add Supervisor accounts to the NT Administrators group. However, each NetWare server retains its unique Supervisor account with its own password, which means you can not centrally manage Supervisor accounts.

- *Workgroup Managers and User Account Managers*—The closest NT equivalent to these NetWare groups is the Account Operators group. As user account administration is centralized in NT server domains, there is no need to migrate Workgroup Managers and User Account Managers to the NT Account Operators group. However, you can opt to do this anyway.

- *Console Operators*—When propagating NetWare servers, you have the choice of making the NetWare File Server Console Operators accounts members of the Console Operators group in NT. Console Operators have the same rights as File Server Console Operators but do not have any special authorities on NT servers. The Console Operators group is created on the NT server when DSMN service is installed.

- *Print Server Operators and Print Queue Operators*—Members of these groups are not added to the NT Print Operators Group. Members of these groups lose their abilities on NetWare servers if they are propagated to the NT domain.

DSMN mapping files function in the same way as the mapping files created by the Migration Tool for NetWare. You can use the Synchronization Manager to create a mapping file, which you can then edit.

Once the NetWare users have been added to the NT domain, you can select which accounts are to be propagated back to the NetWare servers. These could be accounts that originally existed on the NetWare server, as well as NetWare-enabled NT accounts. Table 10.7 details the mapping of NT account restrictions to NetWare account restrictions during the propagation process.

**Table 10.7  Account Restriction Transformations When Propagating from NT to NetWare Servers**

| NT Account Restrictions | NetWare Equivalent | How Propagated |
| --- | --- | --- |
| Username | Username | Propagated intact |
| Full Name | Full Name | Propagated intact |
| Description | None | Not propagated |
| Password | Password | Propagated intact |
| Must Change Password at Next Logon | Password Expiration Date | Password expiration date is current date |
| User Can Not Change Password | Allow User to Change Password | Propagated intact |

*(continued)*

**Table 10.7    Account Restriction Transformations when Propagating from NT to NetWare Servers** *(continued)*

| NT Account Restrictions | NetWare Equivalent | How Propagated |
|---|---|---|
| Password Never Expires | Password Expiration Date | Propagated intact |
| Account Disabled | Account Disabled | Propagated intact |
| Account Locked Out | Intruder Detection/ Lockout | Current setting not propagated |
| Maintain NetWare Compatible Login | None | Must be selected for account to be propagated to NetWare servers |
| Group Memberships | Group Memberships | Propagated intact |
| User Profile Path | None | Not propagated |
| Logon Script Name | None | Not propagated |
| Home Directory | Home Directory | Setting is ignored; NetWare Home Directory Relative Path is propagated |
| Logon Hours | Logon Hours | Propagated intact |
| User May Log On to All Workstations | None | Not propagated |
| User May Log On from All NetWare Workstations | Station Restrictions | Propagated intact |
| Account Expires | Account Expiration Date | Propagated intact |
| Account Type | None | Not propagated |
| NetWare Account Password Expired | None | No effect |
| Grace Logins | Grace Logins | Propagated intact |
| Concurrent Connections | Limit Concurrent Connections | Propagated intact |
| Maximum Password Age | Days between Forced Changes | Propagated intact |
| Minimum Password Age | None | Not propagated |

*(continued)*

**Table 10.7    Account Restriction Transformations when Propagating from NT to NetWare Servers (continued)**

| NT Account Restrictions | NetWare Equivalent | How Propagated |
|---|---|---|
| Minimum Password Length | Minimum Password Length | Propagated intact |
| Password Uniqueness | Require Unique Passwords | Propagated intact for value greater than seven |
| Forcibly Disconnect When Logon Hours Expire | None | Not propagated |
| User Must Log On to Change Password | None | Not propagated |

Of all the built-in NT server groups, only members of the Administrators group are given special rights on NetWare servers. These users are given the equivalent of Supervisor rights on the NetWare servers.

## INSTALLING THE MICROSOFT DIRECTORY SERVICE FOR NETWARE

The Microsoft Directory Service for NetWare service can only function on a PDC. To install the service:

1. In Control Panel, start the Network application.

2. Click on the Add Service button.

3. Click on the Have Disk button.

4. Insert the FPNW CD-ROM into the drive, and enter the path to the CD-ROM drive and the path of the hardware platform (for example, e:\i386).

5. Select Directory Service Manger for NetWare from the OEM list, and click on OK.

6. Enter the DSMN service account password, and then click on OK.

7. Restart the NT server.

## ADMINISTRATION TOOLS

Although DSMN requires an NT server to function, you can install the administration tools that manage it on any other NT server or workstation in the domain. The tools are also installed from the Network application in Control Panel, but instead of selecting the DSMN service to install, select the Administration Tools option instead.

## ADMINISTRATION OF THE DIRECTORY SERVICE MANAGER FOR NETWARE

Two tools are available to aid you in the administration of the DSMN service: the Synchronization Manager and User Manager for Domains. The Synchronization Manager (or Directory Service Manager for NetWare, as it is displayed in the NT Administrative Tools group) is the tool used to add NetWare servers for management within an NT domain. The Synchronization Manager, shown in Figure 10.17, allows for:

• The addition of NetWare servers to a domain

• Performing a trial run of adding NetWare servers

• Removal of a NetWare server from management within a domain

• Specifying accounts to propagate from the NT domain to NetWare servers

• Backing up of the synchronization database

User Manager for Domains has the augmented functionality of allowing you to add, modify, and delete user accounts; add, modify, and delete group accounts; and set account policy.

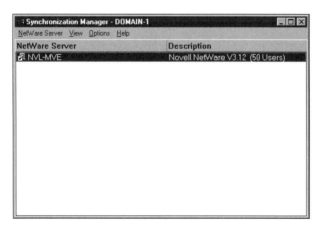

**Figure 10.17**   The DSMN Synchronization Manager.

To illustrate how the DSMN administers the interoperability between NetWare and NT servers, I'll use an example propagation. The scenario includes a NetWare server (NVL-MVE) and an NT server (NT-MVE), which has recently had DSMN installed. The user and group configuration is the same as I used to illustrate the Gateway Service for NetWare (see Table 10.5). Once again, I'll use a mapping file to provide the NetWare users with more meaningful user names when propagated to the NT server.

To add a NetWare server to the NT domain:

1. Start the Synchronization Manager.

2. Select NetWare Server|Add Server to Manage.

3. Select the server NVL-MVE. You are then prompted to enter a user name and password to connect to the NetWare server. For this example, I'll connect using the Supervisor account (whatever account you use must have Supervisor privileges).

4. Once you have successfully attached to the NetWare server, the Propagate NetWare Accounts to Windows NT Domain dialog box is displayed, as shown in Figure 10.18. From here, you specify how the NetWare user accounts will be migrated to the domain.

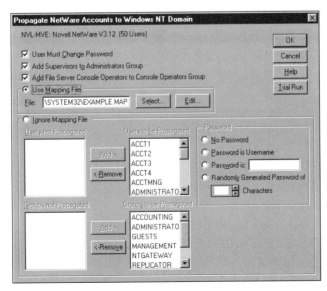

**Figure 10.18** The Propagate NetWare Accounts to Windows NT Domain dialog box defines how the NetWare accounts will be migrated to the NT domain.

5.  Using Figure 10.18 as a guideline, specify that the users must change their password, that Supervisors will be added to the Administrators group, that File Server Console Operators will be added to the Console Operators group, that all users and groups will be propagated, and that we will use the mapping file example.map to update the NetWare user names with more meaningful ones.

6.  Perform a trial migration to evaluate if the propagation will be successful.

7.  If everything looks acceptable, click on OK to start the actual propagation process.

    Once the NetWare to NT propagation has occurred, the Set Propagation Accounts on NetWare server dialog box is displayed. This specifies what groups and their members are migrated back to the NetWare server.

8.  Select all the accounts for propagation, and then select the "Users may only change their passwords via Directory Service Manager for NetWare" option.

9.  Click on OK to perform the migration. Figure 10.19 shows the migration process.

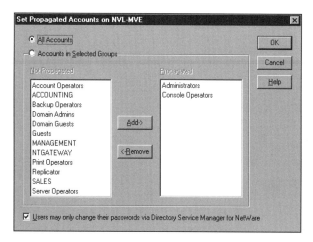

**Figure 10.19**   Migrating all groups to the NetWare server.

As you can see from Figures 10.20 and 10.21, the NetWare users and groups were successfully propagated to the NT domain, where they were renamed, if necessary. These users were then propagated back to the NetWare server.

You can also see that these user names along with any NetWare-enabled NT domain accounts were then propagated back to the NetWare (replacing the old user names). These NetWare accounts can now be administered from NT.

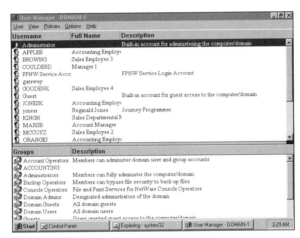

**Figure 10.20**   The NT domain users after the propagation of NetWare accounts to the NT domain.

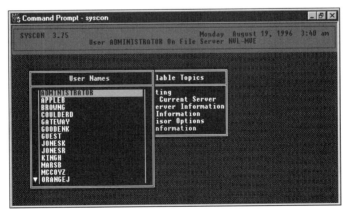

**Figure 10.21**   The user names propagated back from the NT domain to the NetWare server—including any NetWare-enabled NT domain accounts.

For new NT domain accounts to be propagated to NetWare servers, they must be NetWare-enabled.

## HOW USERS SHOULD CHANGE THEIR PASSWORDS

The client software being used dictates how a user should change her password. However, it is important that you try and keep users' NT and NetWare passwords synched, with a minimal amount of administrative effort on your part.

All Microsoft network clients, except for Windows NT workstation users, use the *chgpass* command, which allows the user's password on the NT domain and NetWare servers being propagated. NetWare clients can use either *chgpass* or *mslogin* to change their passwords. The *mslogin* utility is the functional equivalent to similar NetWare utilities. It also changes the password for NT domain and NetWare servers.

# NT and Unix

Unix, arguably the most well-rounded and mature operating system available on the market today, is the yardstick by which open systems are measured. The current thrust for open systems is through the use of the TCP/IP protocol stack, which is tightly integrated with the many flavors of Unix available.

Unfortunately, the TCP/IP services provided within NT 4 systems are fairly limited, providing for the basic TCP/IP applications—FTP and Telnet—which can be used to access Unix systems at the most basic level for character-based terminal emulation and file transfer. Other basic TCP/IP connectivity tools in NT 4 for interaction with Unix machines include *finger, lpr, rcp, rexec, rsh,* and *tftp.*

However, to fully interoperate with Unix systems, you will have to look into the third-party arena to reach any effective connectivity. These services include NFS and X Windows systems.

The integration of NT into a Unix environment holds several challenges of interoperability at the basic configuration. The Windows Internet Naming Service (WINS) does not support Unix workstations and doesn't integrate with DNS services. Therefore, identifying and administering your NT/Unix environment may require employing gateways.

## TCP/IP Printing

The TCP/IP Printing service supplied with NT 4 allows any client computer to print to a network-attached printer or a printer that is directly attached to a Unix host. Only one client on the network (either an NT 4 server or workstation) needs to have TCP/IP and the Microsoft TCP/IP Printing service installed to act as a print server for the printer and to allow other clients to access the printer through it.

### PRINTING IN THE TCP/IP ENVIRONMENT

TCP/IP printing consists of two main components: the Line Printer Daemon (LPD) and the Line Printer Remote (LPR).

The LPR usually resides on the client and sends requests to the LPD print server. Installing Microsoft TCP/IP Printing under NT 4 installs the LPD service. However, the service is set to start manually. To be started automatically, you must reconfigure the TCP/IP settings.

### INSTALLING TCP/IP PRINTING

The Microsoft TCP/IP Printing is added as a service under the NT network configuration. You add TCP/IP printers using the Add Printer wizard. To add a printer, you will need the IP identifier of the LPD server and the printer name on the LPD server.

### HOW TCP/IP PRINTING WORKS

LPR allows a client application on one computer to send a document to a print spooler on another computer (usually called the LPD service). Windows NT provides the LPR.EXE utility and the LPR port monitor, both of which can act as clients that send documents to an LPD service.

## Accessing Applications on Unix Servers

You can access two types of applications on Unix servers:

- Character-based

- Graphical-based

To access character-based applications, you can use a terminal emulation application, such as Telnet, which is shipped as part of the TCP/IP protocol suite in NT 4. To access Unix GUI applications, you will need to implement a third-party PC X server software solution on your NT.

An X server solution can enable NT users to access and display Unix applications in windows on the NT desktop and provide the benefits of the 32-bit features of NT.

## Accessing Directories and Files

The most common way of sharing files, directories, and printers between Unix machines is by using Network File Sharing (NFS). Unfortunately, NT 4 does not support NFS; however, many third-party vendors are now releasing NFS client and server software for NT 4.

An NFS implementation in NT is usually deployed as a kernel-mode or NT service, and can be configured through service administration or through applets in Control Panel. The configuration of an NFS service in NT 4 should include selecting directories to export, creating NFS user accounts, and mapping NT and Unix accounts, including access privileges between environments.

Including an NFS server service on your NT 4 server will allow Unix users to access file and print services on your NT server, as well as allow your Microsoft network clients access to the same resources. An NFS client installed on the NT 4 machine will allow you to access files and printer resources on a Unix machine.

# NT and Banyan VINES

The much maligned Banyan VINES and the related ENS for Unix and NetWare provide arguably the best enterprise network operating system solution on the market. The strength of its StreetTalk naming service, which is still far ahead of anything being offered by Microsoft or Novell, provides a mechanism whereby servers learn about each other in an extremely efficient manner, with the minimum configuration effort on the part of the network administrator.

Unfortunately, the advantages VINES boasts with is enterprise structure is more than balanced by its appalling lack of support on the Intel-based platform, poor user administration facilities, text-based interface, and poor back-up facilities.

However, because VINES is a Unix-based operating system (its underlying operating system is a version of Berkeley Unix), it is capable of running on a wide range of hardware platforms—Banyan VINES and ENS for NetWare on the Intel x86 platforms, and ENS for Unix on Solaris, HP-UX, and SCO platforms.

## VINES StreetTalk

The major feature of VINES and ENS is the StreetTalk service. This is the mechanism that allows servers to learn about each other and their resources. This is similar to the domain relationships implemented in Windows NT, but with one distinct advantage. Relationships between servers in the VINES enterprise design are transitive. Instead of implementing trust relationships between groups of servers, all authentication is carried out on the server where the user is trying to access a resource.

Consider a scenario where four servers (A, B, C, and D) exist in an enterprise, as shown in Figure 10.22. Server A knows of the existence of Server B, and Server B knows of the existence of servers A, C, and D.

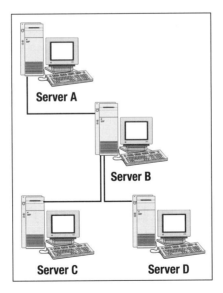

**Figure 10.22**  The connections between servers.

In the VINES enterprise implementation, because B is aware of C and D, A is automatically aware of C and D, and because C knows about B, C also is aware of A and D. These relationships do not require the manual configurations of connections between any other servers except for the ones existing at the start of this example. Therefore, if you were to go into office (server A) from your home office (server D), you could login to a client at the office and access the resources on the server at home, without administrators having to set up a relationship between A and D.

Compare this to the same scenario using the Windows NT domain model. To have the ability to login to a home server from a server in another office, every server in the model must have a trust relationship with every other server manually configured.

This may not seem like such a big deal in a small scenario, but consider the addition of another server to the enterprise—Server E which is at the same location as Server D. To make the rest of the servers in the environment aware of Server E, all that needs to be done is to establish a relationship between D and E. The configuration of E will then be automatically propagated throughout the enterprise. To achieve the same effect with NT, the administrator of the new server would need to coordinate with the administrators of the other servers to establish trust relationships.

Banyan provides two main products for the integration of Banyan VINES and NT:

- StreetTalk Access for Windows NT File and Print

- Banyan Enterprise Client for Windows NT

Let's take a look at both of these products in more detail.

## StreetTalk Access for Windows NT File and Print

The StreetTalk Access for Windows NT File and Print is Banyan's entry into the realm of services for the NT environment. Basically, it allows VINES clients access through VINES servers to NT server resources, using either VINES IP or Microsoft's TCP/IP stack.

The StreetTalk Access for Windows NT File and Print requires the VINES StreetTalk service residing on a VINES or ENS for Unix server.

StreetTalk features include:

- *VINES Requester for Microsoft Windows NT*—Bypasses the requirement for additional configuration of clients wishing to access the NT server. Supports both VINES IP and Microsoft TCP/IP protocols.

- *High Capacity File Service*—Allows for file services exceeding 2 GB (a serious limitation in VINES).

- *Universal File Service*—Files can be shared with other Windows NT users who may not be accessing the NT server through NT (Macintosh and NetWare users, for example).

- *Support for VINES ARLs*—Access rights to the file services on the NT server can be set through VINES access rights lists.

- *Support for RAID and Disk Compression*—Support for NT software-based RAID and disk compression.

- *Support for Additional Printer Types*—Support for printers, through NT, which are not normally supported by VINES.

- *Accounting for Print Jobs*—Generates reports by users, groups, or organizations for accounting purposes.

- *Universal Print Service*—Printers can be shared with users not accessing NT through VINES.

- *StreetTalk Management*—StreetTalk continues to manage users, groups, and file and print services, providing enterprise-wide directory services for NT file and print resources.

- *STDA Searching*—StreetTalk names are applied to the NT file and print services.

- *Single Login*—StreetTalk names are validated for access to the NT resources, as well as VINES and Unix systems.

One of the benefits of the StreetTalk Access for Windows NT File and Print is that it allows VINES clients to access NT resources without requiring the installation of additional network drivers on the client. This makes it a viable option in the move to integrate NT as an application server into the VINES enterprise environment.

The main advantage of employing the StreetTalk Access for Windows NT File and Print is the ability to overcome the 2 GB file system limit inherent in VINES and ENS. Running out of disk space for file services has been a major problem with VINES environments in the past.

## Banyan Enterprise Client for Windows NT

The Banyan Enterprise Client for Windows NT is a workstation solution in the nature of the Client for NetWare that comes with Windows NT. It allows access to Banyan VINES and ENS services from an NT workstation. It is not designed to be a gateway service residing on an NT server.

The client provides access to VINES-based file and print services, as well as the VINES mail store. These rights are achieved through the processing of a VINES logon script.

NT 4 requires a minimum of version 5.56(30) of the client software which itself requires access to a VINES 6.20 server for IP functionality. The 5.56(30) installation files are available from Banyan's Web site (**www.banyan.com**).

It's possible that you use your NT workstation to maintain your network. You could successfully administer the Novell and Unix environments from your workstation, but not VINES. Why? The VINES client is missing some crucial features required to administer the VINES environment that can be achieved from a DOS-based VINES client.

Some of the crucial missing features are:

- The ability to upgrade the client software from files stored on the VINES server

- The ability to apply kernel patches to the VINES server from a client

- The editing of VINES and ENS for NetWare user profiles over 1 KB in size

- No clients are available for NT Workstation running on DEC Alpha and PowerPC platforms

Some of the client features that are included are:

- TCP/IP support (only in environments containing VINES 6.20 servers)

- Support for the synchronization of Banyan and NT passwords

- Common login to Banyan networks with NT user name and password

- Printing to VINES print services from both MS-DOS and Windows NT Print Manager

- VINES IP protocol support

- Universal Naming Convention (UNC) support

## INSTALLATION OF BANYAN ENTERPRISE CLIENT FOR WINDOWS NT

The client requires the following:

- A minimum of 16 MB RAM

- 3 MB of free disk space

- Access to a Banyan server running version 5.30(0) (or 6.20 with the server-to-server option installed if using TCP/IP, which acts as a routing server for the IP clients)

- An Ethernet, Token Ring, or FDDI LAN adapter card with NDIS 3.0 driver supported by NT

## CONSIDERATIONS WHEN RUNNING TCP/IP

Prior to installing the Banyan Enterprise Client for Windows NT with the TCP/IP protocol (actually named the Banyan NT Client with IP), you will need to modify the IP settings for each IP routing server. Specifically, you will need to:

- *Change the Size of the Sequenced Packet Protocol (SPP) Maximum Transfer Unit (MTU)*—The SPP MTU is the maximum size allocated for the SPP data in a packet. The default (and maximum) size of the MTU is 1450 bytes. However, as IP packets processed by Banyan IP Clients require more UDP and IP header information space, the size of the MTU must be reduced on an IP routing server. Normally, when using non-encapsulated VINES networks, the packet header requirement is about 50 bytes. Therefore, the packet header requirement plus the MTU results in an Ethernet packet of maximum size (about 1500 bytes).

  However, in using the Banyan IP Client, the UDP protocol increases the size of each VINES packet it handles by adding its own header.

This results in fewer data bytes available for the packet to carry data. This means that the data contained in the original VINES packet will not be able to fit into on encapsulated packet, which would cause the VINES packet to be fragmented into additional packets. The fragmentation and reassembly of IP or UDP packets can cause a significant slowdown in network performance. This fragmentation can be avoided by reducing the size of the MTU. If the TCP/IP encapsulation type is set to IP and UDP, or UDP only, the MTU should be set to 1436 bytes. If the encapsulation type is for IP only, then an MTU size of 1440 bytes is recommended (see *Specify the Encapsulation Type*).

- *Enable LAN IP*—Any VINES server that will act as a routing server for a Banyan IP Client workstation must have LAN IP enabled. Enabling LAN IP allows the server to exchange IP packets with other IP servers throughout the network, regardless of whether a server-to-server connection had been set up between the servers. If LAN IP is disabled, manual entries must be entered for other servers targeted as IP connections.

- *Specify the Encapsulation Type*—Workstations running DOS/Windows 3.x use IP encapsulation. Workstations running Windows NT or Windows 95 use UDP encapsulation. Therefore, depending on the clients running on the network, it will be necessary to specify IP, UDP, or both. It should be noted that enabling encapsulation requires some resources used to maintain server-to-server connections. Therefore, specify the encapsulation type necessary for the clients attached to the network. For example, if the network contains Windows 95 and NT clients only, do not specify IP as an encapsulation type.

- *Disabling VINES IP on Individual Interfaces*—Disabling a VINES IP on an interface prevents that interface from transmitting VINES IP packets on a network. Consider a network with all TCP/IP clients. In this network, all servers have LAN IP enabled and do not transmit VINES IP packets. For this situation, there is no need to transmit VINES IP packets across the network. Therefore, disabling VINES IP would reduce the amount of unnecessary network traffic.

## INSTALLING THE CLIENT

You must install the client while logged on to the NT workstation with administrator rights. Follows these steps to install the client from the three floppy disks:

1. Insert disk one and run *setup*. The VINES Setup dialog box appears.

2. Click on the Install button. Any running VINES services are stopped and the Install Directory dialog box appears, as shown in Figure 10.23. The default directory is c:\vines. You can change the directory to any directory name conforming to the 8.3 naming convention. Most files are installed to this directory and its subdirectories; however, some files are installed to the NT *system32* directory.

3. Click on the Continue button to access the Network Communications dialog box, and select one of the following:

    *IP Encapsulation*—When you select this option, the Network Adapter section of the dialog box is replaced by a server IP address section, as shown in Figure 10.24. IP encapsulation can only be used with the Microsoft TCP/IP stack. You can enter up to three preferred routing server IP addresses in this and/or the Dial-up Server IP Addresses section. Also, specify whether the client should use LAN IP addresses, Dial-up IP addresses, or both.

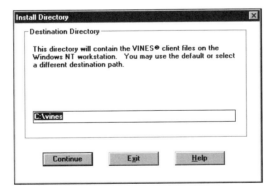

**Figure 10.23**    Selecting the installation directory for the Banyan Enterprise Client for Windows NT.

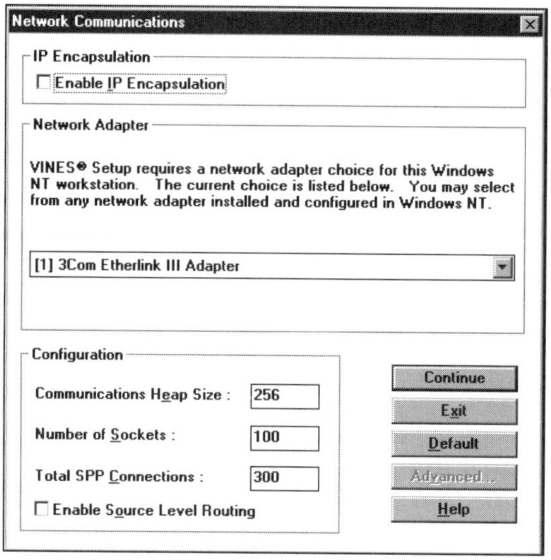

**Figure 10.24**   Selecting the network configuration for the client running IP.

*The LAN Adapter Used by the Workstation*—You must specify this in order to use VINES IP. The default settings for communications buffers allocated, maximum number of sockets, and maximum number of SPP connections can usually be accepted, as shown in Figure 10.25.

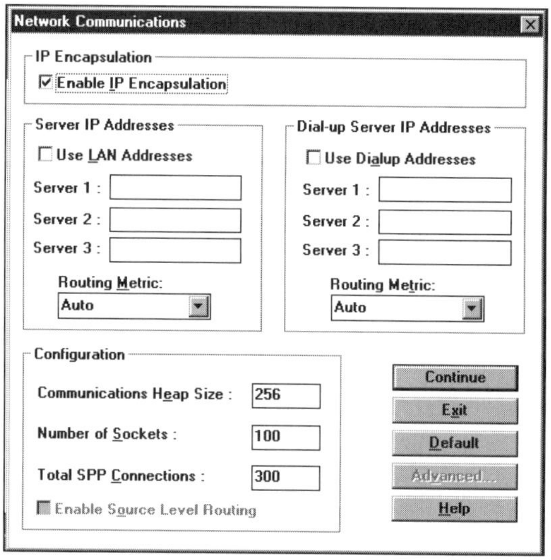

**Figure 10.25**   Selecting the network configuration for the client running VINES IP.

4. Click the Continue button. The VINES Workstation Configuration dialog box appears.

5. Specify the Login Search List. You can select up to three groups that the login program will search through when entering the first part of the three-part StreetTalk user ID. For example, consider the user *jonesr* whose full StreetTalk names is *jonesr@finance@XYZ*. Entering *finance@XYZ* as one of the entries in the Login Search List would require him to only enter *jonesr* as his user name, as shown in Figure 10.26. The VINES user name consists of three parts—user name, group, and organization—formatted like this: id@group@organization.

6. Enable or disable the following Login Options:

   *Load Banyan Workstation During System Start*—Enabling this option loads Banyan workstation software each time the workstation boots.

   *Common Login*—Enabling this option allows the use of Windows NT user name as a common login to the Banyan network. Of course, the NT and Banyan user names and passwords must be the same.

   *Login Status Display Time*—Configures the length of time the Login Status dialog box remains on screen after login process has completed.

7. Click on the Continue button. The VINES Desktop Configuration dialog box appears. This allows you to configure:

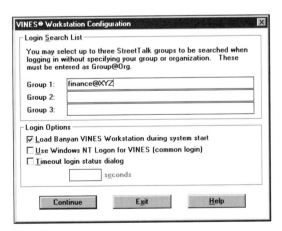

**Figure 10.26** Entering finance@XYZ in the Login Search List.

*VINES Program Group*—Enabling this option creates a program group that contains the Banyan NT Client applications. You can also change the name of the program group.

*Support for 16-bit Banyan DOS and Windows Applications*—Enabling this option loads the TSR program BANSVC.COM. Not configuring this option requires the manual execution of the program before running Banyan Applications Toolkit DOS programs, such as mnet, mail, and mservice.

8.  Click on the Continue button. The Configure Network Computer Name dialog box appears. This dialog box allows you to specify the name for the workstation for communications with distributed applications. I recommend that you leave this option blank unless you are using a third-party Winsock application.

9.  Click on the Continue button. The Toolkit Options dialog box appears. Version 5.56(30) of the client is distributed with the Banyan Windows NT Toolkit, which aids in the development of VINES-aware applications. Select Yes to install the Toolkit on the workstation.

10. After all files have been installed, restart the workstation in order to access the VINES network.

## Using the NT Client

To login to the Banyan VINES network from Windows NT, you have two options:

• Double click on the Login icon in the VINES program group, or run BAN.EXE from the VINES directory. Enter the StreetTalk user name and password. Click on OK, and the profile script will execute. Click on Close when the VINES login script has completed, then close the Login Status dialog box.

• Enable the common login option through the VINES Workstation dialog box. Remember, if this option is selected the Windows NT and VINES user name and passwords must be the same.

You can use the Enterprise client to change the Windows NT and Banyan VINES passwords at the same time by running the Password program in the VINES program group.

## PRINTING

Windows NT uses an object-oriented printing model. Applications print to target printer objects, which may or may not represent a local printer or correspond to a physical printer port. This approach is different from VINES and Windows 3.x models, which redirect physical printer ports to a network printer.

Connecting to a VINES printer from Windows NT is performed through Print Manager. You connect to a VINES print service by selecting the Connect to Printer command within Print Manager and then entering the StreetTalk name of the VINES printer service to be connected. Because Windows NT is unable to use the VINES printer drivers, you must install a printer driver within Windows NT.

The banner page, paper format, and number of copies can be specified in the Printers applet in the VINES Setup window.

## UNIVERSAL NAMING CONVENTION SUPPORT

The structure of UNC support used by Banyan servers is slightly different from the convention used by NT servers. In VINES, the StreetTalk name of the file service is equivalent to the servername\sharename convention used by Windows NT.

For example, a file service exists on a server (Server1), which contains a service (Data1). The StreetTalk name for this service is Data1@Sales@Servers. The Banyan convention for accessing this service through UNC would be:

```
\\Data1@Sales@Servers\*
```

The NT notation for accessing this service would be:

```
\\Server1\Data1\*
```

**TIP** As with Windows NT, any StreetTalk names that contain spaces must be enclosed within quotation marks when using UNC constructions.

## NT into a VINES Environment

Moving an NT server into a Banyan VINES environment could be used to enhance the functionality of the VINES network, or could be the first step in the migration from VINES to NT. In either case, to achieve any level of interoperability between the VINES and NT environments, you will need to employ some type of gateway. As I've previously discussed, the StreetTalk Access for Windows NT File and Print can provide you with the services necessary to achieve this.

Chances are that if you are introducing the NT server into the VINES environment, you're employing the NT server as an application server for the VINES users on the network. This setup lets NT do what it does best, while letting the VINES server do what it does best—functioning as an excellent messaging server. However, the maintenance of users and groups on your network will still have to be maintained on your VINES portion of the network.

# Conclusion

Hopefully, this chapter has helped you understand the issues involved in integrating NT 4 into a multivendor environment. The multivendor environment isn't a heterogeneous, open-systems implementation; there is no one product available that can be used to integrate multiple operating systems.

The support for NetWare in NT is the most complete. NT 4 is shipped with the tools necessary to achieve connectivity between the NT 4 and NetWare servers up to migrating NetWare users and files to the NT server. Also, by using the additional products—File and Print Services for NetWare and Directory Service Manager for NetWare—you can make your NT server appear to NetWare clients as a NetWare server and manage NetWare accounts from within NT.

Unfortunately, the operating system you would expect NT to integrate best with in the multivendor environment—Unix—has fairly minimal capability built in to NT. Apart from the basic TCP/IP applications Telnet and FTP, NT really has very little to offer when integrating with Unix systems.

To provide a more rounded integration philosophy, you will have to look for third-party NFS and X Server products.

Banyan is seriously pushing its products as add-ons to the NT server environment and is even providing tools for users to integrate NT and VINES. Adding an NT server to your VINES network and using the StreetTalk Access for Windows NT File and Print could easily be the first step in scrapping your VINES network for NT.

PART

5

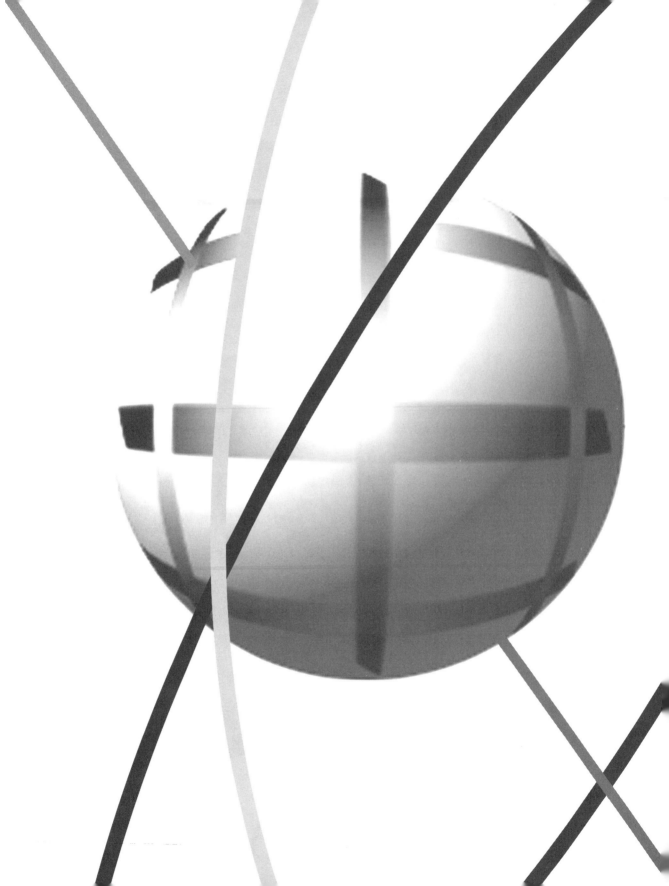

# Network Performance

Picture this: You plan, create, and install a network, and begin attaching NT 4 servers and workstations to it. Everything seems to be going fine, but how do you know if the network is running efficiently? If everyone is satisfied with the performance, should you care if it is really efficient? Yes, you should. At some point, the network users will become dissatisfied with slow network services. Waiting for minutes to move data files or to access server-based applications is a late indication that the network performance does not meet user needs. Save yourself the trouble and work out the kinks *before* you find yourself faced with frustrated users. Profiling a network once you get it up and running is one of the best ways to understand a network's true capacity. Once you understand what your network is capable of, you can compare it to the actual performance to see actual/potential problem areas. In this chapter, I will discuss some of the currently available performance measurement tools to help you thoroughly test and optimize your network.

## A Five Step Plan

Many of today's networks are running at less than optimal efficiency. Whether you want to optimize your network or just test its capacity, you should create a plan to meet your goal. I have developed a plan that I use to test and adjust network performance. My plan includes these five basic steps:

1. Create a profile of your network using a software network performance tool. The proper tool will yield a performance profile curve that describes the capabilities of your network to move data.

2. Monitor your network's normal operation and capture the data.

3. Analyze the results of the normal operation versus the network performance data. Where are you currently on the performance curve? How many network resources can be used before a throughput or slowdown occurs?

4. Make changes to NT 4's configuration to improve performance.

5. Retest the network's normal operation, and compare the results to verify if you have increased or decreased performance.

Steps 4 and 5 are iterative. In other words, you should never quit trying to improve performance. This process is important to your future network plans. When you introduce the next generation of NT or install a new application, the operational performance curve will change. Once again, you will be faced with testing the network's limits and improving on the results.

## Performance Measurement

In this chapter, I present several optional performance benchmarking tools that you can get from third-party software vendors, either directly or over the Internet. Although Microsoft has not included any network performance benchmark tools with their current NT 4 release, these tools are readily available.

A performance benchmarking tool differs from a measurement utility in several ways. The benchmarking tool runs a standard set of activities, usually from several different network computers. The results of these benchmarking runs are to exercise NT and its application software to measure how well it performs while under stress. The stress is planned and is a fundamental part of the benchmarking tool. The majority of these tools allow you the option of customizing how it operates and the level of stress that it will place on the network, NT, and the application. The standard NT measurement utilities, such as Perfmon, only monitor performance; they do not create NT activities or stress, they merely record NT's reactions during normal operation.

Many performance measurement tools require at least three computers—a server and two workstations—to create a network testbed. One workstation is a controller used to collect information. The other workstation (or workstations, if possible) acts as a client, issuing server requests in increasing quantities to create a performance curve. The more workstations you use, the more variations to client activity you can collect.

The results that you get from these measurements depend on which tool you choose. For example, you may see a chart similar to the one shown in Figure 11.1. This chart shows that the network's performance is a function of the number of users attached. The chart's X axis contains the number of users, from 0 to 100, and the Y axis displays the time an average transaction takes to pass through the network. This particular network is running NT 4 servers connected to 85 users at 100 MHz using Ethernet.

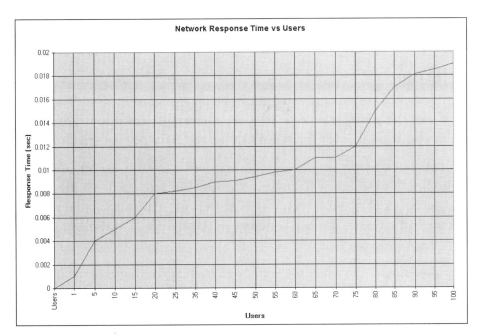

**Figure 11.1**   An example performance curve describes a network's performance as a function of time versus clients, transactions, or bytes.

Once you have created a performance curve, you will need to determine at what point on that curve your network is currently operating. NT 4 provides some excellent tools to monitor network performance. I will cover these tools and explain how you can use them to quantify current usage.

Once you know the network's capacity and at what point on the performance curve you are running, then you will want to change how NT 4 operates. This is called *network tuning*. NT includes a standard set of tools that you can use to adjust its network performance. In the Resource Kit, you will find additional performance tools that will aid you in making and evaluating changes to the NT 4 workstation or server.

Our goal is to consider any and all factors that will cause a network to operate below its maximum potential. Of course, I have to do this within the confines of a chapter. For purposes of clarity, and to avoid any possible confusion, I am restricting this discussion to Ethernet running TCP/IP.

## Third-Party Network Performance Tools

The tools I describe in this section can all be used, to different degrees, to create a reasonably accurate view of your network. Although these tools are not the only possible selections (many other packages are available), they represent the market in terms of familiarity, availability, and cost.

### NETBENCH

The NetBench benchmark program, available from Ziff-Davis publications, measures the performance of network file servers communicating with client workstations. Each client workstation issues file requests to the server.

NetBench, currently version 4.01, uses a controller, file server, and multiple client workstations to create a throughput score of your file server and each of the clients. From these scores, you can plot actual performance and estimate the performance of these devices at different levels of activity.

The documentation available with NetBench is complete and steps you through setup and operation. For more details on this product, review the documentation; it contains a wealth of knowledge. NetBench and its documentation is available from Ziff-Davis at **http://www.zdnet.com/adbot/ netbench/netbench.html**.

## SERVERBENCH

ServerBench, another Ziff-Davis benchmark program, measures the performance of networked clients and application servers. The program, currently version 3.0, creates a set of performance scores for both the application server and the clients. ServerBench also uses a controller to capture performance data, an applications server, and one or more clients located anywhere in the network.

While ServerBench is designed to capture client/server network performance, it can also be used to measure network performance by moving previously scored clients to different parts of the network.

For more information on the ServerBench program and a complete set of documentation, contact Ziff-Davis.

## THE TPC BENCHMARK

The TPC benchmarking tool is available from the Transaction Processing Performance Council. Microsoft states in its Technet CD that the TPC-B benchmark is a standard defined by the Transaction Processing Performance Council. The current version of this tool is TPC-D.

TPC is designed to test an SQL server's ability to handle and process network client transactions, including SQL server products from many different vendors.

Because SQL server is an application, using this tool enables you to test the network's ability to support client transactions with an applications server. While the TPC benchmark was designed to test client and SQL server software, it can also be used to test how a client/server-based application performs across an entire network.

To use this tool to test a network, clients should be located at many physical locations on the network. Client workstations should also be placed in different subnets. Each client transacts a configurable number and type of transactions with a server. Testing clients at different locations in the network and then comparing the benchmarking results can create a comparison of network performance across routers, subnets, and network backbones.

The TPC benchmark's results are calculated at the client workstation, not at a separate controller.

For more information and the documentation for this tool, contact Microsoft's Tech Net, either by purchasing the Tech Net CD or by contacting the TPC at their Web address.

# Monitoring Network Performance

Why would you spend time trying to understand a network's capacity? After all, Ethernet runs at 10 Mbps and token ring runs at either 4 Mbps or 16 Mbps, right? Unfortunately, the answer is both yes and no. Yes, these are the theoretical throughputs for Ethernet and token ring. But no, in a real-world network, they don't move data at these speeds. Data on an Ethernet network is moved one packet at a time. If two network computers see a packet collision, both computers stop and wait to resend their packets for a statistically derived time period. The more traffic an Ethernet network sees, the more likely it is that collisions will occur and the more likely the sending computers will spend a lot of time waiting for available bandwidth.

Depending on who you ask, Ethernet networks see their maximum throughput between 65 and 75 percent network utilization. So, while the theoretical throughput may be 10 Mbps, the reality is only 7.5 Mbps. When you consider that bits are fine, but it's bytes (8 bits) that really count, then, as a rule of thumb, you should divide the Mbps by 10—8 bits for bytes and two bits for the packet overhead. Data contained in each packet can range from 64 bytes up to 1500 bytes per packet. A good guestimate is that Ethernet can pass a minimum of 650 and a maximum of 750 kilobytes per second. This number appears to be substantially slower than the much lauded 10 Mbps.

Token ring has a similar problem with theoretical versus actual throughput. Because the fast pipes are not as fast as expected, you must often take steps to tune the network and minimize overhead. Another alternative is to increase LAN speed to 100 Mbps. Even at this speed, Ethernet limitations on maximum versus actual throughputs apply. But, LAN capacity is still increased by a factor of 10.

## *Real-World Network Capacity*

In considering network capacity or expected throughput, you must consider that many networks are not created on a single contiguous wire. They have routers, bridges, hubs, servers, and workstations, each with their own interface to the network, NICs, or some derivation of interface cards. This means that if you must cross a router, you can expect a delay due to the traffic using that router going between different networks.

As you analyze your network's performance, you will begin to see slow-downs and bottlenecks. Bottlenecks aptly describe points in the network that act like the neck of a bottle by constricting packet throughput. Consider that you are a workstation requesting a file from a file server. You request the file and the server goes to its disk to obtain the file. But the disk is busy, so you must wait. You will find that memory also plays a big factor in server response. Too little memory means that NT is page swapping to meet its demands. Page swapping works via the disk, and disks are slow. Therefore, an already slow network can become even less responsive as you bring in disk latency, which is measured in milliseconds.

## NETWORK TRAFFIC

Most network traffic falls into four categories. Not every message type can be included in these categories, but they are typical for many client/server-based networks. As part of the profiling process, you should capture and analyze your network traffic to determine what portion of the network utilization fits these categories:

- *Normal Operating Traffic*— This consists of server message blocks (SMB). SMB consist of user data sent to and received from server-based applications, such as database servers. These messages often arrive in low volume, with the time between transmissions correlated to users typing in data or selecting screen updates. On many networks, SMB LAN utilization runs at 10 percent or below for normal traffic. Of course, as more users access a server, SMB traffic increases proportionally.

- *Burst Mode Traffic*—This is traffic flowing at burst rates between computers. Burst rates are often caused by large data files being moved between client and server or from server to server. As each packet is sent, the sending computer immediately sends the next packet. Other network users can interrupt this traffic by sending a packet to the network, but during this period a larger number of collisions can be expected.

An excellent example of burst mode traffic can be seen when running file backups across a network between a database server and a backup server. Every spare interval is used by the backup server to request more file data. The database server answers these requests as

quickly as possible. This is one of the reasons that file backups occur either late at night or early in the morning. Network utilization for burst mode transmission can reach as high as 75 percent. Token passing rings or buses were designed to minimize burst mode traffic by requiring a token to be obtained before a computer could transmit and limiting the number of packets per token. While token passing does ease the burst mode problem, it automatically builds in delays. These delays are caused by moving the token into many network nodes that are not sending.

- *Broadcast Traffic*—This is traffic broadcast by one or more network computers and directed to other network computers. Browser broadcasts are used to identify newly attached computers and to verify that the network computers currently listed are still attached. Broadcast packets can be stopped by a router and are limited to their originating subnet. NetBIOS uses broadcast traffic for resolving name claim resolutions and undirected datagrams within a subnet. Name claims and resolutions are sent by directed UDP Broadcast packets. They are sent to network computers and identified by name. Session services send TCP messages or data to specific network computers within the local network segment or across a router. UDP is used to send NET LOGON at both the subnet level and across routers to the PDC. Undirected broadcast traffic is sent to everyone and may or may not expect a reply from those computers receiving the packet.

- *SNMP Traffic*— This is used to collect performance data from network workstations. The amount of SNMP traffic has increased lately on many networks, primarily due to the advances in better SNMP software products. SNMP is often short duration traffic containing small byte counts. On a periodic basis, SNMP commands are directed to specific network nodes from one or more central diagnostic servers.

# Network Monitoring Tools

When you consider the seemingly random nature of computer network messages, how do you monitor and capture data? Several excellent tools come standard with NT 4 to assist you in performing that task:

- Performance Monitor (PERFMON.EXE)

- Network Monitor (NETMON.EXE)

- Windows Performance Viewer (WPERF.EXE)

- Quick Slice (QSLICE.EXE)

- Microsoft System Diagnostic (MSD)

These tools can be used to monitor and diagnose many NT activities, but they can be especially helpful when used in NT networking.

## Performance Monitor

The Performance Monitor utility program, described in depth in Chapter 7, is a standard NT measurement tool with the capability of capturing and monitoring performance data for all parts of the system, including the CPU, memory, disk, and network. NT 4 stores the captured data within its Registry to be used by the Performance Monitor program. As I mentioned in Chapter 7, there are four different modes of operation:

- *Chart Mode*— Displays a set of monitored parameters on a standard XY line chart with the values displayed as a function of time. The chart can also be configured to display histograms, which show instantaneous readings with each value being updated every monitoring interval. The line chart can be exported to either a Comma Separated Variable (CSV) or a Tab Separated Variable (TSV) file, which can then be imported into Excel, Access, and many other software applications. The exported chart data is also time stamped. Figure 11.2 shows the network segment

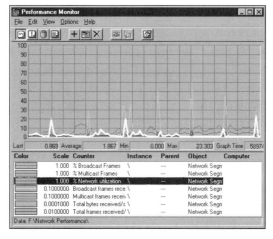

**Figure 11.2**   A Performance Monitor chart showing the entire network segment object and its variables.

objects displayed as a series of line charts. In this figure, the network segment object is showing that the network utilization is running between 1.8 and 23 percent during a three-day period.

- *Alert Mode*—Compares performance data with user-specified upper or lower thresholds. When a monitored value exceeds these thresholds, a screen message is generated. The alert may also begin execution of a program to either perform more detailed analysis or take control actions.

- *Log Mode*—Samples variables during a specified interval and stores these readings as a log file. The log captures all the data associated with a specific object, such as the processor, memory, or network interface. The logging samples are collected during user-defined time periods. To view the captured data, you must use the Performance Monitor Chart, which can specify a view of either all or part of a log file object. A typical use of a log file is to capture data during long periods, play the data back, and export those variables that will be useful. This mode provides an excellent way to correlate error events with network traffic.

- *Report Mode*—Presents captured data in a report format. The report contains selected information chosen by the user and updated every sampling time period. This report is useful for comparing readings, such as network utilization versus the IP, TCP, and UDP components making up the network traffic.

While Performance Monitor is one of the most useful tools in the NT suite of diagnostic tools, it can only monitor the information specified by the user. If the user does not understand Performance Monitor's variables, he cannot create a chart, log, alert, or report that will allow him to capture the desired results. A list of these variables is presented later in this chapter with the network Registry entries.

## Network Monitor

The Network Monitor, introduced in Chapter 7, can be used to monitor network traffic in realtime (while it is actually happening). Network Monitor is useful for troubleshooting network problems and for monitoring the network operation of specific components.

The Network Monitor is a diagnostic tool used to monitor network operation, view the details of network packets, and remotely capture data packets anywhere in the network. You may also use the Network Monitor to collect operating statistics from a network subnet or the overall LAN. It is especially useful in capturing and analyzing potential network bottlenecks.

When tuning a network, you will find that many different connections between computers are continuously being made and dropped. The message traffic may consist of a combination of TCP/IP, IPX/SPX, NetBEUI packets, and other types of network formats. To understand and view network activity, you must have a tool to cut through the bedlam and isolate a desired subset of that traffic. Network Monitor's features include the ability to capture frames from the network, filter the captured frames, and analyze the captured frames. Figure 11.3 shows Network Monitor running in capture mode. This capture mode provides you with a quick look at the number, type, and frequency of the data packets being captured.

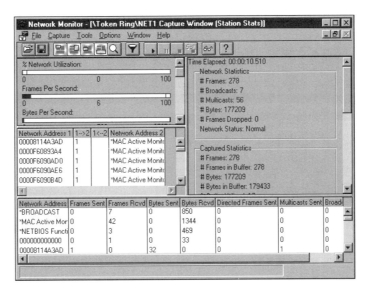

**Figure 11.3**   The Network Monitor, running in capture mode, displays four tiled screens, each with a separate view of the captured network data.

Network Monitor monitors the network data stream. This consists of all of the information transferred over a network at any given time, as shown in Figure 11.4. Prior to transmission, this information is divided by the networking software into smaller segments, called frames or packets. Each frame contains:

- The source address of the computer that sent the message (this is a unique hexadecimal number that identifies the computer on the network)

- The destination address of the computer that received the frame

- Headers from each protocol used to send the frame

- The data or a portion of the information being sent

Depending on protocol and routing, every computer on the network can see all network activity. Only packets being sent to a particular address are passed by the NIC. Network Monitor requires you to use only NICs that are capable of running in promiscuous mode. Promiscuous mode NICs monitor and pass all network traffic. Network Monitor captures, filters, and stores copies of all the frames it captures in a buffer.

| Frame | Time | Src MAC Addr | Dst MAC Addr | Protocol | Description |
|---|---|---|---|---|---|
| 7 | 0.266 | 0000F6093B22 | CCNTMONITOR | NCP | Reply:     Packet Burst Connectic |
| 8 | 0.267 | CCNTMONITOR | 0000F6093B22 | NCP | Request: Negotiate LIP Buffer |
| 9 | 0.267 | 0000F6093B22 | CCNTMONITOR | NCP | Reply:     Negotiate LIP Buffer |
| 10 | 0.267 | CCNTMONITOR | 0000F6093B22 | IPX | NCP Packet - 21000070.0001FA16C |
| 11 | 0.920 | CCNTMONITOR | 0000F6093B22 | IPX | NCP Packet - 21000070.0001FA16C |
| 12 | 0.922 | 0000F6093B22 | CCNTMONITOR | IPX | NCP Packet - 210002F1.00000000C |
| 13 | 0.922 | CCNTMONITOR | 0000F6093B22 | IPX | NCP Packet - 21000070.0001FA16C |
| 14 | 0.927 | 0000F6093B22 | CCNTMONITOR | IPX | NCP Packet - 210002F1.00000000C |
| 15 | 0.931 | CCNTMONITOR | 0000F6093B22 | IPX | NCP Packet - 21000070.0001FA16C |
| 16 | 0.931 | 0000F6093B22 | CCNTMONITOR | IPX | NCP Packet - 210002F1.00000000C |
| 17 | 0.937 | CCNTMONITOR | 0000F6093B22 | IPX | NCP Packet - 21000070.0001FA16C |
| 18 | 0.937 | 0000F6093B22 | CCNTMONITOR | IPX | NCP Packet - 210002F1.00000000C |
| 19 | 0.937 | CCNTMONITOR | 0000F6093B22 | IPX | NCP Packet - 21000070.0001FA16C |
| 20 | 0.949 | 0000F6093B22 | CCNTMONITOR | IPX | NCP Packet - 210002F1.00000000C |
| 21 | 0.949 | CCNTMONITOR | 0000F6093B22 | IPX | NCP Packet - 21000070.0001FA16C |
| 22 | 0.949 | 0000F6093B22 | CCNTMONITOR | IPX | NCP Packet - 210002F1.00000000C |
| 23 | 0.960 | CCNTMONITOR | 0000F6093B22 | IPX | NCP Packet - 21000070.0001FA16C |
| 24 | 1.085 | 10005A4D1338 | 800143000000 | BPDU | Root BPDU: Priority 0x8000, Por |
| 25 | 1.366 | 0000F6093B22 | Sytek BD9816 | SPX | ConCtrl = 0x80, DtaStrm = 0x00, |
| 26 | 1.573 | CCNTMONITOR | 0000F6093B22 | IPX | NCP Packet - 21000070.0001FA16C |
| 27 | 1.588 | 0000F6093B22 | CCNTMONITOR | IPX | NCP Packet - 210002F1.00000000C |
| 28 | 1.588 | CCNTMONITOR | 0000F6093B22 | IPX | NCP Packet - 21000070.0001FA16C |

NetWare Core Protocol (NCP) packet          F#: 9/278          Off: 47 (x2F)          L: 13 (xD)

**Figure 11.4**   The Network Monitor capture buffer display shows a listing of the frames that have been previously captured.

**TIP** Promiscuous mode NICs monitor and manage more network traffic. While this type of NIC is useful to Network Monitor, they can encounter performance problems during periods of high traffic. It pays to acquire a more advanced promiscuous mode, 32-bit NIC to offset the additional requirements.

Although the amount of information Network Monitor can capture is limited only by the amount of memory available on your computer, you will usually need to capture only a small subset of the frames traveling on the network. To single out a subset of frames, you can design a capture filter which functions in the same manner as a database query. You can filter on the basis of source and destination addresses, protocols, and protocol properties, or by specifying a data pattern.

Network Monitor has two filters that can be changed to capture and display network data: the capture data filter and the display data filter.

## Capture Data Filter

If you want to capture only specific events in your network, you can specify a capture data filter. While the capture data filter is limited to specific addresses and a subset of network events, it can reliably capture network traffic on even the busiest networks.

You may also specify a capture trigger that runs and executes a specified action, such as opening a particular executable application whenever it detects a predefined set of conditions. For example, Network Monitor may be configured to identify traffic being transmitted to a server by a specific workstation or workstations. If the specified traffic is observed, it can turn on Performance Monitor to begin collecting performance data from the designated server.

## Display Data Filter

The options available to the capture data filter are somewhat limited due to the size of memory, resources, and the realtime requirement to monitor every packet. The display data filter allows you many more selections because displaying data is not obligated to maintain realtime performance. You can specify and filter only computers that meet the filter's selection criteria. For example, you could filter all broadcast traffic contained within the capture data filter and identify which computer is sending the broadcast messages. In Figure 11.5, you can see the displayed data frames, protocol elements, and contents of the frame.

# Quick Look Tools

Perfmon and Netmon are both excellent tools to use to conduct a detailed analysis of network operations. Unfortunately, you may find that you do not have sufficient time to conduct as thorough an analysis as you would like. Your users are complaining about slow performance and overall network slowdown. You have only a short period of time to identify and correct a problem. In this situation, you would be better off using some quick look tools. A quick look tool is comparable to the differences between an analog and digital watch. A digital watch tells you the precise time in hours, minutes, and seconds. An analog watch is useful at a glance (or quick look) to tell the relative time. Quick look tools perform the same function. You use them to quickly scan computer workloads.

The NT 4 Resource Kit has several excellent tools to aid you during these time-critical periods. Let's take a closer look at several of the quick look tools I find useful.

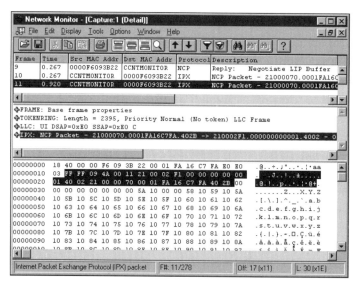

**Figure 11.5**   The Network Monitor capture buffer contains three subwindows that can show the details of each frame.

# *Wperf*

When I first looked at Wperf, I thought it was a poor cousin to Performance Monitor. But, the more I used the utility, the more I came to appreciate its simplicity. Wperf, which is located in the \%root%\i386\perftool\ perftool\meastool\ directory of the Resource Kit, is a collection of small desktop windows, each showing a short history of one of NT 4's many variables. Figure 11.6 shows a typical desktop display.

Wperf tracks the following network performance variables:

- Total processor utilization

- Memory

- Pool memory

- Non-pool memory

- Number of active processes

- Number of threads being executed

I'll provide more detail on these variables later in the chapter. A variable's history is shown in a line chart that extends for about the past 10 minutes.

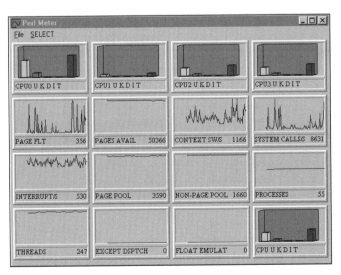

**Figure 11.6**    The Wperf display screen is a set of small windows, each showing the status of a particular NT 4 variable.

The selection of variables shown in these windows is left to the user, who may select from a list of approximately 15 choices, as shown in Figure 11.7.

In addition to the selected variables, Wperf shows the current CPU utilization percentage. The CPU utilization window has several options:

- You can display each CPU and the total processor load of a Symmetric MultiProcessor array (SMP). These are used in many network servers to increase performance; however, Wperf is not restricted to SMP servers. You may also use the utility on your single CPU workstation.

- Both the individual CPU utilization window and the total CPU utilization window can be displayed as either a bar chart or a line chart. The bar chart shows instantaneous (approximately every 10 seconds) CPU utilization. The line chart shows a brief trend history of CPU utilization values over approximately 10 minutes.

Wperf is very useful when left on a desktop to be used as an indicator of processor load. You can display the same variables with Performance Monitor, but you have to switch back and forth between the legend that tells you what line or bar chart is assigned to which variable. Wperf shows the name of each variable under every small window.

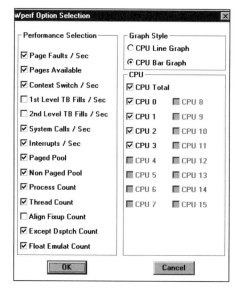

**Figure 11.7**   The Wperf Option Selection lists the types of variables that can be displayed in the utility.

It's safe to say that Wperf will not replace Performance Monitor as an analysis tool. But, for a quick look at a server's or workstation's current operating capacity, Wperf is an excellent choice.

## Qslice

The Qslice utility, which is located in the \% root%\i386\compdiag\ directory of the Resource Kit, displays NT's currently executing processes as a graphical task list.

Qslice is a handy tool to display which processes are being executed by NT 4. As each service, application program, or kernel mode task executes, it creates a process that executes under the NT 4 operating system. When you start a program, Qslice will display the new process. The new process begins sharing a percentage of the NT 4 resources. Each process continues executing until it completes or terminates, either by a user or NT 4. The Qslice display, shown in Figure 11.8, illustrates a typical NT 4 server operating with minimal load. The long System Process bar is an indicator of the idle time.

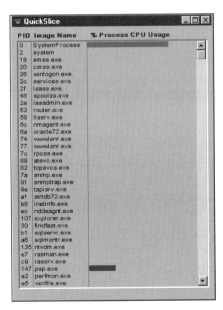

**Figure 11.8** The Qslice main screen displays each of the processes and the relative level of resources being consumed.

As a process executes, it must spawn one or more threads. A thread is a chain of executable software that is owned exclusively by a process. The thread contains executable software, a program counter, two stacks (user-mode and kernel-mode stacks), and its own set of NT register values. A process's threads all have access to its object handles, address space, and any other resources belonging to the process.

Qslice displays each process in a vertical list with a bar chart graph of its activity. As a process creates threads, a bar chart to the right of the process name extends or recedes, showing the percentage of CPU resources being used by the process's threads. The bar is blue for user activity; the red bar is for kernel activity.

By double clicking on one of the processes, a listing of the process's spawned threads will appear in the same name-bar chart format, as shown in Figure 11.9. In the thread, a bar chart shows the activity of each thread, using the red/blue colors to show kernel and user activity, respectively.

What does Qslice do to help you tune a network? Well, networks are a group of computers, some running NT 4 Server, others running NT 4 Workstation. To tune a network, you must have some knowledge of what workload is being executed on each of the networked computers. If a computer's resources are being consumed by its workload, its network response will be slowed. Network tasks must compete for the same limited resources as the workload currently being executed by each computer.

The Qslice utility, combined with Wperf, allows you to quickly spot a computer with a heavy workload. Wperf graphically indicates computer activ-

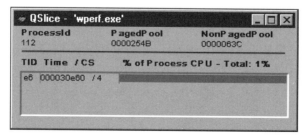

**Figure 11.9**  Double clicking a process displays a listing of the associated threads, along with a bar graph display of thread activity.

ity, and Qslice identifies which processes are causing that activity. If a computer is responding too slowly to network traffic, you may be able to shut down some of its noncritical processes to increase performance. You may also find that the computer's workload is required and that the computer is under-powered for its assigned tasks. You should consider any computer that continuously uses 50 percent or more of its processing resources to complete tasks as a candidate for replacement by a more powerful machine. I am not referring to occasional intense workloads, but to computers that continuously use greater than half of their processing capability.

Qslice also displays the processes associated with networking. These processes provide a quick view and estimate of what percentage of NT's resources are being consumed by network services.

## Microsoft System Diagnostic

The Microsoft System Diagnostic (MSD) was initially released in Windows 3.1 for the purpose of quickly showing a computer's configuration. With each release of MSD, the utility's capability has increased. The MSD released with NT 4 has made some significant improvements in the information it presents on NT's network settings and offers a quick look at the current network statistics. MSD is located in the \%system root%\system32 directory of the Resource Kit.

Figure 11.10 shows MSD's Network tab with the Settings button selected. Each item displays its current Registry setting. This information can be a very valuable aid to quickly reviewing how each workstation or server is configured. Clicking on the Statistics button will display a set of network statistics that includes the latest byte count for the transmitted and received bytes, frames, and other network parameters.

Clicking on the Print button prints a report showing a complete listing of these statistics. A typical report is shown in Figure 11.11.

To see information specific to the general network setup, including machine name and network type, click on the General button. If you want to review the current transport protocol settings, including the IP, mask, and gateway addresses, click on the Transport button.

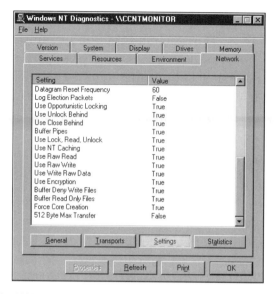

**Figure 11.10**    The MSD Network menu shows a networked computer's current network Registry settings.

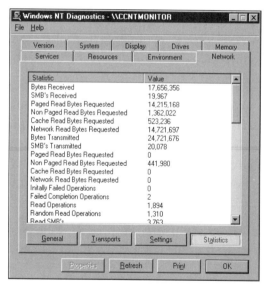

**Figure 11.11**    NT 4's latest network statistics are displayed when you click on the Statistics button.

While this information seems very basic, a quick look utility with this level of information did not exist on NT 3.51 or earlier. If you needed to review the settings on those systems, you had to use the Regedit32 or the Network configuration menu in the control panel. I use this utility to print reports from different workstations and servers to include in my settings log.

# Analyzing a Network Problem

Here is an example of an all too typical network problem: Your network users are complaining about how slow the network is when they request data from a server. At one time, user requests would be completed within seconds. Now, they estimate that it takes from 10 seconds to a minute to obtain the same results. Your mission is (and you must accept it) how do you, as the network administrator, determine the cause of this slowdown. And after determining the cause, what will you do to resolve it?

In such a situation, a performance curve or benchmark is useful when you are using empirical techniques, for example, trial and error. If you keep LAN records, you may be able to detect changes in network operation. The problem may lie in recent additions, changes to the network, or a problem that has been developing over a period of time.

## *Isolating a Network Problem*

The next alternative is to isolate the cause of the slowdown. Ask yourself the following questions:

- Are only a small number of the users reporting slowdown?

- Can you isolate the slowdown to a specific subnet?

- Has the overall network traffic on any subnet increased substantially during the period of this slowdown?

- Is the slowdown only occurring when users are accessing one server or a specific type of server, such as email?

- What are the percentages of network utilization found at each of the subnets? Is the utilization the same at the subnets experiencing this problem?

- Has the number of errors reported by Performance Monitor, or any other types of monitoring tools, increased?

Use Network Monitor to view the communications between one of the computers reporting the problem and the server. You may also, if you have one at your disposal, use a network sniffer to capture network traffic and analyze the results. A network sniffer usually consists of a microcomputer-based terminal running software dedicated to watching and capturing network traffic. While a sniffer performs many of the same functions as the Microsoft Network Monitor, it has the ability to capture more traffic and to display the captured data with more detail. I might add that a sniffer is a substantial investment, but one you should consider as a wise choice when troubleshooting a medium to large network (greater than 200 nodes).

Conduct a simple test of throughput during network off-hours. Send a standard test file across the network, passing through each subnet, and record the time it takes to complete using Performance Monitor. If you regularly perform this test and maintain records, you can compare each result with those recorded earlier.

Using the network's previous performance results, input the number of network workstations and computers, type of network services being required at each network computer, and an observed profile of network traffic from Performance Monitor. The results may point to a segment of the network that is overutilized.

## Network Failures, Changes, or Workload?

Many network problems can be immediately attributed to a bad cable, router, hub, or problematic software. This particular problem may be difficult to solve unless you can readily isolate it to specific recent network changes. If you combine a network performance tool with your normal monitoring tools, the combination enables you to compare real and theoretical results.

Typical network traffic problems can often be attributed to failed components or a component that is being overutilized. Answering the previous set of questions can often help you to quickly located a failed component. However, a problem caused by overutilization of components may require that you complete a network analysis. For this discussion, we'll assume that our slowdown is caused by an overused component. After speaking with the end users and performing some simple diagnostics, we have made the following determinations:

- All users who are using a particular server are experiencing the same problem, regardless of their location on the network.

- The server in question resides on a subnet that is dedicated to database servers. From our first look, it appears that all the database servers on that subnet are performing well, with network utilization below 10 percent.

- The subnet network traffic to the servers has increased 25 percent in the past few weeks.

- Slowdowns appear to be occurring when connecting to any of the servers in that subnet.

- Network utilization of the server subnet is seldom above 10 percent, not a high percentage.

- Error counts for the server subnet have not increased significantly and remain relatively constant during both low and heavy periods of network traffic.

- Using Network Monitor, we find that the servers are receiving requests from all of the other user subnets. However, there are still occasional periods of time when no network requests are made to the server.

- Sending a test file to the subnet results in an increased transmit time of 20 percent over tests conducted previously.

- Our network performance curves show that the server subnet should be capable of sustaining a traffic increase of between 25 to 40 percent. A performance curve of the subnet itself shows that traffic is well within the normally planned range. We try the large file transfer between servers on the same questionable subnet. This test results in transmission times correlating with previously made test results. The router manufacturer's specification indicates that the server subnet's router is capable of handling network traffic increases of 50 percent over the current workload without substantial packet rejection or slowdown.

## *Drawing Conclusions*

From this information, we are able to conclude that the server subnet is not experiencing delays, but users accessing that subnet are. This leads us to believe that the router that separates the subnet may be the bottleneck. However, the performance curves say it can handle a substantially increased traffic flow. So, we begin monitoring the server subnet's router and find that it randomly rejects packets sent from the server users. The application server in question does not see 30 percent of the packets being sent. We compare this information against the performance curves by changing the router curves in question. The comparison provides results that show user wait time increasing by a range of 35 to 45 percent. This correlates to our users' complaints. So, our analysis shows that the server subnet router is not performing its task reliably because it doesn't comply with our predicted performance. We replace the router, and the network slowdown disappears.

While there may be other, more efficient ways to find the bad router, this example points out the combination of empirical and analytic tools. It also contains three reasons to create and use a set of network performance results:

- Creating a network benchmark before we created the network allows us to have a documented expectation of the performance of each component and subnet.

- If we can logically isolate the problem to a limited segment, we can readily show that predicted versus observed performance is different.

- We have the ability to change a component's operating characteristics without disrupting any further network operations. We changed the curves to include the router's observed performance and found that it indeed could be a candidate for causing the delays.

# Possible Network Bottlenecks

Your network's running too slow. Your networked users are complaining that they have to wait too long to get network data. What do you do?

A quick answer is to increase the speed of the network, say from 10 MHz to 100 MHz. That should fix the problem, right? If you make this change without analyzing the network, then you have fixed a symptom but probably haven't fixed the real problem. This isn't to say that network speed isn't a prime tuning parameter, it is. But, many times there is a more basic problem that affects network operations. If we only speed up the network, the problem may resurface later.

Network performance is a sum of many factors. Figure 11.12 depicts a basic network which contains at least two computers: a client workstation and a network server.

This basic network can contain many potential sources of network bottlenecks, shown in the rectangular boxes. As I've mentioned previously, a network bottleneck prevents a network, to some degree, from reaching its optimum performance. However, every bottleneck can also be considered an opportunity to improve performance through either tuning, adjustment, or replacement. So, instead of calling them bottlenecks, I'm going to relabel the bottlenecks as tuning factors.

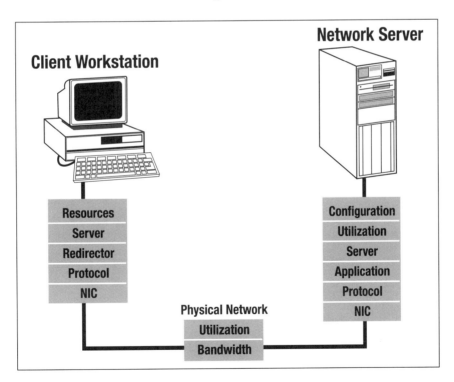

**Figure 11.12**    A simplified overview of the various parameters that affect NT 4's network performance.

## Network Problems

In any network, problems can go undetected for a long time. These problems may be created by either a specific change to the network, increased workload, poor design, improper configuration, or all of the above. Some problems you may encounter are:

- *One or More Overloaded Servers*—Overloading is simply asking a server to provide more services than it has the physical resources to complete.

- *Network Overloading*—Any network can only support a limited amount of data due to its design, extent, and the number of attached computers. When the maximum loading limit is exceeded, everyone sees a slowdown in the network operation.

- *Data Integrity*—One or more network components is misbehaving and causing the network to either drop, lose, or corrupt data.

Of course, these general problems don't include every possible situation you may encounter, but they are often the root cause of most network slowdowns.

## Normal Operation

What is normal for your workstations? This depends on:

- Workstation configuration

- Application software

- The network you are attached to

- The operating system

- Network utilization

- The number and types of errors that the network is experiencing

For all intents and purposes, there are no global settings. Microsoft and, most likely, your workstation's manufacturer have created a version of the NT workstation operating system that is configured to some degree to meet your requirements. Do these configurations create an optimum environment for all applications and users? No. It is virtually impossible to fine-tune a standard operating system to everyone's needs with one set of parameters. However, they've given you a starting point to work from. You have certain tuning options that, when changed, can make your workstation and server run more efficiently. These same settings, if incorrectly changed, may also result in less efficiency and troubled operation.

I recommend the following steps to increase performance:

1. Create a log that contains your current hardware configuration, including any optional boards that the computer contains, and a detailed list of the standard components.

2. Export the NT Registry to a text file and keep a copy with the hardware components in the log.

3. Copy the NT Registry using the Regback utility from the NT Resource Kit. Save this backup with the log.

4. Run Performance Monitor using the logging view for at least a week during a period of normal operations to capture a baseline view of your computer's normal operation. We'll go into which parameters you should log later in this chapter.

5. Measure and record in your log the network responses at several different client workstations. You should try to make these measurements as accurate as possible to the level of seconds. Make these measurements at different times of the day and record the time of day in your log.

 **Don't keep your** log on a computer that will be involved in the network testing. Mistakes happen and your log, Registry backup, and settings may be destroyed. Another approach is to make several copies and keep at least one of them on a floppy disk.

6. Log all changes to NT's operations as they are made. Be sure to include which parameters were changed and both their initial and changed settings.

7.  Decide what tests will be performed on the workstations, servers, and network. Create a test plan and stick to it, logging each result. An excellent way to stress the network and log its performance is to run Performance Monitor from an idle workstation. Log the network segment objects at a one-second interval. Then, move a large (300 MB or larger) file across the network between two other workstations or between a workstation and server. When the move is complete, stop the log. This approach decreases network utilization to a limited degree. The Performance Monitor log now contains the percentage of network utilization and the time it took to move that file on your network. Perform this test at different times of the day. The end result is a network stress test that is one view of network performance.

8.  Configure Performance Monitor to continually run in chart mode, at a frequency of 900 seconds (every 15 minutes) per measurement. This frequency shows an entire 24-hour period in a single screen. Configure the utility to capture the entire set of network segment objects. These objects measure the amount of broadcast, multibroadcast, frames, bytes, and network utilization. This view of your network can tell you at what type, level, and time that network traffic occurs. After each day, export the chart to a CSV file and export it to a spreadsheet application. The CSV file contains the detailed readings, along with a valuable time and date stamp. You may wonder why you should use a frequency of 15 minutes. The reason is that 15 minutes is the longest practical time period. Only after you understand your network's operation should you reduce the capture frequency to five or one minute intervals. The more frequent the interval, the more data there is to both store and review. If you start at the 15 minute frequency time, and work down, your data and the objects monitored can become more specific.

The eight-step plan to test your network's performance is one approach to record your findings, record changes, and prevent repeated steps. The result of this approach is a compiled history that can be sent to outside consultants or other engineers facing the same problems. A recorded history is also helpful in case you need to reload NT because you'll have a record of the changes.

Considering different approaches to a network problem often results in more work, but can yield substantial benefits. Because technology is moving quickly, it is wise to review your network specifications with the goal of improving performance or reducing errors.

For example, you may configure your NIC to utilize a "full duplex" mode, if your NIC will support this mode of operation. Full duplex separates the send and receive functions, increasing the effective bandwidth and allowing your NIC to send and receive data simultaneously. If your NIC supports this feature, then you must also check to see that your router also supports this feature. Full duplexing doesn't double network bandwidth, but it can increase it substantially, depending on the network traffic. This is a relatively new technology for LAN cards that you will be seeing more of in the future.

## The Client Workstation

In most networks, there are many client workstations. Each client may use the network's resources very differently. Clients can share files with a server or with other workstations. Many can access the Internet, an intranet, send and receive mail, and run server-based applications. How the client goes about these activities is an important consideration.

A key factor that distinguishes the client from a network server is utilization. In most cases, each client only supports a single user. While other NT workstations can share resources on workstations, sharing is usually limited. If your workstation is supporting many users, it becomes a server and local activity slows down due to overutilized resources.

Regardless of how the client uses a network, the speed at which the network responds depends on its available resources.

### RESOURCES

The client workstation has a limited set of resources. These resources include:

- The generation and type of CPU being used, such as 386, 486, Alpha, MIPS, etc.

- CPU speed

- The amount of RAM configured

- The amount of free hard drive capacity

- The speed of the workstation's internal bus

- The NOS (in our review, we limit this to only the NT 4 workstation)

- The application software running on the workstation

- The number and type of concurrent user activities

These items constitute the principle resources of a client workstation. There are other factors to consider, such as the computer manufacturer. But for our discussion, all manufacturers are equal.

Your workstation's network performance depends a great deal on the answer to these two basic questions:

- What resources in the previous list does your workstation currently have?

- What amount of these resources are available to support network operations?

Earlier in the chapter, I introduced Performance Monitor. In the Quick Look tools, I introduced Wperf and Qslice, which are both useful in determining the answer to question two. If your resources are being overtaxed, your network performance will be slowed. If you are running applications software that consumes CPU cycles and memory, there are few options for tuning. You must quit the application, increase the speed of your CPU, or install more RAM. If you don't fully understand what software is absorbing these resources, then use the three utilities to gain a better understanding of the internal workings of your computer. Nobody said tuning was easy.

To quickly access resource utilization, start Wperf and watch the CPU utilization bar chart. There are several bars associated with each CPU:

- A bar showing the level of CPU resources used by user processes. The longer the bar, the more resources are currently being used by user applications.

- A bar showing the level of CPU resources used by the NT kernel. The bar length is proportional to the amount of CPU cycles being used by the NT kernel processes.

- A bar showing the level of interrupts occurring. The bar length is proportional to the number of interrupts being received by the CPU.

- A bar showing the level of Delayed Process Calls (DPC) occurring. The bar shows a relative level of DPCs, indicating that pending CPU tasks are queuing, possibly due to overutilization of internal resources.

- A bar showing the sum total of both the CPU resources being used by the kernel and user applications.

**TIP** Write down what levels of activities you normally see and their associated values. Wperf is most useful when these levels change dramatically. If you know what their normal levels are, it is easier to spot over-expenditure of resources.

While there are many variables to select from, the following five indicator line charts provide a wealth of troubleshooting information:

- *Page Faults*—This shows a relative level of memory paging caused by NT swapping out memory to disk. If the line is climbing, the workstation's performance is decreasing due to disk latency or the time it takes to read and write memory pages on the disk.

- *Available Memory*— This is a line chart showing a historic level and actual amount of the workstation's currently available memory. Of the two indicators, the variable's history is the most important. A steadily dropping value will result in more page faults and, eventually, an NT diagnostic screen that informs you that the workstation is running low on virtual memory. If the cause of the increased memory use continues, NT will either dedicate its remaining resources to servicing that application or shut down the system.

- *Processes*—This is a line chart showing a level and the actual number of software processes that NT is currently running. Processes, and their associated threads, commit NT resources as they execute. An increase in the number of processes will result in a decrease in computer resources.

- *Interrupts*—This is both a historical line chart and a current quantity of the interrupts being generated in the workstation. While some of these will be network interrupts, some will result from application and kernel usage. If you see an increase in the CPU's Interrupts bar chart, view the Interrupts line chart to review its short-term history. A substantial increase (30 percent or more) in the number of interrupts usually indicates major resource utilization.

- *Pool Paged Bytes*—These are the number of bytes in the Paged Pool memory. The Paged Pool memory is acquired by the operating system components as required. Paged Pool memory pages can be paged to the hard disk page file when not used for long periods of time. A decrease in this memory pool, coupled with increased kernel activity, usually indicates that NT is running low on resources.

- *Pool Non-paged Bytes*—These indicate the number of bytes in the Non-paged Pool. The Non-paged Pool is an NT memory area where space is allocated to kernel and operating system components as they are required. Non-paged Pool memory pages are not available to user processes, and they can't be paged out to the hard disk. The Non-paged Pool memory resides only in the main memory, when allocated. A decrease in this memory pool, along with a decrease in the Paged Pool and increased kernel activity, indicates that NT is in danger of being resource starved.

I can hear you asking, "If these indicators show that my resources are being reduced, what do I do next?" The best answer is usually to either add more memory or reduce the number of processes running on the computer.

## SERVER

Because we are tuning an NT 4 network, any workstation can be a server to any other workstation to share files, applications, and local printing. In the past, Microsoft imposed a limitation on the NT workstation for the number of users who could simultaneously connect to a single workstation. In NT 4, this limitation has been removed and the Server service's operation is now more crucial than ever. Remember from previous chapters, the workstation's server provides outside users with an access to your hard drives and printers. The more connections, the more resources this service takes. Your workstation may appear to be idle, but, if the disk lights are flashing, you may be sharing data with other users. If Wperf is showing that the CPU is engaged in a substantial level of activity, and Qslice shows that there is a substantial level of kernel activity, you are probably serving one or more network users who are attached to your shared drives.

User share connections can often impose a severe workload on your workstation. To identify the number of user connections and the level of activity, configure Performance Monitor to monitor both the server objects and system objects.

To limit the effects on your workstation, move the shared item to a network server. The network is configured to better handle this type of activity. If this is impossible, use NT's File Manager to change your shared drive settings to limit the number of users who can concurrently share your resources.

## REDIRECTOR

The Redirector is your workstation's main gateway to the network. When your application requests a file or directory not contained physically in your computer, the NT Redirector is called upon to find the requested resource. While many of these network references are already specified, such as the attached shared drive, other resources may require the Redirector to find them at the expense of response time.

While the Redirector primarily affects a single workstation, it can slow down network performance. If the Redirector does its job and sends the proper packets to the correct network computers, why consider it a potential bottleneck? The reason is that it can queue up commands (resulting in long delays) while waiting to attach to a network computer or waiting for even a simple directory to appear. The Redirector can be monitored using Performance Monitor to view the Redirector's current commands. If the number of current commands is substantially increasing, the cause can be an internal delay or a network slowdown. To decide which situation is causing the delays, view the same current commands parameter on several workstations. If they are all exhibiting the same increases, the results point to an overall network slowdown. If only one workstation is queuing the Redirector's commands, then consider further testing of that workstation.

## PROTOCOL

The type of network protocol you configure on your workstation will determine its network response and what variables you should monitor. Each configured protocol has a corresponding object associated with it. Each object, in turn, has several variables that can be monitored.

## NIC

The choice of Network Interface Card contributes greatly to how well, or how poorly, your workstation uses the network. Eight-bit NIC cards are still installed in many networks. State of the art 32-bit NICs are supported by an onboard microprocessor. Verify by checking your NIC's specifications, or with its manufacturer, that your workstations all are configured with at least 16-bit NICs.

Performance Monitor is limited on the number of objects that it can monitor. Several views of your NIC's performance are reported through the network segment and network interface objects. A few manufacturers, such as Compaq, supply add-on objects that work with Performance Monitor to directly monitor NIC operations.

# The Physical Network

Whether you use wire or fiber, your physical network has a finite limitation on the amount of workload it can adequately support. Earlier, I described the limitations of Ethernet. These limitations at the physical network level are a direct result of the network speed (bandwidth) and the current level of utilization the network is supporting.

## Bandwidth

The bandwidth is another name for the speed that the network runs to move traffic from one point to another. For instance, Ethernet has either a 10 Mbps or a 100 Mbps bandwidth. Per our previous discussion, you know that a real-world bandwidth for Ethernet is something less than 75 percent of that theoretical number.

If you want an immediate jump in performance, increase the speed of the network. However, as I stated earlier, this may only mask inefficient configuration, performance, or network failures. The higher the speed, the higher the cost—you must change a number of components to install a higher performance network. In most cases, every NIC must be replaced. Routers, bridges, and servers may need to be upgraded to meet the more demanding speed requirements. If your network wasn't installed using the appropriate specifications, you may have to replace much of your physical wiring plant, as well.

## Utilization

Network utilization is a nondimensional term that includes all of the traffic flowing through the network at any given time. Packets from TCP/IP, NetBEUI, IPX/SPX, broadcast, multibroadcast, ICMP, and SNMP traffic all contribute to this number. Generally, the higher the utilization, the longer it takes to move your data to its final destination.

To monitor this value and the level of many of its contributors, use Performance Monitor to capture the network segment objects. These include the majority of the contributing sources of network traffic and a value for the current network utilization.

Network Monitor is another very useful tool in understanding the cause of a highly utilized network. With this utility, you can capture, identify, and decipher the majority of the traffic on your network. Network Monitor identifies the type of traffic and allows you to decode that traffic to ascertain its importance and purpose.

## The Network Server

Network servers come in all sizes, shapes, and varieties. The NT 4 server is designed to run on many of the server platforms that are installed today. In the first chapter, we noted the differences between NT 4 Server and NT 4 Workstation. Workstation is designed to be used by one user. NT 4 Server is designed to support many users. These differences are found in the way the two flavors of NT perform tasks and how they support attached users.

Some users may use the NT4 server to store, retrieve, and share files. Others may use the server to print documents. The most resource-taxing user runs applications that connect to, or utilize, server-based applications. For example, the Microsoft Office Suite is configured to be shared over a network, and MS SQL Server provides a centralized database for many clients. While these examples are quite different, they share one common parameter: They can substantially stress the NT 4 server.

Storing, retrieving, and sharing files loads a server sporadically. Each time a client wants to store a file, it sends a data stream to a server. The server accepts or rejects the client's request based on the presence of the requested file or the client's security ID.

Printing client documents requires NT server to receive and spool user print jobs, then connect the spooled print jobs with its destination printer.

## CONFIGURATION

Windows NT 4 Server was designed to act in the role of either a network file, print, or applications server. Server performance is different than the workstation in several respects, but server performance affects any user who attaches to it. The server can be changed to provide default priority to either foreground or background tasks. It can also be configured to balance these tasks, providing similar performance for both. Network activity is primarily considered a background task.

## UTILIZATION

The utilization of a server refers to the number, type, and size of the transaction processes that are running on the server's platform. Performance is a direct function of utilization, as the more the computer is tasked to perform, the less time available for each task, and the fewer resources available for new tasks.

## APPLICATION

Applications play a key role in server network performance, as they are the processes running on the server that create a level of utilization. The more efficient the application, the more clients it can support, resulting in less server and network loading.

# Conclusion

In this chapter, I presented network performance as being difficult, but not impossible, to monitor and change. NT 4 is a network operating sys-

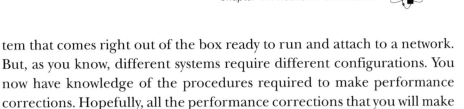

tem that comes right out of the box ready to run and attach to a network. But, as you know, different systems require different configurations. You now have knowledge of the procedures required to make performance corrections. Hopefully, all the performance corrections that you will make will help optimize NT's operation. Unfortunately, my experience has shown that changing a parameter to improve operation often results in a latent problem waiting to be discovered. However, if you follow the procedures for changing Registry and other NT settings, you can readily recover the original settings and repair the damage.

Networks are often difficult to understand and manage, especially when you consider the amount of seemingly random data and protocols. Using the tools I've described can make this task considerably easier. The Perfmon network objects can be found in Appendix B.

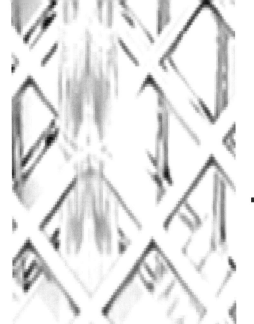

# 12

# The Last Word

## A Recap: Behind the Chapters

When my publisher and I sat down at the round table to discuss the title of this book, we knew we wanted something to convey what the material I was writing was all about—every day issues of networking. What we came up with did just that—*Real-World Networking with NT 4*. I have tried throughout this book to describe the network technologies that form the basis of NT 4 networking.

As a quick overview, let's review the book's contents and describe the purpose of each chapter. Remember, I started with the premise that you, the reader, may or may not understand either NT or its role in networking. That is why, in many chapters, I've included seemingly basic information. This information is beneficial in two ways. First, it familiarizes those of you with little NT or network experience with the basic concepts. Second, while many texts are quick to use networking jargon, few make any effort to provide detailed definitions, and you need to understand the terminology to understand the concepts.

Let me point out one more thing to you. You may have noticed that I avoided dealing with many of the non-networking features of NT. I wasn't being lazy, but I did do it on purpose. I wanted to concentrate on actual networking and avoid writing reams of pages trying to describe a very complicated operating system in general terms. To be honest with you, I wrote the book that I would like to read if I were new to NT or trying to increase my NT networking knowledge.

Throughout this book, I have described NT 4 networking by combining technology with philosophy. I tried to present the NT 4 architectural overview from the perspective that the NT network operating system is not static, but continues to grow and incorporate new technology on every release.

In order to grow and gain acceptance in the computer industry, NT 4 must support the latest in state-of-the-art networking requirements and adapt to changing user needs. NT continues to broaden its appeal through its open architecture, supporting both add-in Microsoft technology with third-party protocols and file system components. Open architecture allows NT to enjoy the support of many independent software vendors (ISVs). More people writing applications, combined with more competition, establishes a software product that is both widely accepted and affordable.

When first introduced, NT faced several well-entrenched competitive network operating systems. Two of its competitors, Novell and Unix, have large established portions of the existing NOS market and are enthusiastically embraced by a legion of devoted followers. The NT NOS is distinct from its competitors by integrating a standard user-oriented GUI interface with extensive network capabilities. The combination enables NT to work equally well as a standalone system or as a fully functional network workstation.

# The NOS Market

To win acceptance in the highly competitive NOS market, NT has to win both the new network and expansion markets. Network decisions are made not only by engineers, but by LAN administrators and network managers. While each of these groups have the same goals, their priorities are often different.

## Engineering Priorities

Engineering priorities generally include performance, integration, and expandability. Performance is important because the faster the LAN operates, the more data can be transferred and, of course, the more users supported. The level of integration between the NOS and the user's workstation is useful in reducing data transfer bottlenecks and user application problems that often plague new networks. Expandability is a good one-word definition of a network's ability to grow in order to meet either new user demands, or the demands of new graphics or database applications.

## LAN Administration Priorities

While LAN administrators are interested in the same issues as engineers, their priories often are availability, security, and maintainability. Availability is another good one-word definition of a network's ability to operate with the fewest problems. The fewer the problems, the less user downtime and, as a result, the less users will complain. Security can prevent unwanted intrusion, data destruction caused by viral infection, and data loss from operator error. Maintainability can be described as how easily an operating environment can be fixed once a server or workstation fails.

## Management Priorities

Managers are interested in cost, low risk, and the support of the network's users. While the definition of cost is obvious, the types of costs included are not always easy to understand. Depending on their industry or corporate philosophy, managers must consider not only the cost to install the network, but also the following costs:

- Yearly maintenance charges

- Upgrading the NOS and workstation software

- Adding new hardware and software

- Employing personnel to operate the network

- Training personnel to use the network and associated software

- Fixing inefficient network operation

To management, risk includes the probability that the network will be installed on time and within the budget. Another major risk consideration is how many bugs will appear that will result in user dissatisfaction. This leads to the third priority: user satisfaction. You may install the world's best network, but if the users can't use it, the network is a failure.

At this point in time, I hope you have a better understanding of NT 4's level of compliance. Let's recap the chapters and then discuss the future of NT.

## Chapter 1: Windows NT Networking Features

In the first chapter, I described the NT 4 network architecture and the fundamental technologies that Microsoft has included in this operating system. This chapter tried to build your knowledge of the networking terminology and provide an insight into how the various applications, services, and utilities work together to present the user with a relatively seamless interface to the network.

## Chapter 2: Internal Networking

In Chapter 2, I explained how NT connects, retrieves, and sends network information. The protocols take the information from the TDI and publish it to the network. We also explored tweaking the system by using the Windows NT 4 Registry.

## Chapter 3: Installing NT Networking

Chapter 3 describes the terminology, utilities, user interface, and parameters behind installing and configuring NT networking services and protocols. While the NT 4 installation is aptly described by Microsoft in their NT 4 installation documentation, there are many varied services that can be added to NT. Each parameter and add-on service or utility has its own special set of configuration parameters. The reason for, and the definition behind, these parameters is not always clear.

The software and services that we installed in Chapter 3 were selected to highlight the installations of a range of features, extending from basic network services to the more complex TCP/IP, WINS, and DNS services. I also covered the installation of the DHCP Server, Gateway Services for NetWare, and TCP/IP Printing.

## Chapter 4: Network Security

Very often, security is the last task to be completed when installing a new network. In Chapter 4, I talked about NT network security and its importance. The chapter described the mechanisms behind NT security that combine to make it the most secure commercial operating system on the market. Your system may be a simple workstation that uses security only to prevent viral infection, or your needs may be far more complex, with multiple domains and thousands of users.

The information presented in Chapter 4 includes many of the concepts and technology behind a range of needs. For instance, NT provides two effective security mechanisms for defeating viruses. The first is the object security that protects file objects from being deleted by processes that do not have sufficient privileges. The second is the memory management function that prevents one program from impinging on the memory and resources of another program. Undoubtedly, viruses will still be designed to infect the NT operating system. But, at least for now, we do have these two protections.

A fundamental part of NT's security requirements is file and directory access. Even in applications that warrant very little need for security, file and directory permissions are needed to prevent unauthorized access. In Chapter 4, I pointed out that unless your network is designed for security, NT 4's security is of limited effectiveness. Your LAN administrative personnel, along with the workstation users, must be in agreement as to what security is needed and its level of implementation.

## Chapter 5: Remote Networking

I started Chapter 5 by reviewing a set of requirements for remotely accessing and managing NT 4 workstations and servers, either across the network or from remote locations. In the industry, there appears to be different concepts of remote applications. Two distinct types of applications can readily be found: the remote control and remote node applications. The distinction between the two isn't always obvious to the casual user, but which choice you make will determine how well, and to what, you can remotely communicate with using NT 4.

This chapter also dealt with the need to remotely manage the NT 4 server. Server tools allow a LAN administrator to operationally manage NT from a remote location. These tools are especially useful if you frequently travel or manage the network from home. This chapter described various standard NT tools and tools that can be obtained through the NT Resource Kit.

## Chapter 6: Network Planning

In Chapter 6, I presented one approach to network planning based on several years of personal experience installing networks for the U.S. government and private industry. This approach consists of six basic steps, which begin with talking to the users. A network project's success or failure should start and end with a high management and employee comfort level. The techniques that I described in this chapter showed different approaches that you can use to increase the user comfort level. If a plan is drawn up that clearly itemizes the tasks, project goals, and network features, then the installation and maintenance phases will go more smoothly. If planning and user requirements are forfeited in lieu of installing only the newest technology, no one will be satisfied.

## Chapter 7: Built-In Maintenance

NT 4 comes standard with many maintenance, diagnostic, and performance tools, and the NT Resource Kit includes additional tools and utilities. In Chapter 7, I described some of the standard tools that you can use to maintain NT 4's network environment. The tools I selected are both versatile and offer the best insight into how NT 4 and networks operate.

## Chapter 8: Testing and Troubleshooting the NT Network

In Chapter 8, I presented several representative network problems and discussed the steps necessary to troubleshoot them. The important issues aren't the solutions but are the tools and procedures used to find them. We use the tools presented in Chapter 7, along with some command-line utilities described in this chapter, to troubleshoot these problems.

Although the NT 4 operating system is feature rich, it is also complex. Complexity can often mask or hide network problems. The ideas presented show that with a standard set of tools, you can often solve very complex problems by knowing what tools are available and how to use them.

## Chapter 9: Configuring NT for the Internet

In Chapter 9, I presented NT 4 in the context of the Internet. This is an excellent operating system to create Web pages and make use of some of the advanced software being released by Microsoft and other ISVs.

The Internet is an important subject in today's networking because, in time, it will interface with virtually all existing networks. In this chapter, I talked about the distinction between the Internet and an intranet. Where the Internet is global and open, intranets help organizations maintain privacy while allowing more use of their information investments. By combining the best of the Web along with the best creation, analysis, and collaboration tools, organizations will be able to reap the full rewards of an Internet and intranet connection. The new capabilities in Windows NT 4.0 build on the existing infrastructure, providing an evolutionary path for Internet solutions with revolutionary results.

The basis of Microsoft's network strategy is an open software platform, based on the Windows NT Server and Workstation operating systems. This will enable network managers to deploy high-speed, multimedia and video-enriched Internet solutions on existing network infrastructures. The deployment of open systems helps to increase options and reduce risk by allowing smooth transitions to new technologies.

## Chapter 10: NT 4 in the Multivendor Environment

In Chapter 10, I talked about the issues and decisions involved in integrating NT 4 into a new or existing multivendor environment. NT 4 was designed to integrate into these environments as a means to improve the network, expand the available network services, and frankly, to sell more NT 4 operating systems. Part of Microsoft's network strategy is to allow LAN administrators and users to gain familiarity and knowledge of NT. This, of course, will help sway them to specify NT in future networks.

This chapter also described NT 4's ability to interface with networks such as Novell, Banyan, and Unix environments.

## Chapter 11: Network Performance

In this chapter, I presented network performance as being difficult but not impossible to monitor and change. NT 4 is a network operating system that comes out of the box ready to run and attach to a network. But, as you know, different systems require different configurations. This chapter provides you with the knowledge and procedures to make performance corrections to optimize NT's operation. Unfortunately, my experience has shown that changing a parameter to improve operation can often result in a latent problem waiting to be discovered. However, if you follow the procedures for changing Registry and other NT settings, you can readily recover the original settings and repair the damage.

Networks are often difficult to understand and manage, especially when you consider the amount of seemingly random data and protocols. Using the tools I described can make this task considerably easier.

# The Future of NT

The views expressed in this chapter are my own and do not reflect any great insight into Microsoft's advanced planning. The ideas are mainly centered around NT's market direction and information releases from Microsoft and other independent sources.

A recurring theme in this book is that NT's development will not stop with the release of version 4. A future release, nicknamed Cairo, is forecasted to heavily use Microsoft's object-oriented technology. The use of a standard object interface will make it easier for ISVs to create applications, while helping individual developers to take advantage of existing operating system and applications objects. What advantage will this give to the user? I see three distinct advantages. The first is that the time needed to develop applications will be reduced, enabling new applications to reach the market more quickly after the release of a new operating system. The second advantage is that the shorter the development time, the less the software should cost. The third advantage is for those users that need software utilities or applications that can't be found in the market; they will be able to more easily create these themselves.

## The Common Object Models (COM and DCOM)

If, as expected, the future NT operating system components will support the Component Object Model (COM) and Distributed Component Object Model (DCOM), then the user can readily make use of the NT internals. The COM and DCOM standardize the way software is written. The two models describe a standard object, including how that object interfaces to new applications and user-developed software. As new releases of Microsoft-developed software occur, new features are simply added into the objects, without eliminating existing features. This approach supports both forward and backward compatibility.

## Clustering

Clustering is a technology that allows a user to combine computers and their operating systems together to work as a system. The clustered system shares its operational load across the combined resources to deliver faster extensible performance. If a component should fail, the other components in the clustered system will automatically assume the failed component's load. Extending system performance by simply adding components is called *extensibility*. Reducing the impact of a failed component on performance or operational integrity is called *availability*. Clustering will be the result of the cooperation between computer hardware and operating systems manufacturers. Allegedly, Microsoft's code name for their clustering software is *Wolfpack*.

### EXTENSIBILITY

Clustering is also a methodology that combines a standard philosophy with a specific set of requirements. To create a clustered computer system, that system must be able to add additional components without destroying or extensively changing existing computers or software.

NT 4 is capable of being run on Symmetric MultiProcessing (SMP) systems, which are computers that use two or more Central Processing Units. You may ask how that differs from clustered computers. The differences are significant. SMP systems combine two or more CPUs into one computer. Each of the processors use the same memory bus, I/O bus, and platform resources, such as disks and peripherals. The multiple CPUs run as a single CPU; only their processing capability is additive. This theoretically means that if a CPU is contributing 100 percent of its processing power to software and you add another CPU, each would contribute 50 percent. You can look at this as adding processing power or adding capability to execute more software instructions. I added the word *theoretically* because you cannot automatically increase the processing power by 100 percent simply by doubling the number of CPUs. The way NT 4 executes processes and threads, the amount of processing increase only approaches 100 percent. I know this distinction seems a little feeble, but the additive power of the second CPU depends on the software being executed.

Clustered computers may individually consist of SMP platforms. But, the clustered computers do not share platform resources. Each clustered computer has its own memory, I/O bus, and platform resources.

Using NT 4, few application programs are written specifically for SMP computers. To the application program, SMP platforms appear as a single processor. There are special applications that distinguish SMP from a single processor, but these are mainly troubleshooting and maintenance utilities.

To take advantage of clustering, programs must be written to use processing power on other computers through the network and to share access to disk files. Programs written for clustered computer systems will be designed to take advantage of the clustering. Today, new applications are often advertised as being *MAPI compliant* because they take advantage of the Messaging Application Programming Interface (MAPI). Future programs will be described as being clustering compliant.

## Availability

The term *availability* refers not only to the ability of a computer to be accessible, but to the ability of the software to also remain available for use. While that seems like a wafer-thin difference, you have to consider the network from the server's viewpoint. Let's say that an applications server supports 200 network users and the server includes two clustered computers. A failure of one processor means that the second computer in the cluster will automatically take over the full load of 200 users. The clustered computer must also have full access to the data both on disk and in the failed computer's memory. The now defunct first computer was executing software when the failure occurred, so this data is as important as the data stored on disk. The existing disk data may be hours old, whereas the data in RAM may be immediate. If the cluster can continue the execution of the software without losing data, or stopping programs, it is considered to be available. Clustering is not simply a hot failover to a spare processor. It involves an intimate working relationship between each clustered computer.

## Conclusion

I hope the information in this book proves helpful to you. While researching it, I've found many new ideas and interesting information. I also hope that this book leads you to do further reading on this subject; a single book cannot possibly encompass all the information available on NT or networking in general. Also, be sure to try the different tools I've outlined. It's going to take good old-fashioned hands-on trial and error before you really know and understand them. Good luck.

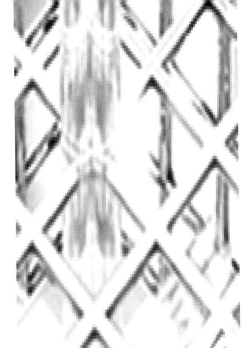

# Glossary

**Access Control Entry (ACE)**—An entry in an access control list (ACL) containing a security ID (SID) and a set of access rights. See also *Access Control List* and *Security ID*.

**Access Control List (ACL)**—A portion of the security descriptor that contains the instructions for accessing and auditing an object. See also *Security Descriptor*.

**Access Right**—A process is granted permission to manipulate a specific object in a certain way. Each object type supports different access rights.

**Access Token**—An object, attached to the user's security ID, that uniquely identifies any user who has logged on.

**Address Resolution Protocol (ARP)**—This protocol enables IP to identify the physical address, a six digit hexadecimal number (for example 00-00-fa-cc-bc-ab) that matches a given IP address, such as 142.38.5.21. See also *Internet Protocol (IP)*.

**Alerter Service**—A network service that sends system messages to another computer.

**API (Application Programming Interface)**—A standard set of procedure calls used by application programs to perform previously written functions.

**Asynchronous I/O**—A method of executing I/O instructions that allows program control to return while the I/O transfer is occurring.

**Auditing**—The ability to detect and record important security-related events. This process enables you to log user selectable security events.

**Authentication**—NT's validation of a user's ID and password information against the logon information contained in the SAM database. See also *SAM* and *SAM Database*.

**Backup Domain Controller (BDC)**—This controller contains a replicated version of the PDC's security files. See also *Primary Domain Controller*.

**Cache Manager**—Manages NT's I/O cache that is used to speed up transfers between the system disk and RAM.

**Callback**—A security procedure that immediately follows a remote user's logon and calls that user back at a preset telephone number.

**Catapult Server Proxy**—A Microsoft service product that provides a private network client with access to the Internet.

**CD-ROM File System (CDFS)**—An NT 4-supported file system for reading data from compact disks.

**CHAP (Challenge Handshake Authentication Protocol)**—An automated authentication protocol that NT uses to create a secure communications channel with another computer. It does this by requiring a challenge response to the server and demanding encryption on the response. See also *PAP*.

**Client**—A network computer that initiates data interchange with a server.

**Client/Server Model**—This term describes the transactions that occur between a server and one or more clients.

**Committed Memory**—A page in a process's virtual memory that has been allocated storage space on a hard drive.

**Component Object Model (COM)**—The underlying design model that provides interoperability among the objects written by multiple independent software vendors (ISVs) to meet the OLE 2.0 specifications. See also *Independent Software Vendor.*

**Computer-Based Training (CBT)**—An interactive course that runs on a computer workstation.

**Configuration Registry**—An NT database that contains operating system and application software configurations.

**Console**—The hardware and software modules that enable a user to manage and monitor Windows NT.

**Context Switching**—The timed procedure that saves one thread's executing environment and transfers operational program control to another thread.

**Control Object**—A kernal object that provides methods for controlling other system objects.

**DARPA (Defense Advanced Research Projects Agency)**—A U.S. governmental organization, originally called the Department of Defense Advanced Research Projects Agency, began researching methods of networking that would be robust, reliable, and able to endure significant damage, in order to maintain our national defenses. The protocols that were developed for DARPA became the standard set of protocols for the Internet.

**Deferred Procedure Call (DPC)**—A part of the Windows NT 4 interrupt architecture that executes at a level between CPU interrupts and process threads. The DPC packets execute when there are no more interrupts to service.

**Demand Paging**—The method used to move data from RAM to the paging file on the hard drive and back to RAM when processes demand its return.

**Desired Access Rights**—The set of access rights requested when opening an object. See also *Access Rights.*

**Detail Pane**—The pane in the Network Monitor window that displays information about the protocols and frames that are contained within the capture file.

**Device Object**—An object that describes a device's characteristics.

**DHCP (Dynamic Host Configuration Protocol)**—Dynamically allocates IP addresses for networked computers.

**Discretionary Access Control**—At the discretion of an object owner, the access rights to an object are assigned to specific users and groups. See also *Access Rights.*

**Disk Mirroring**—Automatically creating a copy of one disk's files to another disk.

**Disk Striping with Parity**—This is a fault-tolerant procedure (also known as RAID-5) that strips data across three or more same-size hard drives to prevent loss of data in the event of a disk failure. See also *RAID.*

**Dispatcher**—A kernel module that manages thread execution and context switching.

**Distributed Component Object Model (DCOM)**—An extension of the Component Object Model (COM) capabilities (which were restricted to local applications only) to also include networked and Internet applications. See also *Component Object Model.*

**Distributed Computing Environment (DCE)**—Provides a common set of application services that will work across a wide range of operating systems, allowing you to mix, manage, and operate multiple operating systems as if they were one unified network.

**DLL (Dynamic Link Library)**—This contains software routines that are called by executable software applications. The DLL concept has replaced the subroutine in many applications because it can be simultaneously called by many applications.

**Domain**—A group of servers and workstations that share common user accounts and policies.

**Domain Controller**—A server in a network domain that accepts user logons and initiates their authentication.

**Domain Trust Relationships**—A communications mechanism that allows users to interact, manage user account security, and share information across domain boundaries.

**Dynamic Data Exchange (DDE)**—Enables the user to link data from one file to a location in another file.

**Encryption**—The scrambling of binary data through either a hardware or software algorithm.

**Enhanced Meta File Spooling (EMF)**—Decomposes a graphic image into components that can be efficiently processed by the graphics subsystem and spooled to a printer.

**Fault Tolerance**—A computer and operating system's ability to minimize destruction during events such as a hardware failure or power outage.

**File Allocation Table System (FAT)**—The file system that maintains a table containing the status of the disk space used for file storage. FAT is compatible with MS-DOS, MS Windows 16 bit, and Windows NT.

**File Handle**—A unique object identifier that can be accessed by local processes or remote clients that have sufficient security privileges to operate on the object.

**Firewall**—A software application that performs data packet filtering for incoming Internet files.

**Gateway**—A network device that is responsible for segmenting local area networks into multiple subnets and routing messages between them.

**Gateway Service for NetWare (GSNW)**—A gateway between Microsoft network workstation clients and the NetWare file and printer servers.

**Granted Access Rights**—The access rights given by an NT object that allow an executing thread to open the object's handle. See also *Access Rights.*

**Graphics Device Drivers**—A device that directly interfaces the graphics hardware.

**Graphics Device Interface (GDI)**—The graphics engine that creates and manages displayed and printed graphics.

**GUI (Graphic User Interface)**—A Windows operator console interface that uses graphics instead of text.

**HAL (Hardware Abstraction Layer)**—The HAL.DLL (dynamic link library) is a layer of software designed to shield applications from differences in hardware and device drivers.

**High Level Data Link Control (HDLC)**—An ISO (International Organization for Standardization) definition of a standard communications interface for transferring data between two computers. See also *International Organization for Standardization.*

**High Performance File System (HPFS)**—The standard file format system for OS/2.

**Independent Software Vendor (ISV)**—An independent software vendor that publishes software for an existing operating system.

**Interface Definition Language (IDL)**—This language enables programmers to develop network applications without writing special interface drivers.

**International Organization for Standardization (ISO)**— This organization developed the OSI seven-layer reference model for Open System Interconnection protocols.

**Internet Control Message Protocol (ICMP)**—This protocol, one of the suite of TCP/IP Protocols, is a mechanism for reporting packet delivery errors.

**Internet Information Server (IIS)**—A network file and application server that transmits and receives information in HTML pages using HTTP, providing Internet access as a configurable option to the NT 4 setup.

**Internet Protocol (IP)**—The primary Internet protocol, IP is routeable. The IP protocol uses a system of logical host addresses, used by the Internet to identify devices and to perform internetwork routing. See also *Address Resolution Protocol* (ARP) and *TCP/IP.*

**Interrupt Dispatch Table (IDT)**—The IDT tracks the specific interrupt service routine that will handle the interrupts that occur at each Interrupt Request (IRQ).

**Interrupt Object**—A kernel object that allows a device driver to connect an interrupt service routine (ISR) with an interrupt request level (IRQL). See also *Interrupt Service Routine* and *Interrupt Request Level.*

**Interrupt Request Level (IRQL)**—A ranking of the computer interrupts by level of priority.

**Interrupt Service Routine (ISR)**—A function designed to handle (service) an interrupt.

**I/O Manager**—The I/O Manager manages fundamental operating system data movement to and from attached hardware devices.

**I/O Request Packet (IRP)**—Data structures that are used for intercommunication between device drivers.

**ISDN (Integrated Services Digital Network)**—A protocol that supports dial-up networks and contains two b-channels, each of which operate at 64 Kbps, and an administrative d-channel that runs at 16 Kbps. ISDN communications can run individual b-channels or combined b-channels at 128 Kbps.

**Kernal Mode**—A high-priority level mode that NT servers and workstations use to execute the operating system.

**LAN (Local Area Network)**—A network that consists of at least two workstations, connected by a communications medium. Most LANs provide connection to one or more servers and usually provide access to printing facilities. LANs support at least one, often multiple, protocols, passing data between workstations via the communication medium.

**Link Control Protocol (LCP)**—This protocol is used by RAS for establishing, configuring, and testing a data-link connection.

**Local Procedure Call Facility (LPC)**—A message-passing facility that allows the user and kernel mode subsystems to communicate with one another on the same machine.

**Logical Link Control (LLC)**—Manages communications services through the use of service access points (SAP). See also *Service Access Points.*

**Logon Process**—A user must supply a user ID and password, processed by the Security subsystem, in order to be granted access. See also *Security Subsystem.*

**Mailslots**—Used to provide connectionless messaging services on a local area network.

**MAP**—Translating a virtual address into a physical address.

**Masking Interrupts**—Raises the processor's interrupt request level (IRQL) to stop processing interrupts at and below the new IRQL. See also *Interrupt Request Level.*

**Medium Access Control (MAC)**—A method of providing access to devices in order to use a network to send and receive data.

**Messenger Service**—A network service that receives messages from other systems and displays them.

**MilNet (Military Network)**—A U.S. government network developed by the Department of Defense (DOD).

**Multi-Provider Router (MPR)**—An NT software component that supports applications that do not use UNC names in their I/O requests.

**MUP (Multiple Universal Name Convention Provider)**—An NT software component that is responsible for decoding UNC names. See also *UNC.*

**Named Pipe**—An interprocess communication implement that permits one process to send data to another local or remote process.

**Naming Service**—This service translates a network computer's name into an IP address.

**National Science Foundation Network (NSFNET)**—The National Science Foundation (NSF) was involved in the commercialization of ARPAnet. NSFNET evolved from this effort and has become the backbone for the commercial Internet.

**NetBIOS Interface (Network Basic Input Output System)**—A programming interface that allows I/O requests to be sent to, and received from, a remote computer. It hides networking hardware from applications.

**NetBEUI (NetBIOS Extended User Interface)**—A small, efficient protocol used on department-sized LANs (20 to 200 workstations) to provide error detection, powerful flow control, and tuning parameters.

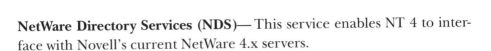

**NetWare Directory Services (NDS)**— This service enables NT 4 to interface with Novell's current NetWare 4.x servers.

**NetWare Loadable Module (NLM)**— A network application used by NT to emulate the NetWare environment.

**Network Alert**—A notification of the occurrence of an event in one computer transmitted to one or more computers, over the network.

**Network Driver Interface Specification (NDIS)**—A Windows NT 4-supported standard interface for network card drivers.

**Network Interface Card (NIC)**—A hardware circuit board that interfaces a computer and its operating system to a physical network.

**Network Server**—An NT 4 service that responds to I/O requests from another network computer.

**NT**—New technology.

**NT Executive Services**—A collection of high-priority, level 0 modules that conduct basic OS services supporting the user mode subsystems and network access.

**NT File System (NTFS)**—A file system used by the Windows NT operating system to support file system recovery and large storage media. NTFS also supports NT 4's security features for directory and file access.

**NT POSIX**—A Windows subsystem designed to run POSIX applications. See also *POSIX*.

**NT Virtual DOS Machine (NTVDM)**—Appears to MS-DOS applications as a fully functional DOS environment.

**Object Attribute**—A field of data in an object that defines, or records, the object's state and can be manipulated by calling an object service.

**Object Directory Object**—An object that stores the names of other objects, much as a file directory stores file names. It provides the means to support a hierarchical naming structure for Windows NT objects.

**Object Domain**—A self-contained set of objects that is accessible through the NT object manager's object name hierarchy, but is managed by a secondary object manager (such as the NT I/O system).

**Object Handle**—An index to a specific object, such as a process. In order to access an object's handle, a thread must possess the necessary access security.

**Object Linking and Embedding (OLE)**—The ability of one application to embed an object created by another application, such as embedding an Excel spreadsheet into a Word document. When an embedded object is selected, it's linked to the creating application.

**Object Manager**—The component of the NT Executive Services that manages operating system resources, which are then stored as objects. Defines what an object is, specifies what operations can be performed upon it, and sets rules for object retention, naming, and security.

**Object Service**—A user mode NT 4 service for handling an object.

**Page Frame**—A block of contiguous physical addresses used to store the contents of a virtual page.

**Page Frame Database**—A data structure used by the NT 4 virtual memory manager to store the status of all physical memory page frames.

**Page Table Entry (PTE)**—The memory to disk page file swap-out.

**PAP (Password Authentication Protocol)**—One of two automated logon methods supported by Windows NT RAS. Unlike CHAP, this method uses unencrypted password authentication. See also *CHAP*.

**Parent Process**—A process that spawns another process (a child process) that inherits some or all of the parent resources.

**Port**—A communication channel that connects one machine to another machine using either a synchronous or asynchronous protocol.

**POSIX (Portable Operating System Interface)**—A set of 12 standards for applications that are portable across Unix environments.

**PPP (Point-to-Point Protocol)**—A method for transmitting and receiving serial datagrams over point-to-point links. Used by NT 4 Remote Access Service (RAS), PPP promotes interoperability with ISV remote access software. NT 4's PPP is compliant with Request For Comment (RFC) 1134, the industry standard for PPP. See also *Independent Software Vendor (ISV)* and *Remote Access Service (RAS)*.

**Presentation Layer**—Translates data obtained from the applications layer into its own intermediate format.

**Primary Domain Controller (PDC)**—An NT server that is responsible for maintaining the user account and security policy databases for the entire domain.

**Process Manager**—Manages the creation and deletion of processes and their associated threads. The Process Manager also works in conjunction with the Security Reference Monitor and the Virtual Memory Manager to provide interprocess protection. See also *Security Reference Monitor* and *Virtual Memory Manager.*

**Provider**—A generic name for software that establishes Windows NT as the client of a remote network server.

**RAID (Redundant Array of Inexpensive Disks)**—This is a fault-tolerant disk system used to protect against disk failure. See also *Disk Striping with Parity.*

**RAS (Remote Access Service)**—A remote node serial dial-up application that is standard with NT 4.

**Redirector**—An NT service that directs requests for remote files, named pipes, or mailslots to a network server on another machine.

**Registry**—The Registry is the area of the operating system where all the settings for hardware and software are stored.

**Remote Procedure Call (RPC)**—Enables individual application procedures to execute on systems anywhere on the network.

**Replication**—An NT service that allows duplication of data from one computer to another. In Windows NT, replication also includes a test that verifies that the replicated copy matches the current file's size and time stamp. If it does not match, the replication service waits for a period of time to allow the source file to stabilize.

**Robustness**—The ability of a program to function well or to continue functioning well in unexpected situations.

**RPC Transport Provider Interface**—A DLL that acts as an interface between the remote procedure call (RPC) facility and network transport software.

**SAM (Security Accounts Manager)**—The NT 4 subsystem that maintains the SAM database and provides access to the WIN32 security API.

**SAM Database**—The NT SAM database that contains user IDs, passwords, and administrator-configured security policies.

**Secure Logon Facility**—Software in a secure operating system that monitors a particular class of logon devices to ensure that all users enter valid identification before they are allowed access to the system.

**Security Descriptor**—A data structure attached to all objects that protects their integrity from unauthorized access.

**Security ID (SID)**—A particular name that identifies a logged on user or group to the security system.

**Security Reference Monitor**—Oversees internal and external network and program access to the operating system and checks user rights before allowing access to files and other security objects.

**Security Subsystem**—A subsystem that accepts a user's ID and password, creates a token, and compares that token against a system security database.

**Service Access Points (SAP)**— The LLC manages communications services through the use of Service Access Points (SAP). A SAP is a pointer to the upper-layer protocol that initiated the data transfer.

**Session Layer**—Manages computer-to-computer interchanges by establishing a communications link.

**SNMP (Simple Network Management Protocol)**—Provides the NT administrator with detailed information regarding local and remote operation of servers and workstations.

**STREAMS**—A driver-development environment that Windows NT supplies for creating or porting network transport drivers.

**Symbolic Link Object**—An NT executive object that translates one object name into another.

**TCP (Transmission Control Protocol)**—A protocol that provides reliable, full-duplex connections and service. TCP supports multiple, simultaneous connections to network hosts. See also *Internet Protocol* (IP).

**TCP/IP (Transmission Control Protocol/Internet Protocol)**—An industry-standard suite of protocols designed for wide-area networking. This suite includes the Transmission Control Protocol (TCP), Internet Protocol (IP), User Datagram Protocol (UDP), Address Resolution Protocol (ARP), Internet Control Message Protocol (ICMP), and the Point-to-Point Protocol (PPP), which is used for dial-up access.

**Terabyte**—One thousand gigabytes.

**Transport Driver Interface (TDI)**—A specification to which the transport protocol device drivers are written.

**Transport Layer**—This layer is responsible for the error-free transfer of data between the higher levels of the model and the network. It is also responsible for reconciling the data packets and recovery, if errors are detected.

**Trusted Domain**—Independent domains that can share users, files, applications, and printing facilities between domain boundaries.

**UNC (Uniform Naming Convention)**—Specifies that remote file names must begin with the string \\, indicating that they exist on another network machine.

**Uninterruptable Power Supply (UPS)**—A backup battery that is attached to a computer and allows memory contents to remain undiminished long enough for the operating system to properly shut down if a power outage occurs.

**URL (Universal Resource Locator)**—An Internet addressing standard.

**User Datagram Protocol (UDP)**—A protocol used at the host-to-host layer which provides fast unreliable network data transfers when error recovery is not required. See also *TCP/IP*.

**User Mode**—The mode that NT uses to run its application software.

**Virtual Circuit**—A virtual communication channel between two machines. Many network sessions can be multiplexed across a single virtual circuit.

**Virtual DOS Machine (VDM)**—A safeguarded subsystem that supplies a complete MS-DOS condition.

**Virtual Memory**—An abstract view of memory that does not directly correspond to physical RAM.

**Virtual Memory Manager (VMM)**—Manages NT's real and virtual memory. When memory is required, the VMM maps memory pages between the two. Once mapped, the VMM can transition the mapped applications to a paging file on the hard drive, providing memory space for other applications.

**WAN (Wide Area Network)**—A WAN extends beyond the limit of a local area network to connect computers across the U.S. and around the world.

**Win32 API**—A 32-bit API that updates the earlier version of the 16-bit Windows API. The Win32 API includes advanced operating system functions, security, and new API features. See also *API*.

**Windows NT**—The high-end Microsoft Network operating system that has maintained backward compatibility with most of the applications that ran under previous versions of Windows NT, Windows 16-bit operating systems, and MS-DOS.

**Windows Sockets**—An API that allows processes to make calls to connect to a socket or pipe at another network computer. Once connected, the networked computers can exchange data through the socket. See also *API*.

**WINS (Windows Internet Naming Service)**—A network service provided by one or more servers to associate IP addresses with computer names.

**Working Set**—A set of virtual pages that are in physical memory at any given moment for a specific process.

**Workstation Service**—A network service that supplies user-mode application API routines to manage the Windows NT redirector. See also *API*.

**WOW (Windows on Win32)**—A protected subsystem that runs within a virtual DOS machine (VDM) process. It provides a 16-bit Windows environment capable of running any number of 16-bit Windows applications on Windows NT. See also *Virtual DOS Machine*.

# Performance Monitors's Network Objects and NT 4 Network Files

**A**dditional information pertaining to this appendix can be found in the Windows NT Registry under:

\HKEY_LOCAL_MACHINE\SOFTWARE\Microsoft\
WindowsNT\CurrentVersion\Perflib\409\Counters\
Network Objects

# Network Objects

**Table B.1  System Object**

| Name | Function |
|---|---|
| System Object | Contains the counters that represent the activity of all processors on the computer. |
| File Read Operations/Second | A total of all the disk file Read operations on the computer. |
| File Write Operations/Second | A total of all the disk file Write operations on the computer. |
| File Control Operations/Second | A total of all other (non-file reads or writes) disk file operations, including file control or inquiries about devices or status. |
| File Read Bytes/Second | A total of the bytes transferred corresponding to the File Read Operations/Second, i.e., the file system Read operations on the computer. |
| File Write Bytes/Second | A total of the bytes transferred corresponding to the File Write Operations/Second, i.e., the file system Write operations on the computer. |
| File Control Bytes/Second | A total of bytes transferred corresponding to the File Control Operations/Second, i.e., non-Read or Write file system operations. |
| Context Switches/Second | The interthread rate at which NT 4 performs context switches. |
| System Calls/Second | The number of calls to Windows NT 4's system service routines. |
| % Total Processor Time | The percentage of total processing time being consumed by the % Total User Time + % Total Privileged Time. For SMP systems, this percentage is an aggregate of the processing time for all CPUs. |

*(continued)*

**Table B.1 System Object** *(continued)*

| Name | Function |
|------|----------|
| % Total User Time | The percentage of total user mode time consumed by the CPU. For SMP systems, this percentage is an aggregate of the processing time for all CPUs. |
| % Total Privileged Time | The percentage of total privileged mode time consumed by the CPU. For SMP systems, this percentage is an aggregate of the processing time for all CPUs. |
| Total Interrupts/Second | The total number of hardware interrupts being received by the CPU. For SMP systems, this percentage is an aggregate of the processing time for all CPUs. |
| File Data Operations/Second | The rate of file system Read and Write operations. |
| System Up Time | The total system operational Second since the last system reboot. |
| Processor Queue Length | The number of threads awaiting execution by the system's processor. (Note: this number does not include the currently executing threads.) |

**Table B.2 Memory Object**

| Name | Function |
|------|----------|
| Memory Object | The counters that describe the parameters of the system's real memory and virtual memory. |
| Available Bytes | The size of the virtual memory currently available to the system, i.e., the sum of the Free, Standby, and Zeroed lists. |
| Committed Bytes | The size of the system's committed (used) virtual memory. |

*(continued)*

**Table B.2 Memory Object** *(continued)*

| Name | Function |
| --- | --- |
| Commit Limit | The amount of virtual memory bytes available to be committed to the system before the paging file must be extended. |
| Page Faults/Second | The number of processor page faults. A page fault occurs when a process accesses a memory page not currently in main memory. |
| Write Copies/Second | The number of processor faults that occur when processes write to page copies. |
| Transition Faults/Second | The number of processor faults made to pages that are queued for the page file. |
| Cache Faults/Second | The number of processor faults that occur when the Cache Manager fails to find a file's page in the cache and requests the Memory Manager to locate the appropriate page in memory or on disk. |
| Demand Zero Faults/Second | The number of processor page faults that occur when pages are required to be filled with zeros. |
| Pages/Second | The sum of Pages Input/Second + Pages Output/Second. The amount of disk paging to satisfy process memory requirements. This counter is the Memory Object's most useful indicator that the system is bottle-necked due to memory activity. |
| Pages Input/Second | The rate at which pages are Read from disk to satisfy process memory demands. This counter can indicate potential memory bottlenecks due to disk reads. |
| Page Reads/Second | The combined rate of page Read operations; includes both single and multiple pages. |

*(continued)*

**Table B.2   Memory Object** *(continued)*

| Name | Function |
| --- | --- |
| Pages Output/Second | The rate of pages being output to disk after being changed in main memory. |
| Page Writes/Second | The rate pages have been written to the disk due to being changed since last retrieved. |
| Paged Pool Bytes | The memory in the Paged Pool can be paged out to the disk when not required. This counter shows the current size of the Paged Pool in bytes. |
| Nonpaged Pool Bytes | The memory in the Nonpaged Pool cannot be paged out to the disk. This counter shows the current size of the Nonpaged Pool in bytes. |
| Paged Pool Allocations/Second | The demand rate to allocate space in the system Paged Pool. This number indicates that the operating system is using more memory by increasing the size of its pool. |
| Paged Pool Frees/Second | The demand rate to free space in the system Paged Pool. This counter can indicate a possible problem due to the lack of virtual memory. |
| Nonpaged Pool Allocations/ Second | The demand rate to allocate space in the system Nonpaged Pool. |
| Nonpaged Pool Frees/Second | The demand rate to free space in the system Nonpaged Pool. This counter can indicate a possible problem due to lack of virtual memory. |
| Free System Page Table Entries | The total Page Table Entries available for use by the memory. The rate of decrease by this counter indicates the rate of system and user process memory demands. |

*(continued)*

**Table B.2    Memory Object** *(continued)*

| Name | Function |
| --- | --- |
| Cache Bytes | The size of the current system cache which buffers data from the disk or the network. The cache memory is allocated from free memory, i.e., not allocated to user or kernel mode processes. |
| Cache Bytes Peak | The maximum size of the system cache. The rate of change in this counter indicates the rate of use by network or disk activities. |

**Table B.3    Redirector Object**

| Name | Function |
| --- | --- |
| Redirector Object | The Redirector manages your computer's network connections to other computers. |
| Bytes Total/Second | Counts the number of bytes being processed per Second by the system Redirector. Changes in this counter indicate the level of computer demands for network resources. |
| File Data Operations/Second | Counts the number of files the Redirector is currently processing every Second. Redirector File Efficiency = (Bytes Total/Second)/ (File Data Operations/Second). The larger the result, the more efficiently this operation is working. |
| Packets/Second | Counts the number of data packets the Redirector is currently processing every Second. Redirector Packet Efficiency = (Bytes Total/ Second)/(Packets/Second). The larger the result, the more efficient the Redirector is operating. |

*(continued)*

**Table B.3    Redirector Object (*continued*)**

| Name | Function |
| --- | --- |
| Bytes Received/Second | Counts the number of bytes sent by the network to the Redirector. |
| Packets Received/Second | The rate of network packets being received by the Redirector. How efficiently the network is handling packets can be obtained by Network Packet Efficiency = (Bytes Received/Second) / (Packets Received/Second). Individual samples seldom contain practical information, but the trend showing an increase or decrease reflects positive or negative changes in network efficiency. |
| Read Bytes Paging/Second | Indicates the number of bytes the Redirector is reading due to page faults. |
| Bytes Nonpaging/Second | Counts network data read by the Redirector to fulfill application file requests. This count only contains data bytes, not protocol overhead. |
| Read Bytes Cache/Second | Counts the data bytes read by your computer from the system cache. |
| Read Bytes Network/Second | Counts data bytes read by local applications from external network sources. Includes only bytes from the network that are not available in the Read Bytes Cache/Second. |
| Bytes Transmitted/Second | Counts the bytes being sent by the Redirector to external network destinations. This count includes both data and protocol overhead. |
| Packets Transmitted/Second | Counts the number of packets the Redirector is sending to external network destinations. |
| Write Bytes Paging/Second | Counts the number of bytes that the Redirector is writing to paged memory. |

*(continued)*

**Table B.3    Redirector Object** *(continued)*

| Name | Function |
| --- | --- |
| Write Bytes Nonpaging/Second | Counts the number of nonpaged bytes written by the Redirector to pages located in memory. |
| Write Bytes Cache/Second | Counts the number of bytes being written by the Redirector to the system Cache. |
| Write Bytes Network/Second | Counts the number bytes written by applications to network computers. |
| File Read Operations/Second | Counts the number of applications requesting data from the Redirector. |
| Read Operations Random/Second | Counts unsequential Redirector file reads. |
| Read Packets/Second | Counts the number of read packet requests the Redirector sends to a network destination. |
| Reads Large/Second | Counts the number of application reads that require more than twice the destination server's negotiated buffer size. |
| Read Packets Small/Second | Counts the number of application reads that require data packets less than one-fourth of the destination server's negotiated buffer size. |
| File Write Operations/Second | Counts the number of application write calls being sent to the Redirector. |
| Write Operations Random/Second | Counts the number of non-sequential file operations being made to the Redirector. |
| Write Packets/Second | Counts the number of writes being sent by the Redirector to remote network computers. |

*(continued)*

**Table B.3   Redirector Object *(continued)***

| Name | Function |
| --- | --- |
| Writes Large/Second | Counts the number of application writes that require more than twice the destination server's negotiated buffer size. |
| Write Packets Small/Second | Counts the number of application writes that require data packets less than one-fourth of the destination server's negotiated buffer size. |
| Reads Denied/Second | Counts the number of times that a server cannot accept raw read requests. |
| Writes Denied/Second | Counts the number of times that a server cannot accept raw read writes. |
| Network Errors/Second | Counts the number of serious network errors that occur between the local Redirector and a network server. Network Errors are also entered in the NT 4 system event log. Use the event log to gain deeper insight into the error and the name of the network server. |
| Server Sessions | Counts the number of Secondurity objects that the local Redirector is actively managing. |
| Server Reconnects | Counts the number of reconnection operations the local Redirector has made to servers to complete an active request. |
| Connects Core | Counts the connections the local Redirector has to MS-Net SMB, Xenix, and Vax network servers. |
| Connects LAN Manager 2.0 | Counts the number of connections that the local Redirector has to LAN Manager 2.0 servers. |

*(continued)*

**Table B.3    Redirector Object** *(continued)*

| Name | Function |
| --- | --- |
| Connects LAN Manager 2.1 | Counts the number of connections that the local Redirector has to LAN Manager 2.1 servers. |
| Connects Windows NT | Counts the connections to Windows NT computers. |
| Server Disconnects | Counts the number of server disconnects from the local Redirector. |
| Server Sessions Hung | Sums the active sessions that were disconnected due to time-outs and lack of response from network servers. |
| Current Commands | Counts the number of requests that are queued by the local Redirector for service. Queued requests greater than the number of NICs identifies a possible NIC bottleneck. |

**Table B.4    Server Object**

| Name | Function |
| --- | --- |
| Server Object | The Server service shares access to local resources with remote network computers. |
| Bytes Total/Second | Counts the bytes which have been sent to and received from the network by the server. |
| Bytes Read/Second | Counts the bytes that the local server has received from other network computers. |
| Bytes Sent/Second | Counts the bytes that the local server has sent to other network computers. |
| Sessions Timed Out | Counts the number of network sessions that have been closed because their idle time exceeds the server's auto-disconnect parameter in the Registry. |

*(continued)*

**Table B.4    Server Object** *(continued)*

| Name | Function |
|------|----------|
| Sessions Errored Out | Counts the number of network sessions that have been closed by the local server because of an unexpected error condition. This counter is a good indicator of client-server network error problems. |
| Sessions Logged Off | Counts the sessions that have been terminated normally. |
| Sessions Forced Off | Counts the number of sessions that have been forced to logoff by the local server due to exceeding logon time limits. A high value in this counter may indicate that a longer logon period may be required. |
| Errors Logon | Counts the number of failed logon attempts made by network clients trying to gain access to the local server. This value can indicate possible Secondurity access problems. |
| Errors Access Permissions | Counts the number of user attempts to access local resources that have been rejected with the diagnostic message STATUS_ACCESS_DENIED. |
| Errors Granted Access | Counts the number of user attempts to access files that successfully opened but were denied. |
| Errors System | Counts the number of detected internal server errors. An increase in this counter may indicate a serious server problem is developing. |
| Blocking Requests Rejected | Counts the number of server-rejected blocking SMBs because of a low quantity of free work items. |

*(continued)*

**Table B.4    Server Object** *(continued)*

| Name | Function |
| --- | --- |
| Work Item Shortages | Counts the number of occurrences of STATUS_DATA_NOT_ACCEPTED that were returned to the Redirector on the remote networked computer. This indicates that work items are unavailable. |
| Files Opened Total | Counts the number of successful open attempts executed by the server for remote network clients. |
| Files Open | Counts the number of currently opened files on the local computer. |
| Server Sessions | Counts the number of currently active server sessions. |
| File Directory Searches | Counts the number of currently active file searches being conducted by the server. |
| Pool Nonpaged Bytes | Counts the number of currently used Nonpage pool memory bytes being used by the server. |
| Pool Nonpaged Failures | Counts the number of times that nonpaged pool memory has failed. An increase in this counter may indicate a low memory problem with physically attached RAM. |
| Pool Nonpaged Peak | Stores the maximum number of nonpaged pool memory bytes the server has used since the last system reboot. |
| Pool Paged Bytes | Counts the number of pageable computer memory bytes the server is currently using. |
| Pool Paged Failures | Counts the number of failed paged pool memory allocations. |
| Pool Paged Peak | Stores the maximum number of paged pool memory bytes the server has used since the last system reboot. |

*(continued)*

**Table B.4   Server Object** *(continued)*

| Name | Function |
|------|----------|
| Context Block Queue/Second | Counts the average time a work context block was queued by the server awaiting execution. Large changes in this value can indicate other serious server problems. |
| Context Blocks Queued/Second | Indicates how fast work context blocks are being queued by the server awaiting execution. |

**Table B.5   NetBEUI Object**

| Name | Function |
|------|----------|
| Datagrams/Second | Indicates how many and how fast datagrams are being processed by the local computer. |
| Datagram Bytes/Second | Indicates how many and how fast datagram bytes are being processed by the computer. The count includes both transmitted and received datagrams. |
| Packets/Second | Indicates how many and how fast packets are being processed by the local computer. This counter includes both transmitted and received packets. |
| Frames/Second | Indicates how many and how fast frames are being processed by the local computer. This counter includes both transmitted and received data-carrying frames. |
| Frame Bytes/Second | Indicates how many and how fast data-carrying frame bytes are being processed by the computer. The count includes both transmitted and received frames. |
| Connections Open | Counts the number of current NetBEUI connections. |

*(continued)*

**Table B.5    NetBEUI Object** *(continued)*

| Name | Function |
| --- | --- |
| Connections No Retries | Counts the total number of successful first-time connections. The counter accumulates the total number of successful first-time connections made since the last reboot. |
| Connections With Retries | Counts the total number of successful connections made after one connection attempt. The counter accumulates the total number of successful first-time connections made since the last reboot. |
| Disconnects Local | Counts the number of locally disconnected sessions made on the local computer. The counter accumulates the total number of disconnections made since the last reboot. |
| Disconnects Remote | Counts the number of remotely disconnected sessions made with the local computer. The counter accumulates the total number of disconnections made since the last reboot. |
| Failures Link | Counts the number of dropped connections attributable to a link failure. The counter accumulates the total number of link failures that have occurred since the last reboot. |
| Failures Adapter | Counts the number of connections dropped because of an adapter failure. The counter accumulates the total number of adapter failure disconnects that have occurred since the last reboot. |
| Connection Session Time-outs | Counts the number of connections that were dropped because of a session time-out. The counter accumulates the total number of time-out session disconnects that have occurred since the last reboot. |

*(continued)*

**Table B.5   NetBEUI Object** *(continued)*

| Name | Function |
|------|----------|
| Connections Canceled | Counts the number of canceled connections made by either local or remote users. The counter accumulates the total number of connections canceled disconnects that have occurred since the last reboot. |
| Failures Resource Remote | Counts the number of failed connections resulting from resource unavailability on remote network computers. The counter accumulates the total number of connections canceled due to remote resource problems that have occurred since the last reboot. |
| Failures Resource Local | Counts the number of connections that have failed due to local computer resource unavailability. The counter accumulates the total number of connections canceled due to local resource problems that have occurred since the last reboot. |
| Failures Not Found | Counts the number of failed connection attempts due to failure of the server to find the designated remote computer. The counter accumulates the total number of connections canceled due to network location problems that have occurred since the last reboot. |
| Failures No Listen | Counts the number of rejected connections due to the remote computer not listening for connection requests. The counter accumulates the total number of connection failure problems that have occurred since the last reboot. |
| Datagrams Sent/Second | Counts the number of datagrams sent by the local computer. |

*(continued)*

**Table B.5    NetBEUI Object** *(continued)*

| Name | Function |
|------|----------|
| Datagram Bytes Sent/Second | Counts the number of datagram bytes sent by the local computer. |
| Datagrams Received/Second | Counts the number of network datagrams received by the local computer. |
| Datagram Bytes Received/Second | Counts the number of datagram bytes received by the local computer. |
| Packets Sent/Second | Counts the number of packets sent by the local computer. This count includes both data and control packets. |
| Packets Received/Second | Counts the number of network packets received by the local computer. This count includes both data and control packets. |
| Frames Sent/Second | Counts the number of frames sent by the local computer. This count includes only data-carrying frames. |
| Frame Bytes Sent/Second | Counts the number of frame-contained data bytes sent by the local computer. |
| Frames Received/Second | Counts the number of network frames received by the local computer. This count includes only data frames. |
| Frame Bytes Received/Second | Counts the number of network frame bytes received by the local computer. This count includes only frame bytes containing data. |
| Frames Re-Sent/Second | Counts the number of data frames that have re-sent by the local computer. |
| Frame Bytes Re-Sent/Second | Counts the number of data frame bytes that have been re-sent by the local computer. |

*(continued)*

### Table B.5    NetBEUI Object *(continued)*

| Name | Function |
| --- | --- |
| Frames Rejected/Second | Counts the number of data-carrying frames rejected by the local computer. |
| Frame Bytes Rejected/Second | Counts the number of data-carrying frame bytes rejected by the local computer. |
| Expirations Response | Counts the number of T1 timer expirations. |
| Expirations Acknowledgements | Counts the number of T2 timer expirations. |
| Window Send Maximum | The maximum number of bytes of data sent to a remote network computer prior to the start of an acknowledgment waiting period. |
| Window Send Average | Contains the running average number of data bytes transmitted to a remote computer before waiting for a remote computer acknowledgment. |
| Piggyback Acknowledgements Queued/Second | Counts the number of queued piggybacked acknowledgments. |
| Piggyback Acknowledgements Timeouts | Counts the number of piggyback acknowledgments that could not be sent due to no outgoing packet destined to the remote computer. |

### Table B.6    NetBEUI Resource Object

| Name | Function |
| --- | --- |
| Used Maximum | Displays the maximum instantaneous number of NetBEUI buffers that are used by the system. |
| Used Average | Displays a running average of the number of NetBEUI buffers being used by the system. |
| Times Exhausted | Counts the number of instances when the NetBEUI buffers were in use and unavailable for new transmissions. |

**Table B.7   NBT Connection Object**

| Name | Function |
| --- | --- |
| Bytes Received/Second | Counts the number of bytes received by the local NBT connection to a remote computer. |
| Bytes Sent/Second | Counts the number of bytes sent by the local NBT connection to a remote computer. |
| Bytes Total/Second | Counts the number of bytes both sent and received by the local NBT connection to a remote computer. |
| Packets Sent/Second | The rate that packets are sent to the network interface instance. |
| Current Bandwidth | Contains an estimate of the interface instance's current bandwidth in bits per Second. |
| Bytes Received/Second | Counts the bytes received on the network interface instance. |
| Packets Received Unicast/Second | Counts the number of subnet packets that are delivered to an upper-layer protocol. |
| Packets Received Non-Unicast/ Second | Counts the number of subnet broadcast or multicast packets that are delivered to an upper-layer protocol. |
| Packets Received Discarded | Counts the number of errorless received packets that were discarded, preventing their delivery to a higher-layer protocol. This number will increase during periods of high computer resource utilization. |
| Packets Received Errors | Counts the number of received packets containing errors that are discarded and not sent to higher-layer protocols. |
| Packets Received Unknown Protocol | Counts the number of received packets from the interface instance discarded due to an unrecognized protocol. |

*(continued)*

**Table B.7    NBT Connection Object** *(continued)*

| Name | Function |
|---|---|
| Bytes Sent/Second | Counts the number of bytes being sent by the interface instance. This counter includes both data and framing bytes. |
| Packets Sent Unicast/Second | Counts the number of packets transmitted to subnet-unicast addresses by upper-level protocols. |
| Packets Sent Non-Unicast/Second | Counts the number of packets transmitted to subnet-broadcast and multicast addresses by upper-level protocols. |
| Packets Outbound Discarded | Counts the number of discarded errorless packets that were to be sent to the network. |
| Packets Outbound Errors | Counts the number of outbound packets not transmitted due to errors found in the packets. |
| Output Queue Length | Counts the current number of packets contained in the output queue. |

**Table B.8    Network Interface Object**

| Name | Function |
|---|---|
| Bytes Total/Second | Counts the bytes being sent and received on the network interface instance. This count includes both data and framing bytes. |
| Packets/Second | Counts the packets that are sent and received on the network interface instance. |
| Packets Received/Second | Counts the packets that are received on the network interface instance. |

**Table B.9    Network Segment Object**

| Name | Function |
|------|----------|
| % Broadcast Frames | Displays an instantaneous percentile of the network bandwidth comprised of broadcast traffic. |
| % Multicast Frames | Displays an instantaneous percentile of the network bandwidth comprised of multicast traffic. |
| % Network Utilization | Displays an instantaneous percentile of the network bandwidth being used by the network. This percentage contains the sum of all protocols divided by the total network bandwidth. |
| Broadcast Frames Received/Second | Counts the number of broadcast frames currently occupying bandwidth on the network. |
| Multicast Frames Received/Second | Counts the number of multicast frames currently occupying bandwidth on the network. |
| Total Bytes Received/Second | Counts the number of bytes currently occupying bandwidth on the network. |
| Total Frames Received/Second | Counts the number of frames currently occupying bandwidth on the network. |

**Table B.10    P Object**

| Name | Function |
|------|----------|
| Datagrams/Second | Counts the number of IP datagrams transmitted from or received by the local computer's network interfaces. |
| Datagrams Received/Second | Counts the number of IP datagrams received by the local computer's network interfaces. |

*(continued)*

**Table B.10    P Object** *(continued)*

| Name | Function |
|------|----------|
| Datagrams Received Header Errors | Counts the number of received datagrams that the system discarded due to IP header errors. This is an accumulating sum started at the last system reboot. |
| Datagrams Received Address Errors | Counts the number of received datagrams which the system discarded due to IP address errors. This is an accumulating sum started at the last system reboot. |
| Datagrams Forwarded/Second | Counts the number of received datagrams that were not destined for the local computer. The local computer attempted to discover a route to the correct IP address. |
| Datagrams Received Unknown Protocol | Counts the number of successfully received datagrams which the system discarded because they contained an unknown or unsupported protocol. This is an accumulating sum started at the last system reboot. |
| Datagrams Received Discarded | Counts the number of received errorless IP datagrams, which were discarded. This is an accumulating sum started at the last system reboot. |
| Datagrams Received Delivered/Second | Counts the number of received datagrams that have been successfully delivered to IP user-protocols within the local computer. |
| Datagrams Sent/Second | Counts the number of IP datagrams sent to the IP protocol for transmission by the local computer. |

*(continued)*

**Table B.10    P Object** *(continued)*

| Name | Function |
| --- | --- |
| Datagrams Outbound Discarded | Counts the number of errorless IP datagrams to be transmitted, but were discarded. This is an accumulating sum started at the last system reboot. |
| Datagrams Outbound No Route | Counts the number of IP datagrams discarded due to the lack of a path to their destination. This is an accumulating sum started at the last system reboot. |
| Fragments Received/Second | Counts the number of received IP fragments that require re-assembly by the local computer. |
| Fragments Re-assembled/Second | Counts the number of IP fragments that have been successfully re-assembled at the local computer. |
| Fragment Re-assembly Failures | Counts the number of failures found by the IP re-assembly algorithm. This is an accumulating sum started at the last system reboot. |
| Fragmented Datagrams/Second | Counts the number of datagrams that have been successfully fragmented by the computer. |
| Fragmentation Failures | Counts the number of discarded IP datagrams due to the inability of the local computer to fragment them. This is an accumulating sum started at the last system reboot. |
| Fragments Created/Second | Counts the number of IP datagram fragments that have been successfully fragmented by the local computer. |

**Table B.11    CMP Object**

| Name | Function |
|------|----------|
| Messages/Second | Counts the number of ICMP messages that are received and transmitted by the local computer. |
| Messages Received/Second | Counts the number of ICMP messages that are received by the local computer. |
| Messages Received Errors | Counts the number of ICMP messages received at the local computer containing errors. This is an accumulating sum reset by the last system reboot. |
| Received Destination Unreachable | Counts the number of ICMP Destination Unreachable messages received by the local computer. This is an accumulating sum reset by the last system reboot. |
| Received Time Exceeded | Counts the number of ICMP Time Exceeded messages received by the local computer. This is an accumulating sum reset by the last system reboot. |
| Received Parameter Problem | Counts the number of ICMP Parameter Problem messages received by the local computer. This is an accumulating sum reset by the last system reboot. |
| Received Source Quench | Counts the number of ICMP Source Quench messages received by the local computer. This is an accumulating sum reset by the last system reboot. |
| Received Redirect | Counts the number of ICMP Redirect messages received by the local computer. This is an accumulating sum reset by the last system reboot. |

*(continued)*

**Table B.11    CMP Object** *(continued)*

| Name | Function |
| --- | --- |
| Received Echo | Counts the number of ICMP Echo messages received by the local computer. This is an accumulating sum reset by the last system reboot. |
| Received Echo Reply | Counts the number of ICMP Echo Reply messages received by the local computer. This is an accumulating sum reset by the last system reboot. |
| Received Timestamp | Counts the number of ICMP-requested Timestamp messages received by the local computer. This is an accumulating sum reset by the last system reboot. |
| Received Timestamp Reply | Counts the number of ICMP Timestamp Reply messages received by the local computer. This is an accumulating sum reset by the last system reboot. |
| Received Address Mask | Counts the number of ICMP Address Mask Request messages received by the local computer. This is an accumulating sum reset by the last system reboot. |
| Received Address Mask Reply | Counts the number of ICMP Address Mask Reply messages received by the local computer. This is an accumulating sum reset by the last system reboot. |
| Messages Sent/Second | Counts the number of ICMP messages are sent by the local computer. |
| Messages Outbound Errors | Counts the number of ICMP messages that were not transmitted by the local computer due to errors found. This is an accumulating sum reset by the last system reboot. |

*(continued)*

**Table B.11    CMP Object** *(continued)*

| Name | Function |
|------|----------|
| Sent Destination Unreachable | Counts the number of ICMP Destination Unreachable messages sent by the local computer. This is an accumulating sum reset by the last system reboot. |
| Sent Time Exceeded | Counts the number of ICMP Time Exceeded messages sent by the local computer. This is an accumulating sum reset by the last system reboot. |
| Sent Parameter Problem | Counts the number of ICMP Parameter Problem messages sent by the local computer. This is an accumulating sum reset by the last system reboot. |
| Sent Source Quench | Counts the number of ICMP Source Quench messages sent by the local computer. This is an accumulating sum reset by the last system reboot. |
| Sent Redirect | Counts the number of ICMP Redirect messages sent by the local computer. This is an accumulating sum reset by the last system reboot. |
| Sent Echo | Counts the number of ICMP Echo messages sent by the local computer. This is an accumulating sum reset by the last system reboot. |
| Sent Echo Reply | Counts the number of ICMP Echo Reply messages sent by the local computer. This is an accumulating sum reset by the last system reboot. |
| Sent Timestamp | Counts the number of ICMP request for Timestamp messages sent by the local computer. This is an accumulating sum reset by the last system reboot. |

*(continued)*

**Table B.11    CMP Object** *(continued)*

| Name | Function |
|------|----------|
| Sent Timestamp Reply | Counts the number of ICMP Timestamp Reply messages sent by the local computer. This is an accumulating sum reset by the last system reboot. |
| Sent Address Mask | Counts the number of ICMP Address Mask Request messages sent by the local computer. This is an accumulating sum reset by the last system reboot. |
| Sent Address Mask Reply | Counts the number of ICMP Address Mask Reply messages sent by the local computer. This is an accumulating sum reset by the last system reboot. |

**Table B.12    TCP Object**

| Name | Function |
|------|----------|
| Segments/Second | Counts the number of TCP segments that are transmitted or received by the local computer, using the TCP protocol. |
| Connections Established | Counts the number of TCP connections with the local computer, whose current state is either ESTABLISHED or CLOSE-WAIT. This is an accumulating sum reset by the last system reboot. |
| Connections Active | Counts the number of TCP connections that have made a transition from the CLOSED state to the SYN-SENT state. |
| Connections Passive | Counts the number of TCP connections that have made a direct transition from the LISTEN state to the SYN-RCVD state. |

*(continued)*

**Table B.12    TCP Object** *(continued)*

| Name | Function |
|------|----------|
| Connection Failures | Counts the number of TCP connections that have made a direct transition from the SYN-SENT or SYN-RCVD state to the CLOSED state. Included in this counter is the number of TCP connections that have made a direct transition from the SYN-RCVD state to the LISTEN state. |
| Connections Reset | Counts the number of TCP connections that have made a direct transition from either the ESTABLISHED state or the CLOSE-WAIT state to the CLOSED state. |
| Segments Received/Second | Counts the number of segments received by the local computer including segments received from established connections. |
| Segments Sent/Second | Counts the number of segments that have been transmitted by the local computer. |
| Segments Retransmitted/Second | Counts the number of segments that have been retransmitted by the local computer. |

**Table B.13    UDP Object**

| Name | Function |
|------|----------|
| Datagrams/Second | Counts the number of UDP datagrams transmitted or received by the local computer. |
| Datagrams Received/Second | Counts the number of UDP datagrams that are delivered to UDP users. |
| Datagrams Received No Port | Counts the number of UDP datagrams that could not find a supporting application at the destination port. |

*(continued)*

**Table B.13    UDP Object** *(continued)*

| Name | Function |
|------|----------|
| Datagrams Received Errors | Counts the number of received undeliverable UDP datagrams that the local computer could not deliver. This count doesn't include packets that were received lacking application support at the destination port. |
| Datagrams Sent/Second | Counts the number of UDP datagrams that are transmitted by the local computer. |

# NT 4 Network Files

**Table B.14    Executables Used by NT for Networking**

| File Name | Function |
|-----------|----------|
| ARP.EXE | TCP/IP network utility to manipulate the ARP cache. |
| CLIPSRV.EXE | Network DDE Clipbook service. |
| DDESHARE.EXE | Network dynamic data exchange share support. |
| DHCPADMN.EXE | Dynamic Host Configuration Protocol (DHCP) Manager. |
| FINGER.EXE | TCP/IP utility that displays information about a user on a specified system running the Finger service. Output varies based on the remote system. |
| FTP.EXE | File Transfer Program, a TCP/IP utility. |
| HOSTNAME.EXE | TCP/IP network utility to determine the system's local hostname. |
| IPCONFIG.EXE | Windows NT IP Configuration. |
| IPXROUTE.EXE | Network IPX. |
| LMREPL.EXE | LAN Manager Replicator service. |

*(continued)*

**Table B.14    Executables Used by NT for Networking *(continued)***

| File Name | Function |
| --- | --- |
| LOCATOR.EXE | Supports Remote Procedure Calls (RPC). |
| LODCTR.EXE | Load Performance Monitor counters. |
| LOGVIEW.EXE | Migration Tool for NetWare Log File Viewer. |
| LPQ.EXE | TCP/IP diagnostic utility used to obtain status of a print queue on a host running the LPD server. |
| LPR.EXE | TCP/IP connectivity utility used to print a file to a host running an LPD server. |
| MACFILE.EXE | Windows NT Macintosh MacFile command-line user interface. |
| MPNOTIFY.EXE | Run by Winlogon to notify multiple providers (such as Banyan®, Novell, and so on) of Secondurity events (such as change password and logon). |
| MUSRMGR.EXE | User Manager (Windows NT base product). |
| NBTSTAT.EXE | NetBIOS over TCP/IP networking statistics application. |
| NCADMIN.EXE | Network Client Administrator. |
| NDDEAGNT.EXE | Network DDE. |
| NDDEAPIR.EXE | Network DDE. |
| NET.EXE | Network command-line utility supporting commands such as net use and net print. |
| NET1.EXE | Net command utility. |
| NETDDE.EXE | Network DDE background application. |
| NETSTAT.EXE | TCP/IP utility for gathering network statistics information. |
| NMAGENT.EXE | Network Monitor service that provides remote access to RNAL.DLL. |
| NW16.EXE | NWCS file. |

*(continued)*

**Table B.14   Executables Used by NT for Networking** *(continued)*

| File Name | Function |
| --- | --- |
| NWCONV.EXE | Migration Tool for NetWare. |
| NWSVC.EXE | NetWare Services. |
| PING.EXE | TCP/IP diagnostic command that verifies connections to one or more remote hosts. |
| RASADMIN.EXE | Remote Access Server Administrator. |
| RASDIAL.EXE | Remote Access Server Dial tool. |
| RASMAN.EXE | Remote Access Server Manager. |
| RASMON.EXE | Remote Access Monitor. |
| RASPHONE.EXE | Remote Access user tool. |
| RASSPRXY.EXE | Remote Access Server supervisor proxy. |
| RASSRV.EXE | Remote Access Server supervisor. |
| RCP.EXE | TCP/IP connectivity command that copies files between a Windows NT computer and a system running RSHD, the remote shell server. |
| REDIR.EXE | Network redirector for Win16 support; not required for startup. |
| REXEC.EXE | TCP/IP connectivity command that runs commands on remote hosts running the REXECD service; authenticates the user name on the remote host by using a password. |
| ROUTE.EXE | TCP/IP diagnostic command used to manipulate network routing tables. |
| RPCSS.EXE | Remote Procedure Call subsystem. |
| RPLCMD.EXE | Remoteboot command-line utility. |
| RPLCNV.EXE | Remoteboot conversion utility. |
| RPLMGR.EXE | Remoteboot Service Manager. |
| RPLSVC.EXE | Remoteboot Service DLL. |
| RSH.EXE | TCP/IP connectivity command that runs commands on remote hosts running the RSH service. |

*(continued)*

**Table B.14   Executables Used by NT for Networking** *(continued)*

| File Name | Function |
| --- | --- |
| SFMPRINT.EXE | Services for Macintosh Print Service. |
| SFMPSEXE.EXE | Services for Macintosh PostScript Raster Image Processor program. |
| SFMSVC.EXE | Services for Macintosh file service. |
| SHARE.EXE | Command-line utility to enable file sharing facilities. |
| SNMP.EXE | SNMP Service; proxy agent that listens for requests and hands them off to the appropriate network provider. |
| SNMPTRAP.EXE | SNMP Trap Service that works with SNMP.EXE to receive Trap Packets. |
| TCPSVCS.EXE | TCP/IP Services application. |
| TELNET.EXE | Starts the Telnet service (if not started already) and Windows Terminal. |
| TERMINAL.EXE | Terminal application. |
| TFTP.EXE | Trivial File Transfer Protocol (TFTP) client over UDP (TCP/IP utility). |
| TRACERT.EXE | TCP/IP Traceroute command. |
| VWIPXSPX.EXE | NWCS file. |
| WINS.EXE | WINS Server. |
| WINSADMN.EXE | Windows Internet Naming Service Manager. |

**Table B.15   Driver Files Used By NT for Networking**

| File Name | Function |
| --- | --- |
| ASYNCMAC.SYS | Remote Access Server Serial network driver. |
| BHNT.SYS | Network Monitor driver for capturing packets. |
| BRHJ770.DLL | Network browser kernel component; Redirector. |
| DLC.SYS | Data Link Control driver. |

*(continued)*

**Table B.15    Driver Files Used By NT for Networking** *(continued)*

| File Name | Function |
| --- | --- |
| EE16.SYS | Network NDIS driver: Intel Ether-Express card. |
| ELNK16.SYS | Network NDIS driver: 3Com Ether-link-16 card. |
| ELNK3.SYS | Network NDIS driver: 3Com Ether-link-III card. |
| ELNKII.SYS | Network NDIS driver: 3Com Ether-link-II card. |
| ELNKMC.SYS | Network NDIS driver: 3Com Ether-link-MC card, 3Com EtherLink MCA driver. |
| IBMTOK.SYS | Network NDIS driver for IBM Token Ring adapter and IBM Token Ring adapter/A. |
| IBMTOK2I.SYS | IBM Token Ring 16/4 Adapter II ISA network driver. |
| LANCE.SYS | Network NDIS driver: DEC Lance adapter driver. |
| LANMAN.DRV | Win16 LAN Manager network driver. |
| LOOP.SYS | Microsoft loop-back network NDIS driver. |
| MSACM32.DRV | Microsoft Audio Compression Manager driver. |
| MSFS.SYS | Mailslot file system driver. |
| MUP.SYS | Network Multiple UNC Provider (required). |
| NBF.SYS | NetBEUI Frame (NBF) driver. |
| NBT.SYS | NetBIOS for TCP/IP driver, used for Windows Networking (RFC1001/1002). |
| NDIS.SYS | NDIS wrapper driver; required for NDIS drivers. |
| NDISTAPI.SYS | NDIS 3.0 connection wrapper driver. |
| NDISWAN.SYS | Remote Access network driver. |

*(continued)*

**Table B.15    Driver Files Used By NT for Networking *(continued)***

| File Name | Function |
| --- | --- |
| NE3200.SYS | Network NDIS drivers for Novell NE1000, NE2000, and NE3200 adapters. |
| NETBIOS.SYS | NetBIOS API driver; Microsoft NetBIOS Transport Interface. |
| NETBT.SYS | NetBT driver. |
| NETDTECT.SYS | Network card detection driver. |
| NETFLX.SYS | Network NDIS driver for COMPAQ NetFlex/DualSpeed Token Ring adapter card. |
| NETWARE.DRV | Netware driver. |
| NPEISA.SYS | Network peripherals FDDI, EISA NDIS driver. |
| NPFS.SYS | Named pipes file system driver. |
| NPMCA.SYS | Network peripherals FDDI, MCA NDIS driver. |
| NTCX.SYS | Network NDIS driver for Digiboard C/X adapter. |
| NTXALL.SYS | Network NDIS driver for Digiboard PC/Xi, PC/2e, PC/4e, PC/8e. |
| NTXEM.SYS | Network NDIS driver for Digiboard PC/Xem. |
| NWLINK.SYS | NWLink library. |
| NWLNKIPX.SYS | NWLINK2 IPX protocol driver. |
| NWLNKNB.SYS | NWLINK2 IPX NetBIOS protocol driver. |
| NWLNKRIP.SYS | NWLINK2 RIP protocol driver. |
| NWLNKSPX.SYS | NWLINK2 SPX protocol driver. |
| NWNBLINK.SYS | NetWare® NetBIOS Link (NWNBLink) network transport driver. |
| NWRDR.SYS | NetWare redirector file system driver. |
| PCIMAC.SYS | Network NDIS driver for Digiboard ISDN adapter. |

*(continued)*

**Table B.15    Driver Files Used By NT for Networking** *(continued)*

| File Name | Function |
| --- | --- |
| RASARP.SYS | Remote Access IP ARP driver. |
| RASHUB.SYS | RAS Hub driver. |
| RDR.SYS | Network Redirector driver. |
| SFMATALK.SYS | Services for Macintosh AppleTalk protocol driver. |
| SFMSRV.SYS | Services for Macintosh file server driver. |
| SMBTRSUP.SYS | SMB trace support; required for RDR.SYS and SRV.SYS. |
| SMC8000N.SYS | Network NDIS driver for SMC (Western Digital) network adapter cards. |
| SRV.SYS | Network Server driver. |
| STREAMS.SYS | Streams driver; used by Streams-based protocols including TCP/IP and NWLink. |
| TCARC.SYS | ARCNET network driver. |
| TCPIP.SYS | TCP/IP driver; includes TCP/IP modules such as IP, UDP, TCP, and ARP. |
| TDI.SYS | Network TDI wrapper (required). |
| WFWNET.DRV | Windows for Workgroups 16-bit network stub driver. |
| ASYNCMAC.SYS | Remote Access server serial netwok driver. |
| BHNT.SYS | Network Monitor driver for capturing packets. |
| EE16.SYS | Network NDIS driver: Intel Ether-Express card. |

### Table B 16  Dynamic Link Libraries Used by NT for Networking

| File Name | Function |
| --- | --- |
| AMDNCDET.DLL | Network Control Panel Tool detection library for AM1500T card. |
| ATKCTRS.DLL | AppleTalk Performance Monitor counter. |
| BHMON.DLL | Network Monitor component that provides network statistics to Performance Monitor. |
| BHNETB.DLL | Network Monitoring NetBIOS remote protocol driver. |
| BHSUPP.DLL | General support DLL for Network Monitor network drivers. |
| BROWSER.DLL | Network browser service. |
| DECPSMON.DLL | Digital network printing SW. |
| DGCONFIG.DLL | Network NDIS driver for Digiboard serial driver. |
| DHCPCSVC.DLL | DHCP client service. |
| DHCPMIB.DLL | DHCP SNMP agent. |
| DHCPSAPI.DLL | DHCP Server API stub dynamic link library. |
| DHCPSSVC.DLL | DHCP Server service. |
| DIGIINST.DLL | Network NDIS driver for Digiboard ISDN. |
| DLCAPI.DLL | Data Link Control API library. |
| FTENG32.DLL | Full-text search engine library. |
| FTPCTRS.DLL | FTP Service performance counters. |
| FTPSMX.DLL | File Transfer Program (FTP) server management extensions for Server Manager. |
| FTPSVAPI.DLL | FTP Service Client API stubs. |
| FTPSVC.DLL | FTP server management API support for Control Panel. |
| ICMP.DLL | ICMP helper DLL used by PING. |
| INETMIB1.DLL | TCP/IP Management Information Base. |

*(continued)*

**Table B.16  Dynamic Link Libraries Used by NT for Networking *(continued)***

| File Name | Function |
| --- | --- |
| IPADRDLL.DLL | IP address custom control. |
| IPXCFG.DLL | IPX configuration DLL. |
| ISDN.DLL | Network NDIS driver for Digiboard ISDN. |
| LMHSVC.DLL | NetBIOS over TCP/IP (NBT) LMHOSTS parsing support. |
| LMMIB2.DLL | LAN Manager management information base. |
| LMUICMN0.DLL | Network user interface DLLs. |
| LMUICMN1.DLL | LAN Manager Common User Interface library. |
| LOCALMON.DLL | Local Monitor; used to send a print job to a port. |
| LOCALSPL.DLL | Local spooling support for printing. |
| LPDSVC.DLL | LPDSVC Service, the server side of TCP/IP printing for Unix clients. |
| LPRHELP.DLL | LPR Print Monitor. |
| LPRMON.DLL | TCP/IP connectivity utility used to print a file to a host running an LPD server. |
| MGMTAPI.DLL | SNMP component; Management API library. |
| MPR.DLL | Multiple Provider Router library; takes Win32 networking APIs and passes the call to the correct network provider (should not be required for startup, except that Program Manager calls restore connections). |
| MPRUI.DLL | Multiple Provider user interface, helper library for MPR.DLL. |
| NAL.DLL | Network Abstraction Layer used to communicate with NDIS30.DLL. |

*(continued)*

**Table B.16    Dynamic Link Libraries Used by NT for Networking *(continued)***

| File Name | Function |
| --- | --- |
| NBTSVC.DLL | NetBIOS over TCP/IP (NBT) service. |
| NDDEAPI.DLL | Network DDE API library. |
| NDDENB32.DLL | Network DDE NetBIOS interface. |
| NDIS30.DLL | Used to communicate with the BHNT.SYS file, the network driver used to capture packets. |
| NETAPI.DLL | OS/2 subsystem thunk DLLs. |
| NETAPI32.DLL | Windows NT 32-bit Network API library. |
| NETDTECT.DLL | Network card auto-detection library. |
| NETEVENT.DLL | Network components error messages library. |
| NETFLX.DLL | NET NDIS driver: COMPAQ detection DLL. |
| NETH.DLL | Help messages for NETCMD (network command-line interface) and network services; needed even without a network adapter card to start and stop services and to add users to groups at the command line. |
| NETLOGON.DLL | Network logon library. |
| NETMSG.DLL | LAN Manager network error messages library. |
| NETRAP.DLL | Routines library used for talking to or from down-level systems; support routines for Rpcxlate and Xactsrv. |
| NETUI0.DLL | Windows NT LM user interface common code (GUI classes). |
| NETUI1.DLL | Windows NT LM user interface common code (GUI classes). |
| NETUI2.DLL | Windows NT LM user interface common code (GUI classes). |
| NWAPI16.DLL | NW Windows/DOS API. |

*(continued)*

**Table B.16    Dynamic Link Libraries Used by NT for Networking** *(continued)*

| File Name | Function |
| --- | --- |
| NWAPI32.DLL | NW Win32 API. |
| NWCFG.DLL | NWC configuration DLL. |
| NWEVENT.DLL | Event messages for Client Service for NetWare. |
| NWLNKCFG.DLL | NWLink configuration library. |
| NWLNKMSG.DLL | NWLink message library. |
| NWNBLINK.DLL | NetWare NetBIOS Link (NWNBLink); Novell NetWare NetBIOS compatible network transport library. |
| NWPROVAU.DLL | Client service for NetWare provider and authentication package DLL. |
| NWSAP.DLL | NW SAP agent DLL. |
| NWWKS.DLL | Client service for NetWare. |
| RASADMIN.DLL | Remote Access Server administrator library. |
| RASAPI16.DLL | Remote Access 16/32 API thunks. |
| RASAPI32.DLL | Remote Access Server API library. |
| RASCAUTH.DLL | Remote Access Server Client authority library. |
| RASCBCP.DLL | Remote Access Server Callback Control Protocol. Negotiates callback information with the remote client. |
| RASCCP.DLL | Remote Access PPP Compression Control Protocol. |
| RASCFG.DLL | Remote Access Server configuration library. |
| RASCHAP.DLL | Remote Access Server Crypto-Handshake Authentication Protocol. |
| RASCTRS.DLL | Remote Access Performance Monitor counters. |
| RASDD.DLL | Raster Printer Device Driver library. |
| RASDDUI.DLL | Raster Printer Device Driver User Interface library. |

*(continued)*

**Table B.16  Dynamic Link Libraries Used by NT for Networking** *(continued)*

| File Name | Function |
|-----------|----------|
| RASFIL32.DLL | Remote Access Server filter library. |
| RASGPRXY.DLL | Remote Access Server NetBIOS gateway proxy. |
| RASGTWY.DLL | Remote Access Server gateway library. |
| RASIPCP.DLL | Remote Access PPP Internet Protocol Control Protocol. |
| RASIPHLP.DLL | Remote Access IP configuration helper. |
| RASIPXCP.DLL | Remote Access PPP Internet Protocol Control Protocol. |
| RASMAN.DLL | Remote Access Server Manager library. |
| RASMSG.DLL | Remote Access Server message library. |
| RASMXS.DLL | Library used by Remote Access. |
| RASNBFCP.DLL | Remote Access NBF control protocol. |
| RASNBIPC.DLL | Remote Access Server NBFCP interface. |
| RASPAP.DLL | Remote Access PPP Password Authentication Protocol. |
| RASPPP.DLL | Remote Access PPP API library. |
| RASPPPEN.DLL | Remote Access PPP engine. |
| RASRES.DLL | Remote Access Server resource library. |
| RASSAUTH.DLL | Remote Access Server authentication library. |
| RASSER.DLL | Remote Access Server serial library. |
| RASSPAP.DLL | Remote Access PPP Shiva Password Authentication Protocol. |
| RASTAPI.DLL | Remote Access TAPI compliance layer. |
| RNAL.DLL | Network monitoring Remote Network Abstraction Layer. |

*(continued)*

**Table B.16  Dynamic Link Libraries Used by NT for Networking** *(continued)*

| File Name | Function |
| --- | --- |
| RPCDCE4.DLL | RPC transport drivers that allow RPC to communicate with TCP/IP and NetBIOS. |
| RPCDGC3.DLL | Remote Procedure Call UDP client DG DLL. |
| RPCDGC6.DLL | Remote Procedure Call IPX client DG DLL. |
| RPCDGS3.DLL | Remote Procedure Call UDP server DG DLL. |
| RPCDGS6.DLL | Remote Procedure Call IPX server DG DLL. |
| RPCLTC1.DLL | Remote Procedure Call client support for Named Pipes (if using LPC for local communication, these won't be needed for minimal startup). |
| RPCLTC3.DLL | RPC transport drivers that allow RPC to talk to TCP/IP and NetBIOS. |
| RPCLTC5.DLL | RPC transport driver. |
| RPCLTC6.DLL | RPC transport driver. |
| RPCLTS1.DLL | Remote Procedure Call server support for Named Pipes (if using LPC for local communication, these won't be needed for minimal startup). |
| RPCLTS3.DLL | RPC transport driver. |
| RPCLTS5.DLL | RPC transport driver. |
| RPCLTS6.DLL | RPC transport driver. |
| RPCNS4.DLL | RPC Name Service support (should not be needed for starting the system). |
| RPCRT4.DLL | RPC run time (if go to LPC for local communication these won't be needed for minimal startup). |

*(continued)*

**Table B.16  Dynamic Link Libraries Used by NT for Networking** *(continued)*

| File Name | Function |
| --- | --- |
| SFMAPI.DLL | Services for Macintosh API library. |
| SFMATCFG.DLL | Services for Macintosh AppleTalk Protocol configuration library. |
| SFMATMSG.DLL | Services for Macintosh AppleTalk Protocol message library. |
| SFMCTRS.DLL | Macintosh file service performance counter. |
| SFMMON.DLL | Services for Macintosh Print Monitor library. |
| SFMMSG.DLL | Services for Macintosh Message library. |
| SFMPSDIB.DLL | Services for Macintosh PostScript Raster Image Processor library. |
| SFMPSFNT.DLL | Services for Macintosh PostScript Font library. |
| SFMPSPRT.DLL | Services for Macintosh PostScript Print Processor library. |
| SFMRES.DLL | Services for Macintosh Setup Dialog Resources library. |
| SFMUTIL.DLL | Services for Macintosh Setup Utilities library. |
| SFMWSHAT.DLL | Services for Macintosh Windows Sockets Helper AppleTalk Protocol library. |
| SIMPTCP.DLL | Simple TCP/IP Services. |
| SOCKUTIL.DLL | Berkeley-style UNIX sockets interface support. |
| SRVSVC.DLL | Server service library. |
| TAPISRV.DLL | Remote Access Server WAN connection wrapper library. |
| TCPCFG.DLL | TCP/IP configuration DLL. |
| TCPIPSVC.DLL | TCP/IP service library. |

*(continued)*

**Table B.16   Dynamic Link Libraries Used by NT for Networking** *(continued)*

| File Name | Function |
| --- | --- |
| VDMREDIR.DLL | Multiple VDM network support (named pipes, mailslots, network APIs, NetBIOS, DLC). |
| VWIPXSPX.DLL | NWCS file. |
| WINSCTRS.DLL | WINS Service performance counters. |
| WINSEVNT.DLL | WINS event log messages. |
| WINSMIB.DLL | WINS SNMP agent. |
| WINSOCK.DLL | 16-bit Windows Sockets interface support (thunks through to WSOCK32.DLL) for TCP/IP. |
| WINSRPC.DLL | WINS RPC library. |
| WINSTRM.DLL | Windows NT TCP/IP interface for the Route utility. |
| WKSSVC.DLL | Network Workstation service library. |
| WSHISN.DLL | NWLINK2 socket helper. |
| WSHNETBS.DLL | NetBIOS Windows sockets helper. |
| WSHNWLNK.DLL | Windows NT Windows Sockets helper for NWLink. |
| WSHTCPIP.DLL | Windows NT Windows Sockets helper for TCP/IP. |
| WSOCK32.DLL | 32-bit Windows Sockets API library. |

# Index